Organizational Success through Effective Human Resources Management

Organizational Success through Effective Human Resources Management

RONALD R. SIMS

QUORUM BOOKS
Westport, Connecticut • London

Library of Congress Cataloging-in-Publication Data

Sims, Ronald R.
 Organizational success through effective human resources management / Ronald R. Sims.
  p. cm.
  Includes index.
  ISBN 1–56720–481–3 (alk. paper)
  1. Personnel management. 2. Human capital. 3. Organizational effectiveness.
 I. Title.
 HF5549.S5925 2002
 658.3—dc21   2001048115

British Library Cataloguing in Publication Data is available.

Library of Congress Catalog Card Number: 2001048115
ISBN: 1–56720–481–3

First published in 2002

Quorum Books, 88 Post Road West, Westport, CT 06881
An imprint of Greenwood Publishing Group, Inc.
www.quorumbooks.com

Printed in the United States of America

The paper used in this book complies with the
Permanent Paper Standard issued by the National
Information Standards Organization (Z39.48–1984).

10 9 8 7 6 5 4 3 2 1

Contents

Acknowledgments

A very special thank you goes to Harrington Bryce, who continues to serve as a colleague, mentor, and valued friend. The administrative support of Larry Pulley, Dean of the School of Business Administration at the College of William & Mary, is also acknowledged. I want to send a special note of appreciation to Eric Valentine, Publisher at Quorum Books, who continues to believe that I have something worth saying and sharing with others.

My thanks and appreciation as usual goes out to my wife, Serbrenia, and to our children, Nandi, Dangaia, Sieya, and Kani, for their continued patience and support during my periods of writing, which always takes time away from them. A special thanks goes out to Ronald, Jr., Marchet, Vellice, Shelley, and Sharisse.

Organizational Success through Effective Human Resources Management

Chapter 1

Organizational Success through Effective Human Resources Management

INTRODUCTION

Anyone who is familiar with the major organizations in their area probably has observed firsthand how dramatically the business environment has changed in recent years. These changes have had a significant impact on organizational efforts to be successful. In practically every instance organizations have tried to more clearly identify and then focus on factors that impact their success. One factor that seems to be receiving more attention than any other are the people who work for organizations. What organizations are realizing is that their likelihood of sustained success is most dependent on learning to get the maximum out of their employees. Such a realization has had a significant impact on the practice of human resources management (HRM). What's more, business forecasters predict that the role of employees, managers, and HRM personnel are likely to see more changes in the decades ahead. Thus, individuals entering the business environment today (and tomorrow) require both an understanding of the importance of human resources and effective HRM to organizational success.

As we move further into the twenty-first century, it's becoming absolutely clear that the effective management of an organization's human resources is a major source of competitive advantage and may even be the single most important determinant of an organization's performance over the long term. This book is designed to be a tool to help teach future employees about the importance of HRM and provide some ways to manage those resources more effectively.

Organizations have started to realize that their success is dependent on their ability to attract, develop, and retain talented employees. Robert Reich emphasizes this point when he suggests that in the future, the organization's ability to attract, develop, and retain a talented workforce will be a critical factor in developing a high-performance organization (Reich, 1998, p. 124). The long-term, sustained success of an organization in today's changing and challenging business environment involves top management's commitment to designing and implementing HRM programs geared to developing both high-performing employees and organizations. This means that top management anticipates the future need for employees and develops specific plans to obtain, develop, and retain the type of employees who meet the needs of a high-performing organization. Only by anticipating and working toward the development and retention of the right type of employees can any organization expect to be successful in a global, dynamic, and continuously changing competitive environment.

An important element of organizational success is an HRM strategy where every manager is an HRM manager. For example, every manager must be expected to set goals for the development and satisfaction of employees. Second, every employee is viewed as a valuable resource, just like buildings and equipment. The organization's success is dependent upon high-performing employees, and without such employees there is no competitive advantage for the organization. Finally, through effective HRM programs the organization's goals are successfully integrated with individual employee needs. It is the thesis of this book that HRM will continue to be an important element in achieving organizational success in the years to come.

This opening chapter first defines HRM and its role in helping organizations to succeed. Next, we offer a look at the history and contemporary growth of HRM. We conclude the chapter with a discussion of the contemporary challenges confronting organizations and their HRM functions.

WHAT IS HRM?

What makes one organization successful whereas another fails to make use of the same opportunities? For our purposes, the key to continued survival and organizational success lies not in the rational, quantitative approaches, but increasingly in a commitment to things like people, employee involvement, and commitment. Success for the organizations of today and tomorrow is being increasingly seen as dependent on effective HRM. Effective HRM positively affects performance in organizations, both large and small.

Human resources management is the term increasingly used to refer to the philosophy, policies, procedures, and practices related to the management of an organization's employees. Human resources management is particularly concerned with all the activities that contribute to successfully attracting, developing, motivating, and maintaining a high-performing workforce that results in organizational success.

In the process of HRM, there is an increasing emphasis on the personal needs of the organization and its members. How effectively employees contribute to organization goals depends to a larger extent upon the ability of its HRM staff. The challenge is to create an organizational environment in which each employee can grow and develop to his or her fullest extent. Such an environment increases the likelihood of a successful organization, and this is what HRM is all about, making organizations successful.

Human resources management efforts are planned, systematic approaches to increasing organizational success. They involve HRM programs aimed at developing HRM strategies for the total organization with an eye toward clarifying an organization's current and potential problems and developing solutions for them. They are oriented toward action, the individual, the global marketplace, and the future. Today it would be difficult to envision any organization achieving success without efficient HRM programs and activities. The strategic and competitive advantage importance of HRM to organizational success will become more evident throughout this book.

The purpose of HRM programs is to increase organizational success and also to develop the potential of all members. Human resources management also emphasizes that HRM planning needs to be closely related to the organization's strategic goals and plans. Finally, there are a series of planned HRM activities that will ultimately influence the success of an organization. These HRM activities are described in succeeding chapters in this book.

The importance of recruiting, selecting, training and developing, rewarding, and compensating employees is recognized by managers in all parts of today's organizations. Human resources management and other functions must work together to achieve organizational success and to compete locally and internationally. Organizational success is described in this book in terms of such criteria and components as legal compliance, performance, employee satisfaction, turnover, absenteeism, grievance rates, and accident rates. In order for an organization to be successful (i.e., prosper and earn a profit), reasonable goals in each of these components must be achieved.

HRM FUNCTIONS

Only recently have organizations looked at HRM practices as a means to contribute to profitability, quality, and other organizational goals through enhancing and supporting organizational operations. Within each functional area of HRM, many activities must be accomplished so that the organization's human resources can make an optimal contribution to the organization's success. These activities are briefly discussed in the remainder of this section.

Strategic Management of Human Resources

Human resources management needs to be closely integrated with managerial planning and decision making (i.e., international human resources, forecasting, planning, and mergers and acquisitions). Increasingly, an organization's top management is aware that the time to consider organizational HRM strengths or limitations is when strategic organizational decisions are being formulated, not after critical policies have been decided. A closer integration between top management's goals and HRM practices helps to elicit and reward the types of behavior necessary for achieving an organization's strategy. For example, if an organization is planning to become known for its high-quality products, HRM staff should design appraisal and reward systems that emphasize quality in order to support this competitive strategy.

Strategic management of human resources includes HRM planning. The HRM planning process involves forecasting HRM needs and developing programs to ensure that the right numbers and types of individuals are available at the right time and place. Such information enables an organization to plan its recruitment, selection, and training strategies. For example, let's say an organization's HRM plan estimates that 12 additional information systems (IS) technicians will be needed during the next year. The organization typically hires recent IS graduates to fill such positions. Because these majors are in high demand, the organization decides to begin its recruiting early in the school year, before other organizations can "snatch away" the best candidates. Chapter 2 discusses in more detail both strategic human resources management (SHRM) and HRM planning in more detail.

Recruiting and Selecting Employees

Once HRM needs are determined, the next step is recruiting employees (i.e., interviewing, recruiting, screening, and selecting the most qualified candidates, filling some positions through transfer or promotion, and temporary employment coordination).

Recruiting and staffing is a far more complex activity than in previous times when HRM staff could rely on recommendations from current employees or a "help wanted" sign in front of the business. The increased complexity of positions to be filled and equal employment opportunity (EEO), require more sophisticated procedures to identify and select prospective employees. Consider, for instance, the impact antidiscrimination laws have on organizations' hiring practices. Prior to the passage of these laws, many organizations hired people in somewhat arbitrary ways. Applicants were often hired because they had an organization handshake or because they graduated from the employer's alma mater. Today, such practices could result in charges of discrimination. For instance, a woman denied a job because of a weak handshake may end up suing the organization for sex discrimination.

To protect themselves from such charges, employers must conduct their selection practices "by the book." This means they should carefully determine needed job qualifications and choose selection methods that accurately measure those qualifications. Chapter 3 discusses the legal environment, specifically EEO laws, associated with recruiting, staffing, and promoting employees.

In order to plan for future selection efforts and training programs and to ensure that performance appraisal and compensation systems are rationally based on job demands, HRM personnel must complete careful descriptions and analysis of current jobs. The development and use of job analysis information as part of HRM planning and as the foundation for all other HRM functions is the focus of Chapter 4.

Organizations may recruit candidates internally (i.e., recruit current employees seeking to advance or change jobs) or externally. While the aim of recruitment is to identify a suitable pool of applicants quickly, cost efficiently, and legally, selection or staffing involves assessing and choosing job candidates. To be effective, selection processes must be technically sound (i.e., accurate) and legal. The activities involved in recruiting and selecting employees is addressed in Chapters 5 and 6.

Training and Development

Many of today's employees look at the chance to develop and move up as important in where they will seek employment. In order to facilitate employee progression, many organizations choose to spend substantial sums to train and develop their employees. Training and development (i.e., orientation, performance management skills training, and productivity enhancement) are planned learning experiences that teach employees how to perform their current and future jobs.

Training focuses on present jobs, whereas development prepares employees for possible future jobs. Procedures for determining training and development needs and then constructing, delivering, and evaluating HRM development programs to meet these needs are the topics of Chapter 7.

Performance Appraisals

Through the performance appraisal process, organizations measure the adequacy of their employees' job performance and communicate these evaluations to them. Performance appraisals are a critical link in the HRM process, as they assess how well employees are performing and determine appropriate rewards or remedial actions to motivate employees to continue appropriate behaviors and correct inappropriate ones. The HRM role in performance appraisal is one of working with other managers in the organization to establish the appraisal process, the performance dimensions to be measured, the procedures to ensure accuracy, and requirements for discussion of appraisal results with employees.

Management may also use performance appraisals as a tool for making HRM-related decisions, such as promotions, demotions, discharges, and pay raises. Performance appraisal continues to not be one of the pleasant activities for managers, yet it is important that it be undertaken in a timely manner and be done as accurately as possible. Chapter 8 addresses issues related to performance appraisal.

Career Development

Organizations are becoming more active in developing career development programs. Many organizations are designing career programs in an attempt to increase overall organizational performance and employee productivity, and to attract, develop, and retain the most qualified employees in this increasingly competitive and global environment.

In addition to being concerned about their own interests organizations are increasingly concerned about the long-term interests of their employees. However, with pressures to improve efficiency and overall effectiveness, organizations have also expected individuals to accept more responsibility for managing their own careers. This means that individuals must do everything they can to grow and realize their full potential in order to improve their value either to their current or future employer. Individuals have begun to view careers as "boundaryless" including several employers and possibly different occupations. Chapter 9 focuses on career development and its importance to individual and organizational success.

Compensation

A logical result of the appraisal process is determining which employees most deserve rewards. Compensation entails pay and benefits (i.e., wage and salary administration, job descriptions, executive compensation, incentive pay, insurance, vacation/leave administration, retirement plans, profit sharing, stock plans). Allocating rewards is a complex and specialized activity. Rewards include both the direct compensation (salary and hourly wages) and the indirect compensation (benefits) that organizations offer to employees. The aim of compensation practices is to help organizations establish and maintain a competent and loyal workforce at an affordable cost.

Like other HRM activities, compensation practices are also affected by legal requirements of equal pay for equal work, minimum wage and overtime provisions, and required benefits such as Social Security. In addition to the level of pay, a successful compensation system is based on fairness. Employees bring a variety of perspectives to bear in deciding whether they are satisfied with the compensation they receive, thus making management of compensation a particularly challenging HRM activity.

Compensation systems need to be designed to mesh with the strategic objectives of the organization. They also need to integrate the realities of prevailing pay levels in the labor market with an organization's profitability and ability to pay. The general issues related to developing compensations systems are the subject of Chapter 10, while specific concerns associated with performance-based systems and benefits are covered in Chapter 11.

Safe and Healthy Work Environment

An important source of workplace change has been the desire to promote a safer and more healthful work environment. Legal, social, and political pressures on organizations ensure that the health and safety of their employees continue to have a great impact on HRM practices. Part of the impact and concern is a result of the Occupational Safety and Health Act of 1970. A second source of change has been societal concern about exposure to hazardous substances or stress in the workplace. Organizations try to respond to pressures and concerns by instituting accident prevention programs and programs designed to ensure the health and mental well-being of their employees. Organizations are taking more responsibility for helping employees deal with problems caused by stress or substance abuse through wellness and employee assistance programs. These issues are discussed in Chapter 12.

Labor Relations and Collective Bargaining

More than ever before, an increasing number of organizations are drawing on and contributing to a global economy. As these organizations have gone global, the number of employees abroad has increased. With more employees abroad, HRM departments have had to tackle new global challenges. Chapter 13 discusses how HRM policies and practices help organizations tackle these new global challenges and more successfully compete in the global marketplace.

International Human Resources Management (IHRM)

Simply put, IHRM is HRM that cuts across national boundaries. But as many organizations and their HRM personnel have found out from first hand experience, it is not simple. International human resources management can be very complex. Globalization has created an array of employment scenarios based on such variables as citizenship, location, to whom the person reports, and the term of the assignment. Multinational corporations (MNCs), usually defined as companies with organizations in more than one country, are growing in numbers and complexity. An example of this complexity is an organization building a manufacturing plant in Spain to produce engine parts designed by another organization in Japan for motorcycles to be sold in Europe and the United States.

The international aspects of HRM in the MNC require a global perspective. A perspective that recognizes the difference between domestic HRM and IHRM is one of complexity. This complexity affects all the major HRM processes. Chapter 14 alerts the reader to some of the complexities of IHRM.

THE ORIGINS AND HISTORY OF PERSONNEL MANAGEMENT/HRM

From the earliest times in Egypt and Babylon, training in craft skills was organized to maintain an adequate supply of craft workers. By the thirteenth century, craft training had become popular in Western Europe. Some authors suggest that the history of HRM can be traced to England, where masons, carpenters, leather workers, and other craftspeople organized themselves into guilds (Jackson and Schuler, 1995). Craft guilds supervised quality and methods of production and regulated conditions of employment for each occupation. The craft guilds were controlled by the master crafts worker, and the recruit entered after a period of training as an apprentice. The craft system was best suited to domestic industry, which the master operated on his own premises, with his assistants residing and working in the same house. The guilds used their unity to improve their work conditions.

The field of HRM further developed with the arrival of the Industrial Revolution in the latter part of the eighteenth century, which laid the basis for a new and complex industrial society. The Industrial Revolution began with the substitution of steam power and machinery for time-consuming hand labor. Working conditions, social patterns, and the division of labor were significantly altered. A new kind of employee—a boss, who wasn't necessarily the owner, as had usually been the case in the past—became a power broker in the new factory system. With these changes also came a widening gap between workers and owners.

As early as the 1890s, in some companies, a few specialized personnel activities were grouped into larger departments. The Civil Service Commission, established by the Pendleton Act of 1883, has had major influence on the development of personnel or human resources management in the United States. Drawing many of its ideas from the British civil service system, the Pendleton Act established the use of competitive examinations for admission into public service; provided job security for public employees, including those who refused to engage in politics; prohibited political activity by the civil service; and encouraged a nonpartisan approach to employee selection. A commissioner was appointed to administer the act (Van Riper, 1958).

The major effect of the Pendleton Act was to foster employees' appointment and career development in federal service on the basis of performance. Over the years this law has stimulated progressive personnel policies in private organizations as well. For example, around 1890 the Civil Service Commission was developing the forerunners of general intelligence tests and trade tests that became popular in private industry.

In response to the growth of trade unionism at the turn of the century, a few organizations—for example, H.J. Heinz, Colorado Fuel & Iron, and International Harvester—created the position of "welfare secretary." Welfare secretaries were supposed to assist workers by suggesting improvements in working conditions, housing, medical care, educational facilities, and recreation. These people, who were the forerunners of today's personnel or human resources management directors, acted as a buffer between the organization and its employees. The B.F. Goodrich Company developed the first employment department in 1900, but its responsibilities consisted only of hiring. In 1902 the National Cash Register Company established the first comprehensive labor department responsible for wage administration, grievances, employment and working conditions, health conditions, record keeping, and worker improvement.

Scientific management and welfare work represent two concurrent approaches that began in the nineteenth century and, along with industrial psychology, merged during the era of the world wars. Scientific management represented an effort to deal with inefficiencies in labor and management primarily through work methods, time and motion study, and specialization. Industrial psychology represented the application of psychological principles toward increasing the ability of workers to perform efficiently and effectively.

Whereas scientific management focused on the job and efficiencies, industrial psychology focused on the worker and individual differences. The maximum well-being of the worker was the focus of industrial psychology.

In 1902 Maryland became the first state to pass a workmen's compensation (now workers' compensation) law, requiring employers to pay workers for lost time and injuries resulting from occupational accidents. The law was subsequently declared unconstitutional. But in 1911 the U.S. Supreme Court upheld the workers' compensation laws of several other states, and from then on safety specialists became very common in industry. Industrial firms wanted to reduce claims against themselves, and they depended on the safety specialist to help ensure safer working conditions in their plants. As a parallel development, physicians were employed by some companies to ensure that employees would be assigned jobs suited to their physical qualifications (Spates, 1960).

The personnel department began to really emerge during the second decade of the twentieth century with drastic changes in technology, the growth of organizations, the rise of unions, and government concern and intervention concerning working people. In 1911 U.S. Steel created a Bureau of Safety, Sanitation, and Welfare. By 1918 International Harvester had established a Department of Industrial Relations, and Ford Motor Company had created a Sociological Department, which combined medical, welfare, safety, and legal aspects of employee relations. By the same year B. Kuppenheimer and Company had a Department of Industrial Relations that included subdivisions such as health, employment, grievances and discipline, and wage and rate setting (Boettiger, 1923).

In 1917 Standard Oil of New Jersey approved a plan that provided for regular conferences between labor and management. At the same time the company established a retirement income plan, substantial insurance benefits, a safety program, and a medical division. To coordinate many of the new programs, Standard Oil created a personnel and training department (Gibb and Knowlton, 1956, p. 136).

As organizations like Ford began to grow they started to hire their employees through newly created specialized units. Ford, for example, called this unit the "employment department." Although these units were initially created to hire employees, they soon began to help manage the existing workforce as well. This trend was influenced by a number of management books published between 1890 and 1912 in Great Britain and the United States. Moreover, the first comprehensive text in the field appeared in 1920—Tead and Metcalf's *Personnel Administration* (1920).

Meanwhile, other developments, many taking place in other parts of the world, provided organizations with some of the tools they would need to better manage these employment processes. For example, in England the work of Charles Darwin popularized the ideas that individuals differed from each other in ways that were important. In France the work of Alfred Binet and Theophile Simon led to the development of the first intelligence tests, and during World War I several armies tried using these tests to better assign soldiers to jobs. These attempts at staffing continued in the private sector after the war, and by 1923 *Personnel Management*, a seminal book by Scott and Clothier, was already spelling out how to match a person's skills and aptitudes with the requirements of the job.

Another earlier contributor to HRM was called the human relations movement. Two Harvard researchers incorporated human factors into work. This movement began as a result of a series of studies conducted at the Hawthorne facility of Western Electric in Chicago between 1924 and 1933. The purpose of the studies was to determine the effects of illumination on workers and their output. The studies pointed out the importance of social interaction and the work group on output and satisfaction.

As businesses grew increasingly large, they began to create specialized units to cope with more than just their hiring needs. They also began to deal with government regulations and to provide a mechanism for dealing with behavioral issues. During the 1930s and 1940s these units gradually began to be called personnel departments (the word *personnel* was derived from an old French word that meant "persons"). They were usually set up as special, self-contained departments charged with the responsibility of hiring new workers and administering basic human resources activities like pay and benefits. The recognition that human resources needed to be managed and the creation of personnel departments also gave rise to a new type of management function—personnel management (Dulebohn, Ferris, and Stodd, 1995). The manager who ran the personnel department was called the personnel manager.

During this period, personnel management was concerned almost exclusively with hiring first-line employees—production workers, sales clerks, custodians, secretaries, blue-collar workers, unskilled labor, and other operating employees. Issues associated with hiring, developing, and promoting managers and executives did not surface until later.

Personnel management took another step forward in its evolution during World War II. Both the military and its major suppliers developed an interest in matching people with jobs. That is, organizations wanted to optimize the fit between the demands and requirements of the jobs that needed to be performed and the skills and interests of people available to perform them. Psychologists were consulted to help develop selection tests, for example, to assess individual skills, interests, and abilities. During the 1950s the wartime lessons were adapted for use in private industry. New, more sophisticated techniques were developed, especially in the area of testing, and organizations also began to experiment with more sophisticated reward and incentive systems. In addition, labor unions became more powerful and demanded a broader array of benefits for their members. At the same time, government legislation expanded and continued to add complexity to the job of the personnel manager.

Building on the findings of the Hawthorne studies, managers began to focus more and more attention on understanding human character of their employees. It was during this era, for example, that Abraham Maslow popularized his "hierarchy of human needs" (Maslow, 1943). Douglas McGregor's well-known Theory X and Theory Y framework also grew from the human relations movement (McGregor, 1960). Briefly, Theory X rests on an essentially negative view of people. It assumes that they have little ambition, dislike work, want to avoid responsibility, and need to be closely directed to work effectively. Theory Y, on the other hand, rests on a positive view of people. It assumes they can exercise self-direction, accept responsibility, and consider work to be as natural as rest or play. McGregor personally believed that Theory Y assumptions better captured the true nature of workers and should guide management practice. As a result, he argued that managers should free up their employees to unleash their full creative and productive potential. Building on the basic premise of the work of the human relations era, researchers such as Maslow and McGregor stressed that if managers could make their employees more satisfied and happier, they would work harder and be more productive. In more recent times, researchers and managers alike recognize that this viewpoint was overly simplistic and that both satisfaction and productivity are complex phenomenon that affect and are affected by many different things. Nonetheless, the increasing awareness of the importance of human behavior during this period helped organizations to become more focused on managing their human resources. These organizations saw effective management of human resources as a means of potentially increasing productivity and, incidentally, as a way of slowing the growth of unionism, which was gaining increasing popularity.

The early history of personnel still obscures the importance of the HRM function to management. Until the 1960s, the personnel function was considered to be concerned with blue-collar or operating employees. It was viewed as a record-keeping unit that handed out 25-year tenure pins and coordinated the annual company picnic. Peter Drucker, a respected management scholar and consultant, made a statement about personnel management that reflected its blue-collar orientation. Drucker stated that the job of personnel was "partly a file clerk's job, partly a housekeeping job, partly a social worker's job, and partly firefighting, heading off union trouble (Foulkes, 1975).

As suggested in Drucker's comments, from its inception until the 1970s, personnel management was not seen as a particularly important or critical function in most business organizations. Although many other managers appreciated personnel management as a necessary vehicle for hiring blue-collar and operating employees, it was also seen primarily as a routine clerical and bookkeeping function—placing newspaper ads to recruit new employees, filling out paperwork on those employees after they were hired, and seeing that everyone got paid on time.

While other organizational units like finance, operations, and marketing grew in status and perceived importance, the personnel department of most organizations was generally relegated to the status of a "necessary evil" that had to be tolerated but which presumably contributed little to the success of the organization. And personnel managers themselves were often stereotyped as individuals who could not succeed in other functional areas and who were assigned to personnel either because the organization had nothing else they could do or as a signal that the individual was not a candidate for promotion to a higher-ranking position.

CONTEMPORARY GROWTH OF HRM

Today, the HRM function is concerned with much more than simple filing, housekeeping, and record keeping. As time has passed, the role of HRM has changed dramatically and become much more important in most organizations. Perhaps the first major stimulus for this increase in importance was the passage in 1964 of the Civil Rights Act, which made it illegal for employers to consider such factors as gender, religion, race, skin color, or national origin in making employment-related decisions. The 1964 Civil Rights Act, combined with several subsequent amendments, executive orders, and legal decisions, made the process of hiring and promoting employees within the organization far more complex than ever before. Organizations quickly realized that those responsible for hiring and promoting employees needed to fully understand the legal context within which they functioned.

As HRM was becoming more important because of the increasingly complex legal environment, many managers were beginning to recognize that HRM had important strategic implications for the organization as well. During the 1960s and 1970s, for example, international competition grew rapidly, and all organizations found it more important than ever to use their resources wisely and to capitalize on their full value. While managers were becoming increasingly concerned with ways to improve productivity and competitiveness, they also began to realize that workers needed to feel that their jobs were a source of personal satisfaction and growth (Starkweather and Steinbacher, 1998). Successful organizations began to realize that they could maximize effectiveness and make work more meaningful and fulfilling for employees.

HRM departments in the 1960s and 1970s also had to become much more professional and more concerned about the legal ramifications of policies and practices. Also, organizations took a new look at employee involvement and quality of work as a result of concerns about the impact of automation and job design on worker productivity.

Given the shift in competitiveness top management in most organizations began to see that HRM practices and policies significantly affected their ability to formulate and implement strategy in any area and that other strategic decisions significantly affected the organization's human resources as well. As a result, HRM began to be elevated to the same level of importance and status as other major functional areas of the organization. The top HRM executive at most companies today has vice president or executive vice president status and is a fully contributing member of the organization's executive committee—the executive body composed of key top managers that makes policy decisions and sets corporate strategy.

The 1980s and 1990s brought some other changes to the HRM function as well. Many organizations found that they were not able to compete well in the new, global marketplace. Some of these organizations went out of business or were acquired by other, more successful organizations as a wave of mergers and acquisitions began in the United States. After the merger of two organizations, there was often not the same need for as many employees, and many employees lost their jobs. Those organizations that could not compete and that were not acquired by some other company closed down, and yet more employees lost their jobs. Finally, those organizations that were struggling to be competitive often concluded that they could be more efficient with fewer employees and contributed to the era of downsizing, rightsizing, or reengineering. Regardless of what it was called, there were fewer and fewer jobs around.

During the 1980s, the strategic role of HRM became essential as organizations reduced staff, closed plants, or "restructured." The job of the HRM function was made more difficult but also had a more profound, direct effect on the HRM function with the increased employee displacement. As these organizations looked for new ways to be competitive and reduce costs, they looked for activities within the organization that could be done more efficiently by outsiders. It also became somewhat common in some organizations to reduce the size of their HRM staffs and turn to outside help for specific projects. This outsourcing resulted in smaller HRM staffs and other organizational employees. However, despite the fact that some HRM activities are being outsourced, the activities carried out by HRM are indeed growing in importance. Containing the costs of health care benefits also grew in importance.

During the 1990s, organizational restructuring continued. The traditional HRM function began shifting its emphasis as HRM managers were expected to be more strategically focused, proactive, and process based in order to contribute to organizational success. Changing demographics and increasing shortages of workers with the needed capabilities also began growing in importance.

CONTEMPORARY CHALLENGES FOR ORGANIZATIONS AND HRM

In recent years increasing attention has been paid to the importance of HRM in determining an organization's competitive advantage. As noted earlier, some have even declared that human resources represent the only enduring source of competitive advantage available to many of today's organizations. A number of factors have contributed to the increased attention on the value of HRM. For example, there are a number of changes in organizations themselves and broader trends causing these changes to occur. Perhaps most importantly, organizations today are under intense pressure to be better, faster, and more competitive. There are more and more efforts to squeeze productivity out of some organizations, while others are merging and downsizing. Why is this the case? Technological changes, deregulation, and globalization are three trends accounting for these competitive pressures. Other trends include diversity, workforce changes, and achieving societal goals through organizations. Let's take a brief look at each of these.

Technological Changes

Technology has been forcing and enabling organizations to become more competitive. Technology is also changing the nature of work. For example, telecommunications already makes it relatively easy for many to work at home, and the use of computer-aided design/computer-aided manufacturing (CAD/CAM) systems plus robotics is booming. Manufacturing advances like these will continue to eliminate blue-collar jobs, replacing them with jobs requiring greater skill, and these new workers will require a degree of training and commitment that their parents never dreamed of. As a result, to remain competitive, jobs and organizational charts will have to continue to be redesigned, new incentive and compensation plans instituted, new job descriptions written, and new employee selection, evaluation, and training programs instituted—all with the help of HRM.

Deregulation

Being better, faster, and more competitive is also more important because for many industries the comfortable protection provided by government regulations continues to be stripped away. In the United States (and in many other industrialized countries such as England, France, and Japan), industries from airlines to banks to utilities must now compete nationally and internationally without the protection of government-regulated prices and entry tariffs.

One big consequence of deregulation has been the sudden and dramatic opening of various markets. One need only look at the long-distance phone companies' efforts to enter the previously protected monopoly of companies like AT&T or the efforts of startups in the airline industry to compete head-to-head with industry giants like Delta and American Airlines. Just as significant has been the impact that deregulation—and the resulting new competition—has had on prices, requiring these organizations to get and stay "lean and mean." Prices for hundreds of services like long-distance calls have dropped in some instances, which means organizations must get their costs down, too.

Globalization

One of the most dramatic challenges facing U.S. organizations as we begin the twenty-first century is how to compete against foreign firms, both domestically and abroad. Many U.S. companies are already being compelled to think globally, something that does not come easily to organizations long accustomed to doing business in a large and expanding domestic market with minimal foreign competition. The Internet is fueling globalization, and most large organizations are actively involved in manufacturing overseas, international joint ventures, or collaboration with foreign organizations on specific projects.

Such globalization has vastly increased global competition. The implications of a global economy on HRM are many. From boosting the productivity of a global labor force to formulating compensation policies for expatriate employees, managing globalization and its effects on competitiveness will thus present major HRM challenges in the years to come.

Workforce Diversity

Managers across the United States are confronted almost daily with the increasing diversity of the workforce. The workforce is continuing to become more diverse as women, minority group members, and older workers flood the workforce. More specifically, one need only note that in many large urban centers, such as Miami, New York, and Los Angeles, the workforce is already at least half composed of minorities. Women with children under age six have also been one of the fastest-growing segments of the workforce. The HRM function will increasingly be called upon to help organizations accommodate these employees with new HRM programs and with basic skills training where such training is required.

As the workforce gets older employees will also likely remain in the workforce well past the age at which their parents retired, due to Social Security and Medicare funding shortfalls and the termination of traditional benefit plans by many employers.

Increased diversity presents both a significant change and a real opportunity for managers. Organizations that formulate and implement HRM strategies that capitalize on employee diversity are more likely to survive and prosper.

Changes in the Nature of Work

Technological changes, deregulation, and globalization are also changing the nature of jobs and work. For one thing, there has been a pronounced shift from manufacturing jobs to service jobs in North America and Western Europe. As the number of manufacturing jobs have decreased over the past two decades, the number of part-time and service industry jobs in fast foods, retailing, legal work, teaching, and consulting has increased. These service jobs will in turn require what have recently been referred to as "knowledge" workers and new HRM methods to manage them as well as a new focus on human capital.

The knowledge, education, training, skills, and expertise of an organization's workers make up an organization's human capital. And human capital is more important than it has ever been before. Service jobs put a bigger premium on worker education and knowledge than do traditional manufacturing jobs. Even entry-level factory jobs have become more demanding. For example, factory jobs in the textile, auto, rubber, and steel industries are being replaced by knowledge-intensive high-tech manufacturing in such industries as telecommunications, pharmaceuticals, medical instruments, aerospace, computers, and home electronics, and even heavy manufacturing jobs are becoming more high tech. Human capital is quickly replacing machines as the basis for most organizations' success.

An important realization for managers and organizations is that these new "knowledge" workers can't be just ordered around and closely monitored like their parents. New HRM systems and skills will be required to select, train, and motivate such employees and to win their commitment.

Changing Employee Expectations

As levels of education have increased within the population, values and expectations among employees have shifted. There has been a steady increase in the number of employees with a college degree. The result has been an emphasis on the increased participation by employees at all levels. Previous notions about managerial authority continue to give way to employee influence and involvement, along with mechanisms for upward communication and due process.

Another expectation of employees is that the electronics and telecommunications revolutions will improve the quality of work life. Innovations in communications and computer technology will accelerate the pace of change and as a result lead to many innovations in HRM.

Finally, organizations are taking steps to support employees' family responsibilities as the proportion of dual-career families continues to increase along with the number of women in the workforce. More and more companies are introducing family-friendly programs that give them a competitive advantage in the labor market. Once able to assume that the demands of male employees' home lives were taken care of by their wives, organizations are now being pushed to pay attention to family issues such as day care, sick children, elder care, schooling, and so forth. One result is that more employees are enjoying the opportunity to work at home. These programs reflect HRM tactics that organizations use to hire and retain the best-qualified employees, male or female, and they often pay off.

Managerial Changes

Management approaches are adding to the challenges facing HRM. Empowerment of employees and self-managed teams are two specific management approaches that are having a significant impact on today's HRM function. Empowerment is a form of decentralization that involves giving employees substantial authority to make decisions. Under empowerment, managers express confidence in the ability of employees to perform their work. Employees are also encouraged to accept responsibility for their work. In many organizations now using self-managed teams, groups of employees do not report to a single manager; rather, groups of peers are responsible for a particular area or task. The breadth of changes in areas like managerial challenges continues to have a powerful impact on today's HRM personnel.

Achieving Societal Goals through Organizations

Much of the growth in the HRM function over the past three decades is the result of the increasing trend toward viewing organizations as vehicles for achieving social and political objectives. Most organizations are deeply concerned with potential liability resulting from HRM decisions that may violate laws enacted by local governments, state legislatures, and the U.S. Congress. Legislation like the 1964 Civil Rights Act requires organizations to respond to larger social, political, and legal issues. Other legislation requires organizations to provide reasonable accommodations for the disabled and for employees with the HIV virus.

How successfully an organization manages its human resources depends to a large extent on its ability to deal effectively with government regulations. Operating within the legal framework requires keeping track of the external legal and social environments and developing internal systems (for example, supervisory training and grievance procedures) to ensure compliance and minimize complaints.

Organizational responses to legislative requirements today generally follow a realization that important issues need national attention. As entities within the larger society, organizations can't help but be influenced by the ideology and culture around them. As changes occur in the larger society, organizations must adapt and change. The results of legislative and social changes are added pressures on organizations. HRM practices are not formed in a vacuum but must represent the societal ideology in which they are embedded.

Legal Trends Impacting HRM

As you will see throughout this book, many laws continue to be passed that effectively impact employees' actions in today's organizations. Mandated health benefits, occupational safety and health requirements, and union-management relations laws are among the legal constants managers and employees must deal with, generally with the assistance of HRM.

The enactment of new state and federal laws will continue to contribute to the importance of HRM. The added reporting requirements of these new laws are so extensive that compliance requires increasing human resources expertise. If organizations fail to comply with these laws, they run the risk of costly legal actions and possibly severe financial penalties.

Human Resources Management Information Systems

In the increasingly high-tech world we live in, more HRM activities will require specialized expertise. For example, many organizations are developing computerized expert systems for making employee selection decisions. These systems integrate interview data, test scores, and application form information. Similarly, many organizations are developing compensation systems with elaborate cafeteria-style benefit packages to replace simple hourly pay or piece-rate incentive systems. Many organizations are developing sophisticated databases to centralize all HRM information to provide real-time information for strategic human resources planning and other reporting activities.

In concluding this chapter it is important to remind the reader that regardless of their size, mission, market, or environment, all organizations strive to achieve their goals by combining various resources into goods and services that will be of value to their customers. Financial resources such as ownership investment, sales revenues, and bank loans are used to provide capital and to cover expenses necessary to conduct business. Material resources such as factories, equipment, raw materials, computers, and offices play an important role in the actual creation of goods and services. And information resources about consumers and the organization's competitive environment help managers make decisions, solve problems, and develop strategies. But no resources are more vital to an organization's success in today's world of work than human resources. Organizations that once paid lip service to human resources issues are increasingly recognizing the dramatic impact that effective HRM can have in all areas of an organization. Indeed, effective HRM has become a vital strategic concern for most organizations today, and there is every indication that the trend will continue in the years to come.

SUMMARY

Effective management of human resources is an important component of organizational success. And the HRM function is an organization's most critical source of information about employment practices, employee behavior, labor relations, and the effective management of all aspects of human resources. Human resources management is made up of an identifiable set of activities that affect and influence the people who work in an organization. These activities include HRM planning, job analysis, recruitment, selection, placement, career management, training and development, designing performance appraisal and compensation systems, and labor relations.

The current challenge of HRM is to integrate programs involving human resources with strategic organizational objectives. More and more, organizations are under tremendous competitive pressure worldwide. HRM personnel must find ways to develop effective international programs that meet this challenge.

The challenges for HRM today and tomorrow involve responding to corporate reorganizations, global competition, increasing diversity in the workforce, employee expectations, and legal and governmental requirements in order to help their host organizations meet their organizational goals. In the end, HRM must help make organizations better, faster, and more competitive.

REFERENCES

Boettiger, L.A. 1923. *Employee welfare work: A critical and historical study.* New York: Ronald Press, pp. 127–133.

Dulebohn, J.H., Ferris, G.R., and Stodd, J.T. 1995. The history and evolution of human resource management. In G.R. Ferris, S.D. Rosen, and D.T. Barnum (eds.), *Handbook of human resource management.* Cambridge, MA: Blackwell Publishers, pp. 18–41.

Foulkes, F.K. 1993. The expanding role of the personnel function. *Harvard Business Review* (March–April): 71–72.

Gibb, G.S., and Knowlton, E.H. 1956. *The resurgent years, 1911–1927: History of Standard Oil Company (New Jersey).* New York: Harper & Brothers.

Jackson, S.E., and Schuler, R.S. 1995. Understanding human resource management in the context of organizations and their environments. In M.R. Rosenzivey and L.W. Porter (eds.), *Annual Review of Psychology.* Stanford, CA: Annual Reviews, pp. 237–264.

Maslow, A. 1943. A theory of human motivation. *Psychological Review* (July): 370–396.

McGregor, D. 1960. *The human side of enterprise.* New York: McGraw-Hill.

Reich, R. 1998. The company of the future. *Fast Company* (November): 124.

Scott, W.D., and Clothier, R.C. 1931. *Personnel management, principles, practices, and point of view.* New York: McGraw-Hill.

Spates, T.G. 1960. *Human values where people work*. New York: Harper & Brothers.

Starkweather, R.A., and Steinbacher, C.L. 1998. Job satisfaction affects the bottom line. *HRMagazine* (September): 110–112.

Tead, O., and Metcalf, H.C. 1920. *Personnel administration*. New York: McGraw-Hill.

Toran, M.W. 1998. Rolling with the changes. *Human Resource Executive* (June 5): 39–41.

Van Riper, P.P. 1958. *History of the United States civil service*. Evanston, IL: Row, Peterson, pp. 96–112.

Chapter 2

Organizational Strategy and Human Resources Management

INTRODUCTION

Clearly, HRM does not occur in a vacuum but instead occurs in a complex and dynamic milieu of forces within the organizational context. An important trend in recent years has been for HRM managers and staff to adopt a strategic perspective of their job and recognize the critical linkages between organizational strategy and HRM strategy. The view that HRM personnel are simply "paper pushers" continues to disappear, to be replaced by the notion that they play a key role in helping to achieve organizational success and determining the organization's competitive advantage.

The new view of HRM personnel sees them as strategic partners working toward the organization's strategic goals and refers to this as strategic human resources management (SHRM). Today, organizations must adopt HRM practices that are consistent with its strategic missions. This chapter is devoted to this new view of HRM. The first section focuses on corporate, business, and functional strategies and their relationship to HRM. Important theoretical views of SHRM are then described. The discussion then turns to SHRM planning. The importance of fostering the partnership between managers and HRM personnel is highlighted. Finally, a framework for how organizations can evaluate HRM is offered.

STRATEGIC DECISION MAKING IN TODAY'S ORGANIZATIONS

Organizational success increasingly requires managers to engage in three levels of strategic decision making: corporate-level, business-level/competitive, and functional. Many organizations consist of several businesses. They therefore need a corporate-level strategy. An organization's corporate-level strategy identifies the portfolio of businesses that, in total, will comprise the organization and the ways in which these businesses will relate to each other.

At the next level down, each of these businesses is then guided by a business/competitive strategy. A competitive strategy identifies how to build and strengthen the business's long-term competitive position in the marketplace.

Finally, each business will in turn be comprised of departments, such as manufacturing, sales, and HRM. Functional strategies identify the basic courses of action that each of the business's departments will pursue in order to help the business attain its competitive goals. Strategies at all three levels, however, impact on the HRM function under the strategic approach to HRM as suggested in the next few paragraphs.

Strategic Planning and Building a Competitive Advantage

If you do not know where you are going, how will you ever get there? Although organizations pursue three levels of strategies, the term strategic planning is usually reserved for the company's corporate-level, organization-wide strategic planning process. It is through strategic planning that managers will ideally seek to balance two sets of forces—the organization's external opportunities and threats and its internal strengths and weaknesses. The strategic planning process helps organizations determine where they are going. When developing a strategic plan, an organization specifies its overall purpose and objectives and indicates how these are to be achieved. It is through the development and implementation of a strategic plan that organizations try to build and sustain a competitive advantage.

Organizations try to achieve competitive advantages for each business they are in. A competitive advantage can be defined as any factor that allows an organization to differentiate its product and service from those of its competitors to increase market share. Organizations can accomplish this aim in one of two ways: through cost leadership or differentiation.

With cost leadership, an organization provides the same services or products as its competitors, but produces them at a lower cost. By doing so, the organization earns a better return on its investment in capital and human resources. For example, Wal-Mart is an industry cost leader; it maintains its competitive advantage through its satellite-based distribution systems and the fact that it generally keeps store location costs to a minimum by placing most stores on low-cost land outside small to medium-sized southern towns. Timex and Hyundai are other examples of businesses that have successfully used a cost leadership strategy.

Differentiation is a second example of a competitive strategy. In a differentiation strategy, an organization seeks to be unique in its industry along dimensions that are widely valued or preferred by buyers. Like Mercedes Benz, organizations can usually charge a premium price if they successfully stake out their claim to being substantially different from their competition in some coveted way. Rolex and BMW are other organizations that have successfully used a differentiation strategy.

Strategy and HRM

Effective HRM practices can enhance an organization's competitive advantage by creating both cost leadership and differentiation. In today's competitive global environment, maintaining a competitive advantage puts a premium on having a committed and competent workforce. Low-cost, high-quality products and services are a result of committed employees all working hard to produce the best products and provide the best services that they can at the lowest possible cost.

The HRM function focuses its activities on ways to help the organization achieve corporate goals like growing operations through recruiting and hiring employees, orienting and training them, and making their initial and future job assignments. When organizations view the HRM area as a true strategic partner, they also use input from HRM managers in their initial formulation of corporate strategy.

HRM contributions to a cost leadership strategy focus on recruiting and retaining employees who can work as efficiently and productively as possible. On the other hand, more experienced employees may demand higher wages, so it might also be possible to reengineer jobs to require minimal skills and then to select employees who can perform the jobs but who may not remain long with the organization. A number of organizations (i.e., fast-food restaurants) often control labor costs with this type of an approach. Training may emphasize efficient production methods, and reward systems may be based more on quantity than on quality of output. One popular approach to reducing costs today is to move production to countries where labor costs are lower than in the home country.

HRM managers contribute to the successful use of a differentiation strategy by recruiting and retaining employees who can perform high-quality work and/or who can provide exemplary customer service. Likewise, employee training will likely focus on quality improvement, and reward systems may be based on factors such as quality of work and customer satisfaction.

As noted earlier, functional strategies address how the organization will manage its basic functional activities, such as marketing, finance, operations, research and development, and human resources management. Thus it is at this level that HRM strategy formulation or planning formally begins to take shape. It is clearly important that an HRM functional strategy be closely integrated and coordinated with the corporate, business, and other functional strategies. Indeed, without such integration and coordination, organizational competitiveness will clearly suffer.

As effective partners in helping organizations successfully achieve their goals, HRM managers need to have a clear understanding of exactly what are the organization's strategies, and then they must ensure that their own efforts are consistent with and provide support for those strategies. To the extent that the HRM function is seen as a strategic partner and/or a center of expertise, of course, its managers should also be actively involved in the formulation of corporate and business strategies as well as other functional strategies.

STRATEGIC HUMAN RESOURCES MANAGEMENT (SHRM)

One prominent figure in the development of the SHRM perspective argues that changes like those discussed at the end of Chapter 1 present a number of competitive challenges that are quite different from those faced by organizations in past years (Ulrich, 1997). All of the challenges continue to place additional pressure on organizations to be innovative and create new ways of doing business with new technologies, new products, and new services to meet an increasingly diverse and demanding group of customers.

The enhanced value of innovation in determining competitive advantage requires organizations to attract, train and develop, and retain employees of the highest quality. Over time and throughout rapidly changing circumstances, organizations must be able to sustain the competitive advantage that the knowledge and skills of these employees provide. In the past, competitive advantage could be gained through finding better, cheaper access to financial capital, or marketing a new product, or inventing some new technological gizmos. While cheap and ready access to capital, high-quality products, and new technology remain important components of any organization's competitive advantage, today's business environment requires a greater focus on the human resources element in business. Out of this realization has come SHRM.

Before one can understand what SHRM is, it is essential to have a clear picture of the "traditional" view of human resources management. Traditional personnel management is still the prevalent form of HRM activity in many organizations. From the traditional perspective, personnel managers handle administrative tasks. The traditional role of the personnel department revolves around the following tasks: human resources planning; recruiting staff; job analysis; establishing performance review systems; wage, salary, and benefits administration; employee training; personnel record keeping; legislative compliance (affirmative action, EEO, etc.); and labor relations.

The traditional personnel department is often both physically and psychologically separated from the "real work" of the organization. Traditional personnel involves a limited number of functional tasks, and personnel activities and staff are relatively isolated from the "profit-making heart" of the organization.

In the strategic view of HRM, the functional duties remain important. Certainly hiring, training, and providing pay and benefits to employees are essential tasks that must be accomplished in any organization. However, given the changes discussed earlier, many organizations are developing new structural and cultural patterns to meet the competitive demands of their dynamic and often global marketplace.

The fact that employees (or human resources) today can be a competitive advantage has led to the development of this new field known as SHRM. Strategic human resources management has been defined as "the linking of HRM with strategic goals and objectives in order to improve business performance and develop organizational cultures that foster innovation and flexibility (Truss and Gratton, 1994, p. 663). Put another way, it is "the pattern of planned human resource deployments and activities intended to enable an organization to achieve its goals" (Wright and McMahan, 1992, p. 292). Strategic human resources management means accepting the HRM function as a strategic partner in both the formulation of the organization's strategies and the implementation of those strategies through HRM activities such as recruiting, selecting, training, and rewarding personnel.

HRM strategies refer to the specific HRM courses of action the organization uses to achieve its aims. As noted earlier the efforts to formulate and implement sound HRM strategies at the three levels (corporate, competitive, and functional) are designed to achieve desirable end results such as high-quality products and services and socially responsible behavior. In other words, sound strategies are intended to result in growth, profits, and survival.

Strategic planning by an organization leads to informed, purposeful actions. By articulating a clear common vision of why the organization exists, now and in the future, a strategic plan provides direction and a cornerstone for making important HRM decisions. Planning HRM activities expands awareness of possibilities, identifies strengths and weaknesses, reveals opportunities, and points to the need to evaluate the probable impact of internal and external forces.

A well-designed organizational strategic plan permits the HRM department to develop HRM plans and be better prepared to cope with changes in both the internal and external environments. More will be said about HRM planning later in this chapter. Today's organizations need more than a traditional personnel model of HRM activities that simply involve putting out small fires—for example, ensuring that people are paid on the right day, that the job advertisement meets the newspaper deadline, that a suitable supervisor is recruited for the night shift by the time it goes ahead, and that the same manager remembers to observe due process before sacking the new rep who didn't work out. In an effort to offer new models of HRM a number of theoretical views of SHRM have been proposed as highlighted in the next section.

Theoretical Views on SHRM

Given the changes in the business environment many organizations are developing new structural and cultural patterns to meet the competitive demands of their dynamic and often international marketplace. As a result of the new strategic view of HRM in organizations, HRM plays a role in helping the organization reach its strategic objectives and it interacts fully with other functional areas within the organization. For example, HRM must help select employees able to innovate, train them to provide top-class customer service, and measure and reward entrepreneurial behavior.

A number of theoretical models have been developed to explain exactly what SHRM requires in an organization and the processes by which SHRM contributes to the bottom-line success of the organization. A summary of these theoretical perspectives is given in Exhibit 2.1.

As is often the case with theories about human behavior in organizations, the question for HRM practitioners is, "Which theoretical approach is correct, and from a practical perspective, what does it suggest are the important aspects of creating a good, strategically oriented HRM function within an organization?" In the case of the theoretical perspectives of SHRM in Exhibit 2.1, the answer to the question is not a simple one. Like many theories about organizations, none are completely correct. Predicting the effect of various HRM practices on an organization's performance and long-term success is not as straightforward as predicting the effect of gravity on a stone dropped from the roof of your house.

Rather than focusing on right or wrong, it is important to recognize that there are many different theoretical perspectives that one can rely on in the process of developing an effective strategic HRM function. What is important to take away from the different theoretical perspectives is that there is no "one best way" to view or operationalize HRM practices.

Today's and tomorrow's managers must learn as much as possible about the HRM best practices discussed throughout this book and then design a practice that's consistent with what their organization wants to achieve. The reality is that organizational success is increasingly dependent upon flexibility in HRM practices (such as the organization's reward system) and the ability of HRM personnel to change as competitive conditions continually pressure an organization to change its strategy.

Exhibit 2.1
Some Common Theoretical Perspectives on SHRM

Perspective	Description
Universalistic	There is one best way to manage human resources. Strategic HRM is the process of transforming traditional HRM practices into a limited set of "correct" HRM procedures and policies.
Strategic fit	Strategic HRM involves matching specific HRM practices to the organization's overall business strategy.
HRM as internal service provider	Strategic HRM involves HRM professionals providing HRM services to organizational units within the organization. The HRM goal is to enhance the effectiveness and efficiency of the operations of their organizational unit customers.
Configurational	There are various configurations or "bundles" of HRM practices that go together and, collectively, can improve organizational performance. Certain bundles are effective in certain industries and/or in certain business conditions, whereas other bundles should be used in other industries or under different business conditions.
Resource/competency	Strategic HRM engenders organizational success by enhancing an organization's ability to acquire, develop, use, and retain employees with high competence levels relevant to organization activities.

It is important to recognize that the viability (and strategic future) of the HRM department means that HRM needs to focus more and more on activities that clearly add value to the organization's success or bottom line—activities such as strategic planning, change management, corporate culture transitions, and developing human capital. One HRM expert has recently noted that "HRM can help deliver organizational excellence in four main ways" (Ulrich, 1998). For example, if strategy implementation requires, say, a team-based organizational structure, HRM would be responsible for bringing state-of-the-art approaches for creating this structure to senior management's attention. Second, HRM should become an expert in the way work is organized and executed, delivering administrative efficiency to ensure that costs are reduced while quality is maintained. Third, with employee behavior increasingly the key to competitive advantage, HRM should become a champion for employees, vigorously representing their concerns to senior management and at the same time working to increase employees' commitment to the organization and their ability to deliver results. Fourth, HRM needs to ensure the organization has the capacity to embrace and capitalize on change, for instance by making sure that "broad vision statements get transformed into specific behaviors" (Ulrich, 1998). As the tasks they face grow more complex, the HRM field is also becoming more professionalized. Thus, thousands of HRM professionals have already passed one or both of the HRM professional certification exams offered by the Human Resource Certification Institute. Those successfully completing all requirements earn the right to be designated a Professional in Human Resources (PHR) or a Senior Professional in Human Resources (SPHR).

Benefits of SHRM Planning

Successful organizations in the future must closely align their HRM strategies and programs (efforts) with the external opportunities, competitive strategies, and their unique characteristics and core competence. Organizations that fail to clearly define HRM strategy or competitive strategy that explicitly incorporates human resources will not be successful. Equally important to organizational success is ensuring that HRM programs or efforts help implement the organization's HRM strategy effectively.

The process of formulating HRM strategies and establishing programs to implement them is SHRM planning. When done correctly SHRM planning provides a number of direct and indirect benefits for an organization.

- Identification of gaps between an organization's current situation and desired future.
- Explicit communication of organizational goals.
- Encouragement of proactive rather than reactive behavior.
- Encouragement of line mangers' participation.
- Stimulation of critical thinking and ongoing examination of assumptions on which they make their decisions.
- Creation of common bonds or a sense of shared values and expectations.
- Identification of the potential problems and opportunities with respect to the people expected to implement the business strategy.

Other benefits of SHRM planning include:

- HRM costs may be lower because management can anticipate imbalances before they become unmanageable and expensive.
- More time is available to locate talent because needs are anticipated and identified before the actual staffing is required.
- Better opportunities exist to include women and minority groups in future growth plans.
- Development of managers can be better planned.

To the extent that these results can be measured, they can form the basis for evaluating the success of SHRM planning. Another approach is to measure projected levels of demand against actual levels at some point in the future. But the most telling evidence of successful SHRM planning in an organization is when the human resources are consistently aligned with the needs of the organization over a period of time. There are several actions HRM personnel can take to link HRM planning to the organization's strategic plans. These are discussed in the next section.

THE SHRM PROCESS

There are four steps in the SHRM process. The four steps are:

1. Determining the impact of the organization's objectives on specific organizational units.
2. Defining the knowledge, skills, expertise, and total number of employees (demand for human resources) required to achieve the organizational and functional or departmental objectives.
3. Determining the additional (net) human resources requirements in light of the organization's current human resources.
4. Developing specific action plans to meet the anticipated human resources needs.

Determining Organizational Objectives

SHRM plans must be based on organizational strategic plans (i.e., cost leadership or differentiation). In reality, this means the objectives of the SHRM plan must be derived from organizational objectives. Specific HRM requirements in terms of numbers and characteristics of employees should be derived from the objectives of the entire organization.

When properly implemented the objective-setting process involves both operating and HRM personnel in the overall planning process. During the early stages, HRM personnel can influence objective setting by providing information about the organization's human resources. For example, if HRM personnel have identified particular strengths and weaknesses in the organization's staff, this information can significantly influence the overall direction of the organization.

Determining the Knowledge, Skills, and Expertise Required (Demand)

After establishing organizational, divisional, and departmental objectives, line or operating managers must determine the knowledge, skills, and expertise required to meet their respective objectives. The key here is not to look at the knowledge, skills, and abilities (KSAs) of current employees but to determine the KSAs required to meet the objectives. For example, suppose an objective of the production department is to increase overall production of a specific product by 15 percent. Once this objective has been established, the production department must determine precisely how this translates into human resources needs. A good starting point is to review current job descriptions. Once this has been accomplished, the production department personnel is in a better position to determine the KSAs necessary to meet their objectives. The final step in this phase is to translate the needed KSAs into types and numbers of employees.

Determining the Additional (Net) Human Resources Requirements

Once a manager or team has determined the types and numbers of employees required, they must analyze these estimates in light of the current and anticipated human resources of the organization. This process involves a thorough analysis of presently employed personnel and a forecast of expected changes.

HRM personnel often rely on the use of a skills inventory to analyze current and future personnel changes. A skills inventory consolidates information about the organization's human resources. It provides basic information on all employees, including, in its simplest form, a list of the names, certain characteristics, and skills of employees. In addition to appraising present human resources through a skills inventory, managers must take future changes into account. Managers can accurately and easily estimate certain changes but cannot so easily forecast other changes. However, information is almost always available to help make these forecasts (i.e., changes such as retirements, transfers and promotions, resignations, discharges, etc.). By combining the forecast for the human resources needed with the information from the skills inventory and from anticipated changes, managers can make a reasonable prediction of their net human resources requirements for a specified time period.

Developing Specific Action Plans

Once the net human resources requirements have been determined, managers and other personnel must develop specific action plans for achieving the desired HRM results. If the net requirements indicate a need for additions, decisions must be made about whether to make permanent hires, temporary hires, or to outsource the work. If the decision is to make permanent or temporary hires, plans must be made to recruit, select, orient, and train the specific numbers and types of personnel needed. If the decision is to outsource, then potential vendors for outsourcing must be identified and evaluated.

If a reduction in human resources is necessary, plans must be made to realize the necessary adjustments. If time is not of the essence, natural attrition can be used to reduce labor personnel. However, if the organization cannot afford the luxury of natural attrition, it can cut overhead either by reducing the total number of employees or by making other adjustments that do not result in employees leaving the organization.

In successful organizations the SHRM plan provides a road map for the future. The plan identifies where employees are likely to be obtained, when employees will be needed, and what training and development employees must have.

Integrating the Evolving SHRM Process

As should be seen from our discussion thus far organization objectives are influenced by many environmental factors (i.e., competition, globalization, changing technology, workforce diversity, etc.). Once the organizational objectives have been established, they are translated into divisional and departmental objectives. Managers and other personnel then determine the human resources necessary to meet their respective objectives. HRM personnel assimilate these different requirements and determine the total human resources demand for the organization. Similarly, HRM personnel determine the additional (net) human resources requirements based on the information submitted by the various organizational units in light of available resources and anticipated changes. If the net requirements are positive, the organization implements recruitment, selection, training, and development. If the requirements are negative, decreasing or downsizing the workforce must be realized through attrition, layoffs, terminations, early retirements, or voluntary resignations. As these changes take place, they should be reflected in the skills inventory. SHRM planning is an ongoing process that must be continuously evaluated as internal and external conditions change.

To be effective and to contribute to organizational success, SHRM plans must be closely tied to and correspond to the broader organizational planning process and plans. This means that like organizational plans SHRM plans should be classified as short range (zero to two years), intermediate range (two to five years), or long range (beyond five years). Ideally, an organization prepares a plan for each of these time horizons and the forecast factors impacting SHRM plans. These forecast factors are demand, supply, and net human resources needs. For example, human resources demand in the intermediate range could be operating needs from budgets and plans. Supply in the intermediate range could be the human resources vacancies expected from individual promotability data derived from development plans. Net results in the intermediate range could then be the numbers, kinds, dates, and levels of human resources needs. In short, there are a number of short-, intermediate-, and long-range factors that affect SHRM planning.

In successful organizations SHRM planning efforts are viewed not as an all-or-nothing process but as falling at some point along a continuum. At one end of the continuum are those organizations that do no SHRM planning; at the other end are those that completely integrate long-range SHRM planning into their strategic business plans.

One expert has identified a number of benchmarks, or stages, along this continuum. Stage 1 companies have no long-term business plans, and they do little or no SHRM planning. Organizations at stage 2 have a long-term business plan, but tend to be skeptical of SHRM planning. At the same time, such organizations do realize to some degree that SHRM planning is important. Stage 3 organizations do engage in some aspects of SHRM planning, but for the most part these efforts are not integrated into the long-range business plan. Stage 4 organizations do a good deal of SHRM planning, and their top managers are enthusiastic about the process. These organizations have at least one human resources component integrated into the long-range plan. Stage 5 organizations treat SHRM planning as an important and vital part of their long-term business plans. Obviously, organizations at stage 5 are highly enthusiastic about SHRM planning and view it as key to their overall success.

Again, successful organizations require that each step in SHRM planning is a joint effort of the HRM personnel and the various managers and other employees in the organization. An important role of HRM personnel is to coordinate, monitor, and integrate the process. HRM personnel often provide the structure and establish the timetable to be followed by departmental or operating managers. This helps ensure a unified effort. As managers determine their human resources needs, they can channel this information through, or even develop this information with, the HRM staff to be coordinated and integrated. By funneling all the information through a central source, they can attain maximum efficiency in the process—efficiency that is key to today's organizational success.

THE CHALLENGES AND POTENTIAL PITFALLS OF SHRM PLANNING

In organizational life there are always challenges and potential pitfalls that must be recognized and addressed if organizations expect to succeed. This is also the case when it comes to SHRM planning.

Successful organizations recognize that in developing an effective HRM strategy, they face several important challenges and potential pitfalls. A number of these are discussed below.

Supporting Overall Strategy

Developing SHRM strategies to support the organization's overall strategy is a challenge for a number of reasons. First, senior management may not always be able to communicate the organization's overall strategy clearly. Second, there may be much uncertainty or disagreement concerning which HRM strategies should be used to support the overall organizational strategy. In other words, it is seldom obvious how particular HRM strategies will contribute to the achievement of organizational strategies. Third, large organizations may have different organizational units, each with its own strategies. Each unit should be able to formulate the HRM strategy that fits its strategy best.

Developing HRM Strategies for Unique Organizational Characteristics

No two organizations are exactly alike. Organizations differ in history, culture, leadership style, technology, strategy, and so on. The chances are high that any ambitious HRM strategy or program that is not molded to organizational characteristics will fail (Butler, Ferris, and Napier, 1991). And therein lies one of the key challenges in formulating HRM strategies: creating a vision of the organization of the future that does not provoke a destructive clash with the organization of the present.

Securing Management Commitment

SHRM planning is not strictly a HRM department function. Thus, HRM strategies that originate in the HRM department will have little chance of succeeding unless managers at all levels—including senior management— support them completely. To ensure managers' commitment, HRM personnel must work closely with them when formulating policies. Unfortunately, HRM personnel tend to become absorbed in their own function and fail to interact or coordinate with others. More will be said later in this chapter about the importance of an effective relationship between the HRM department and managers at all levels of the organization.

Integration with the Organization's Strategic Plan

As emphasized earlier, HRM plans must be derived from organizational plans. Often a strategic plan that looks great on paper fails because of poor implementation. The real test of any strategic plan is whether or not it makes a difference in practice. If the plan does not affect practice, employees and managers will regard it as all talk and no action. Perhaps the greatest challenge and common pitfall in SHRM planning lies not in the formulation of strategy but rather in the development of an appropriate set of programs that will make the strategy work. The key here is to develop good communication channels between the organization planners and the HRM planners.

Coping with the Environment

Just as no two organizations are alike, no two organizations operate in an identical environment. Some must deal with rapid change, as in the computer industry; others operate in a relatively stable market, as in the market for food processors. Some must deal with turbulent demand (for example, fashion designers); others face a virtually guaranteed demand for their products or services (for example, medical providers). A major challenge in developing HRM strategies is crafting strategies that will work in the organization's unique environment to give it a sustainable competitive advantage.

Qualitative versus Quantitative Approaches to HRM

Some people view SHRM planning from a qualitative perspective and focus on individual employee concerns such as individual promotability and career development. Others view SHRM planning as a numbers game designed to track the flow of people in, out, up, down, and across the different organizational units. These people take a strictly quantitative approach to SHRM planning. As is often the case, a balanced approach usually yields the best results, and successful organizations encourage such an approach.

Accommodating Continuous Change

SHRM plans must be flexible enough to accommodate change. HRM planners work in an environment characterized by ambiguous regulations, organizational politics, diverse management styles, and a rapidly changing, demanding broader organizational environment. An organization with an inflexible strategic plan may find itself unable to respond to changes quickly because it is so committed to a particular course of action. This may lead an organization to continue devoting resources to an activity of questionable value simply because so much has been invested in it already. The challenge is to create a strategic vision and develop the plans to achieve it while staying flexible enough to adapt to change.

Maintaining a Competitive Advantage

One realization in today's environment is that any competitive advantage enjoyed by an organization tends to be short-lived because other organizations are likely to imitate it. This is as true for HRM advantages as for marketing and technological advantages. For example, many high-tech organizations have "borrowed" reward programs for key engineers and scientists from other successful high-tech organizations.

The challenge and potential pitfall from an HRM perspective is to avoid excessive concentration on day-to-day problems and develop strategies that offer the organization a sustained competitive advantage. For instance, an organization may develop programs that simply put out fires as opposed to developing programs that maximize the long-term direction of the organization.

WHY SOME ORGANIZATIONS STILL RESIST SHRM

It is not surprising that many U.S. organizations have yet to make the leap to SHRM given the differences between traditional personnel and SHRM. A number of reasons exist as to why the transformation to SHRM still hasn't been made by some organizations. Committed and supportive top management and a highly competent and persistent SHRM leader are important factors for the adoption of SHRM. Unfortunately, many organizations do not have top management support or this type of HRM leader. Internal organizational forces, accompanied by competing coalitions with different self-interests, may also preclude the adoption of many SHRM practices. For example, HRM systems that may help achieve particular organizational objectives may not be supported by unions. Also, organizations that are not labor intensive may be less likely to make the effort to move to a strategic HRM orientation, since human resources are perceived to make up a relatively small portion of the organization's potential competitive advantage.

The traditional role that HRM has played in many organizations may have established a vicious cycle that makes the transition to SHRM extremely difficult. Unless HRM managers are involved directly in the process of strategy formulation, any attempt by senior management to link HRM activities with business strategy simply creates a cycle in which HRM cannot implement the HRM components of the strategy effectively, which causes HRM to lose credibility with non-HRM managers and which isolates HRM further from the strategic planning process, making it increasingly difficult to implement strategy, and so forth.

Organizations experiencing very turbulent business conditions (sudden decline or rapid expansion) often feel that they are "up to their ears in alligators" and do not have the time or resources to invest in an HRM transformation. Unfortunately, for many of these organizations, the lack of attention to HRM issues may be one of the primary factors contributing to their business stress. For example, historically organizations undergoing downsizing often cut HRM staff, since they are viewed as nonessential to the core business. However, after downsizing, employees often need extensive training to manage expanded jobs, and the selection of any new staff becomes particularly critical. Thus, at a time when HRM services are most needed, they are often reduced. Further, highly decentralized organizations made up of autonomous business units may view the move to an organization-wide, relatively unitary model of SHRM as both infeasible and potentially undesirable.

Making the change to SHRM from traditional HRM is a time-consuming and complex process. It is important for both senior managers and HRM personnel to question the benefits of the process of transforming SHRM. Just as it is important to evaluate the effectiveness of a particular HRM practice, organizations must constantly examine the issue of whether SHRM really provides benefits for all the effort that goes into it.

There is evidence that HRM practices do have a direct bottom-line effect on organizational profitability. For example, one study has shown that highly HRM-progressive organizations enjoyed higher sales growth, profit margins, equity growth, and earnings per share than less progressive ones. Other research assessing the level of HRM "technical" and "strategic" effectiveness has found that "high performance work practices" are also associated with an increase in per-employee sales volume, an increase in cash flow, an increase in market value per employee, and a decrease in employee turnover (see for example, Huselid, Jackson, and Schuler, 1997).

While research on the financial impact of HRM practices is not conclusive, the existing results, along with data on the costs of HRM in best versus typical units and practical dollar-saving experience of some organizations, seem to present a strong case for promoting the improvement of HRM activities as a means of contributing to achievement of strategic goals and affecting the financial results of many organizations. The organizational environment that has caused organizations to recognize the importance of human resources as a competitive advantage will continue in the years to come.

To the extent that HRM personnel continue to view themselves as strategic partners committed to measuring aspects of customer reactions, HRM program impact, and dollar value of HRM practices and to benchmarking their own HRM practices with those of their competitors, SHRM is likely to increase its contribution to organizational success. In closing this chapter, it is important to reemphasize the importance of the partnership between the HRM department and managers at all levels of the organization. The next section offers some views on how to build an effective partnership between the HRM personnel and managers.

FOSTERING THE PARTNERSHIP BETWEEN MANAGERS AND THE HRM DEPARTMENT

As noted earlier, traditionally HRM departments had limited involvement in the total organization's business affairs and goals. HRM managers and staff were often only concerned with making staffing plans, providing specific job training programs, or running annual performance appraisal programs (the results of which were sometimes put in the files, never to be used). They focused on the short term—perhaps day-to-day—needs of human resources.

With the growing importance of human resources to the success of the organization, HRM managers and their departments have taken on the role of knowing the needs of the organization and helping address those needs. The importance of the partnership between managers and HRM personnel to long-term organizational success cannot be underestimated. By partnering with managers in the organization, HRM personnel help organizations balance the sometimes competing concerns of "the organization" as defined by employees upon whom the organization's success ultimately depends and by line managers.

For the sake of the organization, managers and the HRM department need to continue to work together closely. Unfortunately, lack of cooperation has been a problem, and even today it is not uncommon for HRM personnel and managers to view each other negatively. These negative perceptions often create a communication gap and hinder the establishment of an effective partnership between the two groups.

Organizations can take specific steps to foster an effective partnership between the HRM department and managers (Bailey, 1991). Specifically, organizations should:

- Analyze the people side of productivity rather than depend solely on technical solutions. This means that managers need to be trained in certain HRM skills. It also requires encouraging managers to value human resources as a key element in organizational effectiveness, success, and performance.

- View HRM professionals as internal consultants who can provide valuable advice and support to improve the management of operations. In other words, managers need to view the HRM department as a source of expertise capable of assisting them in solving personnel-related problems, planning for the future, and improving utilization of productive capacity rather than thinking of the HRM department as a group responsible for enforcing bureaucratic or traditional policies and procedures.

- Instill a shared sense of common fate in the organization rather than focus on a win/lose perspective among individual departments and units. This means developing incentives for HRM personnel and managers to work together to achieve common goals.

- Incorporate some managerial experience as part of the developing HRM personnel. Incorporating managerial experience as part of developing HRM personnel should make them more sensitive to and cognizant of the problems managers face.

- Consistently involve senior and middle managers in formulating, implementing, and reviewing all HRM plans and strategies in close collaboration with the HRM department. This should increase management's commitment to the effective implementation of these plans.

• Accept nothing less than equal participation by HRM executives with other key executives from the various functional areas (finance, marketing, operations) involved in developing and achieving the organization's strategic direction.

The partnership between managers and HRM personnel leads to effective HRM practices and ultimately organizational success.

HRM EVALUATION IN TODAY'S ORGANIZATION

An important trend in recent years is the increased emphasis on evaluating the effectiveness of the HRM function. Historically, HRM was seen as an organizational cost and expense. That is, the organization budgeted a certain amount of money to spend on the management of its HRM function. As long as the HRM function stayed within this budget, things were generally assumed to be fine. More recently, however, many organizations have come to view HRM in a different light. Specifically, because so many HRM functions can now be subcontracted or outsourced to external vendors, organizations are paying more attention to the actual costs and value of an in-house HRM function. Line managers may even be given the option of choosing to use the corporation's HRM department for various functions or to subcontract those functions to external vendors.

In addition to the evaluation of specific HRM functions, however, another recent trend has focused on evaluating entire systems of HRM activities. In these situations organizations that view HRM practices as competitive activities utilize their human resources in ways that create a stronger competitive advantage relative to other organizations. This perspective also suggests a new approach to the evaluation of HRM activities. Rather than show how a specific HRM practice (for example, using certain types of tests to select new employees) results in higher levels of productivity, this approach suggests that "bundles" of HRM practices are related more clearly to an organization's performance. As organizations continue to strive for new levels of success they will also need to search for new ways to evaluate their HRM practices. Failure to do so will increase the likelihood that they will not get the maximum out of their most valuable resource—their human resources.

SUMMARY

Organizational success requires today's managers to increasingly engage in three levels of strategic decision making: corporate, business, and functional. Each of these strategies in turn has an impact on the HRM function and thus results in the need for a strategic approach to HRM.

Trends such as globalization, technological advances, and deregulation mean that organizations must be better, faster, and more competitive to survive and thrive today. Other important trends include growing workforce diversity and changes in the nature of work, such as the movement toward a service society and a growing emphasis on human capital.

Trends like these, along with an increased emphasis on the levels of strategic decision making, require HRM to be a strategic partner with other managers throughout today's organization. The traditional view of HRM as an isolated, record-keeping function within the organization is no longer viable. Although SHRM can be considered simply as the process of helping an organization achieve competitive advantage through its people, there are many different theoretical perspectives on this seemingly simple definition. These different theoretical perspectives each add to an overall view of SHRM's role in organizational success.

With this new view of SHRM, HRM personnel must work with other top managers to formulate company strategy as well as execute it. In serving in their role as strategic partners, HRM personnel must understand the actions they must take to link HRM planning to the organization's strategic plans. This understanding must also include an appreciation of the challenges and pitfalls of SHRM planning.

Further, there is an increased need for managers and HRM personnel to evaluate the effectiveness of the HRM function and its role in helping the organization attain its strategic objectives. This evaluation usually focuses on specific HRM practices and the more recent emphasis on bundles of so-called HRM best practices.

REFERENCES

Bailey, B. 1991. Ask what HR can do for itself. *Personnel Journal* (July): 35–39.

Butler, J.E., Ferris, G.R., and Napier, N.K. 1991. *Strategy and human resources management*. Cincinnati, OH: South-Western.

Huselid, M., Jackson, S., and Schuler, R. 1997. Technical and strategic human resource management effectiveness as determinants of firm performance. *Academy of Management Journal* 40(1): 171–188.

Truss, C., and Gratton, L. 1994. Strategic human resource management: A conceptual approach. *The International Journal of Human Resource Management* 5(3): 663.

Ulrich, D. 1997. *Human resource champions*. Cambridge, MA: Harvard Business School Press.

Ulrich, D. 1998. A new mandate for human resources. *Harvard Business Review* (January–February): 124–134.

Wright, P., and McMahan, G. 1992. Theoretical perspectives for strategic human resource management. *Journal of Management* 18(2): 292.

Chapter 3

The Legal Environment

INTRODUCTION

A jury awarded $120 million in punitive damages to 17 black former employees of a San Francisco bakery that produces Wonder Bread, Twinkies, and Hostess Cupcakes. The plaintiffs claimed they were forced to endure racial epithets, were denied promotions, and were given the worst shifts.

A prospective lawyer passed the bar exam only to have the state examining committee refuse him admission to the bar, holding that his psychological depression made him unfit to practice law. He filed an Americans with Disabilities Act (ADA) suit and submitted a psychiatric opinion that he could, in fact, adequately represent clients.

Examples such as these seem to be commonplace in the media today. They illustrate issues of equal employment opportunity (EEO) and the reality of today's legal environment for many organizations. The legal environment in which organizations find themselves continues to evolve and change, and HRM personnel and other members of the organization must not only be aware of old but also of new emerging issues if they are to help organizations succeed in the coming years. Thus HRM personnel and managers need to be familiar with existing laws and regulations while they continue to monitor current developments, pending legislation, and court decisions. The HRM function must play an especially important role in this process as part of its' efforts to contribute to organizational success.

This chapter discusses the laws and regulations that have affected organizations' employment practices over the years and that have partly contributed to the emergence of the HRM function as a key contributor to organizational success. The HRM function helps organizations, managers, and employees understand the legal environment, and that is the specific focus of this chapter.

Equal employment opportunity is the central part of the legal context of HRM. Managers need to have a clear and specific knowledge about the various regulations and laws that affect their organizations. They should also understand the various forms of illegal discrimination and the protected classes in the workplace. In addition, managers need to be familiar with the various agencies that enforce equal employment legislation.

In the next section we explore some major laws that regulate HRM activities, particularly EEO laws. We first discuss a number of laws that mandate EEO in the United States and then examine corresponding enforcement agencies. The chapter then provides a discussion of practices to prevent discrimination. The chapter concludes with a number of organizational practices for responding to and avoiding potential EEO pitfalls.

EQUAL EMPLOYMENT OPPORTUNITY

EEO laws are one group of laws that affect HRM issues. We will spend the majority of our time discussing EEO laws because these are the ones that most affect a manager's daily behavior. In addition, the EEO laws cut across almost every other issue that we discuss in this book. There are other laws that affect HRM activities, but these laws tend to be more specifically focused, and they will be discussed in the context in which they apply. For instance, we discuss the labor-related laws in Chapter 13 and the Occupational Safety and Health Act in Chapter 12.

Equal employment opportunity refers to the government's attempt to ensure that all individuals have an equal chance for employment, regardless of race, color, religion, sex, or national origin. Although many EEO laws have been passed by state and local governments, we will limit our discussion to those passed by the U.S. Congress. Managers at all levels of the organization, however, should be aware of state EEO laws, since these laws are sometimes more stringent than federal laws. For example, a Texas state law prohibiting age discrimination covers individuals between the ages of 21 and 70. The federal age discrimination law applies only to persons who are age 40 and over. Exhibit 3.1 offers a summarization of most of the EEO laws and regulations discussed below.

Civil Rights Acts of 1866 and 1871

The Civil Rights Act of 1866 was an effort to further the goal of eradicating slavery as set forth in the Thirteenth Amendment. The Civil Rights Act passed in 1866 was later broken into two sections. Section 1982 granted all persons the same property rights as white citizens. Section 1981 granted other rights, including the right to enter into and enforce contracts.

Exhibit 3.1
Summary of EEO Laws and Regulations

Act	Focus
Thirteenth Amendment	Abolished slavery.
Fourteenth Amendment	Provides equal protection for all citizens and requires due process in state action.
Civil Rights Acts (CRAs) of 1866 and 1871 (as amended)	Grants all citizens the right to make, perform, modify, and terminate contracts and enjoy all benefits, terms, and conditions of the contractual relationship.
Equal Pay Act of 1963	Requires the same pay for men and women who do the same job in the same organization.
Civil Rights Act of 1964	Title VII prohibits employment discrimination in hiring, compensation, and terms, conditions, or privileges of employment based on race, religion, color, sex, or national origin.
Executive Order (EO) 11246	Requires affirmative action in hiring women and minorities.
Executive Order 11375	Added sex-based discrimination to EO 11246.
Age Discrimination in Employment Act of 1967	Prohibits discrimination in employment against individuals 40 years of age and older.
Executive Order 11478	Amends part of EO 11246, states practices in the federal government must be based on merit, and prohibits discrimination based on political affiliation, marital status, or physical handicap.
Equal Employment Opportunity Act of 1972	Granted the enforcement powers for the EEOC.
Vocational Rehabilitation Act of 1973	Requires affirmative action in the employment of individuals with disabilities.
Vietnam Era Veterans' Readjustment Assistance Act of 1974	Prohibits federal government contractors and subcontractors with federal government contracts of $10,000 or more from discriminating in hiring and promoting Vietnam and disabled veterans.
Age Discrimination in Employment Act of 1978	Increased mandatory retirement age from 65 to 70. Later amended (1986) to eliminate upper age limit.
Pregnancy Discrimination Act of 1978	Requires employers to treat pregnancy just like any other medical condition with regard to fringe benefits and leave policies.
Immigration Reform Act of 1986	Makes it illegal to hire, recruit, or refer for U.S. employment anyone known to be an unauthorized alien.

Exhibit 3.1 (continued)

Act	Focus
Americans with Disabilities Act of 1990	Prohibits discrimination against individuals with disabilities, and requires organizations to reasonably accommodate individuals.
Older Workers Benefit Protection Act of 1990	Provides protection for employees over 40 years of age in regard to fringe benefits and gives employees time to consider an early retirement offer.
Civil Rights Act of 1991	Nullifies selected Supreme Court decisions. Reinstates burden of proof by employer. Allows for punitive and compensatory damages through jury trials.
Family and Medical Leave Act of 1993	Enables qualified employees to take prolonged unpaid leave for family and health-related reasons without fear of losing their jobs.

This law has been interpreted by the courts as prohibiting racial discrimination by employers, unions, and employment agencies in making of employment contracts. The Civil Rights Act of 1871 granted all citizens the right to sue in federal court if they felt they had been deprived of some civil right. Both of these laws are still used because they allow the plaintiff to recover both compensatory and punitive damages.

Although these earlier actions have been overshadowed by the 1964 Civil Rights Act, they have gained prominence in years past as being laws that white male workers could use to support claims of reverse discrimination. In such cases, white males used the Civil Rights Act of 1866 and the Fourteenth Amendment to support their argument that minorities were given special treatment in employment decisions that placed the white male at a distinct disadvantage (more will be said about reverse discrimination later in this chapter). In addition to allowing individuals to seek punitive and compensatory damages under Section 1981, the Civil Rights Act of 1866 also allowed for the awarding of back pay. However, in 1989, a Supreme Court ruling limited Section 1981 use in discrimination suits, saying that the law does not cover racial discrimination after a person has been hired. The Civil Rights Act of 1991 amended this act to include the making, performance, modification, and termination of contracts, as well as all benefits, privileges, terms, and conditions of the contractual relationship.

Equal Pay Act of 1963

The first of the civil rights laws was the Equal Pay Act, an amendment of the Fair Labor Standards Act. The Equal Pay Act became law in 1963.

It requires that men and women who do the same job in the same organization should receive the same pay. "Same pay" means that no difference is acceptable.

Determining whether two employees are doing the same job can be difficult. The law specifies that jobs are the same if they are equal in terms of skill, effort, responsibility, and working conditions. Thus it is permissible to pay one employee more than another if the first employee has significant extra job duties, such as a supervisory responsibility. Pay can also be different for different work shifts. The law also specifies that equal pay is required only for jobs held in the same geographical region. This allows an organization to make allowances for the local cost of living and the fact that it might be harder to find qualified employees in some areas.

The law contains several explicit exceptions. First, it does not prohibit the use of a merit pay plan. That is, an employer can pay a man more if he is doing a better job than his female co-worker. In addition, organizations are permitted to pay for differences in quantity and quality of production. Seniority plans also are exempted; an organization that ties pay rates to seniority can pay a man more if he has been with the company longer than a female employee in the same job. Finally, the law indicates that any factor other than sex may be used to justify pay rates. Despite the existence of the Equal Pay Act for close to 40 years, general disparities in the rates of pay for men and women still exist.

Title VII of the Civil Rights Act of 1964

No single piece of legislation in the 1960s had a greater effect on reducing employment discrimination than the Civil Rights Act of 1964. The law was enacted in the middle of the seething civil rights conflicts of the 1960s, one year after the civil rights march on Washington. The goal of Title VII prohibits employment discrimination based on race, color, religion, sex, or national origin. It protects employees from discrimination in such terms and conditions of employment as selection, placement, promotion, discharge, training, and pay and benefits. The Equal Employment Opportunity Commission (EEOC) was created by the 1964 law to enforce the provisions of Title VII.

As amended, Title VII applies to private employers that have 15 or more employees on each working day of 20 or more calendar weeks in the current or preceding year. Title VII also applies to labor unions, employment agencies, state and local governments and their agencies, and colleges and universities. It protects all employees and applicants from employment in these organizations. There are some exceptions to this coverage, however. Religious organizations are not covered by certain religious discrimination aspects of Title VII. Elected public officials and their staffs and members of the Communist Party are not protected. Employees who apply for jobs that require national security clearance are subject to special policies.

Charges of discrimination may be filed with the EEOC or a state agency working cooperatively with the EEOC by an individual, and the EEOC may file its own charges that may involve more than one person. The party charging discrimination (the plaintiff) must present reasonable evidence of the event, usually offering some form of statistical data. Once reasonable cause is shown, the burden of proof is transferred to the one being charged with discrimination (the defendant). Now the organization accused of discrimination begins the process of proving that no discrimination occurred. Often the organization presents data to try to show that the employment practice being questioned is a business necessity or is job-related. These issues will be discussed in more detail later in this chapter.

Executive Order 11246 and Revisions

Concurrently with the passage of the Civil Rights Act of 1964, President Lyndon Johnson issued Executive Order (EO) 11246, which forbade discrimination on the part of federal contractors, subcontractors, and federal agencies. Thus, this executive order is similar to Title VII, and it applies to a large number of U.S. employers.

One major difference is that EO 11246 also requires affirmative action, in which covered employers (e.g., contracts of at least $50,000 and 50 employees) are required to prepare an annual Affirmative Action Plan. The plan reflects a more aggressive effort to rectify the "underutilization" of various minority groups and women within organizations. In effect, affirmative action is designed to "play catch-up"—to achieve accelerated progress in employment opportunities for minorities and women, in order to make up for many years of past discrimination. More will be said about affirmative action plans in our discussion of EEO enforcement agencies (EEOC and OFCCP) later in this chapter.

Age Discrimination in Employment Act of 1967

The Age Discrimination in Employment Act (ADEA) was passed in 1967 and amended in 1978 and 1986. This act prohibits discrimination against employees over the age of 40. The act gave protected group status to individuals between the ages of 40 and 65 and prohibited the widespread practice of requiring employees to retire at the age of 65. The act exactly mirrors Title VII in terms of its substantive provisions and the procedures to be followed in pursuing a case. As with Title VII, the EEOC is responsible for enforcing this act.

The ADEA was passed in response to a disquieting trend that was noticed at some organizations in the early 1960s. Specifically, these organizations were beginning to overtly discriminate against older employees when the organizations found it necessary to lay off people or to otherwise scale back their workforce. By targeting older workers who tended to have higher pay because of their seniority with the organization, organizations were substantially cutting their labor costs. In addition, there was some feeling that organizations were also discriminating against older workers in hiring decisions. The specific concern here was that organizations would not hire people in their forties and fifties because (1) organizations would have to pay those individuals more because of their experience and salary history and (2) those individuals would have a shorter potential career with the organization. Consequently, some organizations were found to be guilty of giving preferential treatment to younger workers over older workers.

In recent years, organizations have often offered early retirement incentives, a possible violation of the act because of the focus on older employees. Early retirement incentives require employees to sign an agreement waiving their rights to sue under the ADEA. Courts have tended to uphold the use of early retirement incentives and waivers as long as the individuals were not coerced into signing the agreements, the agreements were presented in a way that the employees could understand, and the employees were given enough time to make a decision.

The Vocational Rehabilitation Act of 1973

The Vocational Rehabilitation Act requires executive agencies and subcontractors and contractors of the federal government with federal contracts over $2,500 to take affirmative action in the employment of disabled persons. The primary responsibility for enforcing this act lies with the Office of Federal Contract Compliance Programs (OFCCP) of the Department of Labor. A federal district court recently held that compensatory damages (a payment for "future pecuniary losses, emotional pain, suffering, inconvenience, mental anguish, loss of employment of life, and other nonpecuniary losses") are available under the 1973 act.

The Vocational Rehabilitation Act took on added prominence because of a ruling that suggested it could be used to prohibit discrimination against people with acquired immunodeficiency syndrome (AIDS). In any case, the EEOC's position today is that the Americans with Disabilities Act (discussed later) prohibits discriminating against people with AIDS. Furthermore, numerous state laws now protect people with AIDS from discrimination. The guidelines issued by the OFCCP also require that AIDS-type diseases be treated according to the provisions of the Vocational Rehabilitation Act (Bureau of National Affairs, 1989, p. 39). The bottom line for most employers is that discriminating against people with AIDS would be viewed as unlawful (Ritter and Turner, 1987).

The Vietnam Era Veterans' Readjustment Assistance Act of 1974

The Vietnam Era Veterans' Readjustment Assistance Act of 1974 prohibits federal government contractors and subcontractors with federal government contracts of $10,000 or more from discriminating in hiring and promoting Vietnam and disabled veterans. Furthermore, the act requires employers with 50 or more employees and contracts that exceed $50,000 to have written affirmative action programs with regard to the people protected by this act. The protected class consists of disabled veterans with a 30 percent or more disability rating, veterans discharged or released for a service-connected disability, and veterans on active duty for any part of the time period between August 5, 1964, and May 7, 1975. Covered contractors and subcontractors must also list job openings with the state employment service. The act is administered by the OFCCP (Commerce Clearing House, 1988, p. 32).

The Pregnancy Discrimination Act of 1978

The Pregnancy Discrimination Act (PDA) was passed as an amendment to the Civil Rights Act of 1964, Title VII. The act broadened the definition of sex discrimination to encompass pregnancy, childbirth, or related medical conditions. The law requires that pregnant women be treated the same as any other employees in the workplace. Therefore, the act specifies that a woman cannot be refused a job or promotion, be fired, or otherwise be discriminated against simply because she is pregnant (or has had an abortion). She also cannot be forced to leave employment with the organization as long as she is physically able to work. Finally, the PDA specifies that if other employees have the right to receive their jobs back after a leave, then this benefit must be accorded to pregnant women as well.

In January 1987, the U.S. Supreme Court ruled in *California Federal Savings and Loan Association v. Guerra* that if an employer offers no disability leave to any of its employees, it can (but need not necessarily) grant pregnancy leave to a woman who requests it when disabled for pregnancy, childbirth, or a related medical condition, although men get no comparable benefits (Bureau of National Affairs, 1987, p. 7; Murphy, Barlow, and Hatch, 1987, p. 18). In one recent high-profile case, actress Hunter Tylo won a $5 million judgment against the producers of the television show *Melrose Place* after they used her pregnancy as a basis for writing her out of the show ("Pregnant Workers," 1999, p. B1).

The Immigration Reform and Control Act of 1986

In response to an increased influx of illegal aliens into the United States, the Immigration Reform and Control Act (IRCA) was passed making it illegal for anyone to hire, recruit, or refer for employment in the United States a person known to be an unauthorized alien. To meet the requirements of the law, an organization must attest, under penalty of perjury, that it has verified that the individual is not an unauthorized alien by one of the following measures:

1. Examining the individual's U.S. passport; certificate of U.S. citizenship; certificate of naturalization; unexpired foreign passport, if the passport has an appropriate, unexpired endorsement of the attorney general authorizing the individual's employment in the United States; or resident alien card.
2. Receiving verification from documents demonstrating employment authorization (Social Security card, birth certificate, or other documentation that the attorney general deems acceptable as proof).
3. Receiving documentation establishing identification (e.g., state driver's license with a photograph or other documentation that the attorney general deems acceptable as proof).

The Americans with Disabilities Act of 1990

The Americans with Disabilities Act of 1990 (ADA) is one of the most far-reaching acts concerning the management of human resources. The ADA was passed in response to growing criticisms and concerns about employment opportunities denied to people with various disabilities. The act protects individuals with disabilities from being discriminated against in the workplace. It prohibits discrimination based on disability in all employment practices, including job application procedures, hiring, firing, promotions, compensation, and training, in addition to other employment activities such as advertising, recruitment, tenure, layoff, leave, and fringe benefits.

The act initially went into effect in 1992, covering employers with 25 or more employees. It was expanded in July 1994 to cover employers with 15 or more employees. The ADA requires that organizations make reasonable accommodations for disabled employees as long as the accommodations themselves do not pose an undue burden on the organization.

The ADA defines disability as a mental or physical impairment that limits one or more major life activities, a record of having such an impairment, or being regarded as having a disability, such as might be the case with individuals who are disfigured or who for some other reason an employer feels will prompt a negative reaction from others. In addition, the ADA covers mental and psychological disorders, such as mental retardation and emotional or mental abuse problems. Obesity and similar non-work-related characteristics are not covered by the ADA.

It is interesting to note that contagious diseases, including AIDS, are considered conditions of being disabled. In advancing the decision in the

1987 court case of *Arline v. Nassau County* (Flygare, 1987, p. 705), the ADA views contagious diseases as any other medical disability. With respect to AIDS, there are exceptions that can be implemented, but most of these are rare. In restaurants, for example, the individual may simply be assigned other duties rather than terminated. Under this law, employers must treat AIDS employees in the same way that they would treat an employee suffering from cancer, and all job actions must be based on job requirements.

As long as a person with a disability can fulfill the essential duties of a job, that person cannot be discriminated against in employment. As noted earlier, employers are also expected to make reasonable accommodations—up to the point where the organization would experience undue hardship—for employees with disabilities. As with all the discrimination laws, these reasonable accommodations have to be determined on a case-by-case basis.

To illustrate the actions managers need to consider to comply with the ADA, here are a few examples of reasonable accommodations (Commerce Clearing House, 1992):

1. *Making facilities accessible and usable.* This might include installing ramps at building entrances, making restrooms accessible, or rearranging office furniture and equipment.
2. *Job restructuring.* An employer may be expected to change when or how essential job functions are performed, say, by shifting duties from morning to afternoon or by providing a person who is mentally challenged with a task checklist for remembering the order of job functions.
3. *Modifying work schedules.* This may be appropriate for people who need special medical treatment or who have special transportation schedules.
4. *Acquiring or modifying equipment and devices.* Many devices can allow people to overcome barriers to performing job functions (e.g., an elastic band allowing a person with cerebral palsy to hold a pencil). The applicant is the best source of information about these devices.
5. *Modifying exams, training materials, or policies.* Applicants with learning disabilities may be given extra time to finish a test, or hearing-impaired trainees may be provided with interpreters or note takers.

The Older Workers Benefit Protection Act

The Older Workers Benefit Protection Act of 1990 (OWBPA) resulted from a 1989 decision of the U.S. Supreme Court. In that decision, an Ohio county agency denied disability benefits to an employee who had been laid off at age 61 because its disability plan cut off at age 60. The Court ruled that the agency had not violated the ADEA because, it said, the law does not cover benefits, just hirings, firings, and promotions.

Under the OWBPA, employers may integrate disability and pension pay by paying the retiree the higher of the two, integrate retiree health insurance and severance pay by deducting the former from the latter, and, in cases of plant closing or mass layoffs, integrate pension and severance pay by deducting from severance pay the amount added to the pension.

The act also gives employees time to consider a company's early retirement package—21 days for an individual or 45 days if a group is involved. Employees also have seven days to change their minds if they have signed a waiver of their right to sue. Coverage of this law is the same as that under the ADEA.

The Civil Rights Act of 1991

The Civil Rights Act of 1991 (CRA) was passed as an amendment to Title VII of the CRA of 1964. Several decisions by the U.S. Supreme Court that essentially redefined parts of the 1964 act led to this amendment. The CRA of 1991 essentially restored the force of the CRA of 1964, which had been reduced by these decisions. The CRA of 1991 makes it easier for individuals who believe that they have been discriminated against to take legal action against organizations.

It also provides, for the first time, the potential payment of compensation and punitive damages in cases of discrimination under Title VII. Title VII itself, as originally passed, provided only for compensation for back pay. But the new law also limits the amount of punitive damages that can be paid to someone. Depending on the size of the organization, the allowable damage range is from $50,000 to $300,000 for each instance of violation of the law. Further, punitive damages can be paid only if the employer intentionally discriminates against someone or if the employer discriminates with malice or reckless indifference to an individual's federally protected rights.

The law also enables employees of U.S. organizations working in foreign countries to bring suit against those organizations for violation of the CRA. The only exception to this provision is the situation in which a country has laws that specifically contradict some aspect of the CRA. For example, Muslim countries often have laws limiting the rights of women. Foreign companies with operations in such countries would almost certainly be required to abide by local laws. As a result, a female employee of a U.S. company working in such a setting would not be directly protected under the CRA. However, her employer would still need to fully inform her of the kinds of discriminatory practices she might face as a result of transferring to the foreign site and then ensure that when this particular foreign assignment is completed her career opportunities will not have been compromised in any way. This act also includes the Glass Ceiling Act, establishing the Glass Ceiling Commission whose purpose is to study a variety of management practices in organizations.

The Family and Medical Leave Act of 1993

The Family and Medical Leave Act of 1993 (FMLA) was passed in part to remedy weaknesses in the Pregnancy Discrimination Act of 1978. The 1993 law requires employers having more than 50 employees to provide up to 12 weeks of unpaid leave for employees after the birth or adoption of a child; to care for a seriously ill child, spouse, or parent; or in the case of an employee's own serious illness. The organization must provide the employee with the same or a comparable job upon the employee's return (Martinez, 1994).

The law also requires the organization to pay the health care coverage of the employee during the leave. However, the employer can require the employee to reimburse these premiums if the employee fails to work after the absence. Organizations are allowed to identify key employees, specifically defined as the highest paid 10 percent of their workforce, on the grounds that granting leave to these individuals would cause serious economic harm to the organization. The law also does not apply to employees who have not worked an average of 25 hours a week in the previous 12 months.

Clearly, then, a substantial body of laws and regulations governs EEO. Many people argue, of course, that all these laws and regulations are necessary. Without them organizations might either intentionally or unintentionally revert to former employment practices that led to illegal discrimination against large numbers of people. On the other hand, some critics argue that the regulatory environment has grown too complex. They point to the myriad and occasionally contradictory rules and regulations that have created a "bureaucratic jungle" that is very hard to navigate.

State and Local Government EEO Laws

In addition to the federal laws, many state and local governments have passed EEO laws. For example, almost all states have some form of protection against employment discrimination on the basis of disability.

In most cases the effect of the state and local laws is to further restrict employers regarding their treatment of job applicants and employees. In many cases, state EEO laws cover employers (like those with fewer than 15 employees) who are not covered by federal legislation (Bureau of National Affairs, 1988). Similarly, some local governments extend the protection of age discrimination laws to young people as well, barring discrimination not only of those over 40, but those over 17 as well. Here, for instance, it would be illegal to advertise for "mature" applicants, because that might discourage some teenagers from applying. The point is that a wide range of actions by many employers that might be legal under federal laws are illegal under state and local laws (Bureau of National Affairs, 1989, p. 39).

State and local equal employment opportunity agencies (often called Human Resources Commissions, Commissions on Human Relations, or Fair Employment Commissions) play a role in the equal employment compliance process. When the EEOC receives a discrimination charge, it usually defers it for a limited time to the state and local agencies that have comparable jurisdiction. If satisfactory remedies are not achieved, the charges are then referred back to the EEOC for resolution.

Enforcing EEO

The executive branch of the federal government (i.e., president of the United States and the many regulatory agencies the president oversees) bears most of the responsibility for enforcing all EEO laws passed by the legislative branch (i.e., House of Representatives and the Senate). Two federal agencies have the primary responsibility for enforcing equal employment opportunity legislation. These agencies are EEOC and OFCCP.

In the majority of EEO cases, individuals who believe that they have been discriminated against bring complaints to the EEOC or the OFCCP (although the OFCCP usually turns individual discrimination complaints over to the EEOC). These agencies examine the facts of each case, decide whether or not illegal discrimination has occurred, and attempt to arrange a settlement between the individual and the organization. If no settlement is reached, the agencies cannot force a settlement on an employer but may take the issue to federal court. The courts can force an organization to make changes in its employee selection procedures and other HRM practices.

The individual who files a complaint with the EEOC or OFCCP is called the complainant or the charging party. In court, this individual may be called the plaintiff. The organization against which the complaint is filed may be referred to as the respondent or, in court, as the defendant.

Equal Employment Opportunity Commission (EEOC)

The EEOC, a division of the Department of Justice, was created by the CRA of 1964 to administer Title VII of the act and is now responsible for enforcing Title VII, the Equal Pay Act, and the ADA. The commission is composed of five members, not more than three of whom may be members of the same political party. Members of the commission are appointed by the president, by and with the advice and consent of the Senate, for a term of five years. The president designates one member to serve as chairperson of the commission and one member to serve as vice chairperson. The chairperson is responsible on behalf of the commission for its administrative operations.

The EEOC has three major responsibilities: investigating and resolving alleged discrimination complaints, gathering information regarding employment patterns and trends in U.S. businesses, and issuing information about new employment guidelines as they become relevant.

Individuals who feel they have been discriminated against must file a complaint with the EEOC or a similar state agency within 180 days of the incident. Failure to file a complaint within the 180 days results in the case's being dismissed immediately, with certain exceptions, such as the enactment of a seniority system that has an intentionally discriminatory purpose. If the charge is first processed by a state or local agency, and if that agency's actions are not satisfactory to the individual, the individual has up to 300 days from the occurrence, or 30 days after the state or local agency has conducted its investigation and rulings, to file with the federal EEOC.

After the complaint has been filed, the EEOC assumes responsibility for investigating the claim. The EEOC can take up to 60 days to investigate a complaint. If the EEOC finds that the complaint is not valid or does not complete the investigation within a 60-day period, the individual has the right to sue in a federal court.

If the EEOC believes that discrimination has in fact occurred, its representative will try to reach reconciliation between the two parties first before taking the case to court. Occasionally, the EEOC may enter into a *consent decree* with the discriminating organization. This consent decree is essentially an agreement between the EEOC and the organization that stipulates that the organization will cease certain discriminatory practices and perhaps implement new affirmative action procedures to rectify its history of discrimination.

On the other hand, if the EEOC cannot reach an agreement with the organization two options may be pursued. First, the EEOC can issue a "right to sue letter" to the victim, which simply certifies that the agency has investigated the complaint and found potential validity in the victim's allegations. Essentially, that course of action involves the EEOC giving its blessing to the individual to file suit on his or her own grounds. Alternatively, in certain limited cases the EEOC itself may assist the victim in bringing suit in federal court.

The EEOC also plays a role in monitoring the hiring of organizations. It does this by requiring organizations with 100 or more employees to file an annual report (EEO-1) indicating the number of women and minorities who hold jobs in nine different job categories. The EEOC tracks these reports to identify potential patterns of discrimination that it can then potentially address through class-action lawsuits.

The third responsibility of the EEOC is to develop and issue guidelines that help organizations determine whether their decisions are violations of the law enforced by the EEOC. These guidelines themselves are not laws, but the courts have generally placed great weight on them when hearing employment discrimination cases. One of the most important sets of guidelines is the *Uniform Guidelines on Employee Selection Procedures* developed by the EEOC, the Department of Labor, the Department of Justice, and the U.S. Civil Service Commission. These guidelines summarize ways an organization should develop and administer selection systems so as not to violate Title VII. The courts often refer to the *Uniform Guidelines* to determine whether a company has engaged in discriminatory conduct or to determine the validity of the procedures it used to validate a selection system. The EEOC also frequently uses the *Federal Register* to issue new guidelines and opinions regarding employment practices that come about as a result of newly passed laws. This practice has been particularly important in recent years as a result of the passage of the ADA. For instance, when the ADA was signed into law in 1990, the EEOC was given the responsibility of issuing regulations that would inform employers exactly what they would (and would not) be expected to do to comply with the law. The EEOC Web site (http://www.EEOC.gov) also provides a list of its regulations.

Finally, the EEOC also disseminates posters to employers. These posters explain to employees how to protect themselves from employment discrimination and how to file a complaint. The EEOC requires employers to display the posters in a prominent place (such as the company cafeteria).

Office of Federal Contract Compliance Procedures (OFCCP)

The OFCCP is responsible for enforcing the laws and executive orders that apply to the federal government and its contractors. Specifically, it enforces EO 11246 and the Vocational Rehabilitation Act, both of which go beyond prohibiting discrimination to requiring affirmative action (AA) programs for covered employees. Businesses with contracts for more than $50,000 cannot discriminate in employment based on race, color, religion, national origin, or sex, and they must have a written affirmative action plan on file.

Many of the regulations written by the OFCCP are very similar to those issued by the EEOC. However, there are two major differences between the enforcement activities of the two agencies. First, in contrast to the EEOC, the OFCCP actively monitors compliance with its regulations. That is, it does not wait for an employer or applicant to file a complaint. Rather, it requires covered employers to submit annual reports on the state of their AA programs. Second, unlike the EEOC, the OFCCP has considerable enforcement power. Being a government contractor is considered a privilege, not a right. The OFCCP can take away that privilege if it determines that an employer is not complying with the law. It can also levy fines and other forms of punishment.

Affirmative action plans. An AA plan generally has three basic elements. The first element is called the utilization analysis. A utilization analysis compares the racial, sex, and ethnic composition of the employer's workforce to that of the available labor supply. For each group of jobs, the organization needs to identify the percentage of its workforce with a particular characteristic (for example, black or female) and identify the percentage of workers in the relevant labor market with that same characteristic. If the percentage in the employer workforce is considerably less than the percentage in the external labor supply, then that minority group is characterized as being underutilized.

The second part of the AA plan is the development of goals and timetables for achieving balance in the workforce concerning those characteristics, especially where underutilization exists. Goals and timetables generally specify the percentage of protected classes of employees that the organization seeks to have in each group and the date by which that percent can be attained. It is important to recognize that these goals and timetables do not automatically constitute quotas. A quota would involve setting aside a special number of jobs to be filled only by members of a particular protected class. Goals and timetables are considerably more flexible than quotas. The idea underlying goals and timetables is that if no discriminatory hiring practices exist, then over time underutilization should be eliminated.

The third part of the AA program is the development of a list of action steps. These steps specify what the organization will do to actually reduce underutilization. Common action steps include making extra efforts in communicating job openings to women and minorities, recruiting at schools that predominantly cater to a particular protected class, participating in programs that are designed to improve employment opportunities for underemployed groups, and taking all necessary steps to remove inappropriate barriers to employment.

The potential sanction for inadequate progress in attaining an organization's goals is cancellation of government contracts. Note that under AA the use of goals and timetables is not the same as "quota hiring." Afirmative action does not require a particular percentage of hires or rigid hiring restrictions in order to produce the "correct number of minorities." Nevertheless, some employers may choose to resort to more rigid quota-like practices in their efforts to reach their hiring goals. This approach could be unfair and legally risky if it results in discrimination (under Title VII) against those in the majority groups.

Clearly, AA has become increasingly controversial, and some organizations' attention to required goals and timetables has diminished. But at the same time, many organizations in recent years have voluntarily implemented various kinds of diversity programs designed to encourage and support a more diverse, multicultural workforce. Much of the impetus for these programs has come from managers' recognition of the demographic changes in the workforce toward more females and minorities. Diversity programs often include various types of training programs and workshops to increase employees' and managers' sensitivity to diverse cultures, values, and lifestyles. These programs are expected to enhance an organizations' ability to attract, retain, and maintain the morale of a more diverse population of employees.

The OFCCP conducts yearly audits of government contractors to ensure that they have been actively pursuing their AA goals. These audits involve examining a company's AA plan and conducting site visits to determine how individual employees perceive the company's AA policies. If the OFCCP finds that its contractors or subcontractors are not complying with the relevant executive orders, then it may notify the EEOC, advise the Department of Justice to institute criminal proceedings, or request that the secretary of labor cancel or suspend contracts with that organization. This latter step is the OFCCP's most important weapon, since it has a clear and immediate impact on an organization's revenue stream.

Although the EEOC and the OFCCP are the two primary regulatory agencies that enforce equal employment legislation, various other government agencies and components come into play. The Department of Justice and the Department of Labor, for example, are both heavily involved in the enforcement of EEO legislation. The U.S. Civil Service Commission is also actively involved in monitoring compliance in government organizations where civil service jobs exist. In addition, the U.S. judicial system plays an important role in enforcing all HRM legislation.

PREVENTING DISCRIMINATORY PRACTICES

The management of EEO practices will continue to play a key role in the performance of organizations in the years to come. Facing a number of laws and regulations, it is critical for HRM to make sure that their organizations avoid discriminatory practices. While avoiding discriminatory practices is a major charge of top management, oftentimes they have not established an organizational culture that encourages EEO and discrimination may result.

One can well imagine the confusion resulting from the tangle of laws and executive orders. Many organizations and individuals still have difficulty understanding what is meant by discrimination despite the efforts of the EEOC in publishing procedures like the *Uniform Guidelines on Employee Selection* and other efforts to further clarify related laws and regulations. It is not unusual for many to still have difficulty answering questions like: How would you know if you had been discriminated against? or How do you know if your organization does discriminate? Are the organization's EEO practices operating properly? Discrimination is a complex or multifaceted issue. It is often not easy to determine the extent to which unfair discrimination affects an employer's decision. The answer to such questions might lie in a better understanding of the concept of disparate impact.

Disparate Impact

What is disparate impact? In order for individuals to claim discrimination, they must establish that selection procedures resulted in a disparate or adverse impact on a protected class. Disparate impact may be defined as the rejection of a higher percentage of a protected class for employment, placement, or promotion. Up until the *Wards Cove Packing v. Antonio* decision in 1989, a person who felt unintentionally discriminated against needed only establish a prima facie case of discrimination: This meant showing that the employer's selection procedures had an adverse impact on a protected minority group. "Adverse impact" refers to the total employment process that results in a significantly higher percentage of a protected group in the candidate population being rejected for employment, placement, or promotion. (For example, if 80 percent of the male applicants passed the test, but only 20 percent of the female applicants passed, a female applicant would have a prima facie case showing adverse impact.)

Then, once the employee had established a case (such as in *Wards Cove Packing*), the burden of proof shifted to the employer. It became the employer's task to prove that any test, application blank, interview, or other hiring procedure was a valid predictor of performance on the job (and that it was applied fairly and equitably to both minorities and nonminorities).

Wards Cove changed this situation. Before *Wards Cove*, a plaintiff might just show statistically that all clerical jobs were filled by women and all higher level jobs by men. Then the employer had to prove its hiring practices (such as a test) were nondiscriminatory. After the *Wards Cove* decision, the burden of proof switched to the plaintiff or employee. So much heat was generated by this decision that some claim *Wards Cove* was a major factor in adding to the passage of the CRA of 1991, which moved things back to a tougher standard. As this illustrates, the job of keeping up never ends.

Proving disparate impact. Because the burden of proof is shifted to the plaintiff or employee, it means the plaintiff must prove her or his case. There are four basic approaches that can be used. These are the "four-fifths rule," restricted policies, population or geographic comparisons, and statistical tests, or what some referred to as the "*McDonnell-Douglas* test." It should be noted that each of these "tests" is simply an indicator that risky practices may have occurred. It is up to some judicial body to make the final determination.

1. *The four-fifths rule (or disparate rejection rates)*. This is one of the first measures of determining potentially discriminatory practices. This involves comparing the rejection rates between a minority group and another group. Issued by the EEOC, in its *Uniform Guidelines on Employee Selection Procedures*, the four-fifths rule serves as a basis for determining if an adverse impact has occurred. Of course, the four-fifths rule is not a definition of discrimination. It is, however, a practical device to keep the attention of the enforcement agencies on serious discrepancies in hiring and promotion rates, or other employment decisions.

2. *Restricted policy*. This approach means demonstrating that the employer has (intentionally or unintentionally) been using an HRM selection policy that excludes members of a protected group. Evidence of restricted policies is evidence of adverse impact. For instance, assume a company is downsizing and laying off an excessive number of employees who are over age 40. Simultaneously, however, the company is recruiting for selected positions on college campuses only. Because of economic difficulties, the company wants to keep salaries low by hiring people just entering the workforce. Those over age 39, who were making higher salaries, are not given the opportunity even to apply for these new jobs. By these actions, a restricted policy has occurred: That is, through its hiring practice (intentional or not), a class of individuals (in this case, those protected by age discrimination legislation) has been excluded from consideration.

3. *Population (or geographical) comparisons*. A third means of supporting discriminatory claims is through the use of population comparisons. This approach involves comparing the percentage of a protected class in an organization with the percentage of that protected class in the population in the surrounding community. If the organization has a proper mix of individuals at all levels in the organization that reflects its recruiting market, then the organization is in compliance. Additionally, that compliance may assist in fostering diversity in the organization. The key factor here is the qualified pool according to varying geographic areas.

4. *Statistical evidence (or* McDonnel–Douglas) *test*. Named for the *McDonnell-Douglas Corp. v. Green* 1973 Supreme Court case, this approach involves using statistical analysis to show underrepresentation of protected groups. It is used in situations of (intentional) disparate treatment rather than (unintentional) disparate impact (for which approaches 1 to 3 above are used). For this test to be used four components must exist: (1) The individual is a member of a protected group; (2) The individual applied for a job for which he or she was qualified; (3) The individual was rejected; and (4) The organization, after rejecting this applicant, continued to seek other applicants with similar qualifications.

If these four conditions are met, an allegation of discrimination is supported. It is up to the organization to refute the evidence by providing a reason for such action. Should that explanation be acceptable to an investigating body, the protected group member must then prove that the reason used by the organization is inappropriate.

If any of the preceding four tests are met, the organization might find itself having to defend its practices. There are then basically three defenses that the organization can use: the bona fide occupational qualification (BFOQ), the business necessity defense, or seniority systems. Any one can be used to justify an employment practice that has been shown to have an adverse impact on the members of a minority group.

Bona Fide Occupational Qualifications

The bona fide occupational qualification (BFOQ) is one defense against discriminatory charges. Under Title VII, a BFOQ is permitted where such requirements are "reasonably necessary to meet the normal operation of that business or enterprise." As originally worded, BFOQs could be used only to support sex discrimination. Today, BFOQ coverage is extended to other categories covered (i.e., religion, age, national origin). Bona fide occupational qualifications cannot, however, be used in cases of race or color.

Bona fide occupational qualifications are a statutory exception to the EEO laws that allows employers to discriminate in certain very specific instances. The BFOQ exception is usually interpreted narrowly by the courts. As a practical matter, it is used primarily (but not exclusively) as a defense against charges of intentional discrimination based on age. Bona fide occupational qualifications are essentially a defense to a disparate treatment case based upon direct evidence of intentional discrimination and not to disparate impact (unintentional) discrimination.

When using a BFOQ defense, the employer argues that it purposely discriminated against all members of a protected group for one of the following four reasons:

1. *All or nearly all.* All or nearly all of the members of that group are not capable of performing the job in question.
2. *Authenticity.* Examples: "Selecting only persons of Japanese heritage to work as a server in an "authentic" Japanese restaurant; hiring only women to model women's clothes.
3. *Propriety.* Example: Hiring only men to work as attendants in a men's restroom.
4. *Safety.* The employment of people in a certain protected group would put the workers or others at risk.

At one time, employers attempted to justify the exclusion of women from jobs traditionally held by men by using the all or nearly all rule. For example, women were excluded from jobs that require above-average strength (e.g., police officer, firefighter, construction worker) because women are generally physically weaker than men. The courts, however, have rarely (if ever) approved this type of BFOQ defense. They mandate that each applicant be evaluated according to his or her ability. In the earlier example, the courts would require that each female applicant be evaluated based on her own strength. This is consistent with courts generally rejecting the BFOQ defense and holding that each individual job applicant should be permitted an opportunity to demonstrate the ability to perform. The courts have also generally rejected customer preference as a BFOQ defense.

Organizational attempts to invoke the other BFOQ defenses (authenticity, propriety, and safety) have occasionally been successful. For example, the "safety" defense has been successfully used in cases where organizations establish an employment age limit (e.g., the employment of applicants who are over 50 years old will not be considered). To win such a case, an employer must be able to prove the safety-related skills (e.g., vision or reaction time) diminish with age and that employing people over the maximum age would thus pose a safety risk to themselves or others (Faley, Kleinman, and Lengnick-Hall, 1984). Thus, when public safety is involved, such as with airline pilots or interstate bus drivers, age may be used as a BFOQ.

Business Necessity

The business necessity defense basically requires showing that there is an overriding business purpose for the discriminatory practice and that the practice is therefore acceptable. The Supreme Court has made it clear that business necessity does not encompass such matters as avoiding inconvenience, annoyance, or expense to the employer. It's not easy proving that a practice is required for "business necessity." For example, an employer can't generally discharge employees whose wages have been garnished merely because garnishment (requiring the employer to divert part of the person's wages to pay his or her debts) creates an inconvenience.

The focus in business necessity is on the validity of various stated job specifications and their relationship to the work performed. Attempts by employers to show that their selection tests or other employment practices are valid represent one example of the business necessity defense. Here the employer is required to show that the test or other practice is related—in other words, that it is a valid predictor of performance on the job. Where such validity can be established, the courts have often supported the use of the test or other employment practice as a business necessity. Used in this context, the word validity basically means the degree to which the test or other employment practice is related to or predicts performance on the job. For example, in using a business necessity defense, an employer would be required to prove that the ability to lift 100 pounds is necessary in performing a warehouse job.

When a BFOQ is established, an employer can refuse to consider all persons of the protected group. When business necessity is established, an employer can exclude all persons who do not meet specifications, regardless of whether the specifications have an adverse impact on a protected group.

Bona Fide Seniority Systems

Finally, the organization's bona fide seniority system can serve as a defense against discrimination charges. So long as employment decisions, like layoffs, are the function of a well-established and consistently applied seniority system, decisions that may adversely affect protected group members may be permissible. However, an organization using seniority as a defense must be able to demonstrate the "appropriateness" of its system.

Although three means are available for organizations themselves, the best approach revolves around job-relatedness. BFOQ and seniority defenses are often subject to great scrutiny and at times are limited in their use.

Additional Considerations in Providing Defenses for Discriminatory Practices

There are three other points to stress in regard to defending against charges of discrimination. First, good intentions are no excuse. As the Supreme Court held in the *Griggs* case: "Good intent or absence of discriminatory intent does not redeem procedures or testing mechanisms that operate as built-in headwinds for minority groups and are unrelated to measuring job capability" (Cascio, 1978, p. 5).

Second, employers cannot count on hiding behind collective bargaining agreements (for instance, by claiming that the discriminatory practice is required by a union agreement). Courts have often held that EEO laws take precedence over the rights embodied in a labor contract. This isn't iron clad, however. For example, the U.S. Supreme Court, in its *Stotts* decision, held that a court cannot require retention of black employees hired under a court's consent decree in preference to higher-seniority white employees who were protected by a bona fide seniority system. It's unclear whether this decision also extends to personnel decisions not governed by seniority systems (Bureau of National Affairs, 1985).

Finally, remember that although a defense is often the most sensible response to charges of discrimination, it is not the only response. When organizations are confronted with the fact that one or more of their HRM practices is discriminatory they can react by agreeing to eliminate the illegal practice and (when required) by compensating the people they discriminated against.

Other Relevant Issues

There are several other issues that are of interest to HRM staff, such as possible employer liability in failing to screen applicants in the selection process. Many managers are still unaware of their unaccountability for the actions of employees. Negligent hiring can result in being liable for employees' unlawful acts if the employer does not reasonably investigate their backgrounds. If, as the result of an inadequate investigation, the employee is put in a position to commit crimes harming others, the employer may be liable. Of prime importance to the question of employer liability is the nature of the job itself and its exposure to others. Many experts believe that an organization should obtain the applicant's written permission to conduct a thorough background investigation including references and, if appropriate, consumer credit reports (Munchus, 1992).

Sexual harassment is another issue of importance in EEO. Sexual harassment is an example of discrimination in the day-to-day treatment of employees.

Sexual Harassment

One of the more current issues in EEO is sexual harassment. Sexual harassment has long been a problem in organizations and has been held to be a violation of Title VII of the CRA of 1964. However, the importance of sexual harassment was brought to center stage during a 1991 confirmation hearing for Supreme Court Justice Clarence Thomas. Sexual harassment is defined by the EEOC as unwelcome sexual advances in the work environment. If the conduct is indeed unwelcome and occurs with sufficient frequency to create an abusive work environment, the employer is responsible for changing the environment by warning, reprimanding, or perhaps firing the harasser.

The courts have ruled and defined that there are two types of sexual harassment. One type of sexual harassment is quid pro quo harassment. In this case the harasser offers to exchange something of value for sexual favors. For example, a male supervisor might tell or imply to a female direct report that he will recommend her for promotion or provide her with a salary increase in exchange for sexual favors. The other, more subtle, type of sexual harassment is the creation of a hostile work environment. For example, a group of male employees who continually make off-color jokes and lewd comments and perhaps decorate the work environment with inappropriate photographs may create a hostile work environment for a female colleague to the point where she is uncomfortable working in that job setting. It is the organization's responsibility to deal with this sort of problem ("Is Sexual Haressment," 1999, p. 92).

Although most sexual harassment cases involve men harassing women, many other situations of sexual harassment can be identified as well. Sometimes women harass men, and sometimes there is same sex harassment. And indeed, several recent cases involving same-sex harassment have focused new attention on this form of sexual harassment. Regardless of the pattern, however, the same rules apply: sexual harassment is illegal.

There still continues to be considerable ambiguity in particular work situations, as to whether or not illegal sexual harassment is occurring. For assessing the existence of a hostile work environment the courts typically examine questions such as:

• How frequent and severe is the behavior?
• Is the behavior threatening or humiliating?
• Is there interference with an employee's work performance?

Despite the legislation against it and all the court decisions, sexual harassment remains a problem in the workplace, and HRM personnel and all others responsible for employment policy must develop policies to prevent its occurrence. In addition to establishing a written policy forbidding harassment, organizations must communicate the policy and train employees. Further, efforts should include establishment of an effective complaint procedure and the investigation of all claims in a timely manner. Finally, managers should take remedial action to correct past harassment. While sometimes the emphasis seems to focus on laws and defensive measures, the effective HRM function knows that a proactive approach is the way to go. This proactive approach can begin with the organization updating and strengthening their anti-harassment policies to include the following components (Casey, 1999):

• Specific definitions and prohibition of sexual harassment;
• Formats for informing all employees of the sexual harassment policy;
• Strong prohibitions of retaliation for reporting allegations of harassment;
• Multiple channels for making complaints;
• Assurances of prompt investigations and appropriate remedial actions;
• Provisions for confidentiality and privacy.

ORGANIZATIONAL PRACTICES AND RESPONSES TO AVOID PITFALLS IN EEO

Part of the complexity of EEO is the reality that most current and potential employees fall into one or more protected classes. As a result, almost any decision made by a manager (or team) that affects an employment status can be challenged in a court of law. In all likelihood sound management practices will not only help organizations avoid and respond to EEO lawsuits but will also contribute to the organization's success. A number of organizational (or management) practices are recommended below.

Conduct Regular Self-Analysis and Document Decisions

An organization should regularly conduct a self-analysis to examine the status of disabled, minority, and female employees and document HRM decisions. For instance, the organization can develop and regularly update special logs on a variety of HRM decisions (i.e., employee discipline/discharge decisions). The nature of any HRM decision, and the rationale for it, should be clearly documented. This information allows the organization to identify areas in which disparate impact or disparate treatment may be occurring and provides the basis for a defense of organization policies in discrimination suits. Both the EEOC and OFCCP have certain reporting requirements. Organizations that conduct a regular self-analysis and have a sound HRM information system in place do not find it difficult to comply with these requirements. Performance appraisal is one important type of documentation. As will be noted in Chapter 8, there are many good reasons for conducting appraisals, only one of which is to provide documentation in case of a lawsuit.

In either case, the legal reason is an important one. In a discrimination case the generic charge is that the employer has based a decision in whole or in part on a non-job-related characteristic (age, sex, race, religion, and so on). The employer's generic defense is that it had a job-related reason for its decision. This defense is much easier to establish if the employer has undertaken a regular self-analysis and can provide written documentation to support its claim.

Develop and Communicate Written EEO Policies

All organizations should develop formal, written policies concerning EEO. However, policies are effective only to the extent that they are understood by employees. Just stating that the organization is committed to a discrimination-free work environment is not enough. In this policy, specific behaviors that are unacceptable must be identified. The more explicit these unacceptable behaviors, the less chance of misinterpretation later on.

Organizations should focus on communicating to employees their commitment to a discrimination-free work environment. For instance, all employees need to be instructed in what sexual harassment is, how to stop it before it becomes a problem, and what to do if it does become a problem.

The organization should make sure that EEO policies are displayed widely and prominently throughout the company. Perhaps one of the best ways to avoid EEO problems is to develop and provide special training programs to transmit knowledge of EEO issues and the organization's EEO policies. The HRM function should provide regular updates on EEO and other labor issues to executives, managers and front-line supervisors, and other employees, since this area of law is in constant flux ("Washington

Scorecard," 1994, p. 4). The Supreme Court regularly decides cases that affect HRM practice. Although managers can try to read periodicals or search the Web to obtain current information, most find their everyday demands too taxing to allow time for this. Training managers about how to deal with discrimination (i.e., sexual harassment) charges and what responsibility they have to the individual and the organization decreases the likelihood of opening the organization up to potential liability. Regular, focused training sessions conducted by the HRM function are the most efficient method of communicating this information to the organization's employees.

Ensure Employment Procedures Are Objective and Job-Related

Employment decisions about hiring, firing, promoting, or providing benefits to employees must be objective and job-related. For instance, major sources of potential lawsuits are the application and interview phases of the hiring process. The general rule is that organizations should ask only for information that is related to job performance. For example, an interviewer should not ask about an applicant's religious affiliation, although he or she may ask if a person can work on specific days of the week. Similarly, an interviewer can ask if the applicant is capable of performing the essential physical aspects of the job (preferably specifically listed), but asking general questions about health would probably be interpreted as a violation of the ADA. Testing procedures used to hire employees should be validated using techniques consistent with the EEOC's *Uniform Guidelines*. When decisions are based on performance evaluations of employees, the procedures used to assess performance should be as objective and directly related to the job as possible. Job analysis should be used to determine the important aspects of job performance. Performance should be assessed by persons who have been trained in performance-rating techniques and have had adequate time to observe the performance of the individual(s) being rated. (Chapter 8 discusses a good performance appraisal system.)

Develop a Grievance Procedure/Complaint Resolution Process

Every organization should establish a process for the internal resolution of EEO and other types of employee complaints. This means that an employer should have a formal grievance procedure that employees can use to deal with possible cases of discrimination. In cases of discharges, promotions, or sexual, racial, ethnic, or religious harassment, the availability of formal grievance procedures often aids in resolving complaints of discrimination so that the EEOC's involvement is not necessary. It is much less expensive to resolve these concerns if the EEOC, OFCCP, and legal counsel are not involved. More importantly, employee satisfaction and morale can be improved when employees are able to pass along their concerns to upper-level management.

Be Proactive

If evidence of discrimination exists, the organization should be proactive in developing policies to correct the situation. These plans should be consistent with guidelines set forth by the EEOC and the OFCCP. Employees (disabled, minority and female) should be involved in the process of developing these plans. Formally bringing employees into the process can provide useful insights and information about how best to recruit and retain disabled, minority, and female employees. Organizations should take into account the Supreme Court decisions like *Steelworkers v. Weber* (1979). In that case, the Court ruled that voluntary quota systems are acceptable to the extent that employers do the following (Kleinman and Faley, 1988):

- Avoid quota systems when no evidence of past discrimination exists.
- Develop plans that do not require the discharge of or have other significant ill effects on majority workers.
- Avoid setting minority quotas of greater than 50 percent.
- Develop plans that are temporary in nature and will end once the negative effects of past discrimination are corrected.

Be Honest

Often, employees will not file an EEO complaint unless they think they have been mistreated. Perceptions of mistreatment often result from situations in which employees' or applicants' expectations have not been met. Therefore, employers should not only provide realistic job previews for employees but also make sure they provide honest performance feedback and expectations. While it may be painful in the short term, providing honest feedback and expectations to employees is a good management practice that may reduce legal problems in the long run.

In the end, organizations can avoid many of the potential problems associated with the HRM legal environment by engaging in sound management practices—management practices that are part of the organization's strategic initiatives, supported by the HRM function.

SUMMARY

Organizations must be proactive in addressing the challenges presented by the legal environment in general and EEO regulations in particular. The basic goal of EEO regulation is to protect people from unfair or inappropriate discrimination in the workplace. Organizations must ensure that they do not knowingly discriminate or unfairly treat any individuals or groups. Avoiding disparate treatment, sexual harassment, and other forms of discrimination require diligence on the part of organizations and their HRM function.

The major laws and related regulations that affect EEO include Title VII of the CRA of 1964, EO 11246, EO 11478, and the Equal Pay Act of 1963, the Age Discrimination in Employment Act, the Vocational Rehabilitation Act of 1973, the Vietnam Era Veterans' Readjustment Assistance Act of 1974, the Pregnancy Discrimination Act of 1978, the Civil Rights Act of 1991, the Americans with Disabilities Act of 1990, and the Family and Medical Leave Act of 1993. The enforcement of EEO legislation is handled by the EEOC and the OFCCP.

There are a number of organizational practices that if implemented can help organizations avoid and respond to EEO lawsuits while also contributing to increased likelihood of organizational success. HRM personnel bear a particular responsibility in ensuring that their organizations do the right thing when it comes to all of their employees.

REFERENCES

Bureau of National Affairs. 1985. *Fire fighters local 1784 v. Stotts* (April 14).

Bureau of National Affairs. 1987. High court upholds pregnancy law. *Fair Employment Practices* (January 22), pp. 7–8.

Bureau of National Affairs. 1988. A wrap-up of state legislation: 1988 anti-bias laws focus on aids. *Fair Employment Practices* (January 5), pp. 3–4.

Bureau of National Affairs. 1989. Guidelines on AIDS. *Fair Employment Practices* (March 30), p. 39.

Cascio, W.F. 1978. *Applied psychology in personnel management.* Reston, VA: Reston, p. 25.

Casey, J.J. 1999. Developing an effective sexual harassment policy. In G.Z. Cox (ed.), *Sexual harassment: Limiting employer liability.* Eagan, MN: Oakstone Legal and Business Publishing, pp. 53–62.

Commerce Clearing House. 1988. Federal contractors must file VETS-100 by March 31. *Ideas and Trends* (February 23), p. 32.

Commerce Clearing House. 1992. *ADA training manual for managers and supervisors.* Chicago: Commerce Clearing House.

Disabilities act abused? 1998. *USA Today* (September 25), pp. 1B, 2B.

Faley, R.H., Kleinman, L.S., and Lengnick-Hall, M.L. 1984. Age discrimination and personnel psychology: A review and synthesis of the legal literature with implications for future research. *Personnel Psychology* 37: 327–350.

Flygare, T.J. 1987. Supreme Court holds that contagious diseases are handicaps. *Phi Delta Kappa* 68 (May): 705.

Is sexual harassment getting worse? 1999. *Forbes* (April 19), p. 92.

Kleinman, L.S., and Faley, R.H. 1988. Voluntary affirmative action and preferential treatment: Legal and research implications. *Personnel Psychology* 41: 481–496.

Ledvinka, J., and Scarpello, V.G. 1991. *Federal regulation of personnel and human resource management*, 2nd ed. Boston: PWS-Kent.

Martinez, M.N. 1994. FMLA—headache or opportunity? *HRMagazine* (February): 42–45.

McDonnell-Douglas Corp. v. Green, 411 U.S. 972, 1973.

Munchus, G., III. 1992. Check references for safer selection. *HRMagazine* 37(6): 75–77.

Murphy, B.S., Barlow, W.E., and Hatch, D.D. 1987. Manager's newsfront: U.S. Supreme Court approves preferential treatment for pregnancy. *Personnel Journal* 66(3): 18.

Pregnant workers clash with employers over job inflexibility. 1999. *Wall Street Journal* (February 10), p. B1.

Ritter, D.B., and Turner, R. 1987. AIDS: Employer concerns and options. *Labor Law Journal* 38(2): 67–83.

Steelworkers v. Weber, 443 U.S. 193, 20 FEP 1, 1979.

Wards Cove Packing v. Antonio, 109 U.S. 2115, 1989.

Washington scorecard. 1994. *HR News* 13 (March): 4.

Chapter 4

Job Analysis

INTRODUCTION

As organizations have increasingly tried to meet the dynamics of an ever changing competitive global world of work they have developed flatter, more agile, and innovative structures and work designs. These new structures and work designs have led to an increased role for HRM personnel in the actual design and redesign of jobs intended to improve organizational success. HRM personnel now find themselves needing to be prepared to modify job descriptions, job specifications (the qualifications needed to perform a job), and recruitment practices and perhaps to adjust pay scales as well. Job analysis plays an important role in all of these activities.

With an understanding of the nature of HRM and the nature of the legal environment that organizations and their HRM personnel must consider, it is now possible to begin a more focused and detailed analysis of the specific activities and operations of the HRM process itself. This chapter addresses job analysis and its importance in determining the jobs the organization needs to have performed to successfully achieve its strategic objectives. We first discuss the nature of job analysis and why organizations must conduct them. Sources of data for collecting job analysis information is provided next. Then the focus turns to the various methods for analyzing jobs and the decision criteria for determining which methods to use in analyzing jobs. The chapter concludes by highlighting the changing nature of jobs and the future of job analysis in contributing to organizational success.

THE NATURE OF JOB ANALYSIS

What is job analysis? Gatewood and Feild (2001) observed that there are probably as many different definitions of job analysis as there are writings on the topic. They suggested a definition that views job analysis as "a purposeful, systematic process for collecting information on the important work-related aspects of a job" (p. 285). Job analysis provides answers to questions such as these (Cornelius, 1988):

- How much time does it take to complete important tasks?
- Which tasks are grouped together and considered a job?
- How can a job be designed or structured so that the employee's performance can be enhanced?
- What kinds of behaviors are needed to perform the job?
- What kind of person (in terms of traits and experience) is best suited for the job?
- How can the information acquired by a job analysis be used in the development of HRM programs?

Thus, an important part of job analysis is to collect information on the characteristics of a job that differentiate it from other jobs. The categories of information usually obtained in job analysis include the following: work activities, interaction with others, performance standards, financial and budgeting impact, machines and equipment used, working conditions, supervision given and received, and knowledge, skills, and abilities needed.

There are many different ways of analyzing jobs using the information resulting from job analysis. As we shall see in the following sections, there are a variety of approaches for structuring information about jobs. Before we describe these approaches, it is important to think about why organizations should conduct job analysis in the first place.

WHY CONDUCT JOB ANALYSIS?

Two major forces have contributed to the need to conduct job analysis: conducting HRM planning on a continuous basis in response to competition and equal employment opportunity concerns. Employers in the United States, faced with increased foreign and domestic competition, must engage in HRM planning on a near-continuous basis while simultaneously trying to ensure that their employees are working efficiently. New technology, shifts in labor demand, and improved work methods, for example, can each alter an organization's human resources needs. As a result, in three months the human resources needs of an organization may be quite different from its needs today. As a result of these changing needs, the way workers perform their jobs may change. Eliminating jobs that are no longer necessary can streamline organizational functioning. Jobs that have changed in response to new technology create a somewhat different problem. Employers must find individuals with the requisite knowledge, skills, and abilities to perform adequately the activities required. It is through effective HRM planning that adjustments and refinements are made, transforming an organization's workforce to meet the projected future needs of the organization. Job analysis is one of the building blocks of the HRM planning process and is a fundamental source of information for this process.

The cornerstone of the organization is the set of jobs performed by its employees. These jobs provide the vehicle for coordinating and linking the various activities of the organization to achieve the overall mission and objectives. Job analysis is such an important activity to HRM that it has been called the building block of everything that personnel does (Cascio, 1991). This statement refers to the fact that almost every HRM program requires some type of information that is gleaned from job analysis.

Despite the tremendous positive impact of job analysis on organizational functioning, perhaps the most profound factor increasing the use of job analysis techniques is the EEO legislation discussed in Chapter 3. Title VII of the Civil Rights Act of 1964, as amended; the Equal Pay Act of 1963; the Age Discrimination in Employment Act of 1967, as amended; the Americans with Disabilities Act of 1990; and other laws passed over the last 35 years have served to dramatically increase the use of job analysis, making it an integral part of establishing the job relatedness of employment practices. The large number of court cases involving allegations of employment discrimination has been highly instrumental in enhancing the importance of job analysis. One judge noted the following in an employment test validation case:

The cornerstone of the construction of a content valid examination [an examination based on qualifications really needed in the job] is the job analysis. Without such an analysis to single out the critical knowledge, skills, and abilities required by the job, their importance to each other, and the level of proficiency demanded as to each attribute, a test constructor is aiming in the dark and can only hope to achieve job-relatedness by blind luck. (*Kirkland v. New York Department of Corrections*, 1974)

It is hard to imagine a stronger endorsement of job analysis, particularly when we consider that the judge's words have the force of law.

In 1978 the federal agencies charged with enforcing EEO laws issued the *Uniform Guidelines on Employee Selection Procedures* (EEOC, Civil Service Commission, Department of Labor, and Department of Justice, 1978), which confirm the place of job analysis as a fundamental prerequisite for proving employment practices to be free of discrimination (Holley and Jennings, 1983). The *Uniform Guidelines* make the following statement:

There should be a job analysis which includes an analysis of the important work behavior(s) required for successful performance and their relative importance and, if the behavior results in work product(s), an analysis of work product(s). Any job analysis should focus on the work behavior(s) and the tasks associated with them. If work behavior(s) are not observable, the job analysis should identify and analyze those aspects of the behavior(s) that can be observed and the observed work product(s). The work behavior(s) selected for measurement should be critical work behaviors and/or important work behavior(s) constituting most of the job. (p. 38302)

The principle that job analysis should precede any HRM practice is thus well established in the federal *Uniform Guidelines*.

The courts have worked to define further the role of job analysis in demonstrating job relatedness. Thompson and Thompson (1982) reviewed a number of employment discrimination lawsuits to determine the criteria the federal courts use in assessing job analysis in the context of selection tests. The following were among their conclusions:

- Expert job analysts must perform the job analysis.
- The results of the analysis should be reduced to written form.
- The job analysis process employed must be described in detail.
- Data should be collected from a variety of sources (i.e., incumbents, supervisors, job experts).
- Information on tasks performed must be included in the job analysis.
- Knowledge, skills, and abilities should be clearly specified and must be operationally defined in terms of work.

More recently, Buckner (1989) reviewed 185 court cases from 1979 through 1987 dealing with hiring, promotion, reclassification, and training issues. Among her findings for content-related validation (job relatedness) studies were that courts generally ruled for employers when the following conditions existed:

- Job content was well defined.
- Work behaviors were defined in behavioral terms.
- KSAs (knowledge, skills, and abilities) were operationally defined.
- Subject matter experts (i.e., incumbents and/or supervisors) rated KSA importance.

These findings, taken together with the Thompson and Thompson (1982) results and the language in the federal *Uniform Guidelines*, present a clear picture of the importance of job analysis in this context. The passage of the Americans with Disabilities Act in 1990 focused even more attention on job analysis outcomes. So long as EEO laws remain on the books, job analysis is here to stay.

THE MAJOR USES AND IMPORTANCE OF JOB ANALYSIS INFORMATION

As noted above, the information gained through job analysis is of utmost importance; it has great value to the organization as a whole and particularly to HRM specialists and line managers. There are a number of specific uses of job analysis information including: job descriptions, job specifications, job classification, job evaluations, job design, recruitment, selection, performance appraisal, training and development, job evaluation, career planning, work redesign, and HRM planning.

Job Description

A job description is an account of the duties and activities associated with a particular job. It concentrates on describing the job as it is currently being performed. While the format for job descriptions varies somewhat, most job descriptions contain sections that include the following: the job name, a brief summary description of the job, a listing of job duties and responsibilities, and an explanation of organizational relationships pertinent to the job. Job descriptions have a number of important uses including development of job specifications, workforce planning and recruitment, orientation of new employees, and development of performance appraisal systems.

Job Specifications

Job specifications describe the characteristics needed to perform the job activities identified in the job description. They focus on the individuals doing the job rather than on the work itself. Job specifications may include information regarding the KSAs or the competency, educational, and experience qualifications the incumbent must possess to perform the job. A job specification may be prepared as a separate document or, as is more often the case, as the concluding section of a job description. It is important to note that accurate job specifications identify what KSAs a person needs to do the job, not necessarily what qualifications the current employee possesses. Job specifications allow HRM specialists to identify persons with the skills they seek and help target efforts to recruit them.

Job Classification

Classification involves grouping similar positions into job classes and grouping comparable job classes into job families. There are several good reasons to group jobs. One is simplicity. If HRM specialists (and managers) had to deal with each position individually, the sheer volume of paperwork would be overwhelming. Grouping positions into job classifications allows HRM specialists to deal with personnel functions at a more general level. One of the HRM functions that can be handled at this level is pay. Individuals employed in a particular job classification typically receive salaries within the pay range established for that classification.

Job Evaluation

HRM specialists often mention job classification and job evaluation in the same breath. The process of job evaluation involves assessing the relative dollar-value of each job to the organization to set up internally equitable pay structures. If pay structures are not equitable, employees will be dissatisfied and quit, or they will not see the benefits of striving for promotions. To put dollar values on jobs, it is necessary to get the information about different jobs to determine which jobs deserve higher pay than others. There are two basic approaches to job evaluation. One involves comparing the target organization's pay practices to those of other organizations. This approach is often referred to as the market pricing method. The second approach involves rating jobs on the basis of factors that indicate the relative worth of different jobs within the organization. This approach has been called the factor comparison or point factor method. Both methods rely heavily on job analysis data.

Suppose that we want to apply the market pricing method. To compare our jobs to those in other organizations, we must be sure that our jobs are indeed analogous to the ones selected for comparison. Job analysis information on both jobs assures us that they are comparable. Suppose that we want to use the factor comparison method. Assessing the relative worth of jobs means analyzing them on a common set of criteria such as know-how, problem solving, accountability, working conditions, or complexity (U.S. Civil Service Commission, 1977). The factors selected for comparison may vary, but job analysis remains a foundation for job evaluation.

Job Design

Job design has as its primary thrust meshing the needs of the individuals performing various jobs with the productivity needs of the organization. In recent years, an important aim for job design has been to provide individuals meaningful work that fits effectively into the flow of the organization. The goal of job design is simplifying, enriching, enlarging, or otherwise changing jobs to make the efforts of each employee fit together better with jobs performed by other workers. Changing one job can make the overall system work more efficiently.

From the organization's viewpoint, jobs, as performed, must lead to efficient operations, quality products, and well-maintained equipment. From the workers' viewpoint, jobs must be meaningful and challenging, provide feedback on performance, and call on their decision-making skills (Davis and Wacker, 1988). HRM specialists design jobs that attempt to meet the needs of both employers and employees. Efficient job design allows organizations to take full advantage of technological breakthroughs without alienating the workers affected by change. Restructuring jobs allows companies to retain skilled workers, while enhancing output.

HRM Planning

In HRM planning, planners analyze an organization's HRM needs in a dynamic environment and develop activities that enable an organization to adapt to change. This planning process requires accurate information about the levels of skill required in various jobs to ensure that enough individuals are available in the organization to meet the HRM needs of the strategic plan. In short, job analysis provides fundamental input to the HRM planning process by helping planners understand exactly what kinds of work must be performed. That is, job analysis helps define for managers the kinds of general work and specific jobs that the organization will be relying on in the future.

Recruitment

The job analysis specifies the staffing required to complete the job duties. Job analysis can help the HRM specialist generate a higher-quality pool of job applicants by making it easy to describe a job in classified ads in a way that more precisely targets qualified job applicants. Job analysis also helps recruiters screen job applicants because it tells them what tasks, duties, and responsibilities the job entails.

Selection

Human resources selection deals with identifying the most qualified applicants for employment. To identify which applicants are more qualified, it is first necessary to determine the tasks that will be performed by the individual hired and the knowledge, skills, and abilities the individual must have to perform the job effectively. This information is gained through job analysis (Gatewood and Feild, 2001). An organization's managers or HRM specialists also use the job analysis information to choose or develop the appropriate selection devices (e.g., interview questions, tests).

Performance Appraisal

Performance appraisal deals with getting information about how well each employee is performing his or her job in order to reward those who are effective, improve the performance of those who are ineffective, or provide a written justification for why the poor performer should be disciplined. Through job analysis, the organization can identify the behaviors and results that distinguish effective performance from ineffective performance (Murphy and Cleveland, 1991). Information obtained from a job analysis can also be used to develop performance appraisal forms, which list the job's tasks or behaviors and specify the expected performance. The performance appraisal standards used to judge employee performance for purposes of promotion, rewards, discipline, or layoff should be job related.

Compensation

Job analysis is essential when determining compensation. As part of identifying appropriate compensation, job analysis information is used to determine job content for internal comparisons of responsibilities and external comparisons with the compensation paid by competing employers. Internally, job analysis information can be used to compare the relative worth of each job's contributions to the company's overall performance. The value of each job's contribution is an important determinant of the job's pay level. In a typical pay structure, jobs that require mastery of more complex skills or that have greater levels of responsibility pay more than jobs that require only basic skills or have low amounts of responsibility.

Training and Development

By defining what activities comprise a job, a job analysis helps the supervisor explain that job to a new employee (Kennedy, 1997). Organizations use job analysis information to assess training needs and to develop and evaluate training programs. Almost every employee hired by an organization will require some training in the job. By comparing the KSAs that employees bring to the job with those that are identified by job analysis, managers can identify their employees' skill gaps. Training programs can then be put in place to improve job performance. Some training programs may be more extensive than others, but all require the trainer to have identified the tasks performed in the job to ensure that the training will prepare individuals to perform the job effectively (Goldstein, 1993).

Career Planning

Career planning entails matching an individual's skills and aspirations with opportunities that are or may become available in the organization.

This matching process requires that those in charge of career planning know the skill requirements of the various jobs. This allows them to guide individuals into jobs in which they will succeed and be satisfied.

Work Redesign

Often an organization will seek to redesign work to make it more efficient or effective. To redesign work, detailed information about the existing job(s) must be available. In addition, redesigning a job will, in fact, be similar to analyzing a job that does not yet exist.

Job Analysis and Line Managers

Job analysis is clearly important to the HRM function's various activities, but it is even more important to line (or operations) managers. There are many reasons. First, managers must have detailed information about all the jobs in their work group to understand the workflow process—specifically, identifying the tasks performed and the knowledge, skills, and abilities required to perform them. In addition, an understanding of this workflow process is essential if a manager chooses to redesign certain aspects to increase efficiency or effectiveness.

Second, managers need to understand the job requirements to make intelligent hiring decisions. Very seldom do employees get hired by the HRM function without a manager's input. Managers will often interview prospective applicants and recommend who should receive a job offer. However, if the manager does not have a clear understanding of what tasks are performed on the job and the skills necessary to perform them, then the hiring decision may result in employees whom the manager "likes" but who are not capable of performing the job successfully.

Third, a manager is responsible for ensuring that each individual is performing his job satisfactorily (or better). This requires the manager to evaluate how well each person is performing and to provide feedback to those whose performance needs improvement. Again, this requires that the manager clearly understand the tasks required in every job.

The uses of job analysis are many and can contribute substantially to an organization's overall success and competitiveness. As noted earlier, however, competition is not the only force acting to increase the importance of job analysis to business and industry.

COLLECTING JOB ANALYSIS DATA

As mentioned previously, job analysis is a systematic process for collecting, analyzing, and interpreting job-related information. Information involving job content, work method and approach, and expected outcome is collected and analyzed. In addition, the KSAs that workers need in order to perform their jobs may also be identified and analyzed. The individuals who collect, analyze, and interpret job data are generally referred to as job analysts. Although there is no such thing as a typical job analyst, preferred analysts are internal HRM specialists or external consultants trained to conduct job analysis. Sims and Veres (1985) and Siegel (1987) have emphasized the importance of training job analysts and have made specific recommendations on a desired curriculum.

Sources of Data

Most methods of job analysis require that a knowledgeable person describe what goes on in the job or make a series of judgments about specific activities required to do the job. Such information can be obtained from anyone who has specific information about what the work involves. A job analyst may consult diverse sources. Among these sources are documents such as technical manuals, organization studies, and training materials. Additional sources of data are job incumbents, supervisors, managers, engineers, and technical experts who provide information about the jobs being studied. The term *job agent* is generally used to refer to an individual who provides or collects the desired job information. In addition, the term *subject matter expert* (SME) is sometimes used to refer to a job agent who is familiar with the target job or possesses special expertise that is relevant to job activities. Each of the sources sees the jobs from a different perspective, and associated with each source are different advantages and disadvantages. There are three classes of job agents typically employed to collect job analysis information: (1) job analysts, (2) job incumbents, and (3) job supervisors (McCormick, 1979).

Job analysts. In many instances, outside consultants or members of the organization's HRM function take on the role of job analyst. Job analysts are specially trained individuals whose mission is to collect and process job information. Formally trained job analysts should require less orientation to the job under study and less time to analyze it because they are already well versed in the method of job analysis being used (Gatewood and Feild, 2001). Gatewood and Feild also point out that job analysts should provide more objective, reliable, and accurate job data. Furthermore, trained analysts are more likely to appreciate fully the legal issues associated with conducting job analysis. However, there are some drawbacks associated with their use as job agents. Certain nuances and subtleties of a job may escape them because job analysts are less familiar with specific jobs than are incumbents or supervisors. Job analysts may rely on preexisting stereotypes of job content, particularly when they have prior experience with particular jobs or when commonly held jobs are studied (Harvey, 1991).

Job incumbents. An employee who performs a job is generally in the best position to describe it. Incumbents are often best able to detail "what is *actually* done, rather than what should be done" (Gatewood and Feild, 2001, p. 293). In addition, involving incumbents in the job analysis process might increase their acceptance of any work changes stemming from the results of the analysis. Large numbers of employees may be available, allowing the job analyst to obtain differing perspectives on a given job. However, it should be noted that incumbents may have a vested interest in not portraying their jobs accurately. They may paint an inflated picture of their jobs if they believe it is beneficial to do so (McCormick, 1979; Smith and Hakel, 1979). Another concern in using incumbents is adequacy of verbal skills because they must convey their impressions to job analysts in written or oral form.

Job supervisors. Individuals who supervise incumbents performing the job under study can provide accurate job data because they observe the work being performed. Gatewood and Feild (2001) note that supervisory assessments assume that supervisors have worked closely enough with incumbents to possess "complete information about employees' jobs" (p. 294), an assumption that may not be correct. Although supervisors have direct information about the duties associated with a job, researchers have observed a tendency for supervisors to describe subordinates' jobs on the basis of what *should* be done rather than what has been done in actuality (Sparks, 1981). Despite this limitation, supervisors can provide the analyst with an additional perspective on a given job. This perspective can be especially important when incumbents have limited verbal skills. Further, supervisors may be in a better position to describe what tasks should be included in the job and what tasks could be included if the job is to be redesigned (Schneider and Konz, 1989).

Cornelius (1988) reviewed the research pertaining to the choice of job agent and summarized that literature with the following conclusion:

1. Supervisors and subordinates agree more about the tasks performed than they do about the personal characteristics necessary for job performance.
2. Incumbents and supervisors may provide higher ratings than analysts on job elements that are high in social desirability.
3. Supervisors and incumbents attach different meanings to various descriptions of work and may organize work activities differently.
4. Trained observers (i.e., job analysts) can give similar estimates of job characteristics.

Cornelius recommends that supervisors and subordinates be used to collect data on job activities and that trained job analysts be used to collect data regarding the knowledge, skills, abilities, or other characteristics (KSAOCs) necessary to perform the job. Moreover, he suggests that the tendency of supervisors and incumbents to inflate their ratings of job characteristics high in social desirability prohibit their use as job agents in situations where job analysis data will be used in certain decisions (for example, salary decisions).

Although job incumbents and supervisors are typically the prime source of job analysis data, a good analyst will consult with multiple sources to collect the information he or she needs to understand the job in question and to complete the job analysis (Bemis, Belenky, and Soder, 1983). In choosing the sources of job data, a job analyst should be familiar with the research on the optimum source for obtaining job data. In cases in which job processes are extremely complex, it may be wise to add technical experts (e.g., production engineers, scientists) as job agents.

Data Collection Techniques

Not surprisingly, numerous techniques exist for collecting job information. HRM specialists tend to prefer different approaches in different situations. Jobs with substantial physical demands require different data collection techniques than those that call primarily on mental skills. Some jobs entail extensive documentation of task completion in the form of detailed paper trails, whereas others do not. Job characteristics play an important role in the selection of a specific technique. Some job analysis techniques include background research, performance of the job, site observations, individual interviews, group interviews, job analysis questionnaires, and employee diary/logs.

Background research. Background research involves a review of job-relevant documents. It should be the first step in any job analysis process. Initially, the analyst should review the job analysis literature to identify previous job analyses or studies of the job in question. Literature might include the *Dictionary of Occupational Titles* (U.S. Department of Labor, 1977); volume two of Sidney Gael's *Job Analysis Handbook for Business, Industry, and Government* (1988); and professional publications such as the *Journal of Applied Psychology, Personnel Psychology,* and *Public Personnel Management.* This initial research serves to familiarize the analyst with the data collection and analytic techniques used by others, the problems they encountered, and their results (Gatewood and Feild, 2001). Familiarity with past research helps the analyst choose the most effective techniques for the analysis effort. The review of the professional literature should be followed by an examination of organization documents such as existing job descriptions, technical manuals, training materials, organization charts, and previous job analyses.

Job performance. Performing the job may be an effective data collection technique when the job involves primarily either physical operations that can be learned readily or psychomotor skills. Performance-related data may prove very useful in cases where no substitute exists for actually performing the job. Equipment operation that demands hand-eye coordination or fine motor skills may require performing the task for full understanding. Generally, however, because of time constraints, it is more efficient to rely on observation or interview techniques than to expend effort in training an analyst to perform the job.

Site observations. Visiting incumbents at their work sites allows the job analyst to observe the specifics of task performance and determine the degree to which tasks are interrelated. Direct observation familiarizes the job analyst with the materials and equipment used on the job, the conditions under which work is performed, and the factors that trigger the performance of a given task. To minimize distortion, the analyst should explain the reasons for the visit and take care to be unobtrusive. Observation is usually not appropriate when the job primarily entails unobservable mental activity (upper-level manager, lawyer, design engineer). Nor is it as useful if the employee engages in important activities that might occur only occasionally, such as a nurse who handles emergencies. Additionally, reactivity—an employee changing what he or she normally does because the analyst is watching—can also be a problem. The effective use of site observations as a part of the job analysis process requires a trained observer and an analyst with the ability to form varying tasks into a structured format.

Individual and group interviews. The interview is probably the most commonly used technique for collecting job data. The job analyst questions experienced job incumbents or supervisors to determine the tasks that are performed on the job as well as the requirements workers must meet to carry out those tasks. Interviews may be structured or unstructured. However, structure is usually desirable to ensure that the analyst obtains the needed information. Interviews are sometimes conducted concurrently with the site visit so that the performance of job activities can be observed and discussed simultaneously.

In the group interview technique, subject matter experts are convened to discuss the job in question. Typically, job incumbents or supervisors serve as subject matter experts. However, technical experts (such as design engineers or top management) are used to identify tasks when a new job is being created or an existing one updated. Like individual interviews, group sessions may be structured or unstructured. Typically, the job analyst directs the session and imposes structure upon the discussion to elicit the necessary information in the desired format.

Interviews are difficult to standardize. Different interviewers may ask different questions and the same interviewer might unintentionally ask different questions of different respondents. There is also a real possibility that the information provided by the respondent will be unintentionally distorted by the interviewer. The interview method can also be quite time consuming, especially if the interviewer talks with two or three employees doing each job. Finally, the costs of interviewing can be very high, especially if group interviews are not practical.

Questionnaires. A questionnaire presents a list of items that are assumed to be job related and asks SMEs to rate each item on its relevance to the job under study. Subject matter experts identify, among the tasks listed on the inventory, the ones that job incumbents perform, and they rate each task on factors such as the importance to successful job performance and the frequency with which the task is performed. In addition, some questionnaires also require SMEs to identify the knowledge, skills, and abilities required for the job and to rate discrete KSAs on factors such as their importance to acceptable job performance and the extent to which their possession distinguishes between superior and adequate job performance. A commercially available questionnaire may be used, or one may be tailored to fit the job of interest. The items on tailor-made questionnaires can be developed on the basis of information derived from background research, job performance, site observations, individual interviews, or group interviews.

A major disadvantage of the questionnaire method is the possibility that either the respondent or the job analyst will misinterpret the information. Also, questionnaires can be time consuming and expensive to develop. Further, the questionnaire method assumes that employees can accurately analyze and communicate information about their jobs. However, employees may vary in their perceptions of the jobs, and even in their literacy. For these reasons, the questionnaire method is usually combined with interviews and observations to clarify and verify the questionnaire information.

Employee diaries or logs. One drawback of observations, interviews, and questionnaires is that the information they yield is likely to be dependent on the time it happens to be collected. Whatever is most salient at the time of the interview is most likely to find its way into the job and organizational analysis results. Diaries/logs offer one solution to this problem.

This method asks employees to keep a diary/log or list of what they do during the day. For every activity the employee engages in, the employee records the activity (along with the time) in a log. This can produce a very complete picture of the job, especially supplemented with subsequent interviews with the employee and his or her supervisor. The employee might, of course, try to exaggerate some activities and underplay others. However, the detailed, chronological nature of the log tends to mediate against this. If job incumbents and supervisors keep a diary over a period of several weeks, the results are less likely to be biased by the timing of the analysis. For jobs that vary at different times of the year, diaries may be especially valuable.

Some organizations today take a high-tech approach to diaries/logs. They give employees pocket dictating machines and pagers. Then, at random times during the day they page the employees, who dictate what they are doing at that time. This approach can avoid one pitfall of the traditional diary/log method, namely relying on the employee to remember what he or she did when the log is filled out at the end of the day.

A concern about this approach is that it may be burdensome for employees to complete an accurate log, especially since many employees are too busy to record accurate diary entries. Also, employees sometimes perceive this approach as creating needless documentation that detracts from the performance of their work. However, if a diary is accurate, it is useful when analyzing jobs that do not lend themselves to direct observation, such as those of managers, engineers, outside salespeople, or scientists.

JOB ANALYSIS METHODS

There are various methods for analyzing jobs, and it is very difficult to identify "one best way." In this section we shall discuss a number of techniques available for analyzing jobs. All of these techniques can yield information useful in completing HRM tasks such as redesigning work, developing performance measures, planning for training programs, and setting pay levels.

Job analysts commonly combine methods of data collection to achieve a comprehensive picture of the job under study. Most approaches to job analysis mix and match various job data sources and data collection techniques. The job analysis methods presented in this section offer systematic ways of formally applying the data collection techniques. By *formal* we mean that the data collection procedure, as well as the organization of the end product, is standardized. For example, in the individual interview, the job analyst is consistent in the questions asked of different subject matter experts. Furthermore, the data that emerges from the interview is generally structured into precise job statements that would be understandable to someone unfamiliar with the job. By *systematic* we mean that data collection techniques proceed in a set pattern. For example, several current approaches to job analysis progress from background research to individual interviews or observation, group interviews, and ultimately questionnaire administration.

As we have noted, a variety of systems have evolved for conducting job analysis and collecting job-related information. Not surprisingly, several systems for classifying job analysis methodology have also been suggested (e.g., Harvey, 1991). We have adopted the approach most commonly encountered, which make a distinction between *work-oriented* and *worker-oriented* methods. Work-oriented job analysis focuses on a description of the work activities performed on a job. Emphasis is on what is accomplished, including a description of the tasks undertaken and the products or outcomes of those tasks. For example, a work-oriented analysis of a secretarial position might generate observable tasks such as "types letters" or "files documents." Other names for this approach include *task-oriented* and *activity-based* job analysis.

Worker-oriented analysis tends to examine the attributes or characteristics the worker must possess to perform job tasks. The primary products of work-oriented methods are the KSAs and other characteristics required for effective job performance. A worker-oriented analysis of a secretarial position might generate worker characteristics such as "skill in typing" or "knowledge of the organization's filing system." Before we discuss the relative pros and cons of each approach, it may be beneficial to describe examples of each in a bit more detail.

Work-Oriented Approaches

Functional job analysis. Functional job analysis (FJA) provides an approach that takes into consideration the organization, its people, and its work (Fine and Wiley, 1971). The FJA approach employs three data collection techniques, including a review by trained analysts of background and reference materials, interviews with employees and their supervisors, and on-site observations of employees. From this data collection, the purpose, goals, and objectives of the organization are identified by the job analyst and top management. Once analysts have gained an understanding of the organization's work system, they develop task statements in consultation with SMEs. To ensure validity and reliability, analysts edit the task statements with the guidance of incumbents, supervisors, and other SMEs. From the task statements, worker functions are identified, primarily through inferences made by analysts. Finally, FJA attempts to place the individual job clearly in the context of the whole organization by focusing on the results of task performance and the way those results contribute to the attainment of organizational goals and objectives. Because FJA provides a method for assessing the level of each task by describing the employee's required level of involvement with other factors on the job, Fine, Holt, and Hutchinson (1974) recommended it for a broad range of applications. The two most prominent features of FJA are its formal task statements and worker function scales.

Functional job analysis has been used to analyze many different jobs. One advantage of FJA is that the results produce a quantitative score for each job. Thus, jobs can be arranged for compensation or other HRM purposes because jobs with similar ratings are assumed to be similar. Another advantage of the FJA method is that it analyzes each task separately. This results in a much more detailed picture of the job and makes the FJA method more widely applicable for organizational purposes. While FJA has a wide range of applications, it is not particularly useful for job classification or evaluation unless combined with other techniques.

Functional job analysis is an important job analysis system in its own right. However, it is also acknowledged for its influence on subsequent systems. A careful review of a number of the methods described in subsequent sections will reveal FJA concepts and techniques that other researchers have incorporated into their searches for the best job analysis approach.

Critical incidents technique. Developed by John Flanagan (1954), the critical incidents technique (CIT) for job analysis relies on information from supervisors and others who are in a position to observe job behavior. Supervisors are asked to identify and classify those behaviors (critical incidents) that result in effective or ineffective job performance. Examples of particularly successful and unsuccessful job performance are used as guides for future performance. Critical incidents represent a high level of behavioral detail, focusing on the action of the worker, the context in which the behavior occurs, and the consequences of the behavior. CIT is widely applied in performance appraisal because of this specificity.

Perhaps the best way to understand the CIT approach is to examine a critical incident for the job of firefighter (Bownas and Bernardin, 1988):

The firefighter studied two units of the "Red Book" during his daily training period for two weeks. At the end of the period, he couldn't perform the tasks outlined in the manuals, and he couldn't answer sample questions on the content. Because he hadn't picked up these skills, he could only be assigned as a helper to another firefighter at a fire scene. (p. 1123)

This example illustrates the characteristics of a good critical incident. It is specific, its focus is on observable behaviors, and the context in which the behavior occurred is described. Finally, it identifies the consequences of the firefighter's behavior.

As noted, the CIT has been used extensively to assess employee performance. Other suggested uses for the technique include training and job design. One very interesting development noted by Gatewood and Feild (2001) is that CIT can prove useful in the development of structured oral interviews. They recommend conducting a traditional selection-oriented job analysis as a first step in determining interview content. Individual interview questions are then generated using CIT. A major advantage of this approach is the creation of more objective rating scales through the use of critical incidents as anchors for illustrating effective and ineffective responses.

One limitation of the CIT is that it does not identify the common, routine behaviors performed on jobs. This limitation in Flanagan's approach can be eliminated easily by extending the CIT procedure to include statements concerning average performance and thus provide a better overall view of job behaviors (Zedeck, Jackson, and Adelman, 1980).

Comprehensive occupational data analysis program. The Task Inventory/

Comprehensive Occupational Data Analysis Program (TI/CODAP) developed by Christal (1974) for application at Air Force installations consists of two basic components: a task inventory and a computer analysis package. Christal's task inventory is a questionnaire that requires SMEs to make judgments about the tasks constituting their job. A task is defined as a meaningful unit of work that can be readily identified by the employee. Task statements for the inventory are constructed by supervisors, incumbents, and other job experts. Once the task inventory has been developed, job incumbents rate the tasks on a 7-, 9-, or 11-point "relative time spent" scale and on other scales as deemed appropriate or applicable. The task inventory also collects background information such as work experience, education, race, sex, and use of equipment or tools as demanded by the job. These ratings are then analyzed through a series of interactive computer programs that organize the job information in a variety of forms.

CODAP programs exist to perform a number of important HRM functions including describing work performed by individuals or groups, comparing work performed by specified groups, empirically identifying jobs in an occupational area, and analyzing task characteristics (Christal and Weissmuller, 1988). The programs that describe work performed can be used to produce group job descriptions and individual position descriptions. Other programs allow for job classification and evaluation. Christal and Weissmuller note that TI/CODAP has been applied to problems ranging from the study of job satisfaction to the fulfillment of EEO requirements and even to the identification of job hazards. When only a few employees are involved, task inventories are not cost-effective because they are expensive to develop. The information obtained from task inventories is very useful in the design of training programs. Although task inventories like the TI/CODAP might indirectly suggest the types of KSAs and other characteristics people might need to perform the job, these KSAOCs do not come directly out of the process. Thus, other approaches that do put the focus squarely on the people requirement associated with jobs have been developed (e.g., worker-oriented approaches). However, the breadth and flexibility of programs has led to the expanded use of TI/CODAP in business and industry.

Worker-Oriented Approaches

Position analysis questionnaire (PAQ). The PAQ is a very structured job analysis questionnaire that contains 194 different items (such as *written materials*), each of which represents a basic element that may or may not play an important role in the job. Designed by E.J. McCormick (McCormick, Jeanneret, and Mecham, 1972), the PAQ seeks to determine the degree to which the different items, or job elements, are involved in performing a particular job. The 194 items (187 items characterize the worker-oriented activities involved in performing a job, and 7 items deal with pay issues) on the PAQ are organized into six sections:

1. Information input—where and how a worker gets information needed to perform the job.
2. Mental processes—reasoning, decision-making, planning, and information-processing activities involved in performing the job.
3. Work output—the physical activities, tools, and devices used by the worker to perform the job.
4. Relationships with other persons—the relationships with other people required in performing the job.
5. Job context—the physical and social contexts where the work is performed.
6. Other characteristics—the activities, conditions, and characteristics other than those previously described that are relevant to the job.

Examples of job dimensions contained in each of these categories include: (1) use of written materials and use of pictorial materials, (2) level of reasoning and use of stored information, (3) use of keyboard devices and integrative manual activities, (4) physical working conditions and interpersonal conflict situations, (5) communications and personal contact, and (6) work schedules and job demands. Each PAQ item is rated on factors such as extent of use, essentiality, and applicability.

The PAQ itself is filled in by a job analyst, a person who should already be acquainted with the particular job to be analyzed. The job analyst is asked to determine whether each item applies to the job being analyzed. The analyst then rates the item on six scales: extent of use, amount of time, importance to the job, possibility of occurrence, applicability, and special code (special rating scales used with a particular item). These ratings are submitted to the PAQ headquarters, where a computer program generates a report regarding the job's scores on the job dimensions.

The advantage of the PAQ is that it provides a quantitative score or profile of any job in terms of how that job rates on five basic job activities: (1) having decision-making/communication/social responsibilities, (2) performing skilled activities, (3) being physically active, (4) operating vehicles/equipment, and (5) processing information. The PAQ's real strength is thus in classifying jobs. In other words, it lets you assign a quantitative score to each job based on its decision-making, skilled activities, physical activity, vehicle/equipment operation, and information-processing characteristics. You can therefore use the PAQ results to compare jobs to one another, and you can then assign pay levels for each job (Butler and Harvey, 1988; Smith and Hakel, 1979).

While the PAQ has been used extensively for personnel selection, job classification, and job evaluation, its use in performance appraisal and training systems is limited. The worker-oriented PAQ items make analyzing a wide variety of jobs easier, but they also make it difficult to translate PAQ scores directly into specific performance standards or training content. Other shortcomings of the PAQ are that the instrument itself is relatively complex and an employee must have a reading level of a college graduate to be able to complete it. Therefore, PAQ executives recommend that only trained experts complete the questionnaire, as opposed to using job incumbents or supervisors for this purpose. Further, although the PAQ is supposed to be applicable to most jobs, there is reason to believe that it is less useful for describing higher-level managerial jobs and white-collar jobs (DeNisi, Cornelius, and Blencoe, 1987).

Job element method. The Job Element Method developed by Primoff (1975) represents a unique approach to job analysis in that its focus is on worker characteristics rather than on job activities. The Job Element Method identifies skills, knowledge, inclinations, and other characteristics of employees in a particular job classification. This method typically relies not on job analysts to gather information but rather on a group of approximately six job incumbents, supervisors, or both who are familiar enough with the job under study to easily recognize characteristics of superior workers (Feild and Gatewood, 1989). These factors are organized into the following six broad categories of job elements (Primoff, 1975, p. 2):

- a knowledge, such as knowledge of accounting principles;
- a skill, such as skill with woodworking tools;
- an ability, such as ability to manage a program;
- a willingness, such as willingness to do simple tasks repetitively;
- an interest, such as an interest in learning new techniques; or
- a personal characteristic, such as reliability or dependability.

Once the job elements have been identified, the subject matter experts generate a corresponding list of subelements for each element. For example, having identified "knowledge of mathematics" as an element, SMEs might more clearly define the parameters of that knowledge by including "knowledge of addition of fractions" as a subelement. Subject matter experts then rate the job elements and subelements along a series of dimensions that are designed to measure the correlation between success on the job and possession of each job element. Through this correlation, the Job Element Method attempts to identify the characteristics that, if possessed by an individual, will probably result in superior job performance.

Primoff originally intended the Job Element Method for use in conducting job element rating sessions, preparing selection devices based on rating results, and testing and refining selection measures (Primoff, 1975). However, a drawback associated with this method was its inability to satisfy the federal *Uniform Guidelines'* requirements for content validation. The *Uniform Guidelines* require that a job analysis focus on work behaviors as well as knowledge, skills, and abilities. Later, however, Primoff began work to integrate the Job Element Method with FJA and CIT to meet content validity requirements (Bemis et al., 1983).

Threshold traits analysis. The Threshold Traits Analysis System (TTAS) is a job analysis approach first designed and implemented in 1971 (Lopez, 1986). TTAS differs from some other worker-oriented approaches in that it has identified 33 relatively enduring traits hypothesized to be related to the performance of a large number of different jobs. These traits are divided into two broad classes: ability and attitude. Ability-oriented traits are considered "can do" factors, whereas attitudinal traits are "willing to do" factors. Within TTAS, traits are assessed for six characteristics: level, practicality, weight, degree, criticality, and availability. Level refers to a trait's complexity. Practicality relates to the estimated proportion of job applicants thought to possess a given trait. Weight is an index of the impact of a particular trait on overall job performance. Degree represents a four-grade assessment of a person's possession of a trait, ranging from unacceptable to superior. Criticality, as the name implies, refers to the relationship between possession of a trait and overall job performance. Availability "describes the supply/demand ratio of each trait level in the employer's labor market" (Lopez, 1988, p. 884).

In TTAS the heart of the job analysis is the evaluation of traits. This technique demands that incumbents, supervisors, or other SMEs rate the relevance, level, and practicality of each of the 33 traits. These ratings are analyzed to produce a basic functional description of the job. The functional job description then serves as the foundation for selection, training, performance evaluation, and compensation.

Other Approaches

The distinction between work- and worker-oriented approaches to job analysis became blurred as personnel consultants and HRM managers recognized the utility of collecting both types of information (Guion, 1978; McCormick, 1979; Prien, 1977). This development led to recommendations for the use of multiple job analysis systems, and new systems were developed in attempts to meet a variety of HRM needs. These so-called multimethod approaches employ data collection techniques that obtain both work- and worker-oriented information.

IMES variants. The Iowa Merit Employment System (IMES) was an early attempt to incorporate both work- and worker-oriented job analysis data. The IMES approach is a systematic multistep process designed to aid in the development of content-valid selection devices (Menne, McCarthy, and

Menne, 1976). IMES emphasizes the use of a group interview in which supervisors and incumbents work jointly to identify relevant job content. First, job tasks are identified. These tasks are then expanded into a standardized form that answers the following questions:

1. What is the action being performed?
2. To whom or what is the action directed?
3. Why is the action being performed?
4. How is the action done?

Once job tasks have been defined as formal task statements, the knowledge, skills, abilities, and personal characteristics (KSAPCs) needed to perform each of the job's tasks are identified. Incumbents and supervisors then rate task statements on dimensions such as importance, time spent, and necessity at entry. The KSAPCs arising from the aforementioned group interview are also rated for their importance and linked to job tasks. The data provided by these ratings are analyzed, and a picture of the job task and job knowledge domain is obtained. Among the variants of the basic IMES approach are the Alabama Merit System Method (Elliott et al., 1980) and Integrated Job Analysis (Buckley, 1986).

Behavioral consistency method. Schmidt et al. (1979) developed the Behavioral Consistency Method (BCM) to identify competencies workers needed to perform mid-level government, professional, and managerial jobs. The method has since been used to identify competencies in private sector managerial and blue-collar jobs. Two basic principles underlie the BCM approach:

1. applicants should be evaluated only on dimensions that clearly differentiate between superior and minimally acceptable performers.
2. These dimensions must be determined through consultation with individuals who have known and observed superior and marginal performers.

The BCM involves four major components: (1) the identification and description of job activities and tasks; (2) the identification of knowledge, skills, abilities, and other characteristics (KSAOCs) needed to perform the work; (3) the rating of KSAOCs by subject matter experts; and (4) the analysis of these ratings to evaluate KSAOCs.

Job agents independently rate each KSAOC on six scales. Scale 1 evaluates the importance of the KSAOC in preventing job failure. Scale 2 determines the percentage of current workers meeting minimum performance standards for each KSAOC. Scale 3 determines whether the KSAOC is necessary for all positions. Scale 4 evaluates the usefulness of the KSAOC in differentiating between superior and minimally acceptable workers. Scale

5 identifies the extent of variability of the KSAOC in the applicant pool. Scale 6 is used only when subspecialties are present in the occupation. The BCM represents a significant breakthrough in reviewing the appropriateness of applicant qualifications. Its use has been limited primarily to this application.

U.S. Civil Service Commission job analysis technique. The U.S. Civil Service Commission job analysis technique provides a standardized procedure by which different jobs can be compared and classified. With this method the information is compiled on a *job analysis record sheet*. Identifying information (like job title) and a brief summary of the job are listed first. Next the analyst lists the job's specific tasks in order of importance. Then, for each task, the analyst specifies the:

1. Knowledge required (for example, the principles the worker must be acquainted with to do his or her job).
2. Skills required (for example, the skills needed to operate machines or vehicles).
3. Abilities required (for example, mathematical, reasoning, problem-solving, or interpersonal abilities).
4. Physical activities involved (for example, pulling, pushing, or carrying).
5. Any special environmental conditions (for example, cramped quarters, vibration, inadequate ventilation, noise, or moving objects).
6. Typical work incidents (for example, performing under stress in emergencies, working with people beyond giving and receiving instructions, or performing repetitive work).
7. Worker interest areas (for example, the preferences the worker should have for activities dealing with things and objects, or the communication of data, or dealing with people). (U.S. Civil Service Commission, 1977)

Almost any job can be broken into its component tasks, each of which can then be analyzed in terms of knowledge required, skills required, and so forth. The Civil Service procedure thus provides a standardized method by which different jobs can be compared and classified. In other words, knowledge, skills, and abilities required to perform, say, an assistant police chief's job can be compared with those required to perform a librarian's job. If the requirements are similar, the jobs might be classified together, for example, for pay purposes.

VERJAS. A successor to the BCM is the Versatile Job Analysis System (VERJAS) developed by Bemis et al. (1983). This system extends some of the principles underlying the BCM to a wider variety of applications including job design, classification and evaluation, recruitment, selection, training, and performance appraisal. A VERJAS job description contains a list of duties, tasks, task ratings for importance and for needed training, job context descriptions, and competencies needed for the job. As noted by

Bemis et al. (1983), "VERJAS is composed of procedures utilized in other job analysis methods integrated into a single system to meet management's total job analysis needs. The system is a job analysis melting pot in both origin and use" (p. 61). The detailed operational definitions of competencies and clear linkage of competencies back to important job tasks are two appealing features of VERJAS. The system is a hybrid; that is, the procedures from other job analysis methods are integrated into a single system. As such, VERJAS provides a wealth of practical information that can be used for many purposes. When using this approach, Bemis et al. (1983) suggest adhering to the following guidelines: (1) identify duties, (2) identify tasks, (3) evaluate tasks, (4) evaluate job content, and (5) evaluate worker competencies (worker requirements).

WHICH METHOD SHOULD JOB ANALYSTS USE?

Most experts agree that the choice of a job analysis method depends upon the purposes to be served by the data. Unfortunately, research has not yet answered the question of which job analysis system is the best (Bernardin and Beatty, 1984). The purposes for the data and the practicality of the various methods for particular organizations must be considered. Because research provides no definitive guidance on what system to use, the *Uniform Guidelines'* requirements and court opinions merit considerable weight. The most definitive findings from the research on the relative effectiveness of the various methods is that multiple methods of job analysis should be used whenever possible. For example, a quantitative approach such as the PAQ should probably be augmented by a qualitative approach such as the CIT, which can provide more specific information about jobs than what typically can be derived from the quantitative method. As mentioned previously, legal considerations would seem to favor multimethod approaches.

There are several factors that may be used to assess job analysis methods (Levine, Ash, Hall, and Sistrunk, 1983). Some criteria that serve as the basis for assessments are presented in Exhibit 4.1. Although these criteria can be helpful in comparing different methods, which method is best depends on the particular objectives of the organization as well as on cost limitations and other factors governing the project. In other words, the choice of a method is determined by circumstances such as the purpose of the analysis and time and budget constraints.

A final criterion that must be considered in identifying an appropriate job analysis method is *legality*. An organization must ask whether a job analysis method would be acceptable to the courts if the data from such a method were provided as evidence to support the personnel selection, training, performance appraisal, or pay practices of the organization. This criterion is so pervasive that it is impacted, in part, by many of the other 10

Exhibit 4.1
Criteria for Assessing Job Analysis Methods

Number	Criterion	Definition
1	Purposes served	Can the data collected be used for a variety of purposes?
2	Versatility	Can a method be used to analyze many different jobs?
3	Standardization	Does a method provide data that can be easily compared to data collected by other methods?
4	User acceptance	Do users of the method accept it as a reasonable way to collect job data?
5	Training required	How much training is needed before individuals can use it to collect data in the organization?
6	Sample size	How large a sampling of information source is needed before an adequate picture of the job can be obtained?
7	Off the shelf	Can the method be used directly off the shelf, or must considerable development work be done to tailor it for use in a particular organization?
8	Reliability	Does the method produce reliable data?
9	Time to complete	How long does it take to analyze a job using the method?
10	Cost	How much does the method cost to implement and use?

identified criteria. Purpose, for example, is an important consideration not only for maximizing the utility of the job analysis but also for legal reasons. An organization must make it clear why a job analysis is being conducted and choose a method of analysis relevant for that purpose. The results of a good job analysis should be used only for the purpose for which it was originally intended or suited. Sample source and size can also have legal ramifications in the job analysis process. Job data should be collected from several sources. Human sources should be representative of workers associated with the job and should be well acquainted with the job about which they are to provide information. The outcome of the job analysis, driven by the process, is of utmost importance in determining the legal acceptability of the job analysis method. A job analysis should include a listing of all tasks performed on the job but should make clear which tasks are most important. When job analysis results are used to justify the use of specific knowledge, skill, and ability tests in selection, there should be a clear and really justifiable link between specific tasks performed on the job and the knowledge, skills, and abilities tested for in selection. The resulting job analysis data should be checked regularly for reliability and validity, and the results of a job analysis should be reported in a written form that is clear and easily understood. By following these guidelines, the job analyst can greatly increase the likelihood that job analysis procedures will be acceptable from a legal perspective.

RECENT TREND IN JOB ANALYSIS METHODS

One recent trend worth noting in the area of job analysis is that the *Dictionary of Occupational Titles* (DOT) has recently been replaced by the U.S. Department of Labor's new job analysis service entitled the *Occupational Information Network*, also known as O*NET. O*NET was first released to the public in the fall of 1998. The function of O*NET is similar to the DOT—"to provide a comprehensive database system for collecting, organizing, describing and disseminating data on job characteristics and worker attributes." O*NET can be accessed online from its Web site at http://www.doleta.gov/programs/onet, but it's not just a new electronic version of the DOT. It represents a new conceptual framework for categorizing jobs. Development of the DOT was heavily influenced by the dominance of traditional manufacturing jobs earlier in the twentieth century. As jobs changed, the DOT gradually became obsolete. The need to reconceptualize and update the job descriptions that are used and disseminated by the U.S. government stimulated development work that eventually culminated in the creation of O*NET. O*NET better captures the role of advanced technologies and the increasing importance of service-based jobs. This new framework describes jobs as having six content areas: experience requirements, worker requirements, worker characteristics, occupation characteristics, occupation specifics, and occupation requirements.

Like the DOT, O*NET is intended to be a resource for employers, but an added objective of O*NET is to serve as a resource for anyone who seeks to make informed employment decisions. People can get facts about occupations and jobs by visiting O*NET's homepage and searching the database. Traditionally, such information is provided by the Bureau of Labor Statistics *Occupational Outlook Handbook*, which can now be accessed through O*NET. For example, a search for information about the occupation of "actuaries" yields five full pages of descriptive information about this occupation. The advanced technology database that the O*NET provides includes sophisticated occupational and career information systems. O*NET is quick, and it's essentially free. Furthermore, the job descriptions available through O*NET are based on hundreds of observations.

THE CHANGING NATURE OF JOBS

Increasingly there is an understanding that the nature of jobs and work is changing so much that the concept of a "job" may be obsolete for many of today's employees. For example, in some high-technology organizations employees shift from project to project and work in cross-functional project teams. The focus in these organizations is less on performing specific tasks and duties and more on fulfilling responsibilities and attaining results. For instance, a project team of eight employees developing software that will allow various credit cards to be used with automated teller machines (ATMs) worldwide will work on many different tasks, some individually and some with other team members. When that project is finished those employees will move to other projects, possibly with other employers. Such shifts may happen several times per year. Therefore, the basis for recruiting, selecting, and compensating these individuals is their competence and skills, not what they do (Nelson, 1997). Even the job of managers changes in such situations, for they must serve their project teams as facilitators, gatherers of resources, and removers of roadblocks.

However, in many organizations that use lower-skilled employees, traditional jobs continue to exist. Job analysis researchers can study these jobs and their work consequences with relative ease because of the repetitiveness of the work and the limited number of tasks each employee performs.

Analyzing the two types of jobs (i.e., lower-skilled and highly technical) requires different approaches. Many of the traditional processes associated with identifying job descriptions are still relevant with the lower-skilled, task-based jobs. However, for more and more of today's fast-moving organizations, a job description is becoming an obsolete concept. Employees in these "virtual jobs" must be able to function without job descriptions and without the traditional parameters that are still useful with less changeable jobs (Behn, 1997). This strategic view of job analysis will be discussed in the next section.

As evidenced by the discussion thus far, the term "job" has taken on new forms, as has the utility of job analysis. Writers have recently stated that the more fluid and changeable nature of modern organizations brings into question the very logic of job analysis (Cardy and Dobbins, 1992, p. 4). William Bridges, in his 1995 book *Job Shift*, suggests that jobs "are artificial units superimposed on this field. They are patches of responsibility that, all together, were supposed to cover the work that needs to be done" (p. 1).

Clearly, in many organizations today, jobs are becoming amorphous and more difficult to define. In other words, the trend is toward *de-jobbing* many organizations. De-jobbing is ultimately a result of the changes taking place in business today. Organizations need to grapple with revolutionary forces—accelerating product and technological change, political instability, globalized competition, deregulation, demographic changes, and trends toward the information age and a service society. Forces like these have dramatically increased the need for organizations to be responsive and capable of competing in a global marketplace. The new organizational approaches are undermining the traditional notions of the job as a well-defined and clearly delineated set of responsibilities. A few examples of how these approaches are contributing to this blurring are (1) movement away from hierarchical organizations, (2) the boundaryless organization, (3) empowered teams, and (4) reengineering.

THE FUTURE OF JOB ANALYSIS: A STRATEGIC VIEW

The business environment today is increasingly characterized by incredible competition and change (Hamel and Prahalad, 1994). And as noted above, organizations are responding in various ways. Accompanying these changes has been a growing concern that traditional job analysis procedures may be unable to play a central role in the new HRM environment (Barnes-Nelson, 1996). In contrast to the traditional approach to job analysis which assumes that a job in the future will be the same as it is now, several HRM researchers have suggested the need for strategic job analysis (Schneider and Konz, 1989). The main objective of strategic job analysis is to identify the tasks, knowledge, skills, and abilities that will be needed to perform the job in the future.

Thus, in a future-oriented job analysis the emphasis shifts from *descriptions* of the present to *prescriptions* about what the future should be like. For example, suppose an organization has decided to downsize. Traditional job analysis could be used to identify all the tasks currently performed by employees. Then, a future-oriented job analysis could be conducted to focus attention on which tasks in the organization should continue to be done and which tasks should be eliminated or outsourced. This same approach can be used to guide other types of organizational change. For example, future-oriented job analysis was used to help a fashion retailer redesign its floor layout, redesign jobs and create new ones, and alter its work processes (Fogli and Whitney, 1998).

Customers as SMEs

With an increased emphasis on satisfying customers as a key strategic objective, the future should see more and more organizations turning to customers as SMEs in the job analysis process. Today, however, this is seldom done. Collecting any type of information from customers has traditionally been viewed as a marketing, rather than an HRM, activity. One need only consider the fact that more and more employees in service industries are spending increased amounts of time interacting with customers and less and less time interacting with their immediate supervisors or managers. For jobs like these, it seems obvious that using customers as job analysis SMEs can provide valuable information about the job the employee performs or the characteristics present or needed in that employee. Thus, customers as SMEs is likely to become more common as organizations increasingly incorporate the perspectives of customers when designing jobs and assessing employee performance.

Today's organizations can use job analysis techniques to assess their current customer role and to develop a description of the ideal role that customers could play. For many organizations, employees are given tasks to do before they arrive on site. Once on site, the organization can ask employees to engage in some behaviors and avoid others. Job analysis procedures can help the organization identify behaviors and/or competencies that increase or decrease the probability of a successful service encounter.

SUMMARY

This chapter has attempted to convey a general idea of the practice of job analysis. Successful organizations must rely on job analysis as the building block of the HRM planning process and recognize it as the fundamental source for that process.

There are a variety of uses for job analysis information, and every HRM activity relies on the data derived from job analysis. There are also a number of sources for collecting job analysis information. Typical sources include job incumbents, job supervisors, and job analysts. Commonly used methods of job analysis include work- and worker-oriented approaches that involve FJA, PAQ, CIT, TI/CODAP, and others.

The changing nature of jobs requires a new strategic view of job analysis, which requires HRM personnel to take a broader and more innovative approach to the job analysis process. They must focus more on how jobs will change to meet the demands of a dynamic organizational competitive environment. Instead of throwing out the traditional job analysis techniques developed and used over the last four decades, they must broaden and adapt them to meet this new work environment. An environment that is increasingly dependent on the HRM function to collect information that will help organizations cultivate more productive, effective, and efficient employees will increase the likelihood of organizational success.

As May (1996) notes, job analysis may be most useful in a work world that does not include jobs, because the information it provides may enable more effective design and management of work processes. We agree with May that:

Job analysis information is the raw material that is essential to build new work processes and create efficiencies that cannot emerge any other way. This much-maligned tool holds great promise for the future of organizations if we seize the opportunity that presents itself. (p. 100)

HRM personnel will find job analyses to be even more important in the years to come as they continue to find ways to help the organization identify those tasks it must perform to be successful.

REFERENCES

Barnes-Nelson, J. 1996. The boundaryless organization: Implications for job analysis, recruitment, and selection. *Human Resource Planning* 20: 39–49.

Behn, R.D. 1997. Job descriptions vs. real performance. *Governing* (January): 60.

Bemis, B.E., Belenky, A.H., & Soder, D.A. 1983. *Job analysis: An effective management tool.* Washington, DC: Bureau of National Affairs.

Bernardin, H.J., and Beatty, R.W. (1984). *Performance appraisal: Assessing human performance at work.* Boston: Kent.

Bownas, D.A., and Bernardin, H.J. 1988. Critical incident technique. In S. Gael (ed.), *The job analysis handbook for business, industry, and government,* Vol. 2. New York: Wiley, pp. 1120–1137.

Bridges, W. 1995. *Job shift: How to prosper in a workplace without jobs.* St. Leonards, Australia: Allen & Unwin.

Buckley, R. 1986. *Integrated job analysis and selection.* Glendale, CA: Psychological Services, Inc.

Buckner, K.E. 1989. *A review and empirical analysis of court standards for employee selection.* Unpublished doctoral dissertation, Auburn University, Auburn, AL.

Butler, S., and Harvey, R.J. 1988. A comparison of holistic versus decomposed rating of Position Analysis Questionnaire work dimensions. *Personnel Psychology* (Winter): 761–772.

Cardy, B., and Dobbins, G. 1992. Job analysis in a dynamic environment. *Human Resources Division News* 16(1): 4.

Carson, K.P., and Stewart, G.L. 1996. Job analysis and the sociotechnical approach to quality: A critical examination. *Journal of Quality Management* 1: 49–64.

Cascio, W. 1991. *Applied psychology in personnel management,* 4th ed. Englewood Cliffs, NJ: Prentice-Hall.

Christal, R.E. 1974. *The United States Air Force occupational research project.* Lackland Air Force Base, TX: Air Human Resources Laboratory.

Christal, R.E., and Weissmuller, J.J. 1988. Job-task inventory analysis. In S. Gael (ed.), *The job analysis handbook for business, industry, and government,* Vol. 2. New York: Wiley, pp. 1036–1050.

Cornelius, E.T. 1988. Practical findings from job analysis research. In S. Gael (ed.), *The job analysis handbook for business, industry, and government,* Vol. 1. New York: Wiley, pp. 48–68.

Davis, L.E., and Wacker, G.J. 1988. Job design. In S. Gael (ed.), *The job analysis handbook for business, industry, and government,* Vol. 1. New York: Wiley, pp. 157–172.

DeNisi, A., Cornelius, E., and Blencoe, A. 1987. A further investigation of common knowledge effects on job analysis ratings: On the applicability of the PAQ for all jobs. *Journal of Applied Psychology* 72: 262–268.

Elliott, R.H., Boyles, W.R., Hill, J.B., Palmer, C., Thomas, P., and Veres, J.G. 1980. *Content oriented personnel selection procedures—A training manual.* Montgomery, AL: Auburn University at Montgomery, Center for Government and Public Affairs.

Equal Employment Opportunity Commission, Civil Service Commission, Department of Labor, and Department of Justice. 1978. Adoption by four agencies of uniform guidelines on employee selection procedures. *Federal Register* 43: 38290–38315.

Feild, H.S., and Gatewood, R.D. 1989. Development of a selection interview: A job content strategy. In R.W. Eder and G.R. Ferris (eds.), *The employment interview: Theory, research, and practice.* Beverly Hills, CA: Sage.

Fine, S.A. 1988. Functional job analysis. In S. Gael (ed.), *The job analysis handbook for business, industry, and government,* Vol. 2. New York: Wiley, pp. 1019–1035.

Fine, S.A., Holt, A.M., and Hutchinson, M.F. 1974. *Functional job analysis: How to standardize task statements.* Kalamazoo, MI: W.E. Upjohn Institute for Employment Research.

Fine, S.A., and Wiley, W.W. 1971. *An introduction to functional job analysis: A scaling of selected tasks from the social welfare field.* Kalamazoo, MI: W.E. Upjohn Institute for Employment Research.

Flanagan, J.C. (1954). The critical incident technique. *Psychological Bulletin* 51: 327–358.

Fogli, L., and Whitney, K. (1998). Assessing and changing managers for new organizational roles. In R. Jeanneret and R. Silzer (eds.), *Individual psychological assessment: Predicting behavior in organizational settings.* San Francisco: Jossey-Bass.

French, W.L. 1982. *The personnel management process: Human resources administration and development.* Boston: Houghton Mifflin.

Gael, S. (ed.). 1988. *The job analysis handbook for business, industry, and government,* Vols. 1 and 2. New York: Wiley.

Gatewood, R.D., and Feild, H.S. 2001. *Human resource selection,* 5th ed. Hinsdale, IL: Dryden.

Goldstein, I.L. 1993. *Training in organizations,* 3rd ed. Pacific Grove, CA: Brooks/Cole.

Guion, R.M. 1978. Scoring of content domain sample: The problem of fairness. *Journal of Applied Psychology* 63: 499–506.

Hamel, G., and Prahalad, C.K. 1994. *Competing for the future.* Boston: Harvard Business School Press.

Harvey, R.J. 1991. Job analysis. In M. Dunnette and L.M. Hough (eds.), *Handbook of industrial and organizational psychology.* Palo Alto, CA: Consulting Psychologists Press, pp. 71–163.

Holley, W.M., and Jennings, K.M. 1983. *Personnel management: Functions and issues.* Chicago: Dryden.

Kennedy, M.M. 1997. Can this new hire be saved? *Across the Board* (May): 53.

Kirkland v. New York Department of Corrections, 374 F. Supp. 1361 (S.D. NY 1974).

Levine, E.L., Ash, R.A., Hall, H., and Sistrunk, F. 1983. Evaluation of job analysis methods by experienced job analysts. *Academy of Management Journal* 26: 339–348.

Lopez, F.M. 1986. *The threshold traits analysis technical manual.* Port Washington, NY: Lopez and Associates.

Lopez, F.M. 1988. Threshold traits analysis system. In S. Gael (ed.), *The job analysis handbook for business, industry, and government*, Vol. 2. New York: Wiley, pp. 880–901.

May, K.E. 1996. Work in the 21st century: Implications for job analysis. *The Industrial-Organizational Psychologist* 33: 98–100.

McCormick, E.J. 1979. *Job analysis: Methods and applications.* New York: American Management Association.

McCormick, E.J., Jeanneret, P.R., and Mecham, R.C. 1972. A study of job characteristics and job dimensions as based on the Position Analysis Questionnaire (PAQ). *Journal of Applied Psychology* 56: 347–368.

Menne, J.W., McCarthy, W., and Menne, J. 1976. A systems approach to the content validation of employee selection procedures. *Public Personnel Management* 5: 387–396.

Murphy, K.R., and Cleveland, J.N. 1991. *Performance appraisal: An organizational perspective.* Boston: Allyn & Bacon.

Nelson, J.B. 1997. The boundary-less organization: Implications for job analysis. *Human Resource Planning* 20: 39–50.

Primoff, E.S. 1975. *How to prepare and conduct job element examinations.* Washington, DC: U.S. Civil Service Commission, Personnel Research and Development Center.

Prion, E.P. 1977. The function of job analysis in content validation. *Personnel Psychology* 30: 167–174.

Schmidt, F.L., Caplan, J.R., Bemis, S.E., Dewir, R., Dunn, L., and Antone, L. 1979. *The behavioral consistency method of unassembled examining.* Washington, DC: U.S. Office of Personnel Management.

Schneider, B., and Konz, A.M. 1989. Strategic job analysis. *Human Resource Management* 28: 51–63.

Siegel, G.B. 1987. Education and training for the job analyst. *Personnel* 64(7): 68–73.

Sims, R.R., and Veres, J.G. 1985. A practical program for training job analysts. *Public Personnel Management* 14: 131–137.

Smith, J.E., and Hakel, M.D. 1979. Convergence among data sources, response bias, and reliability and validity of a structured job analysis questionnaire. *Personnel Psychology* 32: 677–692.

Sparks, P. 1981. Job analysis. In K. Rowland and G. Ferris (eds.), *Personnel management.* Boston: Allyn and Bacon, pp. 78–100.

Thompson, D.E., and Thompson, T.A. 1982. Court standards for job analysis in test validation. *Personnel Psychology* 35: 865–874.

Tiffin, J., and McCormick, E.J. 1965. *Industrial psychology.* Englewood Cliffs, NJ: Prentice-Hall.

U.S. Civil Service Commission. 1977. *Instructions for the factor evaluation system.* Washington, DC: U.S. Government Printing Office.

U.S. Department of Labor, Employment and Training Administration. 1977.

Dictionary of occupational titles, 4th ed. Washington, DC: U.S. Government Printing Office.

Wright, P., and Wexley, K. 1985. How to choose the kind of job analysis you really need. *Personnel* (May): 51–55.

Zedeck, S., Jackson, S.J., and Adelman, A. 1980. *Selection procedures reference manual*. Berkeley: University of California Press.

Chapter 5

Recruiting for Organizational Success

INTRODUCTION

Emphasizing the essential nature of the recruiting function in today's business environment, Peter Drucker notes that "every organization is in competition for its most essential resource: qualified, knowledgeable people" (Drucker, 1992). Today's successful organizations need to hire the most qualified people they can at the most competitive price. Before an organization is able to hire an individual, it must locate qualified applicants who are interested in working for the organization. How does an organization attract these qualified people? Through the recruitment process, and it represents one of the major responsibilities of the HRM function—a responsibility that if not effectively and efficiently completed can almost single-handedly ensure limited success for today's organizations.

Recruitment is the process by which organizations discover, develop, seek, and attract individuals to fill actual or anticipated job vacancies. Or from another perspective, it is a bridge-building activity—bringing together those with jobs to fill and those seeking jobs.

Most organizations have an ongoing need to recruit new employees to fill job vacancies when employees leave or are promoted, to acquire new skills, and to permit organizational growth. In an era when the focus of most organizations has been on efficiently and effectively running the organization, recruiting the right person for the job is a top priority if organizations are to be successful. Recruitment is directly related to both HRM planning and selection.

Recruitment can be quite expensive when one considers the cost of advertising, agency fees, employee referral bonuses, applicant and staff travel, relocation costs, and recruiter salaries. Although recruitment can be quite expensive, organizations have not always treated it as systematically as other HRM functions, such as selection. However, in recent years organizations have increasingly recognized that failure to systematically recruit employees can impact their success. There is every indication that organizations will continue to see the value of recruitment to their success.

The magnitude of an organization's recruiting effort and the methods to be used in that recruiting effort are determined from HRM planning. Recruitment follows HRM planning and job analysis and goes hand in hand with the selection process (discussed in Chapter 6) by which organizations evaluate the suitability of candidates for various jobs.

Successful recruiting is difficult if the jobs to be filled are vaguely defined. Regardless of whether the job to be filled has been in existence or is newly created, its requirements must be defined as precisely as possible for recruiting to be effective. As discussed in Chapter 4, job analysis gives the nature and requirements of specific jobs. HRM planning determines the specific number of jobs to be filled. Without accurate planning, organizations may recruit the wrong number or type of employees. Without successful recruiting to create a sizable pool of candidates, even the most accurate selection system is of little use. Typical questions that are addressed in the recruitment process include: What are the sources of qualified individuals? How are these qualified individuals to be recruited? Who is to be involved in the recruiting process? What inducements does the organization have to attract qualified individuals? The selection process discussed in detail in the next chapter concerns choosing from the pool of qualified candidates the individual or group of individuals who are most likely to succeed in a given job.

This chapter focuses on the recruitment process. The chapter discusses how to plan and conduct recruiting efforts that contribute to organizational success. The chapter highlights methods that can be used to locate candidates from within and outside the organization. It also focuses on the importance of understanding both the employee's goals and realistic job previews (RJPs) as keys to improving the effectiveness of the recruitment process. Alternatives to recruiting, including the use of overtime, temporary workers, employee leasing, and independent contractors, along with the challenge of recruiting a diverse workforce, are also discussed, emphasizing the need for organizations to evaluate the effectiveness of their recruitment efforts.

FACTORS AND ISSUES AFFECTING RECRUITING EFFORTS

Many factors and issues must be taken into consideration by an organization if it is going to be successful in its recruiting efforts. For example, the nature of the organization's recruiting activities must be aligned to its strategy and philosophy as well as other important features such as the organization's reputation and the environmental factors that influence recruitment success. In this section we will discuss several issues and factors related to successful recruitment.

Organizational Reputation

Probably the most important factor affecting the success of the recruitment program is the organization's reputation in terms of its products or services. If the organization has a negative image it may be limited in its HRM recruitment efforts. For example, the pool of qualified candidates may not include the "best" candidates; or the "best" candidate may not want to be employed by the organization. Overall, the organization projects a certain image to the community at large and this influences its ability to attract qualified employees. In many cases, good advertising and successful public relations efforts can increase community knowledge of the organization, raise public appreciation, and thus make a dramatic impact on recruitment.

The image of the organization should be recognized as a potential barrier. If that image is perceived to be low, the likelihood of attracting a large number of applicants is reduced ("Code Words," 1995). For example, if a potential employee's image of an organization is pessimistic or negative because the organization has a reputation for being in a declining industry, for engaging in practices that result in polluting the environment, poor-quality products, and unsafe working conditions, or for being indifferent to employee's needs, then these potential employees may not be interested in pursuing job opportunities in the organization.

An organization's relations with labor unions can be critical to public perceptions of the organization, as can the organization's reputation for offering high or low wages. Subtle elements in the organizational culture and climate are also important. Since many people hear about job possibilities from friends or relatives already working at the organization, attitudes about the organization are passed along through this informal network. For example, as suggested in the previous paragraph if an organization has a reputation for being indifferent to employee's needs or employees are annoyed by what they perceive as lack of recognition for their efforts, their casual comments may discourage their friends from applying. In the end, such reputations can and do reduce the organization's abilities to attract the best individuals available (Turban and Greening, 1997).

Attractiveness of the Job

Social attitudes about particular types of employment will also affect the supply of potential employees. If the job to be filled is considered uninteresting, oppressive, or unattractive, recruiting a large and qualified pool of applicants will be difficult. In recent years, for instance, many organizations have been complaining about the difficulty of finding suitably qualified individuals for "manual labor" jobs. In a job market where unemployment rates are low and where a wide range of opportunities exist creating competition for workers, a shortage results. Moreover, any job that is viewed as boring, hazardous, anxiety-provoking, low-status, low-paying, or lacking in promotion potential will seldom attract a qualified pool of applicants, since most potential employees will shun it unless the wages are extremely attractive. Even during economic slumps, people have refused to take many of these jobs (Holoviak and DeCenzo, 1990, p. 5).

Costs of Recruiting

Cost is an important factor in recruitment. Recruiting efforts by an organization are expensive. A small organization, for example, may not have the resources to interview candidates at colleges outside the region or to pay the travel expenses of candidates who might be invited from outside the area. Sometimes a long search is not possible because of budget restrictions. Accordingly, when an organization considers various recruiting sources, it does so with some sense of effectiveness in mind—such as maximizing its recruiting travel budget by first interviewing employees over the phone or through videoconferencing. Each organization will need to analyze the costs involved in alternative methods of recruitment.

Recruiting Goals

Among the key issues in recruitment are the goals of the recruitment program. A successful recruiting program needs to serve many and sometimes conflicting goals. The most basic and fundamental goal of an organization's recruiting effort is to accomplish exactly what is stated in the definition—discover, develop, seek, and attract individuals to fill actual or anticipated job vacancies. In short, the goal is to optimize the pool of qualified applicants. If an organization has, say, ten openings and somehow ends up attracting several thousand applicants for these jobs, then the organization has actually created a large problem for itself. In this situation the applicant pool can be too large and thus very costly to process. Enormous amounts of time and resources will be necessary to process the large number of applicants for the positions, and if this processing is not handled effectively and efficiently, then ill will for the organization will be created as well. Thus, the HRM department handling the recruitment process does not really want to attract a pool of applicants that is too large.

Recruiting also must attract a high proportion of well-qualified candidates who are seriously interested in accepting a job offer. Posthiring goals also must be considered. The recruiting process must yield employees who can then be further assessed in the selection process, individuals who will be good performers and who will stay with the organization for a reasonable length of time.

Another goal of the recruiting process is to offer an honest and candid assessment to prospective applicants of what kinds of jobs and what kinds of opportunities the organization can potentially make available to them. It does no one any good to trick or mislead job applicants into thinking that they are going to have more challenging or higher-level jobs than are actually available or that they will be earning higher salaries than the organization is actually prepared to pay. Thus the recruiting process needs to paint a realistic picture of what the potential job actually entails. This goal will be discussed in more detail later when we discuss realistic job previews.

An additional goal is that recruiting efforts should have beneficial "spillover" effects; that is, the organization's general image should be enhanced, and even unsuccessful applicants should develop positive attitudes toward the organization and its products. Further, all the preceding goals should be reached with the greatest speed and at the least possible cost to the organization (Rynes and Barber, 1990).

Recruitment Philosophy

Another key issue is the organization's recruitment philosophy (i.e., whether to hire from outside the organization for vacancies at all levels or to promote from within the organization). Some prefer to hire proven talent from the outside. Other organizations put great emphasis on developing and socializing managers and other employees within the organization, from the ground up. The advantages and disadvantages of external and internal recruiting will be discussed later in this chapter.

Another aspect of an organization's recruitment philosophy focuses on where the emphasis is: on hiring for long-term careers or merely filling vacancies. Is the organization interested in seeking individuals with knowledge, skills, and abilities (KSAs) for present vacancies, or does it try to attract the type of talented candidates who can feed the ongoing management or leadership needs of the organization? A short-term view may emphasize filling vacancies quickly, whereas a longer-term view may tolerate delay in the interests of finding just the right people to bring into the organization for the long haul (Breaugh, 1992).

An additional aspect of an organization's recruitment philosophy concerns depth of commitment to seeking and hiring a diverse range of employees. Some organizations are still at the EEO/affirmative action stage of mere compliance with the law, whereas others have graduated to valuing diversity as a central principle of organizational life. Their recruiting practices, both internal and external, actively encourage participation by all types of individuals. Perhaps more important, extensive training and consultative processes strive to create a climate that is welcoming to and supportive of all candidates (Thomas, 1990).

A fourth aspect of an organization's recruitment philosophy is whether applicants are viewed as commodities to be purchased or as customers to be wooed. Organizations that adopt a marketing orientation with respect to recruiting will spend substantial time and money to determine what their customers (potential applicants) want and to tailor their recruiting practices and messages to various segments of the market.

A final aspect of an organization's recruitment philosophy has ethical overtones, in terms of fairness and honesty in the recruitment process. For example, one of the ethical challenges that can arise in the recruiting process is that both parties to recruiting may be motivated to present their best sides while concealing weaknesses, and this may lead to a temptation to lie or mislead by omission or commission.

EXTERNAL FACTORS

In addition to factors within an organization, the external environment influences recruitment success in a variety of ways. Labor market conditions, labor unions, economic trends, and government influences all impact the recruiting process.

Labor Market Conditions

Most obviously, the condition of the labor market affects the supply of qualified applicants. If there is a surplus of labor at recruiting time, even informal attempts at recruiting will probably attract more than enough. However, when full employment is nearly reached in an area, skillful and prolonged recruiting may be necessary to attract any applicants who fulfill the expectations of the organization. If an organization cannot find enough skilled applicants in the immediate area, it may need a regional or national search program. Competition from other organizations can reduce the pool of qualified employees or raise salary expectations beyond what the organization is willing to pay. Obviously, how many applicants are available also depends on whether the economy is growing. When organizations are not creating new jobs, there is often an oversupply of qualified labor.

Labor Unions

In some industries, unions may control the labor supply of applicants. In the garment and construction trades, for example, potential employees are often referred by the union hiring hall. Although discrimination against nonunion members is illegal, the union can evaluate applicants in terms of work experience and acquired skills, and under these conditions the applicants who are referred will usually be union members. Labor unions will be discussed in more detail in Chapter 13.

Economic Trends

Economic trends can influence both the number of people pursuing certain occupations and the demand for their services. While computer specialists are in demand, textile and steel workers have faced layoffs over the past decade. In recent years, the rapid pace of technological change has accelerated these trends. Not only do products become obsolete from one year to the next, but manufacturing processes and the skills needed to carry them out can undergo similar change. Since the labor market may not keep pace with these developments, special training programs may be necessary. Organizations can encourage vocational schools and colleges to offer courses in new specialties. At times, however, an organization may need to restructure some of its jobs to adapt them to the people available.

Government Influences

The government's influence in the recruiting process should not be overlooked. Federal and state regulations concerning EEO and AA set the framework within which a recruitment program must function. An employer can no longer seek out preferred individuals based on non-job-related factors such as physical appearance, sex, or religious background. An airline wishing to staff all its flight attendant positions with attractive females will find itself breaking the law if comparably qualified male candidates are rejected on the basis of sex—or female candidates are rejected on the basis of age.

STRATEGIC IMPORTANCE OF RECRUITMENT

When designing a recruitment program, the first step is establishing the objectives. Recruitment objectives should flow directly from the organization's strategic planning process. Questions addressed at this stage might include:

1. How many new employees do we need in the near term and three to five years from now?
2. Do we want to recruit people who will stay with the organization for a long time, or are we looking for a short-term commitment?
3. Are we prepared to pay top dollar, or should we look for people who will be attracted to our organization despite the modest compensation we offer?

4. Are we interested in finding people who are different from our current employees to bring in new perspectives, or is it important to maintain our status quo?

Effective recruitment efforts are consistent with the strategy, the vision, and the values of the organization. Strategic discussions focus on the general needs of the organization. Once those needs are understood, the focus turns to defining the needs of specific units or departments and the requirements for specific positions. As introduced earlier, at this stage, job analysis results become relevant. An appropriate job analysis yields answers to questions such as:

1. What are the characteristics of the ideal recruit?
2. Which competencies must people have when they first enter the organization, and how important is it that new hires be eager to learn new competencies?
3. What career opportunities can we discuss with applicants?

Events that occur during recruitment can determine whether the best applicants happily accept the organization's employment offer or choose to reject it. Recruitment activities should create positive experiences for all applicants—even those who aren't offered positions. If the organization's recruitment methods promote a favorable image of the organization, rejected applicants may try again in the future and encourage their friends to view the organization as an employer of choice. In other words, recruitment addresses current labor needs, while also anticipating future labor needs. Effective recruiting leads all applicants—whether they are hired or not—to perceive the organization as an employer of choice.

RESPONSIBILITY FOR RECRUITMENT

The role of HRM in recruiting is crucial. Walk-ins/write-ins and respondents to advertising or individuals interacting with HRM personnel outside of the organization develop an impression of the organization through their contacts with the HRM personnel responsible for employment. If the applicant is treated indifferently or rudely, he or she may develop a lasting negative impression. On the other hand, if the applicant is pleasantly greeted, provided with pertinent information about job openings, and treated with dignity and respect, she or he may develop a lasting positive impression. Having knowledgeable and skilled employees trained in effective communication and interpersonal skills is essential in the recruiting process.

In smaller organizations, the recruitment effort may be the responsibility of one or two individuals who normally have many other responsibilities. Also, it is not unusual for the line managers in small organizations to recruit and interview job applicants.

While responsibility for the overall recruitment process normally is assigned to the HRM department, HRM would never be able to achieve its recruiting goals without the cooperation of other managers, who are in the best position to predict the needs of their own departments. They are responsible for deciding how tasks should be accomplished and what kinds of people are needed to fill each type of position. They can often anticipate retirements, resignations, and other kinds of vacancies and can determine whether any of their current staff members are ready for promotions. Typically, when a vacancy occurs, the appropriate supervisor or manager completes a personnel requisition form, which usually requires higher management approval.

SOURCES AND METHODS FOR RECRUITING

Once the recruitment objectives are specified and job analysis results have been considered, one fundamental decision that an organization must make as part of its recruiting strategy is whether to focus recruiting efforts internally or externally. In some cases, there is no decision to be made. For instance, entry-level jobs must be filled externally, and for other positions, the organization's policy or union contract may require that internal sources be used first. Most organizations use a mixture of internal and external sources—promoting from within when qualified employees are available and recruiting from external sources when new KSAs are needed or growth is rapid. Whenever there is an inadequate supply of labor and KSAs inside the organization, it must effectively "get its message across" to external candidates. It is here that the organization's choice of a particular method of recruitment can make all the difference in the success of the recruiting efforts. As will be highlighted in our discussion of both internal and external recruiting below, each type of source has its advantages and disadvantages.

Internal Sources of Recruiting

Internal recruiting is the process of looking inside the organization for existing qualified employees who might be promoted to higher-level positions. For jobs other than those at the entry level, current employees may be a source of applicants. They become candidates for promotions, transfers, and job rotations. Having expressed their interest in a position, internal applicants typically go through the recruitment process in much the same way as external applicants.

Advantages of internal recruiting. Internal recruiting has several advantages. First, the organization should have a good idea of the strengths and weaknesses of its employees. If the organization maintains a skills inventory, it can use this as a starting point for recruiting from within. In addition, performance evaluations of employees are available. Present and prior managers of the employee being considered can be interviewed to obtain their evaluations of the employee's potential for promotion. Since the employer has observed the employee in one position, there is less guesswork involved in assessing his or her suitability for a second position. In general, more accurate data are available concerning current employees, thus reducing the chance of making a wrong decision.

Another major advantage of internal recruiting is motivation. Many employees want—and some expect—to advance and to move up the organizational ladder to higher-level positions. An opportunity to do just that, then, is likely to be seen as a viable reward and an important source of motivation for many people. Employees also have an incentive for good performance. Skilled and ambitious employees are less likely to quit and more likely to become involved in developmental activities if they believe that promotion is likely (Chan, 1996). Hence an organization that regularly and routinely promotes from within through internal recruiting will usually find that it is more likely to have a committed and motivated workforce.

Not only does the organization know more about its employees, but the employees know more about the organization and how it operates. Thus, another advantage of internal recruiting is that as employees are promoted to higher-level positions, they bring with them an existing familiarity and understanding of the organization, its heritage, its culture, its policies and procedures, its strategies, and its ways of doing business. As a result, their transition to higher-level positions is somewhat easier as compared to employees recruited externally, and the organization can often rely on the fact that these individuals will continue to promote and enhance the organizational culture in a positive and beneficial manner.

Training and socialization time is reduced when openings are filled internally because a current employee has less to learn about the organization and its idiosyncratic procedures than a newcomer. Recruiting may also be faster and less expensive if an internal candidate can be found. Also, in times of impending retrenchment, filling as many jobs as possible internally maximizes job security for present employees.

Another advantage relates to the fact that most organizations have a sizable investment in their workforce. Full use of the abilities of the organization's employees improves the organization's return on investment.

Disadvantages of internal recruiting. There are also disadvantages to internal recruiting. One drawback associated with promotion from within is that infighting for promotions can become overly intense and have a negative effect on the morale and performance of people who are not promoted. If the organization is expanding, there may be an insufficient internal supply of qualified individuals above the entry level. This situation may result in individuals being promoted before they are ready or not being allowed to stay in a position long enough to learn how to do a job well.

If opportunities for advancement are few, promoting an individual who is not clearly the most qualified, nor the group's choice, may cause resentment. Another drawback of internal recruiting is the so-called ripple effect. For example, when one vacancy is filled internally, a second vacancy is created—the position of the individual who was promoted or transferred to fill the first vacancy. If this slot is also filled internally, then another vacancy occurs. In the end, the organization still has an open position to fill. Thus, relatively few promotions can sometimes result in a large-scale set of transfers and movements from position to position within the organization.

Even for large organizations, an overreliance on internal recruitment can be harmful. Another drawback involves the inbreeding of ideas. For example, when all managers have been brought up through the ranks, there may be a tendency to maintain the status quo when innovation and a new direction are needed. Thus, when recruiting comes only from internal sources, precautions must be taken to ensure that new ideas and innovations are not stifled by such attitudes as "We've never done it before" or "We do all right without it." Without occasional new talent from the outside, management may become stagnant and out of touch with the competition and the marketplace. Another drawback of internal recruiting is that some organizations' internal recruiting procedures are extremely cumbersome. They may involve a "bureaucratic nightmare" of forms, waiting times, eligibility lists, and requirements of permission to interview from the candidate's current superior (Lord, 1989). Finally, meeting affirmative action goals usually can be accomplished only by aggressive external recruiting.

External Sources of Recruiting

Using external recruiting sources involves looking outside the organization for prospective employees. Organizations have at their disposal a wide range of external sources for recruiting individuals. External recruiting is needed in organizations that are growing rapidly or have a large demand for technical, skilled, or managerial employees. Not surprisingly, external recruiting has advantages and disadvantages that are directly counter to those of internal recruiting.

Advantages of external recruiting. One inherent advantage of recruiting from the outside is that the pool of talent is much larger than that available from internal sources. External recruiting can bring in new ideas, new perspectives and viewpoints, and new ways of doing things. Hence the organization can enhance its vitality, creativity, and potential ability to innovate by routinely bringing in new people from the outside. In addition, it is often cheaper and easier to hire technical, skilled, or managerial people from the outside rather than training and developing them internally. This is especially true when the organization has an immediate demand for this type of talent.

External recruiting also avoids the confusion that accompanies the ripple effect, helps meet affirmative action goals, and helps cope with the demands of rapid growth without overusing inexperienced personnel. There may be instances that require a severe shakeup or turnaround. Particularly at the upper management level, an outsider with no prior commitment to present employees or ongoing projects may be the only individual with enough objectivity (and even ruthlessness) to bring about needed changes and enunciate a new vision for the organization (Chung, Labatkin, Rogers, and Owens, 1987).

Disadvantages of external recruiting. One disadvantage of external recruitment is that attracting, contacting, and evaluating potential employees is more difficult. With external recruiting, there is also the risk of hiring a candidate who does not live up to the apparent high potential displayed during the selection process.

Another potential disadvantage is that employees hired from the outside need a longer adjustment or orientation period. This can cause problems because even jobs that do not appear to be unique to the organization require familiarity with the people, procedures, policies, and special characteristics of the organization in which they are performed.

External recruiting also may result in motivational problems within the organization. Existing employees may believe that they have been denied opportunities and that they are more qualified than the outsiders who are brought into the organization at higher levels. Finally, another disadvantage of external recruiting is the cost, which tends to be a bit more expensive than internal recruiting because of the advertising and other search processes that must be undertaken. Recruiting externally usually takes longer and costs more because the external labor market is much larger and harder to reach than the internal one.

METHODS OF RECRUITING

Once an organization decides it needs additional or replacement employees, it is faced with the decision of how to generate the necessary applicants. As stated earlier, an organization may fill a particular job either with someone already employed by the organization or with someone from outside. Internal recruiting is usually handled by using one set of recruiting methods, and external recruiting typically relies on different methods. In this section we first discuss methods used for internal recruiting and then look at other methods that are more likely to be used for external recruiting.

Methods for Internal Recruiting

Pursuing internal recruiting with the advantages mentioned earlier means focusing on current employees and others with previous contact with an employing organization. Friends of current employees, former employees, and previous applicants may be sources. Promotions, demotions, and transfers also can provide additional people for an organizational unit, if not for the entire organization. The most common methods of internal recruiting are job posting and bidding, supervisory recommendations, employee referrals, internal databases, and promotions and transfers.

Job posting and bidding. Job posting and bidding is an internal method of recruitment in which notices of available jobs are posted in central locations throughout the organization and employees are given a specified length of time to apply for the available jobs. In the past, job posting involved little more than the use of bulletin boards and company publications for advertising job openings. Today, however, job posting has become one of the more innovative recruiting techniques being used by organizations. Many organizations now see job posting as an integrated component of an effective career management system.

A job posting system gives each employee an opportunity to move to a better job within the organization. Without some sort of job posting and bidding, it is difficult to find out what jobs are open elsewhere in the organization. The organization can notify employees of all job vacancies by posting notices, circulating publications, or in some other way inviting employees to apply for jobs. The most common method employers use to notify employees of openings is to post notices on bulletin boards in locations such as employee lounges, cafeterias, and near elevators.

Computer software is now available to handle posting and bidding on PCs and intranets (Lotus Development Corporation, 1998, p. 9). Computer software allows the employees to match an available job with their skills and experience. It then highlights where gaps exist so that employees know what is necessary if they wish to be competitive for a given job. More recently, some larger organizations have developed job posting systems via electronic mail.

In a unionized organization, job posting and bidding can be quite formal; the procedure often is spelled out in the labor agreement. Because they are concerned about the subjective judgments of managers, unions normally insist that seniority be one of the primary determinants used in selecting people to fill available jobs.

Normally the job notice specifies the job title, rate of pay, and necessary qualifications. The usual procedure is for all applicants to be sent to the HRM department for an initial review. The next step is an interview by the prospective manager. Then a decision is made based on qualifications, performance, length of service, and other pertinent criteria. Some organizations that rely heavily on internal recruiting go so far as to require that jobs be posted internally before any external recruiting may be undertaken.

Job posting and bidding systems can be ineffective if handled improperly. Once a job is posted internally the organization must allow a reasonable period of time for existing employees to check notices of available jobs before it considers external applicants. When employees' bids are turned down, they should have discussions with their supervisors or someone in the HRM area regarding KSAs they need in order to improve their opportunities in the future.

In conclusion, job posting systems have the advantage of reinforcing the notion that the organization promotes from within. This belief not only motivates employees to maintain and improve their performance but also tends to reduce turnover.

Supervisory recommendations. Another method of internal recruiting is through supervisory recommendations. In this case, when a new position needs to be filled, a supervisor simply nominates or recommends internal candidates in response to his or her manager's requests for potential internal candidates. These supervisors look at the individuals for whom they are responsible, and if any of them are particularly well suited for the new job opening, then the supervisors recommend that individual to the higher-level manager.

This method is very popular among supervisors. They like it because it gives them total discretion in selecting the individual who will report to them. Moreover, the supervisor is generally in a good position to know the capabilities of potential candidates, especially ones who already work for them and are seeking promotion.

However, a supervisor's recommendation is usually very subjective, and is thus susceptible to bias and possible discrimination. Moreover, some qualified employees may be overlooked. That is, supervisors may bypass good candidates in order to get their "favorites" promoted, or they may simply be unaware of the capabilities possessed by some individuals.

The courts have frowned on this method of internal recruitment. In a landmark decision, *Rowe v. General Motors* (1984), the Supreme Court found GM guilty of discrimination because under a system where supervisory recommendations were needed for promotions, supervisors failed to recommend qualified black candidates as frequently as they recommended white candidates. As a result, at the time of the suit there were almost no black supervisors at most GM facilities. The courts prefer the use of a system in which all potentially qualified internal candidates are notified of promotional opportunities and are given a fair chance to apply (*Baxter v. Savannah Sugar Refining Corp.*, 1984). In the end, it is important that supervisors give equal consideration to all potential candidates.

Employee referrals. Before going outside to recruit, many organizations ask present employees to encourage friends or relatives to apply. This is a reliable source of people to fill vacancies. Employees can acquaint potential applicants with the advantages of a job with the organization, furnish letters of introduction, and encourage them to apply. These are external applicants recruited using an internal information source.

Informal communications among managers can lead to the discovery that the best candidate for a job is already working in a different part of the organization. In some cases, referrals are made through "support networks" established by certain groups of employees; in recent years women's groups have had a noticeable influence in this area. Employee referrals do appear to have universal application. Lower-level and managerial-level positions can, and often are, filled by the recommendation of a current employee. In higher-level positions, however, it is more likely that the referral will be a professional acquaintance rather than a friend with whom the recommender has close social contact.

Many organizations pay bonuses or "finders fees" in the form of monetary incentives for a successful referral. Other organizations pay employees incentives for referring individuals with specialized skills that are difficult to recruit through normal means. High-tech organizations use this device the most and probably pay the largest bonuses. For example, an organization might pay between $1,000 to $5,000 depending on its need for extraordinary computer talent.

There are, of course, some potentially negative features of employee referral. For one thing, recommenders may confuse friendship with job performance, thus the current employee may recommend a friend for a position without giving an unbiased consideration to the friend's job-related competence. Employee referrals may also lead to nepotism; that is, hiring individuals who are related to people already employed by the organization. Although such actions may not necessarily align with the objectives of hiring the most qualified applicant, interest in the organization and loyalty to it may be long-term advantages.

Organizations must be careful, however, not to accidentally violate EEO laws while they are using employee referrals. For example, in *EEOC v. Detroit Edison* (1975), the U.S. Court of Appeals, Sixth Circuit, found a history of racial discrimination that was related to recruitment. The court stated: "The practice of relying on referrals by a predominantly white workforce rather than seeking new employees in the marketplace for jobs was found to be discriminating." The case suggests that employee referrals should be used cautiously, especially if the workforce is already racially or culturally imbalanced. This can violate equal employment regulations if protected-class individuals are underrepresented in the organizational workforce. The case also suggests that it might not be wise to rely exclusively on word-of-mouth referrals but rather to use them as supplements to other kinds of recruiting activities or that some external recruiting might be necessary to avoid legal problems in this area.

Internal database (skill or talent inventories). Almost every organization has a pool of internal talent that it can tap when recruiting to fill open positions. Like savings accounts, internal talent pools contain easily accessed resources that can be "withdrawn" as needed. Many organizations have developed computerized internal talent or skill banks, or applicant tracking systems, to keep track of their internal talent and furnish a listing of the KSAs available. Information on every employee's skills, educational background, work history, and other important factors is stored in a database, which can then be used to identify employees with the attributes needed for a particular job. Organizations that must deal with a large number of applicants and job openings have found it beneficial to use computer software as part of a human resources information system (HRIS).

Software of this type allows organizations to enter resumes and then sort the resumes by occupational fields, skills, areas of interests, and previous work history. In the past few years, resume-tracking software programs such as *Restrac* and *Resumix* have been developed to store and search resumes electronically. Resumes are either submitted by e-mail or scanned in from paper copies. An artificial intelligence program picks out and catalogs key words from the documents (Talbot, 1996).

One advantage of a computerized talent or skill database is that the system ensures that suitable internal candidates won't be overlooked before recruiting begins outside the organization. Another advantage of these computerized databases is that they allow recruiters to identify potential candidates more quickly than they could by manually sorting numerous stacks and files of resumes.

Promotions and transfers. Many organizations choose to fill vacancies through promotions and transfers from within whenever possible. A promotion generally involves moving into a position that is recognized as having higher status—and often, higher pay. To plan for employee promotions, some organizations use replacement planning charts in addition to maintaining a talent or skills inventory. Replacement planning charts list the current and potential occupants of positions in the organization. The charts also list each person's promotion potential and developmental needs.

A transfer involves moving into a position that's of similar status, often with no increase in pay. Many organizations have replaced the traditional system of jobs that are organized into clear status hierarchies with job families. With job families, taking a new position with the organization often involves a lateral job transfer rather than a promotion. After several transfers, employees develop a broader perspective and can better understand how the entire organization functions as a system.

Some organizations schedule two or three years of planned job transfers to help employees develop a broad array of competencies. When they are included as part of a planned development process, transfers often last for only a few months. Some organizations refer to such transfers as job rotations. Everyone involved realizes that the assignment is intended to be temporary and that employee development is one of the primary objectives. Unlike other job openings and placements, those associated with job rotation programs seldom involve formal recruitment and competition among employees.

External Recruiting Methods

Somewhat different methods are likely to be used by an organization engaged in external recruiting because the organization needs to reach potential applicants from outside the company. These methods are discussed below.

Advertisements. Advertisements in newspapers and related publications are a popular method for external recruiting. Any local newspaper is likely to have help-wanted sections ranging from perhaps a few listings to as many as several pages, sometimes organized by different kinds of job openings such as professional/nonprofessional, sales, technical, and so forth. Depending on the job, these advertisements might be placed in local newspapers or national newspapers such as the *Wall Street Journal.*

Some professional periodicals and publications also have similar kinds of spaces set aside for help-wanted recruiting ads. This form of advertising tends to be relatively expensive and, perhaps suprisingly, attracts somewhat fewer qualified applicants than some of the other methods of recruiting. However, it does enable the organization to cast a wide net, to publicize its affirmative action programs, and to demonstrate an effort to reach every sector of the labor market. By targeting specialized publications that might appeal primarily to members of groups that are underrepresented in the workforce, the organization might also actually advance its affirmative action goals. On the other hand, restricting advertisements to publications that are not widely available could be considered discriminatory.

The two most important questions to ask in designing a job advertisement are: What do we need to say? and To whom do we need to say it? With respect to the first question, many organizations fail to adequately communicate the specifics of the vacancy. Ideally, persons reading an ad should get enough information to evaluate the job and its requirements, allowing them to make a well-informed judgment regarding their qualifications. This could mean running long advertisements, which costs more. However, these additional costs should be evaluated against the costs of processing a huge number of applicants who are not reasonably qualified or who would not find the job acceptable once they learn more about it.

Employment agencies. Public, nonprofit, and private employment agencies and executive search firms can be helpful in recruiting new employees.

Every state has a publicly funded agency that is affiliated with the U.S. Employment Service. Although each state administers its respective agencies, the agencies must comply with the policies and guidelines of the Employment and Training Administration of the U.S. Department of Labor to receive federal funds. The Social Security Act of 1935 requires all eligible individuals to register with the state employment agency before they can receive unemployment compensation. Thus, state employment agencies generally have an up-to-date list of unemployed persons. They also provide free service for individuals seeking employment and for business organizations seeking employees.

Other employment agencies are associated with nonprofit organizations. For example, most professional and technical societies have units that help their members find jobs. Similarly, many public welfare agencies try to place people who are in special categories, such as those who are physically disabled or are war veterans.

Private employment agencies are also found in most cities. For a fee collected from either the employee or the employer (usually the employer) these agencies do some preliminary screening for an organization and put the organization in touch with applicants. Private employment agencies differ considerably in the level of service, costs, policies, and types of applicants they provide. Employers can reduce the range of possible problems from these sources by giving a precise definition of the position to be filled.

Executive search firms recruit managerial talent for positions paying $50,000 to $150,000 or more per year. They view the organization rather than the candidate as their client. In fact, most executive search firms are not interested in receiving unsolicited applications or resumes. Instead, they conduct a separate nationwide or even international search for each position that they contract to fill.

An important advantage of an executive search firm is confidentiality. The organization that is seeking a new employee may be able to pursue an individual in a quiet and discreet manner. Likewise, the individual who is being pursued may also want to keep a relatively low profile and maintain a reasonable degree of confidentiality.

On the other hand, executive search firms tend to be among the most expensive methods for external recruiting. In addition, one caveat that applies to any type of agency relates to potential discrimination. There have been many stories in the popular press about employment agencies (both public and private) that referred individuals of one race, ethnicity, or gender for some jobs, but not for others. If an organization engages the services of an employment agency that discriminates, the organization almost certainly will be held liable for the discrimination.

External referrals. Referrals do not necessarily have to come just from current employees. The importance of good community relations to recruitment can be seen in the experience of organizations like Papa John's

Pizza. Papa John's, one of the fastest-growing companies in the United States, once relied on classified ads to find drivers and store employees. This method was highly unreliable, however, because the organization did not have the facilities to develop sophisticated tests of people's skills and attitudes. Store managers are now encouraged to make professional contacts within their communities, such as with the principal or guidance counselor at the local high school, leaders of church groups, and coaches in youth sports leagues. Store managers can then use these contacts to help generate referrals among promising young applicants. These community relationships help connect Papa John's to young people who have established good reputations in their community for reliability and trustworthiness. As one industry analyst notes, "I think the greatest advantage for Papa John's is recruitment. Once you get your feet wet recruiting that way, you can move on to bigger and better things" (Sunoo, 1995).

Campus recruiting. Campus recruiting is widely used by large and medium-sized organizations that need highly educated entry-level employees. Most colleges and universities maintain placement offices in which employers and applicants can meet. Campus recruiting can be very productive for an organization, since many good candidates can be interviewed in a short period of time and at a single location. Furthermore, it is convenient and relatively inexpensive because the university recruitment center or placement office typically provides the facilities, schedules the appointments, and so forth (Leonard, 1995). The organization need only send the interviewer to campus and have that individual sit in the interview room and meet prospective applicants. For students this method of job search is also quite efficient. The student can visit the local placement office on a regular basis, keep apprised of which companies are coming to interview, and sign up for interviews according to whatever methods and protocols the college or university has established.

One disadvantage of campus recruiting is that candidates are available to start work only at certain times of the year. Other disadvantages include the lack of experience and the inflated expectations often held by new graduates, the high cost of hiring graduates for positions that may not really require a college degree, and the difficulty of evaluating candidates who do not possess much relevant work history.

As with other forms of recruiting, organizations are becoming more creative in their use of college and university recruiting. Many of the changes are designed to reduce overall recruiting costs while maintaining a strong flow of applicants into the organization. For instance, to reduce some of the costs associated with college recruiting some employers and college or university placement services are developing programs using video interviews. With these systems, students can be interviewed by interviewers hundreds of miles away. There are advantages for both the company and students. The organizations save travel costs and still get the value of seeing and hearing students. For students, the system provides a means of discussing their credentials and job openings without having to miss classes. A side benefit of cooperative and internship programs is that they keep the company well publicized on campuses at no additional cost (Hite, 1986).

If the HRM department uses campus recruiting, it should take steps to ensure that recruiters are knowledgeable concerning the organization and the jobs to be filled and that they understand and use effective interviewing skills. This is especially important, since recruiters themselves are often a main problem in on-campus recruiting because they are sometimes ineffective or worse, are unprepared, show little interest in the candidate, and act superior. Many recruiters also don't effectively screen their student candidates. Such concerns underscore the need to train recruiters before sending them to the campus.

Internet recruiting. Perhaps no method has ever had as revolutionary an effect on organizational recruitment practices as the Internet. Many organizational recruiters are now using the Internet as an easy and subtle method to contact employment candidates. Some organizations are not only posting jobs and accepting resumes and cover letters online but also are conducting employment interviews online. There are a number of ways in which the Internet is used by both jobseekers and employers, including the following: (1) resume bulletin boards on which candidates can list their qualifications and availabilities, (2) sites that provide online access to the help-wanted sections of many major newspapers, (3) sites that seek both original job listings from employers and resumes from applicants and provide search and matching services for a fee, and (4) company Web sites that contain an employment opportunities' page.

Advantages of Internet recruiting for employers include: (1) reaching more applicants, (2) having lower costs and faster response time frames, and (3) tapping an applicant pool conversant with the Net. Another advantage of Internet recruiting is that it may improve the chances of contacting "passive job seekers"—those people who are not actively seeking work.

PROSPECTIVE EMPLOYEES' GOALS AND JOB CHOICES

Organizations and their HRM personnel must never forget that recruiting is a two-way process. Just as the organization is seeking qualified applicants who are interested in employment with the organization, so too are individuals likely to be approaching a number of organizations, trying to entice as many of them as possible to offer the individual employment (Barber, Daly, Giannatonio, and Phillips, 1994).

Thus, just as the organization is attempting to develop a pool of qualified applicants, individuals are simultaneously attempting to create a pool of potentially interesting and attractive job opportunities from which they can select. As a result, it is important for the HRM staff to understand the prospective employee's goals as part of the organization's recruiting process.

In many cases a prospective employee's goals are relatively straightforward. The most common goals include financial income, job security, opportunity for promotion, benefits, and challenging work assignments. In addition, some individuals put a great deal of emphasis on the location of a particular job opportunity (i.e., jobs that are located close to their hometown, close to where they went to school, in a big or small city, near family, or near recreational opportunities).

In the end, it is ultimately up to the applicant to accept an offer of employment from an organization. That is, once an organization attracts a recruit and subsequently decides to offer a job to that person, the prospective employee still must decide whether or not to accept the job. Organizations should remember that the messages sent to a potential employee during this process will provide him or her with much of the information needed to make a decision. The realistic job preview described in the next section can serve as an important tool in building a good rapport with prospective and current employees.

Realistic Job Previews

Today many organizations are concerned about increasing the effectiveness of all recruiting methods. These organizations are finding that it is imperative to provide prospective employees with what is called a realistic job preview (RJP). Realistic job previews provide complete job information, both positive and negative, to the job applicant.

Traditionally, organizations have attempted to sell the organization and the job to the prospective employee by making both look good. They made the job sound glamorous, exciting, fun, challenging, and rewarding. In reality, however, once employees accepted the job they often found just the opposite to be true. The job they were hired to fill proved to be boring, tedious, monotonous, and routine. Normally, trying to make the organization and the job both look good is done to obtain a favorable selection ratio; that is, a large number of applicants in relation to the number of job openings. Then, of course, the organization can select the cream of the crop.

Because the new employees' initial job expectations were set so high and the reality they faced proved to be so different, these employees were extremely dissatisfied with their work and consequently were prone to high turnover. These problems can be partly minimized, however, if recruiters paint a more realistic picture of what the job entails. This means that recruiters must provide prospective employees with pertinent information about the job without distortion or exaggeration. In reality, some jobs are attractive, interesting, and stimulating. However, most jobs have some unattractive features (Reibstein, 1987).

One relatively straightforward method for providing a RJP is to provide job applicants with an opportunity to actually observe others performing the work. This might be accomplished by taking them to the job site and letting them watch people work for a while or showing a videotape of people actually performing the job. If neither of these alternatives is feasible, then, at a minimum, the recruiter should describe in as realistic terms as possible the job itself and the circumstances under which it will be performed.

Considerable research has been done to document the benefits of RJPs. For example, research on the effectiveness of RJPs indicates that it seems to reduce new employee turnover (Popovich and Wanous, 1982). Other research has also been done to document the benefits of RJPs. For example, employees who are hired following an RJP also report higher levels of job satisfaction, higher levels of trust in the organization, and a more realistic set of expectations. Realistic job previews do not reduce the flow of higher capable applicants. The effectiveness of RJPs has been demonstrated with such jobs as bank teller, Army recruit, and prison guard (Meglino, DeNisi, and Ravlin, 1993). These findings suggest that RJPs can be used as an inoculation against disappointment with the realities of a job.

ALTERNATIVES TO RECRUITING

Much of the discussion on recruiting methods thus far implies that these efforts are designed to bring into the organization full-time, permanent employees. It is also the case, given the economic realities confronting many organizations today, that they should fully explore various alternatives to recruiting permanent employees. It does no one any good, neither the employee nor organization, for the organization to hire someone only to have to lay off or fire that person because of a downturn in work. Further, an organization's HRM plan may suggest that additional or replacement employees are needed. In either case, because of the cost and permanence of recruiting individuals, organizations today are looking at overtime, hiring temporary help (including retirees), leasing employees, and using the services of independent contractors.

Overtime

When an organization faces pressures to meet a production goal, it may mean that employees need to work overtime. Overtime simply means asking current workers to put in longer hours. This alternative is especially beneficial when the increased need for human resources is of a very short-term nature. By having employees work overtime, organizations avoid the costs of recruiting and having additional employees. Because the existing employees already know how to do their work, the organization does not have to provide them with additional training. Overtime can also provide employees with additional income. Some employees welcome this opportunity and are thankful to the organization for making it available.

On the other hand, overtime may have some negative characteristics as well. For one thing, the labor costs per hour are likely to increase. The Fair Labor Standards Act (FLSA) stipulates that employees who work more than 40 hours a week must be compensated at a rate of one-and-a-half times their normal hourly rate. Other potential problems with overtime include fatigue, anxiety, increased accidents, and increased absenteeism.

On a limited, short-term basis, having some employees work overtime may be an alternative to recruitment. Continuous overtime, though, often results in higher labor costs and reduced productivity.

Temporary Workers

Another increasingly popular alternative to the recruitment of full-time employees is a growing reliance on temporary employees. The idea behind temporary employment is that an organization can hire someone for only a specific period of time. Historically, temporary employment agencies were seen only as sources of semiskilled clerical help during peak work periods. Today, organizations like the Kelly Temporary Services, Accountemps, Temp-Force Inc., and others are a valuable source of employees when individuals are needed on a temporary basis to fill professional, technical, and higher executive positions. For example, it is now possible to hire temporary nurses, computer programmers, librarians, drafting technicians, and even CEOs.

A major advantage of temporary employment for the organization is that such workers can usually be paid a lower rate and are often not subject to benefits that are provided to permanent and full-time employees. Considerable flexibility is also involved because these employees themselves realize that their jobs are not permanent and therefore the organization can terminate their relationship as work demands mandate. On the other hand, temporary employees tend not to understand the organization's culture as well as permanent employees. This unfamiliarity detracts from their commitment to organizational and departmental goals. In addition, temporary employees are not as likely to be as productive as are permanent full-time employees of the organization.

Employee Leasing

Whereas temporary employees come into an organization for a specific short-term project, leased employees typically remain with an organization for longer periods of time. In employee leasing, sometimes called "staff sourcing," the organization pays a fee to a leasing company that provides a pool of employees to the organization. This pool of employees usually constitutes a group or crew intended to handle all or most of the organization's work needs in a particular area—for example, handling payroll, employee benefits, and routing HRM functions for the client company.

Leased employees are well-trained. They are screened by the leasing organization, trained appropriately, and often go to organizations with an unconditional guarantee. Thus, if one of these individuals doesn't work out, the organization can get a new employee or make arrangements to have its fee returned. There are also benefits from the employee's point of view. Some of today's workers prefer more flexibility in their lives. Working with a leasing company and being sent out on various jobs allows these workers to work when they want, for the length of time they desire.

Care must be exercised in choosing a leasing company. Because the individuals are not employees of the organization, they are likely to be less committed and attached to the organization. In addition, the cost of the leasing arrangement might be a bit higher than if the employees had been hired directly by the organization itself.

Independent Contractors

Using independent contractors is another means of recruiting. Often referred to as consultants, independent contractors are taking on a new meaning. Organizations may hire independent contractors to do very specific work at a location or off the company's premises. For instance, medical and legal transcription activities can easily be done at one's home and forwarded to the employer on a routine basis. With the growing use of personal computers, fax machines, and voice mail, employers can ensure that home work is being done in a timely fashion.

Independent contractor arrangements benefit both the organization and the individual. Because the organization does not have to regard this individual as an employee, it saves costs associated with full- or part-time personnel, such as Social Security taxes and workers' compensation premiums. Additionally, this opportunity is also a means of keeping good individuals associated with your organization. This cannot be done through typical work arrangements, but allowing the individual to work at home, on his or her time, can generate a win-win solution to the problem.

RECRUITING A MORE DIVERSE WORKFORCE

Recruiting a diverse workforce is not just socially responsible, it's a necessity, given the rapid growth of minority and female candidates, along with increased globalization. Therefore, smart employers have to actively recruit a more diverse workforce if they are going to be successful. This means taking special steps to recruit older workers, minorities, and women.

A network of laws and regulations helps to prevent discrimination in employment on the basis or race, color, religion, sex, national origin, age, or physical ability. Most organizations, except the smallest, are covered by these government restrictions, and compliance with the law is a major concern in recruitment.

The growing difficulty that many employers have had in attracting and retaining workers has led them to tap a wide variety of sources. Especially difficult has been recruiting protected-class individuals under EEO laws and regulations. If outside agencies are used, EEO and AA concerns of the actual employers must still be met. What is interesting, though, is that even if the legal stipulations were not present, employers who recruit workers with diverse backgrounds have found these recruits to be valuable employees. Three specific groups that have been attracted into the workforce effectively by some employers are persons who are members of racial/ethnic minorities, persons with disabilities, and individuals over 55 years of age.

Recruiting Minorities

Organizations that do business with federal and state governments must have AA plans. Consequently, those organizations face pressures to increase the number of women employees and employees from racial/ethnic minorities. These pressures often are stronger for managerial, professional, and technical jobs than for unskilled, clerical, and blue-collar jobs.

Organizations that are successful in diversifying their workforce use recruiting that targets the appropriate types of applicants. For example, an organization that needs to ensure hiring of minority accountants may use special minority-oriented publications or recruit at colleges with large numbers of minority students. Other means of recruiting have included participating in job fairs sponsored by certain racial/ethnic organizations, establishing a minority internship program, and using current minority employees to recruit others of similar backgrounds.

Recruiting Individuals with Disabilities

Publicity for persons with disabilities has increased in recent years, yet the disabled may face more discrimination than other groups. Their problems are very often compounded by the physical obstacles they must overcome in the buildings where they work. Over 40 million individuals with disabilities are covered by the Americans with Disabilities Act (ADA). Many of them are in the workforce, but others have not been able to find employment, particularly those with severe or multiple disabilities.

Two keys to successfully recruiting and utilizing people with disabilities are well-designed jobs and working with associations representing these people. Jobs must be such that accommodation can be made for people with a disability. Not every disability lends itself to every job, even with accommodation. However, in many cases changes in job duties, work stations, and equipment might result in a job that a person with a disability can do—and very well. Associations of people with various disabilities can sometimes refer people whose disability will fit with a particular job. Such groups can also often make recommendations for accommodation. Individuals with disabilities have generally been found to be reliable and productive employees when properly placed in the right job (Patton, 1999).

Recruiting Older Workers

Demographic data reveals that the percentage of the population over the age of 55 continues to increase each year due to increasing life experiences. Older workers are increasingly mentioned as a possible solution to labor shortages and organizations are looking to older workers as a source of recruits. Employers say they value older workers because of their skills, scheduling flexibility, low absenteeism, high motivation and loyalty, and ability to mentor young workers. Typically, older workers or retirees require little training, will work for less than their previous salary or wage, and have been found to be highly committed to quality performance (Cyr, 1996).

Older workers may not be reached by traditional recruitment advertising because they tend to assume that employers are not interested in them. Thus recruitment messages should specifically mention the value placed on experience and maturity, the chance to build a second or third career, the opportunity for flexible scheduling, and the opportunity to work while keeping one's Social Security benefits. These messages can be delivered through the senior employment networks in operation in many areas; through clubs, organizations, and publications for seniors; and also through more general advertising outlets.

CHOOSING THE RIGHT RECRUITING SOURCE AND METHOD

Many studies have considered whether recruiting from different sources results in different employee outcomes, such as performance, turnover, loyalty, and job satisfaction. If different sources of applicants were found to have different outcomes, organizations could target their recruitment efforts to the most appropriate sources, given their strategic needs. Overall, however, research shows no clear differences in the employment experiences of new employees recruited from different sources (Barber, 1995).

Instead of targeting one source of applicants, most employers recruit from multiple sources using multiple methods. This approach helps the organization generate a large applicant pool. In addition, recruiting from multiple sources is a good way to increase the diversity of the applicant pool.

The choice of an external recruitment method depends largely on the circumstances surrounding the hiring situation. The following factors are the most relevant: (1) the type of job being filled, (2) how quickly the job needs to be filled, (3) the geographic region of recruitment, (4) the cost of implementing the recruitment method, and (5) whether the method will attract the right mix of candidates from an EEO perspective.

Legally, employers must ensure that their recruitment efforts extend to females and minority groups, especially when certain groups within the organization are underutilized. Overreliance on employee referrals and applicant-initiated recruitment methods may put an employer at risk of EEO violations because these methods offer no assurances that a proper mix of individuals will apply. Help-wanted ads, on the other hand, have a much greater potential for successfully reaching these individuals.

EEO and Recruitment

Especially for larger organizations, recruitment is a complex and continuing process that demands extensive planning. EEO legislation has significantly impacted and continues to influence an organization's recruitment activities. All recruitment procedures for each job category should be analyzed and reviewed to identify and eliminate discriminatory barriers. For example, the EEOC encourages organizations to avoid recruiting primarily by employee referral and walk-ins because these practices tend to perpetuate the existing composition of an organization's workforce. If minorities and women are not well represented at all levels of the organization, reliance on such recruitment procedures has been ruled by the courts to be a discriminatory practice.

Recruitment interviewing is also more complex and challenging as a result of EEO legislation and court decisions relating to this legislation. For example, if an interviewer asks for certain information such as age, marital status, and number of children during the interview, the organization risks the chance of an employment discrimination suit. Prior to employment, interviewers should not ask for information that is potentially prejudiced unless the organization is prepared to prove (in court, if necessary) that the requested information is job related.

Just as EEOC influences an organization's recruiting sources, it also suggests that the content of help-wanted ads should not indicate any age, race, or sex preference for the job unless age or sex is a bona fide occupational qualification (BFOQ). Organizations are also encouraged to advertise in media directed toward minorities and women. Advertising should indicate that the organization is an equal opportunity employer and does not discriminate.

Organizations are encouraged to contact nontraditional recruitment sources, such as organizations that place physically and mentally handicapped persons. It is likely that hiring of both women and minority groups will continue to receive attention, and increased emphasis will be placed on hiring those groups.

Campus recruiting visits should be scheduled at colleges and universities with large minority and female enrollments. The EEOC also recommends that organizations develop and maintain contacts with female, minority, and community organizations as sources of recruits.

Increasingly, organizations will also have to be especially sensitive to issues that affect dual-career couples. This means that they will need to pay more attention to the spouse or significant other, male or female, of the person being recruited. More and more organizations are finding that they must be prepared to assist in finding jobs for spouses or significant others of recruits. In hiring employees at all levels of the organization and especially at the managerial level or in professional jobs, it will be necessary to consider the spouse or significant other as well.

EVALUATING RECRUITING EFFORTS

Evaluating the success of recruiting efforts is important. That is the primary way to find out whether efforts are cost-effective in terms of time and money spent. Essentially, an effective recruiting process is one that results in a reasonable pool of qualified employees being available to the organization and from which the organization is able to hire individuals that it wants to perform different jobs. Moreover, this recruiting process needs to be executed with relatively low cost. Thus if an organization is having a difficult time attracting people to apply for its jobs or is having too many people apply for its jobs, then its recruiting efforts are probably less than ideal. Similarly, if the recruiting expenses being incurred by the organization are excessive or higher than they should be for the kinds of employees being recruited, then the organization should look carefully at its recruiting methods to see whether efficiencies or cost savings might be justified.

The effectiveness of recruiters is one way to evaluate recruiting efforts. Organizations assign goals for recruiting different types of employees. For example, a goal for a recruiter might be to hire 350 unskilled and semi-skilled employees, or 100 technicians, or 100 machinists, or 100 managerial employees per year. Then the organization can decide who are the best recruiters. They may be those who meet or exceed quotas and those whose recruits stay with the organization and are evaluated well by their superiors.

In addition, it is possible and often useful to assess the effectiveness of different recruiting sources. The process could involve simply calculating the yield, or the number of applicants, generated by each source. In college recruiting, the organization can divide the number of job acceptances by the number of campus interviews to compute the cost per hire at each college. Then it drops from the list those campuses that are not productive. As noted thus far, general areas of concern for recruiting that should be considered by organizations include the following:

1. Quantity of applicants: Is it sufficient to fill job vacancies?
2. Quality of applicants: Do the applicants meet job specifications and can they perform the jobs?
3. EEO goals met: Is recruiting providing qualified applicants with an appropriate mix of protected-class individuals?
4. Time required to fill openings: Are openings filled quickly with qualified candidates, so that the work and productivity of the organization are not delayed by vacancies?
5. Cost per applicant hired: Is the cost for recruiting employees from any single source excessive?

In the end, organizations should evaluate their recruitment processes along with all their other HRM activities. Collecting appropriate evaluation measures on past recruiting efforts can help an organization predict the time and budget needed to fill future openings, identify the recruiting methods that yield the greatest number or the best quality of candidates, and evaluate the job performance of individual recruiters. Benchmarking against similar organizations also can be informative.

SUMMARY

Organizational recruiting efforts should be guided by a clear recruitment philosophy and goals and keyed to the strategy and values of the organization. An organization's recruiting philosophy and goals will influence the approach it takes in recruiting. In some cases, recruiting may not be necessary if the organization explores creative ways of dealing with labor shortages, such as outsourcing, temporaries, or employee leasing.

One of the first decisions organizations must make in filling a job vacancy is whether to seek a current employee through internal recruiting or seek a new hire from the external labor market. There are advantages and disadvantages to internal and external recruiting. Several techniques have been discussed in this chapter. Organizations and their HRM personnel must be sensitive to changes in the market, people, and competition, and be aware of the need to be adaptive and flexible in their recruiting efforts.

If an organization chooses to recruit externally, it must plan carefully and may consider a wider variety of informal and formal methods. Some of the methods available are employee referrals, advertising (either in print or on the Internet), using employment agencies, and campus recruiting. Special recruiting efforts targeting, for example, older people or the disabled are also important to organizations committed to recruiting a more diverse workforce. Such efforts also help the organization avoid potential equal employment problems.

Organizations should evaluate all of their recruitment efforts. They should evaluate both their recruiters and the methods used by recruiters. In this way, the organization can exclude from future recruiting efforts costly methods or those that produced few or low-quality applicants.

REFERENCES

Barber, A.E. 1995. *Recruiting employees: Individual and organizational perspectives.* Thousand Oaks, CA: Sage.

Barber, A.E., Daly, C., Giannatonio, C., and Phillips, J. 1994. Job search activities: An examination of changes over time. *Personnel Psychology* 47: 739–750.

Baxter v. Savannah Sugar Refining Corporation, 350 F. Supp. 139, 1984.

Breaugh, J.A. 1992. *Recruitment: Science and practice.* Boston: PWS-Kent.

Chan, W. 1996. External recruitment versus internal promotion. *Journal of Labor Economics* 14(4): 555–570.

Chung, K.H., Labatkin, M., Rogers, R.C., and Owens, J.E. 1987. Do insiders make better CEOs than outsiders? *Academy of Management Executive* (November): 325–331.

Code words. 1995. *Wall Street Journal* (September 12), p. A1.

Cyr, D. 1996. Lost and found—retired employees. *Personnel Journal* (November): 40–47.

Drucker, P.F. 1992. The new society of organizations. *Harvard Business Review* (September–October): 95–104.

EEOC v. Detroit Edison Company, U.S. Court of Appeals, Sixth Circuit (Cincinnati), 515F, 2d, 301, 1975.

Hite, R.E. 1986. How to hire using college internship programs. *Personnel Journal* (February): 110–112.

Holoviak, S.J., and DeCenzo, D.A. 1990. Service industry seeks summer help. *Audio Human Resource Report* 1(9): 5.

Leonard, B. 1995. The sell gets tough on college campuses. *HRMagazine* (June): 61–63.

Lotus Development Corporation. 1998. Enterprise-wide recruiting. *Lotus* (Cambridge, MA), p. 9.

Lord, J.S. 1989. Internal and external recruitment. In W.F. Cascio (ed.), *Human resource planning, employment, and practice*, 9th ed. Washington, DC: Bureau of National Affairs, pp. 73–102.

Meglino, B.M., DeNisi, A., and Ravlin, E.C. 1993. The effects of previous job exposure and subsequent job status on the functioning of realistic job previews. *Personnel Psychology* 46: 803–822.

Patton, C. 1999. Challenged workers. *Human Resource Executive* (January): 67–70.

Popovich, P., and Wanous, J.P. 1982. The realistic job preview as a persuasive communication. *Academy of Management Review* 7: 572.

Reibstein, L. 1987. Crushed hopes: When a new job proves to be something different. *Wall Street Journal* (June 10), p. 25.

Rowe v. General Motors, 457 F.2d 348, 1984.

Rynes, S.L., and Barber, A.E. 1990. Applicant attraction strategies: An organizational perspective. *Academy of Management Review* (April): 286–310.

Sunoo, B.P. 1995. Papa John's rolls out hot HR menu. *Personnel Journal* (September): 38–47.

Talbot, S.P. 1996. Get the most from automated resume-tracking software. *Recruitment and Staffing Sourcebook* (supplement to the March issue of *Personnel Journal*): 18–20.

Thomas, R.R. 1990. From affirmative action to affirming diversity. *Harvard Business Review* (March–April): 107–117.

Turban, D.B., and Greening, D.W. 1997. Corporate social performance and organizational attractiveness to prospective employers. *Academy of Management Journal* 40(3): 658–672.

Vecchio, R.P. 1995. The impact of referral sources on employee attitudes: Evidence from a national sample. *Journal of Management* 21(5): 953–965.

Chapter 6

Selecting and Placing Human Resources

INTRODUCTION

One of the important points noted in Chapter 2 in our discussion about SHRM is that it is important for HRM personnel to understand the organization's strategy so that they can hire people with the right skills and retrain people inside the organization to be effective. Selection and placement procedures provide the essence of an organization—its human resources.

Increasingly, organizations have recognized that their success depends on well-trained, highly motivated human resources. In the recruiting process discussed in Chapter 5, HRM has identified a number of sources of potential candidates. If they have achieved their goal and located a number of qualified applicants, it is time to begin to formally whittle down the applicant pool by using the screening tools explained in this chapter, which include interviewing, tests, assessment centers, and background reference checks. This is called selection.

Selection is the process of obtaining and using information about job applicants in order to determine who should be hired for short- or long-term positions. Placement involves matching individuals to jobs, based on the demands of the job (KSAs) and the competencies, preferences, interests, and personality of the individual. Selection and placement yield a match between the organization's needs for specific qualified individuals and the different needs of employees that determine the type of work that's satisfying for them (Schmitt and Chan, 1998).

SELECTION AND PLACEMENT: THE STRATEGIC IMPORTANCE

The selection process is a critical one for the organization as a whole and for all managers. Recognizing the importance of these decisions, today's successful organizations invest substantial amounts of time, effort, and money in selecting their human resources. By making good selection decisions, organizations help ensure that their financial investments in employees pay off (Snow and Snell, 1993). Effective selection also minimizes the risk of lawsuits brought by victims of criminal, violent, or negligent acts perpetrated by employees who should not have been hired or kept in their jobs. By using fair and legal procedures when making selection decisions, employers can also minimize the risk of discrimination lawsuits.

The organization must take into account the fact that not only can an incorrect decision lead to a tremendous cost in terms of resources and opportunity but it can also affect many people. The right choice can mean growth and increased productivity for specific work groups associated with the new hire as well as success for the organization. The wrong selection can result in months of frustration, repetitive training, documentation, and low morale prior to the eventual termination of the recently hired individual, after which the selection process begins all over again. Employee selection is a decision that needs to be made right the first time. Although this is true in organizations of any size, the impact of a wrong selection decision is magnified in a smaller organization. In a larger organization, one inappropriate placement can perhaps be reassigned or retrained. In the smaller organization, there may be no such luxury. Selection is critical.

Selecting the right people is also critical to successful strategy implementation. The organization's strategy may affect job duties and design, and the job should drive selection. For instance, if an organization plans to compete on the basis of prompt, polite, personalized service, then service and communication skills should be featured in the job specification, and selection devices that can identify these skills in front-line applicants should be chosen. This argument is based on the assumption that the organization's strategy is clear, well known, and fairly stable so that people who fit the strategy can be selected. However, some scholars have pointed out that in a rapidly changing, uncertain world, not all organizations are able to stick to a single strategy long enough for staffing practices to catch up and bear fruit.

A recent approach to strategic staffing suggests that human resources come first and drive strategy rather than the reverse: "Companies are beginning to realize that the foundation of their competitive strategy is the quality of their human capital" (Snow and Snell, 1993). Having top-notch, flexible, innovative human resources may be a competitive advantage that is more sustainable than technological or marketing advantages. Such people will be able to generate and implement a wide range of new strategies to respond quickly to a changing environment. This suggests that hiring the best individuals one can find makes more sense than hiring those who fit a specific job or strategy that exists today but may be gone tomorrow. "Best" in this new context means best in intelligence and best in interpersonal skills, since many jobs in rapidly changing organizations involve teamwork, negotiation, and relationship management.

Effective employee selection or screening is especially important because it is so costly to recruit and hire employees. Hiring and training even a clerk can cost $5,000 or more in fees and supervisory time. The total cost of hiring a manager could easily be 10 times as high, once search fees, interviewing time, reference checking, and travel and moving expenses are tallied.

As alluded to earlier, careful selection is also strategically important because of the legal implications of incompetent hiring. For one thing (as noted in Chapter 3), EEO legislation and court decisions require an organization to systematically evaluate their selection procedure's effectiveness to ensure that they are not unfairly discriminating against any protected group. Furthermore, courts are increasingly finding employers liable when employees with criminal records or other problems take advantage of access to customers' homes or other similar opportunities to commit crimes. Hiring workers with such backgrounds without proper safeguards is called negligent hiring (Ryan and Lasek, 1991).

THE SELECTION PROCESS

The selection process is concerned with identifying the best candidate or candidates for jobs from the pool of qualified applicants developed during the recruitment process. This section discusses important considerations that are critical to successful selection and placement and includes basic selection criteria, choosing selection techniques, reliability and validity of selection techniques, making the final selection decision, and evaluating the selection and placement activities.

Basic Selection Criteria

At the heart of any effective selection system is an understanding of what characteristics are essential for high performance. This is where the critical role of job analysis in selection becomes most obvious because that list of characteristics should have been identified during the process of job analysis and should now be accurately reflected in the job specification. This information helps an organization go about selecting a given individual from a pool of qualified applicants. Thus, from a performance perspective, the goal of an organization's selection system is to accurately determine which job applicants possess the KSAs dictated by the job—for example, education and experience, specific skills and abilities, and personal characteristics— needed to perform a specific or current (or future) job successfully. Additionally, an organization's selection system must be capable of distinguishing between characteristics that are needed at the time of hiring, those that are systematically acquired during training, and those that are routinely developed after an individual has been placed on the job.

Formal education, experience, and past performance. An organization selecting from a pool of qualified candidates wants to find the individual who has the right abilities and attitudes to be successful. A large number of cognitive, motor, physical, and interpersonal attributes are present because of what a person has learned at home, at school, on the job, and so on. One of the more common ways to screen for many of these abilities is by using educational accomplishment as a surrogate for or summary of the measures of those abilities. In a selection context formal education refers to the classroom training an individual has received in public or private schools and college, university, and/or technical school.

For some jobs, the organization may stipulate that people have a high school diploma. Other jobs require a two-year associate degree from a junior or community college, and still other jobs might require a four-year college education. In some instances the organization might leave the educational fields open, whereas in other cases they must be within a specified area such as accounting, mechanical engineering, French, or HRM. Occasionally, jobs may require advanced degrees such as a master's degree or perhaps a doctorate in a specific field of study. In other cases a technical certification may also be a good indicator of education. For example, many technical and vocational schools offer certificates when they train people for craft work such as plumbing, mechanical work, electrical work, and so on. The organization might also prefer that the degree be from certain institutions, that the grade point average be higher than some minimum, and that certain honors have been achieved. What is important for organizations to remember is that to be legal, educational or other standards must be related to successful job performance. Care must be exercised not to set standards that are higher than actually required by the job.

While education is likely to continue to play an important role in the selection process, there is increased concern that general education level— such as specifying that an individual needs a high school diploma or two years of college—might be a bit too removed from what many employers today actually need from an individual on the job. Instead, an alternative model to focusing on education per se is to assess "competencies." Although the definitions of competencies vary from organization to organization, they basically refer to relatively broad capabilities that are necessary for effective job performance.

Experience and past performance is another useful criterion for selecting employees. Selection specialists believe that past performance on a similar job is often one of the best indicators of future performance. Experience refers to the amount of time the individual has spent working, either in a general capacity or in a particular field of study. Experience is presumably an indicator of an individual's familiarity with work, his or her ability to work, and a surrogate measure of a person's competencies as an employee. In some cases it may be necessary that the individual have a predetermined level of experience in a certain field of study. For example, an organization looking for a director of marketing is quite likely to expect applicants to have experience in the marketing field. In other cases, however, the experience requirement may be more general. Simply having a certain number of years of experience in full-time work activities might be sufficient evidence of an individual's employability. And some entry-level jobs may require no experience at all.

A large number of research studies support the assumption that experience is related to job performance (Quinones, Ford, and Teachout, 1995). But the organization must have a rational basis for defining what it means by "relevant experience." Not all previous experiences are equally good perdictors of performance on a given job. For example, should two applicants applying for a job as an accountant be given the same credit for previous work experience if both have six years experience in the accounting profession but one has been an internal auditor for another organization and the other an accounting consultant for the General Accounting Office (GAO)?

Skills and abilities. Skills and abilities are another set of selection criteria. Skills and abilities relate more precisely than do experience or education to the specific qualifications and capabilities of an individual to perform a specific job (Dunn, Mount, Barrick, and Ones, 1995). For example, even though an individual may have a college degree and a wealth of work experience, he or she may not have good skills and abilities regarding spatial relations (the ability to mentally manipulate three-dimensional objects in space). To the extent that the organization needs someone who has high levels of spatial relations (which would be the case for many assembly-line jobs), an applicant who lacks that skill will not be an attractive candidate for the organization.

As organizations move more toward teamwork and team-based operating systems, many of them are also putting more emphasis on hiring individuals with the skills necessary to function effectively in a group situation. Some organizations are using existing team members to help hire new members. The rationale for this practice is that current team members are well placed to assess a given individual's ability to fit in and become an effective member of the team.

Personal characteristics. The final criterion category is personal characteristics. In some organizations it is also important to assess the personal characteristics of individual job applicants. These personal characteristics are usually thought to reflect the individual's personality and may be an important factor in certain kinds of jobs. Personal characteristics include marital status, sex, age, and so on. Some organizations have, for example, preferred "stable" married employees over single people because they have assumed that married people have a lower turnover rate. On the other hand, other employers might seek out single people for some jobs, since a single person might be more likely to accept a transfer or a lengthy overseas assignment.

Of course, when basing a selection decision on something such as personal characteristics, the organization must be able to clearly document a performance-related basis for the decision. For example, if a department store manager cannot demonstrate empirically that an outgoing individual will be a more productive salesperson than a shy and introverted individual will be, then that qualification may be of questionable legality. Indeed, as will be discussed later, personal characteristics are among the most complex and sensitive selection criteria to assess and to validate.

Hiring for fit versus skill is an interesting controversy in selection today. Traditionally, HRM personnel believed that they should hire the person with the best set of job-specific skills relative to the work that needed to be performed. But others today are arguing that better candidates are those who best fit into the organization itself. HRM personnel believe that selection decisions should therefore be based on other factors such as personal characteristics, values, and so forth (Behling, 1998).

As with other personal characteristics, selection using any aspect of personality should always be based on whether it is really necessary for high performance. Many personality measures run an even greater risk of being legally challenged as an invasion of privacy than other kinds of selection tools. Thus, the organization wishing to use personality as a criterion must be certain that successful and unsuccessful employees can be distinguished in terms of their personalities. It is probably unwise to use personality as a general criterion for screening out "undesirable" applicants, since the same personality characteristic that leads to failure in one job might lead to success in another (Bourbeau, 1996). In part because of this fact, there is still considerable debate whether general, broad personality measures or more specific ones are the best to use in selection (Paunonen, Rothstein, and Jackson, 1999).

In the end, organizations need to have a clear understanding of the basic selection criteria relevant for their organizations. Such criteria typically include factors such as formal education and past experience, skills and abilities, and personal characteristics, although fit with the overall organization may be even more important.

Reliability and Validity of Selection Criteria

It is necessary to understand that there are a variety of techniques an organization can use in making selection decisions. However, before discussing some of these popular techniques, we will highlight the importance of ensuring that the selection techniques used are valid and reliable. Without such evidence the organization is holding itself open to the possibility of discrimination. As noted in Chapter 3, when there is evidence of disparate impact, the organization must prove that it is not discriminating. Organizations can do so by demonstrating that the selection technique is job related. In practice, however, they must prove that the selection technique is a valid predictor of performance on the job. That is, the information gathered about an applicant should be focused on finding predictors of the likelihood that the applicant will be able to perform the job well. Predictors can take many forms, but they should be job related, reliable, and valid. Previous experience can be a predictor of success if it is related to the necessary performance on the current job. Any selection tool used (for example, application form, test, interview, education requirements, or years of experience required) should be used only if it is a valid predictor of job performance. Using invalid predictors can result in selecting the "wrong" candidate and rejecting the "right" one.

Regardless of the method or technique chosen for collecting information about applicants, the organization must be certain that the information is reliable and valid. We begin our discussion with reliability because a test that is not reliable can never be valid.

Reliability. The main goal of selection is to make accurate predictions about people. The organization wants to make its best guess about who will be a successful employee. In this way, the organization can avoid hiring the wrong person for a job. In other words, the main purpose of selection is to make decisions about people. If these decisions are going to be correct, the techniques used for making them must yield reliable information.

Reliability refers to the consistency of a particular selection device. That is, the reliability of a predictor is the extent to which it repeatedly produces the same results. Specifically, reliability means that the selection device measures whatever it is supposed to measure, without random error. For example, if the same person took a test in December and scored 100, but upon taking it in March scored significantly lower, the test would not be highly reliable. Thus, as noted above, reliability has to do with consistency, and predictors that are useful in selection should be consistent.

Reliability can be assessed in a variety of ways. One common method of assessing the reliability of a selection technique is called test-retest reliability. In this case the same individual or individuals are subjected to the selection technique at two points in time. If there is a high positive correlation between their scores or evaluation between the two time points, then reliability can be inferred. That is, test results seem to be consistent over time and thus may be taken as being reliable. Any random error component would change over time, resulting in inconsistencies, so the degree of consistency is an indication of how much of the score is due to what is being measured, rather than to error. Another method of establishing reliability, particularly for employment tests, is called alternative-form reliability. Alternative-form reliability is determined by correlating scores from two alternate forms of the same test. Most standard academic achievement tests like the Scholastic Aptitude Test (SAT) and the Graduate Management Admission Test (GMAT) have numerous forms, all of which are assumed to be reliable. An applicant's score should not vary much according to which form of the test he or she happens to take. When a measuring tool relies on the judgments of people (such as in an employment interview), reliability is often determined by using interrater reliability. This refers to the extent to which two or more interviewers' assessments are consistent with each other. Each rater is treated like a test, and the scores of the raters are correlated to check for consistency. Differences between the raters are considered error. For example, in a group interview situation, all the interviewers were present for the same interview and therefore should agree on their ratings of the applicant's experience and qualifications. Interrater reliability is also important in assessment centers, where multiple raters assess a candidate's capabilities in several different situations. Assessment centers will be discussed later in this chapter.

Validity. For a selection tool to be useful, it is not sufficient for it to be repeatable or stable. Both legally and organizationally, the measures that it yields must also be valid. Validity refers to the extent to which a measure or indicator is, in fact, a real reflection of what is assumed to be. Validity occurs to the extent that a predictor actually predicts what it is supposed to predict. Validity depends on the situation in which the selection device is being used (Murphy and Sharella, 1997). For example, a test designed to predict aptitude for child care jobs might not be valid in predicting sales potential in a candidate for a sales representative position.

The first condition for a measure to be valid is that it be reliable, as described above. If a test is measuring pure error, it cannot be measuring what is relevant to the selection process. There are three general methods of determining validity, but they tend to overlap, and in a particular situation they may all be appropriate.

Criterion-related validity refers to the correlation between scores on the selection device and ratings on a particular criterion of job performance. For example, if a ballet company wanted to decide whether gregarious people are better fundraisers, it could ask all its current fundraisers to take a personality test. Then it could correlate the fundraisers' scores on gregariousness with their performance as fundraisers. If gregariousness and fundraising performance were correlated, criterion-related validity would be established. Criterion-related validity replaces judgments about which predictors are most useful with statistical analyses that demonstrate the predictive usefulness of criteria. Because the validity of job criteria themselves can be called into question, however, validation studies must be designed carefully (Society for Industrial and Organizational Psychology, 1987).

It is also important to note that even if establishing criterion-related validity were not important in civil rights cases, organizations would still need to be sure of the relationship between scores on their selection devices and performance on the job. If this relationship is missing, the selection device will not help to select better performers. In other words, if organizations select individuals merely on the basis of chance (for example, the flip of a coin) they will produce a workforce that is as effective as that selected using the test. Since it costs time and money to administer any selection device, the organization would be throwing away money on a selection system that produced no benefits in terms of performance.

Content validity is another type of validity. Content validity is the extent to which a selection technique such as a test or interview actually measures the knowledge, skills, and abilities that are necessary to perform the job. For a secretarial position, a typing test would have a high content validity if the secretary had to produce many letters a day. But for a job as administrative assistant involving minimal typing, the same test would have little content validity. This is the simplest kind of validity to determine, but it cannot apply to tests that measure learning ability or general problem solving.

The third kind of validity is called construct validity. Construct validity is the extent to which a relationship exists between scores on the measure and the underlying trait the measure is supposed to tap. For example, if an organization wanted to measure the "conscientiousness" of applicants but was not happy with existing measures, it might set about to develop its own measure of this personality test. The question would be whether the measure that was developed really assessed conscientiousness, which is the fundamental issue in construct validity. Because traits cannot be directly observed, construct validity cannot be established in a single study but can be assumed to exist only on the basis of a large body of empirical work yielding consistent results (Society for Industrial and Organizational Psychology, 1987).

The *Uniform Guidelines on Employee Selection Procedures* have established three stringent requirements for demonstrating the construct validity of a selection technique (Abram, 1979).

1. A job analysis must systematically define both the work behaviors involved in the job and the constructs that are believed to be important to job performance.

2. The test must measure one of those constructs. In selecting a project manager, for instance, there must be evidence that the test validly measures leadership. For example, scores on the test might correlate with leadership ratings given to other employees in other organizations upon previous administration of the test.

3. The construct must be related to performance of critical work behaviors. For example, it must be shown that leadership ability is correlated with job performance for the position of project manager. That is, it is necessary to conduct a criterion validity study between leadership and performance, or to use such data collected by another test to support the claim of construct validity.

Single versus combined predictors. If an organization chooses to use only one predictor (for example, a test) to select who will be hired, the decision is straightforward. If the test is valid and encompasses a major dimension of a job and the applicant does well on the test, she or he can be hired. This is the single predictor approach. Selection accuracy depends on how valid that single predictor is at predicting performance.

In reality, no selection technique is perfectly reliable and valid. Hence most organizations rely on a number of selection techniques and, in fact, may use all or most of the selection techniques available. Hence a person who applies for a job may be (1) subjected to a preliminary screening interview to make sure that he or she meets the minimum qualifications, (2) asked to complete an application and agree to background checks, and (3) required to undergo employment tests and/or participate in work simulations. For example, a large number of the best companies to work for in America rely heavily on multiple predictors when making hiring decisions (Martin, 1998).

An individual who is found to be qualified for employment, based on his or her performance on these various selection techniques, may be subjected to more in-depth interviews, followed by reference and recommendation checks. Finally, physical examinations might be authorized for those who are about to be offered employment. By combining or using multiple predictors in this way, the organization is presumably able to counterbalance the measurement error in one selection technique against another. For example, if a particular candidate for the job scores well on all selection techniques except one, the organization may choose either to ignore the results of that one technique or to try to learn more about why the individual did not perform better. Thus the basic reasoning behind combining predictors is to enhance the validity and reliability of the overall selection process by taking advantage of a wider variety of information. However, it should be noted that having too many predictors—especially those with lower accuracy rates—may actually harm the quality of selection decisions (Mornell, 1998). It is important to ensure that only predictors that genuinely distinguish between successful and unsuccessful employees are used.

Selection Methods

Organizations use a variety of methods in selection. Indeed, most organizations rely on a comprehensive system involving multiple selection techniques to ensure that they gather all the relevant data and that they assess this data rigorously, objectively, and in a nondiscriminatory fashion. In the sections that follow we identify and discuss some of the most popular and commonly used selection methods. Each approach has its limitations as well as its advantages.

Application forms. Application forms are widely used. Properly prepared the application form serves four purposes:

1. It is a record of the applicant's desire to obtain a position.
2. It provides the interviewer with a profile of the applicant that can be used in the interview.
3. It is a basic employee record for applicants who are hired.
4. It can be used for research on the effectiveness of the selection process.

The information received on application forms may not always be completely accurate. However, in an attempt to prevent inaccuracies, many application forms carry a statement that the applicant is required to sign. In effect, the statement reads: "I realize that falsification of this record is grounds for dismissal if I am hired." The statement has been used by organizations to terminate people. In fact, in a recent court case, the court held that when a company can show it would not have hired an applicant if it had known the applicant lied on the application form, the employee's claim of discriminatory discharge will not stand.

Application forms traditionally have asked for references and requested that the applicant give permission to contact them. Rather than asking for personal or general references, though, it may be more useful to request the names of previous supervisors on the application form.

In recent years, some organizations have experimented with new and more sophisticated versions of the traditional employment application. For example, one method that some organizations are experimenting with is the so-called weighted application blank (Hunter and Hunter, 1984). A weighted application blank relies on the determination of numerical indices to indicate the relative importance of various personal factors for predicting a person's ability to perform a job effectively. Using information gathered from current high and low performers in the organization, an organization may be able to determine whether various specific levels of education, experience, and so forth are related to a person's ability to perform a job effectively.

Another, recent variation on the traditional application form is the biodata application form (Russell, Mattison, Devlin, and Atwater, 1990). This is essentially a more detailed version of the application form in which applicants respond to a series of questions about their background, experiences, and preferences. Responses to these questions are then scored. For instance, candidates might be asked how willing they are to travel on the job, what leisure activities they prefer, and how much experience they have had with computers. As with any selection tool, the biodata most relevant to the job should be identified through job analysis before the application form is created. Biodata have moderate validity in predicting job performance.

Note that weighted and biodata applications focus on responses that help predict performance on the job. For example, an organization would not be interested in why individuals who once collected stamps perform better than other applicants and would certainly not suggest that collecting stamps leads to the better performance. The organization only cares that certain patterns of responses seem to be associated with high performance and so seeks applicants with these patterns while seeking other information as well.

The questions asked on an application form—or with any selection device—should be clearly job related. Federal and state laws, administrative rulings, and court decisions have drastically modified the kinds of preemployment questions that may be asked through such devices as application blanks, reference checks, and interviews. Illegal questions typically found on application forms ask for the following: marital status, height/weight, number and ages of dependents, child care arrangements, military discharge, membership in organizations, pregnancy, information on spouse, date of high school graduation, contact in case of emergency, and arrests.

The concern about such questions is that they can have an adverse impact on some protected groups. For example, the question about dependents can be used to identify women with small children. These women may not be hired because of a manager's perception that they will not be as dependable as those without small children. The high school graduation date gives a close identification of a person's age, which can be used to discriminate against individuals over 40. Or the question about emergency contact might reveal marital status or other personal information that is inappropriate to ask.

Reference and background verification. Reference checking, which involves collecting information from applicants' previous employers (usually by phone), provides another potentially useful means of assessment. Most employers check applicant references in the final stages of the hiring process to evaluate candidates on their "short list," the list of job finalists (Pyron, 1970).

Reference checks serve two important purposes. One is to verify information provided by applicants to ensure that they have not fabricated their qualifications and past work histories. Reference checks also provide information about applicants that might predict job performance. For instance, an employer may ask references to discuss an applicant's previous job behaviors in order to better assess his or her technical competence, honesty, reliability, conscientiousness, and ability to get along with others. The topics typically addressed during a reference check are: dates of employment, job titles held, rate of pay, attendance, performance evaluations, discipline problems, character traits, ability to get along with others, strengths and weaknesses, overall opinion of candidate, person's reason for leaving, and willingness to rehire that person.

Because some job applicants falsify their qualifications and misrepresent their past, employers have stepped up efforts to check references thoroughly. Instead of relying on unstructured reference letters, which are seldom negative, some organizations hire outside investigators to verify credentials. Other organizations personally contact prior employers to get reference information firsthand. Unfortunately, the potential for defamation-of-character suits has made getting information from past employers more and more difficult. Reference checks of an applicant's prior employment record are not an infringement on privacy if the information provided relates specifically to work behavior and to the reasons for leaving a previous job. Nevertheless, to avoid possible lawsuits many organizations strictly limit the type of information they give out about former employees (Walley and Smith, 1998).

Employment or ability tests. Various employment or ability tests are another popular selection method used by many organizations. An employment test is a device for measuring characteristics of an individual to include factors such as personality, verbal and quantitative skills, intelligence, or aptitude. Such tests are generally administered before the final stage of interviewing. The testing of applicants offers two advantages: test results seem to be objective and free from personal bias, and they are usually expressed numerically so that they lend themselves to statistical analyses and thus can be validated. Nevertheless, testing has been the most controversial part of the selection process. Despite the decline in testing during the 1970s and 1980s as a result of court cases and government challenges, the use of tests has increased again in recent years as organizations have adjusted to the legal restrictions. Part of the resurgence in testing has been due to the positive results of the validity testing program of the U.S. Employment Service (Solomon, 1993).

Cognitive ability tests measure a candidate's potential in a certain area, such as math, and are valid predictors of job performance when the abilities tested are based on a job analysis. Cognitive or mental ability tests measure reasoning capabilities. Knowing how a specific tool is used reflects a cognitive ability, but being able to actually use the tool is a psychomotor ability. An extremely important cognitive ability is intelligence. General intelligence, or "g," refers to reasoning or problem-solving skills but is typically measured in terms of things one learns in school. The Scholastic Aptitude Test (SAT) is a test of general intelligence. Scores on SATs can be expressed in terms of IQ, or intelligence quotient. People with high levels of "g" have been found to be better job performers, at least in part because few jobs are static today (Hunter, 1986).

Some more specific tests measure physical and mechanical abilities. For example, the physical ability tests used by fire and police departments measure strength and endurance. The results of these tests are considered indicators of how productively and safely a person could perform a job's physical tasks. However, organizations can often get a more direct measure of applicants' performance ability by observing how well they perform on actual job tasks. These types of direct performance tests, called work sample tests, ask applicants to perform the exact same tasks that they will be performing on the job—for example, requiring a person applying for a truck driver's job to back a truck up to a loading dock. An "in basket" test is a work sample test in which a job candidate is asked to respond to memos in a hypothetical in-basket that are typical of the problems faced by people holding that job. The key for any work sample test is the behavioral consistency between the criteria in the job and the requirements of the test.

Work sample tests (sometimes referred to as work simulations) are widely viewed as fair and valid measures of job performance, as long as the work samples adequately capture the variety and complexity of tasks in the actual job. Work sample scores have even been used as criteria for assessing the validity of general mental ability selection measures (Harville, 1996). However, physical ability measures have been found to screen out more women and minorities than white men. Physical preparation before the testing has been found to reduce this adverse impact significantly (Hogan and Quigley, 1994).

Two primary disadvantages are associated with work sample tests. First, they are quite expensive. Second, there could be a safety problem. For instance, it may not be wise to use a work sample test for a telephone pole climber's job; unqualified candidates could fall and break their necks!

Personality tests. Personality refers to the unique blend of characteristics that define an individual and determine his or her pattern of interactions with the environment. Personality tests are designed to assess a variety of personality characteristics (independence, assertiveness, self-confidence, etc.) that are important for applicants for certain jobs (Anatasi, 1982). A variety of approaches for psychological assessment can be used to measure personality, but paper-and-pencil tests are probably the most common (Hogan, Hogan, and Roberts, 1996).

Although most people believe personality plays an important role in job success or failure, for many years U.S. employers shied away from measuring it largely because research indicated that personality seldom predicted performance. But this early conclusion may have been inaccurate (McCrae and Costa, 1997). Recent advances in the understanding of the nature of personality suggest that organizations may have abandoned personality measures too early. The most significant advance has been the realization that most aspects of personality can be captured using only a few basic dimensions which are often referred to as the Big Five.

A great deal of attention has been paid to instruments that measure the Big Five personality traits. These traits tend to be more behavioral than cognitive or emotional, and recent research has suggested that they are likely to be more important for job performance than are more traditional personality traits (Barrick and Mount, 1991). The Big Five traits are extraversion (tendency to be outgoing, sociable, and upbeat), friendliness or agreeableness (tendency to be altruistic and cooperative), neuroticism (disposition to experience things like anxiety and guilt rather than being better adjusted emotionally), conscientiousness (tendency to be purposeful, dependable, and attentive to detail), and openness to experience (tendency to be imaginative and intellectually curious).

When past selection research is categorized into these five factors, there is evidence that some personality dimensions are consistently related to job success. For instance, conscientiousness is related to success in job training, to job performance, and to personnel data such as absenteeism and disciplinary actions on virtually all jobs. Openness to experience predicts success in training, while extraversion is positively related to success in management and sales (Barrick and Mount, 1991). None of these correlations is large, but they do exist and may be of use when combined with appropriate ability measures. There is also evidence that personality-type measures of "customer service orientation" can be useful in predicting the performance of service employees (McDaniel and Frei, 1994).

One problem that limits the validity of personality tests concerns faking. Many applicants answer questions dishonestly in an effort to make themselves look good. For example, some tests ask questions like "Do you frequently goof off?" Few applicants would say "yes" even if it were true.

There is also a possible legal problem with their use. For example, some personality tests ask very personal questions that could be considered an invasion of privacy in some states. For example, a California privacy law forbids businesses from collecting unnecessary information from applicants. The information collected must specifically, directly, and narrowly relate to performance on the job. Personality tests that ask "Does your soul sometimes leave your body?" and "Do you sometimes hate your mother?" have been found to violate that law.

Personal integrity and honesty is another personality characteristic that's attracting a lot of attention among employees. Many organizations are interested in screening out job candidates who may be likely to steal from them. Organizations that subscribe to the "bad apple" theory believe that rejecting potential thieves and hiring only honest employees will greatly reduce losses. This view is only partly correct, since research has shown that positive factors such as pay equity, job satisfaction, and opportunity to steal also play a role in determining actual theft (Hollinger and Clark, 1983).

Two methods have traditionally been used to identify potentially dishonest employees: polygraph examinations and paper-and-pencil tests. The polygraph, or lie detector, measures and graphs respiration, blood pressure, and perspiration while the person being tested answers questions. Doubts about the validity of the polygraph and horror stories of honest individuals who were discharged or denied employment because of erroneous polygraph results have led to legal restrictions on the use of polygraphs. Applicants favor paper-and-pencil integrity tests over more invasive procedures, such as lie detectors (which were found to be highly unreliable and banned as selection tools under the Employee Polygraph Protection Act (EPPA) of 1988) and background checks (Iacono and Lykken, 1997).

The EPPA bans most private-sector (but not public-sector) employers from using polygraph tests in the selection of candidates. EPPA restrictions do not apply in all circumstances. Pharmaceutical companies that test applicants for jobs that would allow access to controlled substances are exempt, as are employers who provide security services when they assess prospective guards. When used under these circumstances, the exam must be "properly" administered by licensed polygraph examiners, according to the EPPA.

Since polygraph testing has been restricted, paper-and-pencil honesty tests have increased in popularity. The tests may be either overt or personality-based measures. Overt tests inquire directly about attitudes toward theft and about prior dishonest behavior, such as "Have you ever stolen property valued at more than $5 from a previous employer?" Because the purpose of these questions is often transparent, answers can be easily faked.

Personality-based measures do not contain any obvious references toward theft and thus are less prone to faking. Personality-based measures assume that certain personality characteristics predispose people to engage in theft (Hogan and Hogan, 1989). These tests use items from personality tests that have been found to correlate with other indices of dishonesty (Sackett, Burns, and Callahan, 1989).

Paper-and-pencil tests are being used with increasing frequency now that polygraph testing has been largely banned. Critics of these tests point out that while many people who fail the test are potential thieves, a significant portion are "innocent" victims (Sackett, Burns, and Callahan, 1989). Organizations must wrestle with this ethical concern before using these tests.

Personality tests predict not only theft but also composite measures of other types of counterproductive behavior such as abuse of sick leave, excessive grievance filing, drug use at work, and rule breaking (Hogan and Hogan, 1989). These behaviors are more common than outright theft and can cost organizations a great deal of money and aggravation. Another behavior that these measures predict is violence.

Violence in the workplace (threats, verbal abuse, harassment, physical attacks, and homicide) is another problem that many organizations face today. Organizations are increasingly interested in screening applicants for violent tendencies, both to reduce the incidence of violence and to reduce liability for negligent hiring. While preemployment screening with personality tests and background checks may be a partial answer, a complete solution must include education, recognition of early warning signs, effective supervision, and appropriate preventative action (DiLorenzo and Carroll, 1995).

Statistically, it is very hard to accurately predict extremely rare events like workplace homicide, but it is possible to measure personality traits that tend to be associated with generally noncompliant, hostile, and impulsive behavior. Recent research on specially constructed violence scales as well as personality-type honesty scales has shown that these instruments do have validity for predicting violent and counterproductive behavior at work. The research also has shown that these scales tap the Big Five personality dimensions of low conscientiousness, low agreeableness, and neuroticism (Arvey, 1994).

Personal interviews. The most widely used selection method in most organizations is the employment interview. Interviews are face-to-face conversations between prospective job applicants and representatives of the organization (McDaniel, Whetzel, Schmidt, and Maurer, 1994). Nearly all organizations consider the employment interview to be a vital selection tool. Rarely would an applicant be hired without having first been interviewed. In fact, viable candidates are usually interviewed by several members of an organization: HRM staff, manager of a vacant position, and one or more upper-level managers. Selection is then based on the consensus of these individuals. Three basic types of interviews are commonly used: structured, semistructured, and unstructured.

The structured interview uses a set of standardized questions that are asked of all applicants. Every applicant is asked the same basic questions, so that comparisons among applicants can more easily be made. This type of interview allows an interviewer to prepare job-related questions in advance and then complete a standardized interviewee evaluation form. Completion of such a form provides documentation if anyone, including an EEO enforcement body, should question why one applicant was selected over another.

The structured interview is especially useful in the initial screening, because of the large number of applicants in this step of the selection process.

Obviously, it is less flexible than more traditional interview formats, and therefore it may be less appropriate for second or later interviews.

Two types of approaches to designing structured selection interviews are the situational approach and the experience-based approach. The situational approach asks candidates to imagine a hypothetical situation that is described by the interviewer and then state how they would behave in that situation. The experience-based approach asks the candidate to describe examples of behaviors that actually occurred. Although either approach can be effective, the experience-based approach appears to have higher validity (Pulakos and Schmitt, 1995).

An unstructured interview involves little preparation. The interviewer merely prepares a list of possible topics to cover and, depending on how the conversation proceeds, asks or does not ask them. Compared to other interview types the unstructured interview is likely to be more spontaneous and more wide-ranging in its focus. Although this provides for flexibility, the resulting digressions, discontinuity, and lack of focus may be frustrating to the interviewer and interviewee. More important, unstructured interviews result in inconsistencies in the information collected about candidates.

Another approach, which minimizes snap judgments, is the semistructured selection interview. Questions are prepared in advance, the same questions are asked of all candidates, and responses are recorded. However, follow-up questions are allowed to probe specific areas in depth. This approach provides enough flexibility to develop insights, along with the structure needed to acquire comparative information. A popular strategy used in some organizations today, especially high-tech firms, is to ask challenging and unusual questions designed to assess creativity and insight. For example, Microsoft interviewers often ask applicants, "Why are manhole covers round?" There are then four different relatively correct answers, each of which allows the interviewer to probe more in different areas ("Think Fast!" 1994). In general, structured and semistructured interviews are more valid than unstructured interviews (McDaniel et al., 1994).

The interview, like a pencil-and-paper test and an application form, is a type of predictor and must meet the standards of job relatedness and non-discrimination. Some court decisions and EEOC rulings have attacked the interviewing practices of some organizations as discriminatory.

An interviewer making a hiring recommendation must be able to identify the factors that shaped the decision. If that decision is challenged, the organization must be able to show justification. Everything written or said can be probed for evidence in a lawsuit. Lawyers recommend the following to minimize EEO concerns with interviewing:

1. Identify objective criteria related to the job to be looked for in the interview.
2. Put criteria in writing.

3. Provide multiple levels of review for difficult or controversial decisions.
4. Use structured interviews, with the same questions asked of all those interviewed for a specific job.

Assessment centers. Assessment centers evaluate how well applicants or current employees might perform in a managerial or higher-level position (or in teams). According to Thornton and Byham (1982), an assessment center is "a comprehensive, standardized procedure in which multiple assessment techniques, such as situational exercises and job simulations (i.e., business games, discussion groups, reports, and presentations), are used to evaluate individual employees for various purposes.

Assessment centers usually involve six to 12 attendees, although they may involve more. Customarily, they're conducted off the premises for two to five days, during which time a group of candidates take a battery of work sample tests and other selection devices, such as interviews and various written tests. Usually managers from throughout the organization are trained and asked to assess the employees or job applicants. Increasingly, team members who will work with new hires also assess participants (Mayes, 1997).

The most common work sample tests used in assessment centers are:

1. *In-basket exercise.* In-basket exercises create a realistic situation designed to elicit typical on-the-job behaviors. Participants are provided with a set of memos, typical of those found in a manager's in-basket. The participants are required to prioritize and respond to the information. The test attempts to measure planning and organizing skills, judgment, and/or work standards.
2. *The leaderless group discussion (LGD).* In a LGD, a group of individuals is asked to discuss a topic for a given period of time. Their behavior is rated by trained observers who evaluate such characteristics as communication skills, leadership, persuasiveness, and/or sensitivity.
3. *Business (or management) games.* Business games are living cases. These involve some activity, such as buying and selling supplies, where individuals (or subgroups) compete in trying to maximize gains (e.g., profits, market share). This type of test often measures risk taking, initiative, analytical skills, and/or leadership.

Because in-basket exercises, business games, and LGDs tend to be useful in managerial selection, they are often used together in an assessment center. As noted earlier, as candidates go through these exercises a trained team of assessors rates their performance. After the program ends, the assessors discuss the candidates and prepare written evaluations based on their combined judgments of the candidates. The composite performance on the exercises and tests is often used to determine an assessment center attendee's future promotability.

Assessment centers appear to work because they reflect the actual job environment and measure performance on multiple job dimensions and because two or more trained raters with a common frame of reference evaluate each participant's behavior. Although assessment centers are expensive to operate, the cost seems to be justified, since studies have shown that the data do predict both short- and long-term success and advancement in management positions. Validities are often quite high. Furthermore, assessment centers are equally valid for both sexes and all races and do not seem to produce adverse impact (Fisher, Schoenfeldt, and Shaw, 1999).

Physical examinations. A final popular selection method is a physical examination. Although not all organizations require physical tests or medical exams, these are being given in increasing numbers. The Americans with Disabilities Act (ADA) prohibits an organization from rejecting an individual because of a disability and from asking job applicants any questions relative to current or past medical history until a conditional job offer is made. The ADA also prohibits the use of preemployment medical exams, except for drug tests, until a job has been conditionally offered.

Organizations require physical exams (1) to determine if the person is physically healthy enough to perform a job, (2) to determine whether or not the applicant has any serious communicable diseases, and/or (3) to determine the extent to which the person may have appropriate levels of stamina and physical condition for performing hazardous or strenuous jobs.

A related type of physical examination that organizations rely on is drug testing. Drug testing may be part of a medical exam, or it may be done separately. Using drug testing as part of the selection process has increased during the past decade, though not without controversy.

Like other types of physical examinations, drug tests are commonly given to people to whom the organization is prepared to make an offer of employment. Of course, as with all selection techniques, reliance on a drug test as a condition of employment requires that the organization be absolutely sure the test that is being administered is valid and reliable. That is, the organization must be prepared to demonstrate that the test is conducted under rigorous conditions and that its results are true and verifiable. This is especially important because such tests are not infallible. The accuracy of drug tests varies according to the type of test used, the item tested, and the quality of the laboratory where the test samples are sent. If an individual tests positive for drug use, then a second, more detailed analysis should be administered by an independent medical laboratory.

Drug testing has legal implications, as alluded above. In a number of cases, courts have ruled that individuals with previous substance-abuse problems who have received rehabilitation are disabled and thus covered by the ADA. Also, preemployment drug testing must be administered in a nondiscriminatory manner, not used selectively with certain groups. The results of drug tests also must be used consistently, so that all individuals testing positive are treated uniformly.

Another controversial area of medical testing is genetic testing or screening. Some large organizations currently are using genetic tests and many more are considering their use in the future. Organizations that use genetic screening tests do so for several reasons. First, the tests may link workplace health hazards and individuals with certain characteristics. For example, genetic testing identifies individuals who are hypersensitive to harmful pollutants in the workplace. Once identified, these individuals can be screened out of chemically dangerous jobs and placed in positions in which environmental toxins do not present specific hazards. Genetic testing may also be used to make employees aware of genetic problems that could occur in certain work situations. The third use is the most controversial: to exclude individuals from certain jobs if they have genetic conditions that increase their health risks.

Genetic screening isn't prohibited by the ADA, however, because people cannot change their genetic makeup, the potential for discrimination based, for example, on race or sex is very real. For instance, sickle-cell anemia is a condition found primarily in African Americans. If chemicals in a particular work environment can cause health problems for individuals with sickle-cell anemia, African Americans might be screened out on that basis. In the end, the question is who should make that decision: the individual or the organization.

Making the Final Selection Decision

After subjecting the pool of candidates to the organization's selection system, one individual must be selected for the job. In some cases the decision may be relatively simple. If the organization is seeking to hire only one individual for a particular position, then the top-ranked candidate from the pool of applicants is the person likely to be hired. On the other hand, if the selection process is part of a larger program in which the organization may be hiring a dozen or so individuals or even more for similar kinds of positions, then the selection decision may consist of choosing where to draw the line between those who qualify for employment and those who do not.

The responsibility for making the final selection decision is assigned to different levels of management in different organizations. In many organizations, the HRM department handles the completion of application forms, conducts preliminary interviews, testing, and reference checking, and arranges for physical exams. The interview(s) or final selection decision(s) are usually left to the manager of the department with the job opening. Such a system relieves the manager of the time-consuming responsibilities of screening out unqualified and uninterested applicants.

In other organizations, the HRM staff handles all of the steps up to the final decision. Under this system, the HRM function gives the manager with a job opening a list of three to five qualified applicants. The manager then chooses the individual she or he believes will be the best employee based on all the information provided by the HRM staff. Many organizations leave the final choice to the manager with the job opening, subject to the approval of those at higher levels of management.

An alternative approach is to involve peers in the final selection decision. In some cases operating employees and potential colleagues of the prospective candidate may be involved throughout the selection process. With the increased emphasis on self-managed teams, many organizations have turned over considerable responsibility for the selection process, including final selection of applicants to be offered employment, to members of particular work groups or intact teams.

Occasionally, none of the candidates who reach the finalist pool for the job are suitable for employment. In this case the organization may actually decide to not make an employment offer to anyone in its pool but instead start over with a different group of applicants.

It is important for managers to recognize that after using various selection techniques to gauge the relative quality of prospective employees, they must still make the actual selection decision. This is an important step because of the costs of recruiting and selecting, the legal considerations, the relatively short probationary time in most organizations, and the turnover rate of many new employees.

Evaluation of Selection and Placement Efforts

Employee selection is clearly one of the most important functions that organizations engage in. The ability to attract qualified human resources and to select the individuals who are most suitable for employment goes a long way toward determining the future vitality, effectiveness, and success of the organization. The effective and ongoing infusion of new talent, new attitudes, and new perspectives can be a major ingredient in the success of an organization.

On the other hand, if the selection initiative results in inbreeding or the continued process of hiring ineffective employees, then the organization and all who work for it will eventually pay the price. Thus organizations must regularly examine their selection efforts to ensure effectiveness. The evaluation of selection efforts is best approached from the standpoint of operating managers who rely on it to supply them with effective new employees.

To the extent that these managers report that the HRM function is indeed providing them with qualified employees, then there is implied evidence for the effectiveness of the organization's selection process. On the other hand, if operating managers report that the HRM function is not providing them with effective employees or if managers are unhappy with the process in other ways, then there may be evidence to suggest that changes in the selection process are warranted.

Additionally, initial job placement can also be evaluated in much the same way. If individuals who begin their employment with the organization express satisfaction with the organization and positive feelings about their initial job experiences, then initial job placement may have been undertaken appropriately and effectively. But if many new employees are unhappy and complaining that their initial job assignment isn't what they expected it to be, then in addition to the possibility that the organization is not providing realistic job previews, it may be the case that initial job placement is not being handled satisfactorily.

SUMMARY

This chapter has focused on the importance of employee selection and placement to organizational success. An organization's selection and placement efforts must be directly tied to its strategic objectives.

The basic selection criteria most organizations use in deciding whom to hire are education and experience, skills and abilities, and personal characteristics. Organizations use a variety of techniques for gathering information about job candidates, including employment applications, background checks, employment tests, work simulations, employment interviews, and physical examinations. Each technique has unique strengths and weaknesses, but each can play an important role in selection.

Regardless of which technique or techniques an organization uses in making selection decisions, it must ensure that those techniques are reliable and valid. Most organizations rely on a number of selection techniques and, in fact, may use all or most of the selection techniques discussed in this chapter.

Organizations must make a final selection decision after reviewing the pool of qualified candidates. Another important part of the selection process is placement of an individual in her or his first job in the organization. It is equally important that the organization regularly evaluate its selection and placement efforts.

REFERENCES

Abram, T.G. 1979. Overview of uniform selection guidelines: Pitfalls for the unwary employer. *Labor Law Journal* (August): 495–502.

Anatasi, A. 1982. *Psychological testing*, 5th ed. New York: Macmillan.

Arvey, R.D. 1994. Violence in the workplace. Paper presented at the Annual Meeting of the Academy of Management, Dallas, August.

Barrick, M.R., and Mount, M.K. 1991. The big five personality dimensions and job performance: A meta-analysis. *Personnel Psychology* (44): 1–26.

Behling, O. 1998. Employee selection: Will intelligence and conscientiousness do the job? *Academy of Management Executive* (February): 77–87.

Bourbeau, J. 1996. *Employment testing manual.* Cumulative supplement. Boston: Warren, Gorham, and Lamont, p. 9.08.

DiLorenzo, L.P., and Carroll, D.J. 1995. Screening applicants for a safer workplace. *HRMagazine* (March): 55–58.

Dunn, W., Mount, M., Barrick, M., and Ones, D. 1995. Relative importance of personality and general mental ability in managers' judgments of applicant qualifications. *Journal of Applied Psychology* 80(4): 500–509.

Fisher, C.D., Schoenfeldt, L.F., and Shaw, J.B. 1999. *Human resource management,* 4th ed. Boston: Houghton Mifflin.

Harville, D.L. 1996. Ability test equity in predicting job performance work samples. *Educational and Psychological Measurement* 56: 344–348.

Hogan, J., and Hogan, R.T. 1989. How to measure employee reliability. *Journal of Applied Psychology* 74: 273–279.

Hogan, J., and Quigley, A. 1994. Effects of preparing for physical ability tests. *Public Personnel Management* 23: 85–104.

Hogan, R.T., Hogan, J., and Roberts, B.W. 1996. Personality measurement and employment decisions. *American Psychologist* 51: 469–477.

Hollinger, R.C., and Clark, J.P. 1983. *Theft by employees.* Lexington, MA: Lexington Books.

Hunter, J.E. 1986. Cognitive ability, cognitive aptitudes, job knowledge, and job performance. *Journal of Vocational Behavior* 29: 340–362.

Hunter, J.E., and Hunter, R.F. 1984. Validity and utility of alternative predictors of job performance. *Psychological Bulletin* (Spring): 72–98.

Iacono, W.G., and Lykken, D.T. 1997. The validity of the lie detector: Two surveys of scientific opinion. *Journal of Applied Psychology* 82: 426–433.

Martin, J. 1998. So, you want to work for the best. *Fortune* (January 12), pp. 77–85.

Mayes, B.T. 1997. Insights into the history and future of assessment centers: An interview with Dr. Douglas Bray and D. William Byham. *Journal of Social Behavior and Personality* (Special Issue): 3–12.

McCrae, R.R., and Costa, P.T., Jr. 1997. Personality trait structure as a human universal. *American Psychologist* 52: 509–535.

McDaniel, M.A., and Frei, R.L. 1994. Validity of customer service measures in personnel selection: A meta-analysis. Paper presented at the Ninth Annual Conference of the Society for Industrial and Organizational Psychology, Nashville, April.

McDaniel, M.A., Whetzel, D., Schmidt, F., and Maurer, S. 1994. The validity of employment interviews: A comprehensive review and meta-analysis. *Journal of Applied Psychology* 79(4): 599–616.

Mornell, P. 1998. No room for compromise. *Inc.* (August): 116.

Murphy, K.R., and Sharella, A.N. 1997. Implications of the multidimensional nature of job performance for the validity of selection tests. *Personnel Psychology* 50: 455.

Paunonen, S.V., Rothstein, M.G., and Jackson, D.N. 1999. Narrow reasoning about the use of broad personality measures for personnel selection. *Journal of Organizational Behavior* (May): 389–405.

Pulakos, E., and Schmitt, N. 1995. Experience-based and situational interview questions: Studies of validity. *Personnel Psychology* 50: 289–308.

Pyron, H.C. 1970. The use and misuse of previous employer references in hiring. *Management of Personnel Selection Quarterly* (Summer): 15–22.

Quinones, M.A., Ford, K.J., and Teachout, M.A. 1995. The relationship between work experience and job performance: A conceptual and meta-analytic review. *Personnel Psychology* (Winter): 887–910.

Russell, C.J., Mattison, J., Devlin, S.F., and Atwater, D. 1990. Predictive validity of biodata items generated from retrospective life experience essays. *Journal of Applied Psychology* 75: 569–580.

Ryan, A.M., and Lasek, M. 1991. Negligent hiring and defamation: Areas of liability related to pre-employment inquiries. *Personnel Psychology* 44(2): 293–319.

Sackett, P.R., Burns, L.R., and Callahan, C. 1989. Integrity testing for personnel selection: An update. *Personnel Psychology* 42: 491–530.

Schmitt, N., and Chan, D. 1998. *Personnel selection: A theoretical approach*. Thousand Oaks, CA: Sage.

Schmitt, N., Schneider, J.R., and Cohen, S.A. 1990. Factors affecting validity of a regionally administered assessment center. *Personnel Psychology* (Spring): 1–12.

Snow, C.C., and Snell, S.A. 1993. Staffing as strategy. In N.Schmitt, W.C. Borman and Associates (eds.), *Personnel selection in organizations*. San Francisco: Jossey-Bass, pp. 448–478.

Society for Industrial and Organizational Psychology. 1987. *Principles for the validation and use of personnel selection procedures*, 3rd ed. College Park, MD: Author, pp. 6–18.

Solomon, C.M. 1993. Testing is not at odds with diversity efforts. *Personnel Journal* 72 (March): 100–104.

Think fast! 1994. *Forbes* (March): 146–151.

Thornton, G.C., and Byham, W.C. 1982. *Assessment centers and managerial performance*. New York: Academic Press.

Walley, L., and Smith, M. 1998. *Deception in selection*. New York: John Wiley.

Chapter 7

Human Resources Development

INTRODUCTION

Organizations today are increasingly recognizing the importance of developing their human resources. The training function, now popularly referred to as human resources development (HRD), coordinates the organization's efforts to provide training and development experiences for its employees. Although training is often used in conjunction with development, the terms are not synonymous. Employee training can be defined as a planned attempt to facilitate employee learning of job-related knowledge, skills, and behaviors or helping them correct deficiencies in their performance. In contrast, development is an effort to provide employees with the skills needed for both present and future jobs.

This chapter stresses the point that in the future the only winning organizations will be those that respond quickly to the issue of training and development–related problems. If an organization wants to succeed, it must recognize the importance of investing in its greatest resource—the force working for it. In this chapter, we discuss developing human resources as key to organizational success. Developing human resources is the next stage in the process of achieving organizational success. We first discuss human resources development and organizational strategy. We then take a look at the role of EEO in organizational efforts to develop human potential. Then we discuss a special form of employee development, new employee orientation. Next we examine how organizations go about assessing their training and development needs. Then we discuss setting training and development goals. Next we discuss the actual development of training and development programs and include a look at the importance of learning principles. Training and development techniques and methods are then introduced and discussed. Before concluding with a discussion on the evaluation of training and development efforts, we look more closely at team training and the challenge of management development.

HRD AND ORGANIZATIONAL STRATEGY

With the movement away from traditional training to that of HRD, organizations during the past decade have recognized that in order to gain a competitive advantage training must encompass a broader focus than just basic skills development. Therefore, to gain a competitive advantage, training is now viewed broadly as a way to create intellectual capital. Intellectual capital includes the KSAs to perform one's job, advanced skills such as how to effectively use technology to share information with other members of the organization, and an understanding of customers and organizational processes key to the organization's success.

Organizations provide training for many reasons: to orient new hires to the organization or teach them how to perform in their initial job assignment, to improve the current performance of employees who may not be working as effectively as desired, or to prepare employees for future promotions or for upcoming changes in design, processes, or technology in their present jobs. Recent changes in the business environment have made the training function even more important in helping organizations maintain competitiveness and prepare for the future.

Restructuring and downsizing over the past decade or so have meant that many employees need to be trained to take on expanded responsibilities as organizations have created internal environments of "doing more with less." The presence of global competition is also changing the way organizations operate and the KSAs that their employees need. For instance, more and more organizations are providing quality management and customer service training in an attempt to keep up with rising consumer expectations. Additionally, ongoing technological innovations require training, with employees often needing more sophisticated KSAs in troubleshooting and problem solving than they did previously.

Like HRM, training must be an outgrowth of the organization's overall strategy. Some have referred to this as high-leverage training (Carnevale, 1990). High-leverage training is linked to strategic business goals and objectives, uses an instructional design process to ensure training is effective, and compares and benchmarks the organization's training programs against training programs in other organizations. Today, training must be tailored to fit the organization's strategy and structure. For instance, an organization whose strategy involves providing exceptional service through a committed, long-service cadre of extremely well-qualified employees will need more complex training and career development systems than an organization that competes on the basis of simple, low-cost services provided by transient, unskilled employees. When strategy changes, training in most cases also has to change to equip employees with the KSAs necessary to meet new demands. This is most evident in team-based high-involvement organizations who have found that extensive training in team skills as well as in individual job skills is necessary to make innovative organizational structures function as intended.

In an age of network organizations, alliances, and long-term relationships with just-in-time suppliers, leading organizations are finding that they need to train people other than their own employees. Some organizations offer quality training to their suppliers to ensure the quality of critical inputs. Other organizations with a strong focus on customer service may provide training for purchasers.

Another example of training and strategy is evident in the recent emphasis on continuous learning and the learning organization. Continuous learning requires employees to understand the entire work system including the relationships among their jobs, their work units, and the organization. Employees are expected to acquire new KSAs, apply them on the job, and share information with other employees and often customers. A learning organization is one whose employees are continuously attempting to learn new things and apply what they have learned to improve products or service quality. Improvements do not stop when formal training is completed (Senge, 1991).

A learning organization is also a company that has an enhanced capacity to learn, adapt, and change. Training processes are carefully scrutinized and aligned with organization goals (Gephart, Marsick, Van Buren, and Spiro, 1996). In a learning organization training is seen as one part of a system designed to create intellectual capital and achieve strategic objectives.

Finally, training is seen as pivotal in implementing organization-wide culture change efforts, such as adopting total quality management, developing a commitment to customer service, or making a transition to self-directed work teams. Today's proactive training functions have moved from simply providing training on demand to solving organizational problems. Trainers see themselves as internal consultants or performance-improvement specialists rather than just instructional designers or classroom presenters. Training is only one of many remedies that may be applied by the new breed of HRD practitioners (Linde, Horney, and Koonce, 1997).

Training and EEO

Some of our previous discussions of EEO have centered on the selection process. Undoubtedly, it is most prevalent in the hiring process, but its application to training cannot be overlooked. The major requirement under EEO is that employees must have access to training and development programs in a nondiscriminatory fashion. Equal opportunity regulations and antidiscrimination laws apply to the training process, just as they do to all other HRM functions.

Determining whether a training program has adverse impact is a primary means of deciding if a process is discriminatory. If relatively few women and minorities are given training opportunities, it would appear that there is discrimination in terms of development offered to different groups of employees. This situation could trigger an investigation and the organization may have to demonstrate that development opportunities are offered on a job-relevant and nondiscriminatory basis.

Organizational training programs may be required for promotions, job bidding (especially in unionized jobs), or for salary increases. Under any of these scenarios, it is the responsibility of the organization to ensure that training selection criteria are related to the job. Furthermore, as noted earlier, equal training opportunities must exist for all employees.

Another concern for organizations in regard to EEO laws and regulations is differences in pay based on training to which protected-class members have not had equal access. Additionally, there is the use of training as a criterion for selecting individuals for promotions.

Organizations should pay close attention to training completion rates. If protected group members fail to pass training programs more frequently than the "majority group," this might indicate dissimilarities in the training that is offered. Once again, organizations should monitor these activities, and perform periodic audits to ensure full compliance with EEO regulations.

NEW EMPLOYEE ORIENTATION

A very common type of training is new employee orientation. All employees, whether managerial or nonmanagerial, should be provided with systematic orientation when they first join an organization. Orientation introduces new employees to the organization and to their new tasks, managers, and co-workers so that they can quickly become effective contributors. Effective orientation can play a very important role in employee job satisfaction, performance, retention, and similar areas (Tyler, 1998).

Job applicants get some orientation to the organization even before they are hired. The organization has a reputation as to the type of employer it is and the types of products or services it provides. During the selection process, the new employee usually also learns other general aspects of the organization and what the duties, working conditions, and pay will be. After hiring the employee, the organization begins a formal orientation program.

Orientation can also serve the role of providing favorable initial job experiences for new employees. As noted in our previous discussion of realistic job previews (Chapter 5), organizations can avoid problems of disenchantment and disappointment when people encounter jobs that are different from what they expected. In similar fashion an effective orientation program can complement and reinforce this process by making sure that a new employee's initial job experiences are positive and effective. The orientation program, for example, will help newcomers feel like part of a team; allow them to quickly meet their co-workers, their supervisor, and other new employees; and in a variety of other ways ease the transition from being an outsider to being an insider.

Responsibilities for New Employee Orientation

The organization must decide who will actually conduct orientation sessions. In many situations a number of individuals are a part of the orientation process. In a small organization without an HRM unit the new employee's supervisor or manager has the total responsibility for orientation. In large organizations, the HRM function and the new employee's immediate supervisor (or manager) normally share responsibilities for orientation. In some unionized organizations, union officials are involved. The HRM staff also helps train supervisors and managers for more effective orientation. It is important that managers and supervisors (and union officials) as well as the HRM unit work as a team in employee orientation.

The HRM function is usually responsible for initiating and coordinating orientation along with other responsibilities that include: (1) designing formal orientation program, (2) placing employees on payroll, (3) explaining benefits and company organization, (4) developing orientation checklist, (5) evaluating orientation activities, and (6) following up the initial orientation with new employees.

The new employee's supervisor or manager is usually responsible for conducting the departmental and job orientation and their responsibilities include: (1) preparing co-workers for new employees, (2) introducing new employees to co-workers, and (3) providing overview of job setting and work rules.

Together they must develop an orientation process that will communicate what the employee needs to learn. Supervisors may not know all the details about health insurance or benefit options, for example, but they usually can best present information on safety rules; the HRM department then can explain benefits. Some organizations have instituted a "buddy system" in which the orientation to the job or work unit is conducted by one of the new employee's co-workers. If a buddy system is to work successfully, the employee chosen for this role must be carefully selected and properly trained for such orientation responsibilities.

Orientation Evaluation and Follow-up

An effective and systematic orientation program should have an evaluation and/or reorientation phase at some point after the initial orientation. An HRM representative or manager can evaluate the effectiveness of the orientation by conducting follow-up interviews with new employees a few weeks or months after the orientation. Employee questionnaires can also be used. Some organizations even give new employees a written test on the company handbook two weeks after orientation. Unfortunately there are many organizations that do limited or no evaluation of the effectiveness of orientation.

The organization should make sure that at least once a year it reviews the orientation program to determine if it is meeting its objectives and to identify future improvements. To improve orientation, organizations need candid, comprehensive feedback from everyone involved in the program. There are several ways to provide this kind of feedback: through roundtable discussions with new employees after their first year on the job, through in-depth interviews with randomly selected employees and supervisors, and through questionnaires for mass coverage of all recent hires.

THE NEEDS ASSESSMENT PHASE

Because the objective of training is to contribute to the organization's overall goals, training programs should be developed systematically with the organization's true needs in mind. However, often they are not. Instead, training objectives may be undetermined or hazy, and the programs themselves may not be evaluated rigorously or at all. In fact, it sometimes seems that what is important is that the training program is attention getting, dramatic, contemporary, or fun. Effective training can raise performance, improve morale, and increase an organization's potential. To maximize the benefits of training, organizations must closely monitor the training process. The training process consists of three parts: needs assessment (or analysis), design and implementation, and evaluation.

Needs Assessment

Needs assessment takes time and money. Unfortunately, a great many organizations undertake training without this necessary preliminary investment. Training that is undertaken without a careful analysis of whether or not it is needed is likely to be ineffective and a waste of money. In the needs assessment phase the organization conducts a systematic analysis of an organization's job-related needs and specifies the objectives of the training effort.

As part of the assessment, those responsible for conducting the assessment must carefully assess the organization's strategy, the resources it has available for training, and its general philosophy regarding employee training and development. By philosophy, we are referring to the extent to which the organization views training as a true investment in human resources or simply as necessary to alter or change a specific outcome or criterion measure. Workforce analysis involves a careful assessment of the capabilities, strengths, and weaknesses characterizing the organization's current workforce. That is, it is important to understand the extent to which the organization's existing workforce is skilled or unskilled, motivated or unmotivated, committed or not committed to the organization, and so forth.

An organization can use a variety of sources for gathering information and several sources of information for needs assessment. The choice of assessment methods and sources depends partly on the purpose of the training. If the purpose is to improve employees' performance in their present jobs, then clearly the trainer must begin by looking at present performance and identifying performance deficiencies or areas where there seems to be room for improvement. Sources of information on performance deficiencies include supervisors' and customers' complaints, performance appraisal data, objective measures of output or quality, and even special performance tests given to determine the current KSA level of employees. In addition, HRM personnel might collect critical incidents of poor job performance and look at accident reports to locate possible knowledge, skill or ability problems.

Individual or group interviews with employees (supervisors, incumbents, or even customers) can be conducted by HRM specialists or outside experts. Interviews are a good way of gathering information on performance discrepancies and perceived training needs. Group techniques are especially helpful for anticipating future training needs, for prioritizing training demands, or for ambiguous situations. A group of top managers, for instance, might work together to predict and prioritize new skills that will be needed by top managers in the organization over the next decade. Similarly, members of self-managed teams might do the same to predict and prioritize new skills that will be needed in six months or a year to successfully complete future projects, and so on.

An example of some basic interview questions that could be asked in reference to a particular job are as follows: What problems is the employee having in his or her job? What additional KSAs does the employee need to better perform the job? What training does the employee believe is needed? Of course, in conducting interviews, every organization would have several additional questions about specific issues. In addition, if interviews are to provide useful information, employees must believe their input will be valued and not be used against them.

When a large number of potential trainees are involved, or when they are geographically dispersed, a subsample may be selected for needs assessment interviews, or a questionnaire or survey on needs assessment may be developed for wider distribution. Typically, existing data will be scrutinized and some interviews will be held prior to designing the questionnaire.

Using surveys and/or questionnaires involves developing a list of KSAs required to perform particular jobs effectively and asking employees to check those KSAs in which they believe training is needed. When using employee attitude surveys, organizations often bring in an outside party or organization to conduct and analyze the surveys. Customer surveys can also indicate problem areas that may not be obvious to employees of the organization. Responses to a customer survey may indicate areas of training for the organization as a whole or for particular functional units.

Observations are also frequently used in needs assessment for determining training needs. HRM specialists or managers may learn a great deal by observing current employees to see how they appear to be working. To be effective observations must be conducted by individuals trained in observing employee behavior and translating observed behavior into specific training needs. HRM specialists who have been trained in performing job analysis should be particularly adept at observing to identify training needs.

Focus groups can also be used to determine training needs. Focus groups are composed of employees from various departments and various levels within the organization. An HRM specialist or an outside expert can conduct the focus group sessions. Focus group topics should address issues such as the following: What KSAs will our employees need for our organization to stay competitive over the next few years? What problems does our organization have that can be solved through training?

It is also useful to examine existing records or documents on absenteeism, turnover, and accident rates to determine if problems exist and whether any problems identified can be addressed through training. Another useful source to examine is performance appraisal information gathered through the organization's performance appraisal system. Performance problems common to many employees are likely areas to address through training.

Once an organization has identified a performance deficiency, the next step is to determine whether the deficiency should be addressed by training. In some cases, motivation, constraints, or poor task design cause the deficiency. In such situations, training in job skills would not solve the problem.

If training is being planned for current employees destined for promotion or transfer, needs assessment is more complex. In this situation an HRM specialist must measure the demands of the future job and then attempt to assess the ability of the employees to meet those demands. Because the employees being assessed do not yet hold the future job, their current level of performance may or may not indicate their ability to do the future job. Therefore, the HRM specialist may have to use special techniques to assess the employees' level of KSAs relative to the demands of the future job. Such techniques include assessment centers and possibly tests or supervisory ratings of relevant KSAs.

When training is being designed for new hires, the methods used must be slightly different. Training is designed on the basis of a careful analysis of job content and the assumed characteristics of the trainees. If the trainees are not yet hired, it is difficult to assess their current level of KSAs. Thus the HRM specialists must coordinate closely with those who set hiring criteria and evaluate candidates.

Regardless of the method employed, a systematic and accurate needs assessment should be undertaken before any training is conducted. Following the needs assessment, objectives or goals must be established for meeting those needs.

SETTING TRAINING AND DEVELOPMENT GOALS

The establishment of training or development objectives or goals is one of the most important steps in any program. Unfortunately, many organizational training programs have no objectives. "Training for training's sake" appears to be the maxim. This philosophy makes it virtually impossible to evaluate the strengths and weaknesses of a training program.

For the organization to manage its investment properly, it should know in advance (that is, prior to training) what it expects of its employees. It is surprisingly difficult to evaluate the effectiveness of training if the organization has no predetermined goals. Thus the HRM specialists responsible for planning training must look at the current state of affairs, decide what changes are necessary, and then formulate these changes in the form of specific training goals.

The HRM specialist should make every reasonable effort to ensure that the training program's goals are objective, verifiable, and specific. For example, a vague and general goal such as "improving employee performance" or "enhancing employee attitudes" is very difficult to evaluate. On the other hand, specific, objective and verifiable goals such as increasing performance by 7 percent, cutting turnover by 5 percent, cutting customer complaints by 3 percent, and improving accuracy or quality by 10 percent are likely to be effective goals for a training and development program, at least in terms of the organization's abilities to evaluate the effectiveness of the training.

When clearly defined objectives are lacking, it is impossible to evaluate a program efficiently. Furthermore, there is no basis for selecting materials, content, or training methods. However, with clear training objectives or goals in hand HRM specialists can begin to plan the actual development, implementation, and evaluation of training.

In-House versus Outsourced Training and Development Programs

An important decision that the organization must make is the extent to which the training and development programs should be conducted in house or outsourced. An in-house training or development program is conducted on the premises of the organization primarily by the organization's own employees. The organization assumes the responsibility for training and developing its employees, making use of its own training staff or managers (or other employees) who are familiar with the organization, its jobs, and its employees.

There are several advantages to in-house training and development. One major advantage is that the organization can be assured that the content of its training and development efforts are precisely and specifically tailored to fit the organization's needs. That is, by definition there will be a close working relationship between operating managers and the training and development personnel as the various training and development programs are planned and conducted for existing employees. Another advantage is flexibility, particularly regarding scheduling, because the training and development programs can be taught at times that are most convenient for the employees.

The alternative approach to in-house training and development is to use an outsourcing strategy. An outsourced training and development program involves having people from outside the organization perform the training. This approach might involve sending employees to training and development programs at a consulting firm's headquarters, at colleges and universities, or at similar locations. The primary advantage of outsourced programs is cost. Because the organization does not have to maintain its own training and development staff, or even its own training and development facilities, the cost is typically lower than would be possible with an in-house training and development program.

Another advantage is quality assurance. Although an organization has reasonable control over its own training and development personnel, the individuals who are assigned the responsibility of doing the training and development might not be particularly skilled trainers or educators. Thus the effectiveness of the training and development effort might be compromised. Professional trainers, however, are almost always highly trained themselves and are also skilled educators. On the other hand, outsourced programs may be more likely to be a bit general and even generic and thus have less applicability and direct relevance to the organization.

THE PROGRAM DEVELOPMENT AND IMPLEMENTATION PHASE

Once HRM specialists have identified training needs, established objectives for the training, and decided the extent to which the training and development should be conducted in house or outcourced, the next step is the development (or design) and implementation of training or development programs that will achieve those objectives. This is accomplished by first outlining and defining training and development program content, then selecting the most appropriate instructors to complete the process, and then selecting training methods and developing training materials that convey the KSAs identified in the training objectives.

Determining Training and Development Program Content

An important first step in developing training and development programs is to create a detailed outline of the intended program (Smith, 1995). This outline should include items such as a summary of the training objectives, a specification of the intended audience for the training, a specification of the proposed content of the training, and estimates of the amount of time necessary to conduct the training. In addition, the outline should also specify factors such as evaluation criteria, cost estimates, and the extent to which the training can be conducted in house or whether it should be outsourced.

Once the training and development program has been outlined, the next step in the development of the program is to define its content. At a superficial level the definition of content would seem to be a relatively straightforward undertaking. In reality, however, defining the content of a training and development program is both extremely important and quite difficult. Simply stated, the content of a training and development program specifies the material that is intended to be taught.

Another way to approach this task is to focus on what is to be learned. For example, consider a training and development program designed to prepare employees to use a certain word processing package. The content specification would need to fully describe those parts of the word processing package that are intended to be taught. Thus the definition should specify all the parameters of the program including the kinds of machines that are appropriate, intended uses of the software, and indicators of how well the material has been mastered.

Using a model of instructional content suggested by Gagne (1984), our word processing example should include the following learning categories:

1. Intellectual skills include concepts, rules, and procedures and are often referred to as procedural knowledge.

2. Verbal information enables the individual to state something about a subject and is also referred to as declarative information.

3. Cognitive strategies enable a learner to know when and how to use intellectual skills and verbal information.

4. Motor skills include basic human physical activities such as writing, lifting, and using tools.

5. Attitudes are learned preferences for different activities.

Using this framework, the learning goals of the training program for word processing would include the intellectual skills needed to understand how the software is to be used, the cognitive strategies needed to know how to apply the knowledge about the programs, and the motor skills needed to operate the machines. Therefore, it is useful to approach the developing of training programs, both from the perspective of what is to be taught as well as from the perspective of what is to be learned.

More complex training and development programs require a more complex definition of content and of learning goals. For example, a program aimed at enhancing the decision-making capabilities of senior executives would need to fully specify the range of decisions that the executives must make, the circumstances under which those decisions are most likely to be made, and various other factors associated with the decision-making process. Given that decision making is an inherently more complex undertaking than using a particular piece of software, it would follow that the content of a decision-making program would need to be more abstract and tap into a higher level of cognitive ability than the content of a program to teach the use of a piece of software.

Deciding on the Training and Development Instructors

A very important aspect of developing training and development programs is the selection of instructors to deliver the material. Eventual success of any training and development effort is effective instruction. Therefore, great care must be exercised in choosing instructors. Effective instructors are those individuals who deliver the content of a training or development program in a way that facilitates learning. Ineffective instructors, in contrast, serve as barriers or impediments to learning.

Personal characteristics (learning and training style, the ability to speak well, to write convincingly, to organize the work of others, to be inventive, to inspire others to greater achievement, to facilitate a climate for learning) are important factors in the selection of instructors.

The instructor or trainer sets the pace, provides the guidance and assistance, and often furnishes the subject-matter expertise. The instructor also plays an important role in evaluating the training and development program during the evaluation phase. Therefore, the quality of the total training or development effort depends largely on the competence of the trainers.

A common choice regarding instructors involves whether to use full-time professional trainers who might either be hired from an external organization or available on an in-house training staff or to use operating managers (or other employees). The other choice is to use a professional trainer. The major advantage to using operating managers or related employees is expertise. These individuals presumably understand the organization and the task to be performed and are thus extremely qualified to present instructional material aimed at those skills and requirements. On the other hand, such individuals, although they may be experts on the task to be taught, may also be poorly trained instructors. Thus they may do a poor job of developing training materials, may not be able to deliver those materials effectively, and may otherwise do an inadequate job of classroom instruction.

The major advantage of using professional trainers is that they are likely to be very qualified instructors. They understand the importance of instructional goals and learning principles (discussed below), are able to deliver the material in an effective manner, and are otherwise capable of facilitating the learning process. On the other hand, these individuals may lack the technical expertise that is associated with the task being taught. Thus, although they might be able to deliver the material in a straightforward and perhaps superficial manner, they may be inadequately prepared to answer questions or to deal with unexpected issues that might arise during the training program.

UNDERSTANDING LEARNING THEORY AND TRAINING AND DEVELOPMENT

Regardless of whether it is training or development, the same outcome is required. That is, the HRM specialists or managers are attempting to help individuals learn! Learning is critical to everyone's success, and it's something that will be with the employees throughout their working lives. But learning for learning's sake does not happen in a vacuum. It is important to understand how people learn—that is, to understand learning principles—in order to design an effective training program.

Learning Principles

Learning is a relatively permanent change in behavior or behavioral potential that results from direct or indirect experience. The intention of training and development is for employees to learn behaviors that are more effective. Thus HRM specialists and managers interested in training and development must understand the fundamentals of learning theory as they apply to training and development. In addition, some organizations in the last few years have begun to pay particular attention to the importance of learning and have even gone so far as to attempt to redefine their organizations as learning organizations. A learning organization is one whose employees continuously attempt to learn new things and to use what they learn to improve product or service quality. Such an organization and its employees see learning not as a discrete activity that starts and stops with conduct of a specific training program but rather as a fundamental and continuous part of the organization and the employee work relationship (Atkinson, 1994).

Beyond this general and fundamental strategic approach to learning, however, a number of more specific learning techniques and principles also relate to employee training and development, such as the use of sound learning principles during the development and implementation of training and development programs. One basic learning principle has to do with motivation. In order to learn, a person must want to learn. In the context of training and development, motivation influences a person's enthusiasm for training and development, keeps attention focused on the training and development activities, and reinforces what is learned. Motivation is influenced by the beliefs and perceptions of the trainee. If a trainee is not motivated, little can be accomplished in a training or development program.

The learning that occurs during training and development must also be reinforced in the organization. Researchers have demonstrated that people learn best with fairly immediate reinforcement of appropriate behavior. Suppose an employee learns how to do a new job in a way that takes a bit more effort but that provides a dramatic improvement in output. When the employee takes this behavior back to the workplace, the employee's supervisor recognizes the new behavior and provides some sort of reinforcement or reward, such as praise and positive comments. To the extent that the manager ignores the new behavior, or even worse, questions or challenges it, then it will not have been reinforced and will likely not be repeated in the future.

In addition, the behaviors that the individual is attempting to learn must be meaningful. That is, the individual who is undergoing the training and development must recognize the behavior and its associated information as being important and relevant to the job situation that she or he faces. Appropriate materials for sequential learning (reading lists, discussion outlines, problems, and cases) must be provided. The trainer acts as a facilitator in the learning process.

Even if the material is meaningful and important, if this message is not communicated effectively to the trainee, she or he will not work hard to master the material, which will presumably cause problems later. The individual must be able to effectively receive the information being imparted and must respond favorably to that material. To a large extent, effective communication depends on matching the training technique with the material to be transmitted. Any learning methods used should also be as varied as possible. It is boredom that destroys learning, not fatigue. Failure to recognize such requirements, along with the inability to effectively use the training technique in question, results in major obstructions to the communication of information. Furthermore, information must be communicated in a unified way and over enough time to allow absorption.

Another important learning principle related to employee training and development is the notion of practice and repetition. The old adage "practice makes perfect" is applicable in learning. It takes time for people to fully internalize what they have learned in training and development. They need time to practice it, to actually use it, and to see how it really affects their work performance. Having trainees perform a particular operation helps them concentrate on the subject. Repeating a task several times develops facility in performing it. Practice and repetition always enhance effective learning.

Another issue that those responsible for training and development must consider is how much practice is enough. Overlearning is practicing beyond the point at which the trainee has mastered and performed the task correctly several times. This concept helps explain the traditional wisdom that once people learn to ride a bicycle or to swim, they never forget how to do so. Overlearning should be used in training and development when the trainee is learning a task in which the first reactions must be absolutely correct. Overlearning is important because (1) it increases retention over time, (2) it makes the behavior more automatic, (3) it increases the quality of performance under stress, and (4) it helps trainees transfer what they have learned to the job setting.

Finally, the material that is being taught must be transferable to the job setting of the individual employee. Mastering material in a training setting is pointless unless the trainee can then apply that material on the job. Two important considerations can facilitate this transfer of training. First, the training setting, or at least the setting in which the new skill or behavior is practiced, should resemble the actual job setting as closely as possible. Managers or trainers cannot always know all the settings in which the material will be applied, but it is nonetheless important to try to anticipate the actual conditions on the job and replicate them in training.

Training is also facilitated if the behaviors learned in training are close to those that will be required on the job. That is, it would be pointless to teach employees to do a job on a piece of equipment if they will be using different equipment that requires different procedures when they actually return to the job setting. In fact, such training would result in negative transfer, which would interfere with performance on the job. But, over time, equipment changes and so procedures learned for one piece of equipment might no longer apply when new equipment is introduced. In this situation it is important to retrain the employees to avoid problems of negative transfer.

Besides the traditional learning theory recommendations for maximizing transfer of learning, there are other guidelines organizations can follow to enhance transfer. Some of these occur during training, whereas others have to do with the pre- and post-training environment. Also, during the training, the trainer should work on building trainee self-efficacy, since it has been shown that efficacy at the end of training predicts the extent to which trainees attempt to use their new skills back on the job (Hill, Smith, and Mann, 1987). In addition, as trainees learn skills, the trainer should ask them to develop an action plan, including measurable goals, for performing the new behaviors back on the job. After the training, trainees should be encouraged to assess themselves against these personal goals on a regular basis (Garavaglia, 1993).

The relapse prevention model suggests that training time should be devoted both to anticipating situations that could cause relapse and to planning strategies for dealing with these situations in advance (Marx, 1982). For instance, if managers who have just been taught to use a participative leadership style expect a relapse to the old autocratic style when working under a tight deadline, they can plan how to avoid the relapse.

Back on the job, a number of factors can affect transfer. One important factor is the opportunity to perform trained tasks. If one is taught how to use a new computer program but does not have on-the-job access to the program for several months after the training, clearly some benefits of the training will be lost. A supportive climate for the new behaviors back in the workplace is another key factor for successful transfer of training. If superiors and peers do not accept or reward new behaviors by trainees, the new behaviors will be given up quickly or may not be tried at all. To facilitate transfer, trainees should be counseled both before and after the training by their immediate superior and receive encouragement to follow through with what they have learned.

Whenever possible, groups or teams that will be working together should be trained together so that they can learn both the training content and how to apply it in the unique mix of personalities and KSAs found in their own team. Intact group training should also facilitate development of group norms that support the new behaviors. Providing reminders or job aids to cue and to support performance also enhances transfer of training. If employees have been taught time management techniques, a cue might be a screen message to each computer user first thing in the morning, asking, "Have you made your to-do list today?" A wallet card listing the steps in a systematic decision-making process or a template to lead the performer through a task would be examples of performance supporting job aids.

Trainers should plan as carefully for transfer of training as they do for the formal portion of the training. The key concept is embedding. Training programs are more effective when they are thoroughly embedded in the work setting. Programs must be consistent with the organization's culture and values; be understood, sold, and supported by trainees' superiors beforehand; and be reinforced by peers, superiors, opportunities, and reward systems afterward.

TRAINING METHODS

This section considers the choice of methods for employee training. With training objectives defined, program content created, instructors selected, and learning principles in mind, those responsible for training must choose appropriate training methods.

New methods available to those in the training profession appear every year. While some are well founded in learning theory or models of behavior change (e.g., behavior modeling), others result more from technological than theoretical developments (e.g., videotapes, computer-based business games). In either case, trainers have a wide variety of methods, materials, and media from which to choose in designing and delivering training initiatives. Which training techniques best suit a particular initiative depends on the learning objectives and cost considerations. Most training initiatives use multiple methods and training aids.

Although no single training method is by nature superior to any other, the goals of a particular training and development effort may be better served by one method than another or one combination of methods versus another combination. The most commonly used training methods are discussed below along with their strengths and weaknesses, beginning with on-the-job training.

On-the-Job Training

On-the-job training (OJT) is hardly a new idea. In fact, it has been around so long that it has become a catch-all term for everything an employee learns outside a formal classroom or group training environment. On-the-job training is considered a work-based training approach because it ties the training and development activities directly to performance of the task. Some experts suggest that as much as 90 percent of all industrial training is conducted on the job (Barron, Berger, and Black, 1997).

More often than not, OJT takes the form of one-on-one instruction: the supervisor or an experienced employee works directly with the trainee, explaining and demonstrating the job, allowing the trainee to practice, checking and correcting the trainee's work. The experienced employee's major role is that of watching over the individual to provide guidance during practice or learning. For example, sales employees use coaching calls in which a senior sales employee coaches a new sales employee (Bernardin and Russell, 1998). Five steps are utilized: (1) observation of the new employee, (2) feedback obtained by the new employee, (3) consensus (i.e., the coach and the new employee arrived at an agreement as to the positives and negatives for the sales call), (4) rehearsal of a new sales call, and (5) review of the employee's performance.

Many forms of OJT focus on exposure to developmental experiences—for example, job enrichment, job rotation, and apprenticeships. Job enrichment gradually builds new duties or more challenging responsibilities into an employee's current position, allowing the person to acquire new skills while on the job. Job rotation allows employees to gain experience at different kinds of narrowly defined jobs in the organization. It is often used to give future managers a broad background. Japanese companies are among the best in the world for providing job rotation. Once employees join a firm, the Japanese company spends an enormous amount of money and time training them and exposing them to various job functions. The training is "just-in-time" so employees are taught skills and then apply their learning within a short period (Overman, 1995).

Many companies in the United States have begun to show greater interest in having their employees be able to perform several job functions so that their workforce is more flexible and interchangeable. General Electric requires all managerial trainees to participate in an extensive job rotation program in which the trainees must perform all jobs they will eventually supervise. This helps managers develop a broader background required for future managerial positions (Bernardin and Russell, 1998).

On-the-job training can save money, since it requires no special training equipment and makes a new hire at least partly productive right away. For mentoring, coaching, and buddy systems, however, these savings must be weighed against the lost productivity of the skilled person assigned to the trainee. For job enrichment and job rotation, the company must anticipate lowered productivity in whatever position the trainee holds. Quality of training can suffer unless a company trains the right employees and managers to serve as coaches and mentors, and selects the right experiences and skills to include in a job rotation or enrichment program.

Properly used OJT can be one of the most effective forms of training. That is why it continues to be one of the most widely used training methods in many organizations.

Programmed or Self-Instruction

Self-instruction lets trainees learn at their own pace. Topics can range from the simple (vocabulary building) to the complex (strategic planning). Programmed instruction (PI) can be carried out by the use of computers or booklets, depending on the need. The method is to present a small amount of information, followed by a simple question that requires an answer on the part of the learner. There is immediate feedback for each response as the learner finds the answer on the next page or elsewhere. The learner knows whether he or she is right or wrong immediately. Since the program is designed to have a low error rate, the learner is motivated further. The main advantage to such an individualized program is that it is self-pacing. For remedial instruction, enrichment material, or short segments, this method works well.

Relative to other training methods, self-instruction offers high mobility and flexibility. It can take place with or without instructors, in a wide variety of learning environments: learning centers, workstations, homes. It can use formats ranging from print texts to instructional tapes to computers and interactive videodiscs. This flexibility minimizes the disruption to work schedules that training programs can often create. While trainers take a back seat to learners in self-instruction, such programs should have someone monitoring and tracking participants' progress.

Programmed instruction is a useful method for self-instruction when the development cost of the materials has been paid by another organization and the materials are available. It might also be a useful method if there are enough trainees to amortize the development cost and if the material presented is suitable to the method.

With traditional training unable to keep pace with demand, computers have been used to fill the gap. Computer-assisted instruction (CAI) has become the fastest-growing segment of the training industry. Although the costs of CAI are high, compared to costs for formulating and delivering teacher-led courses over a period of several years, the results favor CAI.

Knowledge-based or expert computer systems based on artificial intelligence contain information on particular subjects and can give user-specific advice. Combined with interactive video, expert systems can be used as "intelligent" tutors to teach tasks and skills. The systems can also be used in training that is moving from the transfer of knowledge to the application of the system to goal-oriented tasks in the actual work environment (Becker and Eveleth, 1995).

Computer-Based Training

The rise of computers at work has not only increased the need for computer skills training but also created new training formats. Computer-based training (CBT), or computer-assisted instruction, is interactive, self-paced instruction using software teaching tools. In this situation a trainee sits at a personal computer and operates special training software.

Computer-based training can take a variety of forms: Some employers have formed software libraries containing copies of different tutorial programs that trainees can check out to work on at home. Other companies have staffed computer labs where employees can drop by to practice, with personal assistance available if needed. Still other organizations install learning software on workstation computers, which allows employees to switch back and forth between job applications and training programs as their workload demands. Some organizations even conduct online training, making training programs available to employees via the Internet or the company intranet.

Computer-Based Performance Support Systems. Some companies are attempting to improve the links between training and job applications with "performance support systems," a form of interactive learning. This computer-based tool, also called an electronic support system, a performance support tool, or a knowledge support system, helps employees on the job at the time they need specific information. Although individual programs vary by job, all systems contain a database and a help system.

Performance support systems are useful because participants in a training program can retain only a limited amount of information—and usually not as much as has been taught. With a performance support system, however, employees can get training help and information at the exact time needed—the "trainable moment."

Computer-related "knowledge" jobs in which employees follow certain specified procedures—such as a bank teller position—lend themselves most readily to performance support systems. But these systems also help train employees on job tasks that require problem-solving and decision-making skills, such as performance appraisals. Although the costs of developing or purchasing a performance support system can be very high, this expense often is offset by savings realized through improved training delivered in a shorter time.

Distance Learning

As many organizations hone their in-house training and development efforts, they are increasingly receptive to so-called "distance learning." What distance learning really does is bring learning closer, often as close as your computer screen. The other thing is that organizations have continued to wrestle with the realization that face-to-face education is time out of doing work. And when you factor in traveling time and consumption costs like hotels and meals when large groups get together, the cost of traditional training and development delivery rises even higher.

With distance learning, a single trainer at one or a number of broadcast sites can deliver a single program, either in real time or synchronously, to multiple learning sites around the world. While it is not clear at this time whether distance learning will ever be a full substitute for traditional live classroom training, it is very likely that at the least modularized components will be delivered electronically more and more often as technology improves.

While there are those who believe distance learning will completely replace the old-fashioned classroom-style training we are all familiar with, the reality is that people are always going to value reaching out and shaking hands, gauging body language, etc. That extrasensory element is very important for training professionals, as well. They very often need that feedback to judge and direct the way a course is proceeding.

Given the current state of technology, it is questionable whether distance learning is viable for all types of training and development. Casual evidence suggests that distance learning works better with more technical course material (e.g., accounting or statistics) that can be presented via lecture/discussion and less well with "softer" course material (e.g., team building and strategic thinking) that lends itself to more interactive learning between the trainer and the participants and among the participants themselves. Furthermore, it appears that distance learning is more effective and better received at the lower and middle levels of employees, especially when the focus is on hard, technical skills training.

However, given the potential cost reduction, greater efficiency, and convenience of distance learning efforts, it is a good bet that many organizations will gravitate toward this method and will continue to explore ways of making it more effective. In the near term, experimentation with different formats and applications will continue. In the long run, technological breakthroughs will likely give impetus to dramatic change.

The Internet

The Internet offers ways to increase learning, link resources, and share valuable knowledge within and outside an organization. People can use the Internet to deliver training in the following ways, either individually or in combination with other instruction methods: (1) e-mail for accessing course material and sharing information; (2) bulletin boards, forums, and news groups for posting comments and questions; (3) interactive tutorials that let trainees take courses online; (4) real-time conferencing placing all participants in the same virtual classroom; and (5) documents, tutorials, and software that trainees can download.

The emergence of inexpensive Internet technologies has enabled training professionals to effectively conduct training and provide support to their trainees via the Internet. The advantages of Internet-based training (IBT) are universal language, easy and affordable distribution, fresh content, and cheap technology. Five basic levels of IBT have been developed (Kruse, 1997). The first level involves the facilitation of communication between trainers and trainees, while the second is described by the creation of a complete online library of hyperlinked references. The third level involves the automation of the administration of tests and surveys, while the fourth is about the distribution of computer-based training. Finally, the fifth level offers delivery of interactive multimedia in real-time across an organizational network.

Many of the benefits of IBT are a result of interactivity. This is the user's ability to respond to or interact with the software. For example, reading text on the computer is not interactive because the reader passively absorbs information. Computer games, on the other hand, are highly interactive, because the user decides how events will unfold.

The more engaging and interactive the training, the more effective the learning. With IBT, some applications such as hypertext documentation are passive and should be considered support tools. Only when an IBT application is interactive will companies reduce learning time and increase retention through their Internet-based training.

Intranets

In simple terms, an intranet is the descriptive term being used for the implementation of Internet technologies within a corporate organization rather than for external connection to the global Internet (Gery, 1996). The primary advantage of an intranet lies in the ability to focus the content to a particular purpose while conquering many of the technology limitations inherent in the World Wide Web. Intranet developers are able to limit the access of users, permitting the passing of sensitive information. They also can control bandwidth reservation, assuring quality connection between client and server (Sonntag, 1997).

It is a continual challenge for training professionals to keep courseware and training materials up to date, regardless of changes to company products, or strategic direction. A Web site on an intranet is an effective tool to tackle this problem. Those responsible for training and development in their organizations have an obligation to make information readily and meaningfully accessible. With an intranet, trainers can provide employees access to current training materials that incorporate text, graphics, video and audio, and make them available in a self-directed mode at the PC and accessible regardless of geographic location. Through an intranet, training professionals can permit a high degree of interactivity, enabling topical discussion on bulletin boards, testing, research, etc. For example, a new field-sales hire in Germany may want to simply review the "Value Added Selling" portion of the new hire orientation training. At the click of a hypertext link, and at his or her convenience, the new hire finds the information without having to rummage through reams of desktop manuals.

Some intranets can also support the delivery of CD-ROM–based training. As CD-ROM programs continue to become more sophisticated, trainers can learn more about them through the use of "authoring" software, which ranges in difficulty from straightforward, template-based programs to more complex applications requiring expert programming skills.

Experts warn that although technologies like intranets may provide cost savings, these technologies should not be thought of as cheap alternatives (Greco, 1997). In many instances the mistake people make with intranets is that they don't design programming to maximize the benefits. For example, there needs to be a lot less reading, and information has to be broken down into chunks. Designers who use such technologies should also make sure that their sites include lots of graphics and offer a good use of the screen in terms of navigation.

Simulations

Particularly effective in training are simulations. Simulations are training tools that attempt to replicate the actual job duties and/or working environment. They vary from simple and inexpensive to highly complex and costly designs. Organizations often use simulations when the information to be mastered is complex, the equipment used on the job is expensive, and/or the cost of a wrong decision is quite high.

The airline industry has long used simulators to train pilots. Flight simulations often include motion in addition to visual and auditory realism. This aspect substantially increases the cost of the simulation but makes the training even more realistic. Another type of simulation confronts trainee doctors with an accident victim arriving at the emergency room. The trainees choose from a menu of options, with the patient dying if the decision is delayed too long or is incorrect.

Traditionally, simulators have been considered separate from CBT. With recent advances in multimedia technology, however, the distinctions between these two methods have blurred considerably. In fact, as the technology develops, simulators are becoming more affordable, and hence accessible, for a wider range of organizations.

In-baskets, one of the least expensive simulations, consist of nothing more than the incoming materials, all demanding action, that might get deposited daily on a manager's or secretary's desk. Vestibule training, on the other hand, involves setting up a classroom that reproduces the equipment and work environment, whether an assembly line, switchboard, or city block, found on the job. For certain positions, such as nuclear power plant operator or airline pilot, where the consequences of mistakes could destroy costly machinery or endanger lives, trainees use "simulators" that imitate the functions performed by actual equipment.

With the exception of OJT, simulations are the most realistic and relevant training technique. Unlike OJT, however, simulations allow trainees time to practice skills, receive feedback, and engage in trial-and-error learning—without the embarrassment, cost, time pressures, or other negative consequences of making mistakes while performing a job.

Virtual Reality

Virtual reality (VR) uses a number of technologies to replicate the entire real-life working environment rather than just several aspects of it, as in simulations. Within these three-dimensional environments, a user can interact with and manipulate objects in real time.

Tasks that are good candidates for VR training are those that require rehearsal and practice, working from a remote location, or visualizing objects and processes that are not usually accessible. VR training is also excellent for tasks in which there is a high potential for damage to equipment or danger to individuals. One such task is marshaling, an Air Force operational job in which a person on the ground uses hand and arm signals to help a plane land. Imagine the stress you'd feel the first time you rehearsed these maneuvers with a multiton aircraft approaching you at high speed! It's easy to see why VR training is used to prepare people to handle the real situation (Middleton, 1992).

Early studies have indicated a great deal of success with VR training. The immersion of trainees in a virtual world may be the key to this success. The VR experience provides a sense of self-location in a simulated environment in which objects appear solid and can be navigated around, touched, lifted, and so on. This sense of immersion is probably connected to the excitement and motivation often reported by VR trainees. For example, following VR training of space shuttle flight control and engineering personnel at NASA, trainees commented on how good the training was and how it was the "neatest" training experience they'd ever had (Psotka, 1995). Such trainee experiences can only add to the effectiveness of VR training.

One drawback of VR training is that the technology is meant for one user at a time rather than multiple participants. Thus, VR training has not been applicable to team training situations. This limitation may soon be overcome, however. The U.S. military is currently developing a VR training system that allows for the cooperative efforts of multiple trainees (Mastaglio and Callahan, 1995). The system includes over 50 different human–computer interfaces and can use one of three simulated terrains, with each terrain representing over 15,000 square kilometers of virtual space. The training exercises are based on scenarios used with combat units in field training. While the system is still being refined, it may represent the next wave of virtual training. The prevalence of teams in the workplace demands effective techniques for improving cooperation among people and work groups. VR training may soon be able to meet this need (Gomez-Mejia, Balkin, and Cardy, 1998).

Games and Exercises

Games and exercises are one of the most creative and enjoyable training methods. Most training games and exercises have competition (either individual or group), "playing rules," and a designated finish time or final score. These games simulate competition between departments or with other organizations. At least two teams, each of which represents an organization, make decisions concerning their company's operation. Decisions can be made about production, marketing, finance, human resources utilization, and other challenges. Decisions are based on a set of specified economic theories, presented as a model of the economy.

Some simple management games are not based on analyzing complex problems. Instead, emphasis is placed on making good judgments in a minimum amount of time, based on specific problems and limited rules. In simple games, effective strategies can be reached without making too many decisions and without having to use large amounts of managerial know-how. These management games may oversimplify business relationships and give the impression that running a company can be easy—when, in fact, even the simplest management decisions require the consideration of many factors.

When the model is fairly simple, a referee can be responsible for calculating outcomes. When the model is complex, a computer may be used. The game can be continuous: Teams receive all or part of the results of their decisions on which they make new decisions, thus continuing the game.

As learning activities, games offer a number of advantages. They add variety and zest to training programs and get learners actively involved. They allow trainees to acquire knowledge, practice and apply skills, review materials, and ultimately achieve course objectives. They are versatile and easily incorporated into different types of training, whether an instructor-led classroom course or a computer-based instructional program.

While games can enhance training by making learning fun, they will only waste time unless trainers relate these exercises to course objectives. After the game has ended, a trainer should review what happened during the game, have participants say what they learned, and ask trainees how they can apply this learning to their jobs.

Case Studies

Case studies use factual, real-life events to illustrate organizational problems and issues. Case studies can be presented through lecture, film, or video, but most case studies are written and handed out as course materials. Participants read the case study and use what they have learned in the program to analyze the situation.

A case study can involve guided analysis, with formal questions prepared by the instructor for individuals or groups to answer. More challenging case studies use a less structured format and exercise two types of problem-solving skills:

1. Diagnostic analyses ask trainees to identify the underlying cause of a particular problem. Prescriptive analyses require learners to figure out solutions to a particular problem.
2. Case studies tie course concepts and skills into practical situations. This link, along with the chance to exchange ideas and practice problem solving, enhances trainees' interest and involvement in the program.

Trainers can use this technique for either individual or small-group instruction. However, case studies often are complicated and work best when trainees have good analytical reasoning abilities. When presented in a written format, case studies also require that trainees possess well-developed verbal communication and reading comprehension skills.

Classroom Instruction

Classroom lectures are used in many organizations to impart information to trainees. Classroom lectures are oral presentations covering particular topics and concepts. Lectures can last an entire class period and are ideal for presenting large amounts of information to groups. Lecturettes are short lectures lasting less than 15 minutes. They provide participants with the theoretical background needed for learning new skills. Lecturettes can be combined with question-and-answer sessions, discussions, or other instructional methods.

Discussions involve more interchange and less structure than other oral instructional methods. Discussions encourage participants and trainers to freely exchange knowledge, ideas, and opinions on a particular subject. Discussions work well when the information presented can be applied in different ways. Discussions also give trainers feedback on how employees are using the knowledge or skills they have learned.

Although widely viewed as "boring," classroom instruction can be exciting if other presentation techniques are integrated with the lecture. For example, a videotape could complement the discussion by providing realistic examples of the lecture material.

Demonstrations, Behavior Modeling, and Role-Plays

Demonstrations are visual instructional techniques: The instructor performs the behavior or skills to be learned and the trainees learn by watching. Modeling takes demonstrations one step further by having trainees learn by doing, not just by watching. First, the trainer demonstrates the desired performance, and then participants model the skill or behavior. The trainer provides feedback to trainees, with additional modeling and practice as needed.

Role-plays are the most sophisticated of these three instructional methods. After the trainer models the desired skills or behaviors, trainees are asked not just to imitate the trainer's performance but also to apply these skills and behaviors to a sample situation in which different individuals play certain roles. Solving and discussing problems helps trainees learn technical material and content, and role-plays are an excellent way to apply the interpersonal skills being emphasized in the training. If done well, role-plays give trainees the opportunity to integrate new information with job behavior (Estabrooke and Fay, 1992).

All three techniques can be used in either one-on-one or group instruction. Each method can enhance training by illustrating how to apply instruction in practice. Demonstrations are ideal for basic skills training, while role playing works well for building complex behaviors, such as interpersonal or management skills. Of the three tools, demonstrations are the least threatening to trainees, since they are not called upon to perform themselves. Modeling and role-plays, on the other hand, allow trainers to assess participants' skill levels and to make sure that trainees can apply what they have seen.

SELECTING AND COMBINING METHODS

To choose the training and development method (or combination of methods) that best fits a given situation, trainers should first define carefully what they wish to teach. That is the purpose of the needs assessment phase discussed earlier in this chapter. Only then can those responsible for training and development choose a method that best fits these requirements. To be useful, the method should meet the minimal conditions needed for effective learning to take place. That is, the training method(s) should: motivate the trainee to improve his or her performance, clearly illustrate desired KSAOCs, allow the trainee to participate actively, provide an opportunity for practice, provide timely feedback on the trainee's performance; provide some means for reinforcement while the trainee learns; be structured from simple to complex tasks, be adaptable to specific problems, and encourage positive transfer from the training to the job.

As evidenced from the discussion to this point there are a wide variety of methods, materials, and media from which to choose in designing and delivering training. Which training techniques best suit a particular program depends on course content and cost considerations. Most training initiatives can use multiple instructional methods and training aids.

Each of the methods described has certain strengths and weaknesses. As a result of the strengths and weaknesses of the various methods, those responsible for training and development can handle the trade-offs in at least two ways. They can perform a systematic trade-off analysis and choose the most appropriate training methodology. They can also combine training methods. It is apparent from the discussion of the training methods earlier that with a careful analysis, trainers should be able to combine different methods and come up with a more complete and efficient training system. This is in fact what many of those responsible for training are currently doing. In many cases those responsible for training and development efforts will use several different techniques. For example, teaching supervisors how to give performance feedback may first begin with a lecture or overview of the performance appraisal process, followed by small-group discussions or videotapes depicting effective coaching, and then role-plays to have supervisors practice their feedback skills (Bernardin and Russell, 1998).

TEAM TRAINING AND DEVELOPMENT

Team training involves coordinating the performance of individuals who work together to achieve a common goal. Such training is an important issue when information must be shared and individuals affect the overall performance of the group.

There is a core set of skills that characterize effective teamwork. These skills include adaptability, shared awareness of situations, performance monitoring and feedback, leadership/team management, interpersonal skills, coordination, communication, and decision-making skills. Attitudinal skills that characterize effective teamwork include beliefs about the importance of teamwork skills, belief in placing the team's goals above those of individual members, mutual trust, and shared vision.

Team training takes many forms. Two specific team training strategies include cross-training and coordination training (Clements, Wagner, and Roland, 1995). Cross-training involves having team members understand and practice each other's skills so that members are prepared to step in and take another's place should someone temporarily or permanently leave the team. Coordination training involves training the team in how to share information and decision-making responsibilities to maximize team performance. Coordination training is especially important for commercial aviation and surgical teams who are in charge of monitoring different aspects of equipment and the environment but also must share information to make the most effective decision regarding patient care or aircraft safety and performance. Team leader training refers to training that the team manager or facilitator receives. This may involve training the manager how to resolve conflict within the team or how to help the team coordinate activities or other team skills.

MANAGEMENT DEVELOPMENT

Manager effectiveness has an enormous impact on contemporary organizational success and competitive advantage. As an organization grows and matures, high-quality management talent is crucial to its success. Organizations must therefore provide instruction for their managers and their high-potential management candidates to help these individuals perform their current or future jobs with the utmost proficiency (Kleinman and Faley, 1992).

Management development is important for new managers because these individuals really need instruction in how to perform their new supervisory jobs. Yet, organizations often allow these individuals to make the transition to management with little or no training, leaving them with feelings of frustration, inadequacy, and dismay (Phillips, 1986).

Formal training of supervisors and junior managers is often done by in-house trainers or by training consultants. Development of senior managers and executives sometimes takes place at universities, in programs of one to four weeks' duration. Some of the largest and most successful organizations have what amounts to their own "university," such as General Electric's Crotonville Management Development Institute in New York State. There is an increasing trend toward corporate universities and customized courses for senior managers and away from generic MBA-type courses for management development (O'Reilly, 1993). World-class management development systems are driven by clearly defined business needs and focus on the skills needed to perform now and in the future business environment.

EVALUATING TRAINING AND DEVELOPMENT PHASE

Evaluation is the final phase in the training and development process. Evaluation is the determination of the extent to which the training and development activities have met their goals. Unfortunately, the evaluation is often done poorly or ignored altogether. One reason for this is that organizations simply tend to assume that training and development will work. Another is that an individual who champions a training and development program may feel threatened by the prospect of an objective evaluation of the program's effectiveness.

The basic approach to evaluation should be to determine the extent to which the training or development program has met the objectives identified prior to the training and development. Planning for the evaluation should start at the same time that planning for the training and development program begins. If the goals of the program are clearly stated as specific objectives, the appropriate evaluation method can be implemented at the same time as the program.

Many ways of evaluating training and development programs have been proposed, including immediate reactions to the training, changes in productivity, changes in attitudes (e.g., satisfaction with job, stress, role conflict, knowledge of work procedures, satisfaction with supervisor, and satisfaction with diversity programs), benefit gains, and cost savings (Gerson and McCleskey, 1998). However, there are usually three types of criteria for evaluating training: internal, external, and participants' reaction. Internal criteria are directly associated with the content of the program—for example, whether the employee learned the facts or guidelines covered in the program. External criteria are related more to the ultimate purpose of the program—for example, improving the effectiveness of the employee. Possible external criteria include job performance rating, the degree of learning transferred from training and development sessions to on-the-job situations, and increases in sales volume or decreases in turnover. Participants' reaction, or how the trainees feel about the benefits of a specific training or development experience, is commonly used as an internal criterion.

Most experts argue that it is more effective to use multiple criteria to evaluate training (Kirkpatrick, 1996). Others contend that a single criterion, such as the extent of transfer of training to on-the-job performance or other aspects of performance, is a satisfactory approach to evaluation.

One view that most experts agree on is that a systematic or multiple-criterion approach to training evaluation such as that developed by Kirkpatrick (1996) should be used. He suggests measuring the following:

- *Reaction to training*: Did the trainees like the program? Was the instruction clear and helpful? Do the trainees believe that they learned the material?
- *Learning*: Did the trainees actually acquire the KSAs that were taught? Can they talk about things they could not talk about before? Can they demonstrate appropriate behaviors in training (role-play)?
- *Behavior or performance change*: Can trainees now do things they could not do before (e.g., negotiate or conduct an appraisal interview)? Can they demonstrate new behaviors on the job? Is performance on the job better?
- *Results*: Did the training produce tangible results in terms of productivity, cost savings, response time, safety, employee retention, and/or customer satisfaction?

Kirkpatrick suggests that the last three levels of evaluation may form a hierarchy. Change farther up the hierarchy of outcomes is unlikely unless change has occurred lower in the hierarchy. That is, if no learning has occurred, it is unlikely that on-the-job behavior will change. If behavior does not change, it is unlikely that measurable improvements in results will be observed. In the end, regardless of which approach or criteria organizations decide to use to evaluate training and development initiatives, they must recognize that evaluation provides the opportunity to make decisions about whether to continue such efforts and how to improve them.

SUMMARY

Training and developing human resources is key to organizational success. Learning is the key to successful training and development and to the organization's continued survival. New employee orientation is one important part of an organization's training and development efforts. In planning an orientation for new employees, HRM personnel and other managers must deal with basic issues that include the content of the orientation, the length of the orientation, who will actually conduct the orientation, and evaluation or follow-up of the effort.

Training needs assessment is the starting point for any employee training and development program. This process involves consideration of the needs analysis, the determination of training and development goals, and decisions regarding in-house training versus outsourced training and development.

The actual design and implementation of training and development are key components of effective programs. Besides determining the training content and methods, consideration must be given to learning principles that will impact the success of the training and development programs.

There are a number of techniques and methods that can be used for the actual delivery of information, and most training and development programs use a variety of these techniques and methods. Team training and management development are two other special types of training and development that organizations use to improve their human resources in general and the organization in particular.

Organizations need to do a good job of evaluating their training and development initiatives. There is no reason to neglect this important activity, given the high cost of most training and development programs and how easy it is to measure their effectiveness.

REFERENCES

Atkinson, M. 1994. Build learning into work. *HRMagazine* (September): 60–64.

Barron, J.M., Berger, M.C., and Black, D.A. 1997. *On-the-job training*. Kalamazoo, MI: Upjohn Institute.

Becker, T.E., and Eveleth, D.M. 1995. Foci and bases of employee commitment: Implications for job performance. *Academy of Management Journal*, Best Paper Proceedings, pp. 307–312.

Bernardin, H.J., and Russell, J.E. 1998. *Human resource management: An experiential approach*. Boston: Irwin McGraw-Hill.

Carnevale, A.P. 1990. America and the new economy. *Training and Development Journal* (November): 31–52.

Clements, C., Wagner, R.J., and Roland, C.C. 1995. The ins and outs of experiential training. *Training and Development* (February): 52–56.

Estabrooke, R.M., and Fay, N.F. 1992. Answering the call of "tailored training." *Training* (October): 29, 85–88.

Gagne, R.M. 1984. Learning outcomes and their effects: Useful categories of human performance. *American Psychologist* 39: 377–385.

Garavaglia, P.L. 1993. How to ensure transfer of training. *Training and Development* (October): 63–68.

Gephart, M.A., Marsick, V.J., Van Buren, M.E., and Spiro, M.S. 1996. Learning organizations come alive. *Training and Development* 50: 35–45.

Gerson, G., and McCleskey, C. 1998. Numbers help make a training decision that counts. *HRMagazine* (July): 51–58.

Gery, G. 1996. *Electronic performance support systems.* Boston: Weingarten Publications, Inc.

Gomez-Mejia, L.R., Balkin, D.B., and Cardy, R.L. 1998. *Managing human resources.* Upper Saddle River, NJ: Prentice Hall.

Greco, J. 1997. Long-distance learning. *Journal of Business Strategy* 18:53–54.

Hill, T., Smith, N.D., and Mann, M.F. 1987. Role of efficacy expectations in predicting the decision to use advanced technologies: The case of computers. *Journal of Applied Psychology* 72: 307–313.

Kirkpatrick, D.L. 1996. Great ideas revisited. *Training and Development* (January): 54–59.

Kleinman, L.S., and Faley, R.H. 1992. Identifying the training needs of managers in high technology firms: A case study. In L.R. Gomez-Mejia and M.W. Lawless (eds.), *Advances in global high-technology management*, Vol. 1. Greenwich, CT: JAI Press.

Kruse, K. 1997. Five levels of Internet-based training. *Training and Development* (February): 60–61.

Linde, K.V., Horney, N., and Koonce, R. 1997. Seven ways to make your training department one of the best. *Training and Development* (August): 20–28.

Marx, R.D. 1982. Relapse prevention for managerial training: A model for maintenance of behavior changes. *Academy of Management Review* 7: 443–451.

Mastaglio, T.W., and Callahan, R. 1995. A large scale complex virtual environment for team training. *Computer* 28: 49–56.

Middleton, T. 1992. The potential of virtual reality technology for training. *Journal of Interactive Instructional Development* (Spring): 8–11.

O'Reilly, B. 1993. How execs learn now. *Fortune* (April 15): 52–58.

Overman, S. 1995. Japan shares ways to improve job training. *HRMagazine* (January): 60, 62, 64.

Phillips, J.J. 1986. Corporate boot camp for new appointed supervisors. *Personnel Journal* (March): 70–74.

Psotka, J. 1995. Immersive training systems: Virtual reality and education and training. *Instructional Science* 23: 405–431.

Senge, D. 1991. The learning organization made plain and simple. *Training and Development Journal* (October): 37, 44.

Smith, T.L. 1995. The basics of basic skills training. *Training and Development* (April): 44–49.

Sonntag, E. 1997. Emerging PC training technologies. http://www.trainingnet.com.

Tyler, K. 1998. Take new employee orientation off the back burner. *HRMagazine* (May): 49–54.

Chapter 8

Performance Appraisal

INTRODUCTION

This chapter focuses on performance management systems in general and their key component, performance appraisal, in particular—the HRM activity designed to provide performance feedback to employees. This feedback serves a variety of purposes and makes potentially significant contributions to organizations and individual employees alike. Indeed, we can almost think of performance-related feedback as being like a ship's navigational system. Without such a system, the ship's captain would have no way of knowing where the ship was, where it had come from, and where it was heading. Similarly, without an effective performance management system, organizations and individual employees would have no way of knowing how well they were doing or where improvements might be needed.

Performance appraisal is the process by which an employee's contribution to the organization during a specified period of time is assessed. Some organizations actually use the term performance appraisal, whereas others prefer to use terms such as performance evaluation, performance review, annual review, employee appraisal, or employee evaluation. Regardless of the term used, this chapter is concerned with preparing managers and other employees to cope with today's workforce diversity in the management and appraisal of performance. More specifically, the purpose of this chapter is to provide an understanding of performance management in general and its key component, performance appraisal, in particular. This includes the major appraisal techniques, discussing various rating methods, identifying several performance evaluation problems, reviewing how to conduct effective performance appraisals, and explaining how to evaluate an organization's performance appraisal system.

THE IMPORTANCE OF PERFORMANCE APPRAISAL

Strategically, it is hard to imagine a more important HRM system than performance appraisal. Organizations strive to do the following at all levels: (1) design jobs and work systems to accomplish organizational goals, (2) hire individuals with the abilities and desire to perform effectively, and (3) train, motivate, and reward employees for performance and productivity. It is this sequence that allows organizations to disperse their strategic goals throughout the organization. Within this context, the evaluation of performance is a control mechanism that provides not only feedback to individuals but also an organizational assessment of how things are progressing. Without performance information, managers of an organization can only guess whether employees are working toward the right goals, in the correct way, and to the desired standard (Gephart, 1995).

One of the most important activities of HRM personnel is maintaining and enhancing the workforce. After all the effort and costs involved in the recruiting and selection process, it is important to develop employees so that they are using their fullest capabilities, thus improving the effectiveness of the organization. The development of a standard performance appraisal process will help organizations improve their bottom-line performance, uplift motivational efforts, and resolve most morale problems.

In the future, the only successful organizations will be those that are able to increase productivity through improving the performance of their human resources. Therefore, all managers need to understand and appreciate the importance of performance appraisal as well as the various goals associated with effective performance appraisal. Moreover, HRM personnel can best serve their role as a center of expertise by ensuring that everyone in the organization has confidence in the performance appraisal systems used and that their performance appraisals fulfill their goals.

Traditionally, the HRM literature has considered as separate and distinct the issues of which types of performance to measure, methods of measuring importance, who should rate performance, and methods of performance. Today, however, organizations have moved to focusing on developing performance management systems that are broader and more encompassing and that are the ultimate goal of performance appraisal activities. Performance management is discussed in the next section.

PERFORMANCE MANAGEMENT

Employee job performance is an important issue for all employers. However, satisfactory performance does not happen automatically; it is more likely with a good performance management system. Performance management is the integration of performance appraisal systems with broader HRM systems as a means of aligning employees' work behaviors with the organization's goals. Thus, a performance management system consists of the processes used to identify, encourage, measure, evaluate, improve, and reward employee performance at work.

There is no one best way to manage performance. Whatever system is adopted needs to be congruent with the culture and principles that pervade the organization (Ghorparde and Chen, 1995). However, most systems of performance management have several parts:

1. *Defining performance.* It is desirable to carefully define performance so that it supports the organization's strategic goals. The setting of clear goals for individual employees is a critical component of performance management.
2. *Empowering employees.* It is desirable to empower workers to deal with performance contingencies. Thus, if interaction with a supplier about timeliness of deliveries is required for an employee to achieve goals successfully, the employee is authorized to handle the situation.
3. *Measuring performance.* Measuring performance does not need to be narrowly conceived but can bring together multiple types of performance measured in various ways. The key is to measure often and use the information for midcourse corrections.
4. *Feedback and coaching.* In order to improve performance, employees need information (feedback) about their performance, along with guidance in reaching the next level of result. Without frequent feedback, employees are unlikely to know that behavior is out of synchronization with relevant goals or what to do about it (Cardy and Dobbins, 1997).

The purpose of performance management is to make sure that employee goals, employee behaviors used to achieve those goals, and feedback of information about performance are all linked to the organizational strategy. It is important to note that although performance management typically relies heavily upon performance appraisals, performance management is a broader and more encompassing process and is the ultimate goal of performance appraisal activities.

THE PURPOSE OF EMPLOYEE PERFORMANCE APPRAISALS

Two decades ago, the typical supervisor or manager would sit down annually with his or her employees, individually, and critique their job performance. The purpose was to review how well they did toward achieving their work goals. Those employees who failed to achieve their goals found the performance appraisal to result in little more than their supervisor documenting a list of their shortcomings. Of course, since the performance appraisal is a key determinant in pay adjustments and promotion decisions, anything to do with appraising job performance struck fear into the hearts of employees. Not surprisingly, in this climate managers often wanted to avoid the whole appraisal process, and in many instances formal appraisal programs yielded disappointing results. Their failure was often due to a lack of top-management information and support, unclear performance standards, lack of important skills for managers, too many forms to complete, or the use of appraisal for conflicting purposes.

Today, successful organizations and managers treat the performance appraisal as an evaluation and development tool, as well as a formal legal document. Appraisals review past performance—emphasizing positive accomplishments as well as deficiencies and drafting detailed plans for future development. By emphasizing the future as well as the past, documenting performance effectively, and providing feedback in a constructive manner, employees are less likely to respond defensively to feedback, and the appraisal process is more likely to motivate employees to improve where necessary. The performance evaluation also serves a vital organizational need by providing the documentation necessary for any personnel action that might be taken against an employee.

Given the importance of performance appraisal, the goals of performance appraisal are almost self-evident. For example, a basic goal of any appraisal system is to provide valid and reliable measures of employee performance along several dimensions. Appraisals tell managers who is performing well and who is not as well as indicate the areas of specific strengths and weaknesses for each person being rated. Another goal of appraisals is to provide information in a form that is useful and appropriate for the organization with regard to HRM planning, recruiting and selection, compensation, training and development, and the legal context. But the ultimate goal for any organization using performance appraisals is to be able to improve performance on the job.

All managers need to understand and appreciate the importance of performance appraisal as well as the various goals associated with effective performance appraisal. Moreover, HRM personnel can best serve their role as a center of expertise by ensuring that everyone in the organization has confidence in the performance appraisal systems used and that performance appraisals fulfill their goals.

When Should Appraisals Occur?

Ideally, performance appraisals should occur both formally and informally. Formal performance reviews should be conducted once a year at a minimum, but twice a year is better. Informal performance appraisals and feedback should complement the formal appraisal system. The ultimate goal is to establish an effective "performance management system" where performance is monitored and managed overall, not just appraised in a once a year session.

Continuous feedback is primarily important in letting employees know how they are doing. Without constructive feedback, employees tend to assume that their performance is acceptable, and problems may continue. Without positive feedback or praise, employees begin to feel that their hard work is unappreciated and may decide to stop putting forth so much effort. Employees need and expect frequent communication and feedback about their performance—not just during the formal appraisal interview session. Managers must make it a habit to get out among their employees throughout the day or week and not wait for their employees to come to them. This type of frequent interaction also tells employees that their manager thinks they are important.

Who Performs the Performance Appraisal?

Performance appraisal can be done by anyone familiar with the performance of individual employees. Possibilities include (1) supervisors who rate their employees, (2) employees who rate their superiors, (3) team members who rate each other, (4) employees who rate themselves, and (5) customers.

Supervisory ratings of employees. Traditional rating of employees is based on the assumption that the immediate supervisor is the person most qualified to evaluate the employee's performance realistically, objectively, and fairly. An employee's immediate supervisor is usually in the best position to observe and judge how well the employee has performed on the job. There are some situations in which a "consensus" or "pooled" type of appraisal may be done by a group of managers—for example, if an employee works for several managers because of rotating work-shift schedules or because the organization has a matrix structure. Some organizations have implemented work team concepts that expand the manager's span of control, and some have become leaner and eliminated middle-level management positions. It is not practical for a manager to track the performance of 20, 30, or even 50 employees and evaluate their performance objectively. This restructuring of authority and responsibility could lead to grave inequities in the performance appraisal system. To ensure that employees feel that the appraisal process is fair and just, each evaluator must understand what is necessary for successful job performance and be able to apply the standards. A supervisor's appraisal typically is reviewed by his or her immediate boss to make sure that a proper job of appraisal has been done.

Employees who rate their superiors. The concept of having supervisors and managers rated by employees or group members is being used in a number of organizations today. A prime example of this type of rating takes place in colleges and universities, where students evaluate the performance of professors in the classroom. Industry also uses employee ratings for management development purposes.

Team/peer ratings. The use of peer groups as raters is another type of appraisal with potential both to help and to hurt. For example, if a group of salespeople meets as a committee to talk about one another's ratings, then they may share ideas that could be used to improve the performance of lower-rated individuals. Alternatively, the criticisms could lead to future work relationships being affected negatively. An advantage of using peers or team members in a performance appraisal process is that by definition they do have expert knowledge of job content, and they may have more of an opportunity than their supervisor to observe the performance of a given worker on a day-to-day basis.

Peer ratings are especially useful when supervisors do not have the opportunity to observe each employee's performance, but other work group members do. Team/peer evaluations are best used for development purposes rather than for administrative purposes. However, some contend that any performance appraisal, including team/peer ratings, can affect teamwork and participative management efforts negatively.

Employee self-appraisal. In this case, the employee evaluates herself or himself with the techniques used by other evaluators. The rationale behind this approach is that more than any other single person in the organization, an individual is in the best position to understand his or her own strengths and weaknesses and the extent to which he or she has been performing at an appropriate level. Of course, the biggest negative aspect of using self-ratings is that there is a tendency on the part of many people to inflate their own performance.

Self-appraisals seem to be used more often for developmental (as opposed to evaluative) aspects of performance evaluation. They are also used to evaluate an employee who works in physical isolation.

Customers. A final source of information in the performance appraisal system is customers. The dramatic increase in the service sector of the U.S. economy in recent years has resulted in a major push toward the use of customers as a source of information in performance appraisal. The inclusion of customers might be accomplished through such things as having customers fill out feedback forms. Some restaurants, like Chili's and Red Lobster, for example, insert brief feedback forms in their meal-check folders and ask customers to rate the server, the cook, and other restaurant personnel on various characteristics relevant to the meal. The advantage of this method is that customers are the lifeblood of an organization, and it is very helpful to managers to know the extent to which customers feel that employees are doing a good job. On the other hand, this method may be expensive to develop and reproduce and may ignore aspects of the job the customer doesn't see (e.g., cooperation with other employees).

Multisource, or 360-degree, feedback. One important thing for any manager to recognize is that each source of performance appraisal information is subject to various weaknesses and shortcomings. Consequently, many organizations find it appropriate and effective to rely on a variety of information sources in the conduct of a performance appraisal. That is, organizations may gather information from both supervisors and peers. Indeed, some organizations gather information from all the sources described in this section. Multisource feedback recognizes that the manager is no longer the sole source of performance appraisal information. For 360-degree feedback to be effective, the person managing the review process should ensure that the responses are anonymous. Employees especially may be afraid to respond honestly if they think that the person being reviewed will retaliate for negative comments. Anonymity is greater if the responses are pooled into a single report rather than presented one by one. Collecting appraisals from more than three or four people also increases the likelihood of protecting respondents' privacy.

Multisource approaches to performance appraisal are possible solutions to well-documented dissatisfaction with today's legally necessary administrative performance appraisal. But a number of questions arise as multisource appraisals become more common. One concern is whether 360-degree appraisals improve the process or simply multiply the number of problems by the total number of raters. Also, some wonder if multisource appraisals really create better decisions than conventional methods, given the additional time investment (LaMountain, 1997). It seems reasonable to assume that these issues are of less concern when the 360-degree feedback is used only for development because the process is usually less threatening. But those concerns may negate multisource appraisals as an administrative tool in many situations (Jackson and Greller, 1998).

TYPES OF APPRAISALS

Many techniques have been developed for appraising performance. The HRM department or higher-level management usually dictate which types the organization will use. An organization that has all managers use the same approach establishes a way to keep records showing performance over time, especially when an employee reports to more than one manager during his or her employment. Although a manager has to use the appraisal format selected for the whole organization, he or she may be able to supplement it with other helpful information. A manager can use the "Comments" section of a preprinted form or attach additional information to it, as one manager does when appraising employees.

Performance appraisals are generally conducted using a predetermined method such as one or more of those described in this section.

Graphic Rating Scale

The graphic rating scale (GRS) is the simplest, most popular technique for appraising performance. There are actually two types of GRSs in use today. They are sometimes both used in rating the same person. The first and most common type lists job criteria (quantity of work, quality of work, etc.). The second is more behavioral, with specific behaviors listed and the effectiveness of each rated.

The GRS presents appraisers with a list of traits assumed to be necessary to successful job performance (e.g., adaptability, maturity, cooperativeness, motivation). Each trait is listed and accompanied by a 5- or 7-point rating scale. The evaluator then goes down the list and rates each on incremental scales. The scales typically specify five points, so a factor such as job knowledge might be rated 1 ("poorly informed about work duties") to 5 ("has complete mastery of all phases of the job").

While GRSs don't provide the depth of information other performance evaluation methods do, many organizations use them because they are practical and cost little to develop. HRM staff can develop such forms quickly, and because the traits and anchors are written at a general level, a single form is applicable to all or most jobs within an organization. Another advantage of a GRS is that it is relatively easy to use. In addition, the scores provide a basis for deciding whether an employee has improved in various areas.

There are some obvious drawbacks to the GRS as well. Often, separate traits or factors are grouped together, and the rater is given only one box to check. Another drawback is that the descriptive words sometimes used in such scales may have different meanings to different raters. Terms such as initiative and cooperation are subject to many interpretations, especially if used in conjunction with words such as outstanding, average, and poor. Also, many managers tend to rate everyone at least a little above average. Some appraisal forms attempt to overcome these problems by containing descriptions of excellent or poor behavior in each area. Other rating scales pose a different problem by labeling performance in terms of how well an employee "meets requirements." Presumably, the manager wants *all* employees to meet the requirements of the job. However, scoring everyone high on this scale may be seen as a rating bias (on the assumption that not everyone can be a "top performer") rather than successful management of human resources.

Critical Incidents

Critical incidents focus the evaluator's attention on those behaviors that are key in making the difference between executing a job effectively and executing it ineffectively. That is, the appraiser writes down anecdotes that describe what the employee did that was especially effective or ineffective. The key here is that only specific behaviors, not vaguely defined personality traits, are cited. A list of critical incidents provides a rich set of examples from which the employee can be shown those behaviors that are desirable and those that call for improvement.

To successfully conduct a critical-incident appraisal, a rating supervisor must keep a written record of incidents that show positive and negative ways an employee has acted. The record should include dates, people involved, actions taken, and any other relevant details. At the time of the appraisal, a manager reviews the record to reach an overall evaluation of an employee's behavior. During the appraisal interview, the manager should give an employee a chance to offer her or his views of each incident recorded. The critical incident method can be used with other methods to document the reasons why an employee was rated in a certain way.

There are several disadvantages with this technique. First, what constitutes a critical incident is not defined in the same way by all supervisors. Next, keeping records of critical incidents can be time consuming, and even if a supervisor is diligent, important incidents could be overlooked. Also, supervisors tend to record negative events more than positive ones, resulting in an overly harsh appraisal. Further, employees may become overly concerned about what the superior writes and begin to fear the manager's "black book."

Paired-Comparison Approach

The paired-comparison approach measures the relative performance of employees in a group. A manager lists the employees in the group and then ranks them. One method is to compare the performance of the first two employees on the list. A manager places a checkmark next to the name of the employee whose performance is better, then repeats the process, comparing the first employee's performance with that of the other employees. Next, the supervisor compares the second employee on the list with all the others, and so on until each pair of employees has been compared. The employee with the most checkmarks is considered the most valuable.

A manager also can compare employees in terms of several criteria, such as work quantity and quality. For each criterion, a manager ranks the employees from best to worst, assigning a 1 to the lowest-ranked employee and the highest score to the best employee in that category. Then all the scores for each employee are totaled to see who has the highest total score.

The paired-comparison approach is appropriate when a manager needs to find one outstanding employee in a group. It can be used to identify the best candidate for a promotion or special assignment. However, paired comparison makes some employees look good at the expense of others, which makes this technique less useful as a means of providing feedback to individual employees. It is especially inappropriate as a routine form of appraisal in situations calling for cooperation and teamwork.

FORCED-CHOICE APPROACH

In the forced-choice approach, the appraisal form gives a manager sets of statements describing employee behavior. For each set of statements, a manager must choose one that is most characteristic and one that is least characteristic of the employee. When this approach is used by managers to appraise employees, managers deal with all their direct reports. Therefore, if a rater has 20 employees, only four can go in the top fifth and, of course, four must also be relegated to the bottom fifth.

These questionnaires tend to be set up in a way that prevents a manager from saying only positive things about employees. Thus, the forced-choice approach is used when an organization determines that managers have been rating an unbelievably high proportion of employees as above average.

Written Essays

Probably the simplest method of evaluation is to write a narrative describing an employee's strengths, weaknesses, past performance, potential, and suggestions for improvement. In short, managers answer questions such as "What are the major strengths of this employee?" or "In what area does this employee need improvement?" The written essay requires no complex forms or extensive training to complete.

Essay or "free-form" appraisals often are used along with other types of appraisals, notably graphic rating scales. They provide an opportunity for a supervisor to describe aspects of performance that are not thoroughly covered by an appraisal questionnaire. The main drawback of essay appraisals is that their quality depends on a supervisor's writing skills.

Behaviorally Anchored Rating Scales (BARS)

Another method for appraising performance involves the use of behaviorally anchored rating scales, or BARS. BARS appraisal systems (also known as "behavioral expectation scales") represent a combination of the GRS and the critical incident method. These scales rate employee performance in several areas, such as work quantity and quality, using a series of statements that describe effective and ineffective performance in each area. In each area, a manager selects the statement that best describes how an employee performs. Behavioral descriptions might include the following: anticipates, plans, executes, solves immediate problems, carries out orders, and handles emergency situations. The statements in the rating scales are different for each job title in the organization.

A significant advantage of BARS is that they dramatically increase reliability by providing specific behavioral examples to reflect effective and less-effective behaviors. Also, BARS can be tailored to the organization's objectives for employees. In addition, the BARS approach is less subjective than some other approaches because it uses statements describing behavior. However, developing the scales is time consuming and therefore relatively expensive.

Behavioral Observation Scale

The Behavioral Observation Scale (BOS) is another behavioral approach to assessing employee performance. Like BARS, a BOS is developed from critical incidents. However, rather than only using a sample of behaviors that reflect effective or ineffective behavior, a BOS uses substantially more behaviors to specifically define all the measures that are necessary for effective performance. A second difference between a BOS and BARS is that rather than assessing which behavior best describes an individual's performance, a BOS allows managers to rate the frequency with which the individual employee has exhibited each behavior during the rating period. The manager then averages these ratings to calculate an overall performance rating for the individual. Although the BOS approach avoids the limitations of the BARS approach, the BOS takes even more time and can be even more expensive to develop.

Checklist Appraisal

A checklist appraisal contains a series of questions about an employee's performance. A supervisor answers yes or no to the questions. Thus, a checklist is merely a record of performance, not an evaluation by a supervisor. The HRM department has a key for scoring the items on the checklist, and the score results in a rating of an employee's performance. The following are typical checklist statements: "can be expected to finish work on time," "seldom agrees to work overtime," "is cooperative and helpful," "accepts criticism," and "strives for self-improvement."

The checklist can be modified so that varying weights are assigned to the statements or words. The results can then be quantified. Usually the weights are not known by the rating supervisor because they are tabulated by someone else, such as a member of the HRM department.

While the checklist appraisal is easy to complete, it has several disadvantages. As with the GRS, the words or statements may have different meanings to different raters. The checklist can be difficult to prepare, and each job category will probably require a different set of questions. Also, a rating supervisor has no way to adjust the answers for any special circumstances that affect performance. Additionally, raters do not assign the weights to the factors. These difficulties limit the use of the information when a rater discusses the checklist with the employee, creating a barrier to effective development counseling.

Management by Objectives (MBO)

A very popular individualized method of evaluating performance of employees (particularly managers and professionals) is management by objectives (MBO). In an MBO system an employee meets with his or her manager, and they collectively set goals for the employee for a coming period of time, usually one year. These goals are usually quantifiable, they are objective, and they are almost always written. During the year the manager and the employee periodically meet to review the employee's performance relative to attaining the goals. At the end of the year, a more formal meeting is scheduled in which the manager and employee assess the actual degree of goal attainment. The degree of goal attainment then becomes the individual's performance appraisal. That is, if an individual has attained all of his or her goals, then the person's performance is deemed to be very good. Otherwise, the individual is directly responsible for his or her performance deficiency, and the person's performance is judged to be less than adequate or acceptable.

No management tool is perfect, and certainly MBO is not appropriate for all employees or all organizations. Jobs with little or no flexibility are not compatible with MBO. For example, an assembly-line worker usually has so little job flexibility that performance standards and objectives are already determined. The MBO process seems to be most useful with managerial personnel and employees who have a fairly wide range of flexibility and control over their jobs. When imposed on a rigid and autocratic management system, MBO may fail. Extreme emphasis on penalties for not meeting objectives defeats the developmental and participative nature of MBO.

Which Performance Appraisal Method Is Best?

Determining the best appraisal method depends upon the objectives of the system. A combination of the methods is usually superior to any one method. For development objectives, critical incidents and MBO work well. For administrative decisions, a ranking method based on rating scales or BARS works well. The real success of performance appraisal does not lie in the method or form used; it depends upon the supervisor's interpersonal skills.

SOURCES OF BIAS IN PERFORMANCE APPRAISALS

Ideally, rating supervisors should be completely objective in their appraisals of employees. Each appraisal should directly reflect an employee's performance, not any biases of a supervisor. Of course, this is impossible to do perfectly. We all make compromises in our decision-making strategies and have biases in evaluating what other people do. Raters need to be aware of these biases so that their effect on the appraisals can be limited or eliminated.

Unclear standards. Although the graphic rating scale seems objective, it would probably result in unfair appraisals because the traits and degrees of merit are open to interpretation. For example, different supervisors would probably define "good" performance, "fair" performance, and so on differently. The same is true of such traits as "quality of work" or "creativity."

There are several ways to rectify this problem. The best way is to develop and include descriptive phrases that define each trait. For example, by specifying on the evaluation form what is meant by such things as "outstanding," "superior," and "good" quality of work. This specificity results in appraisals that are more consistent and more easily explained.

Harshness or leniency bias. Some managers are prone to a harshness bias; that is, rating employees more severely than their performance merits. New supervisors or managers are especially susceptible to this error because they may feel a need to be taken seriously. Unfortunately, the harshness bias also tends to frustrate and discourage employees, who resent the unfair assessments of their performance.

At the other extreme is the leniency bias. Managers with this bias rate their employees more favorably than their performance merits. A manager who does this may want credit for developing a department full of "excellent" employees. Or the manager may simply be uncomfortable confronting employees with their shortcomings. The leniency bias may feel like an advantage to the employees who receive the favorable ratings, but it cheats the employees and department of the benefits of truly developing and coaching employees.

The harshness/leniency problem is especially serious with graphic rating scales, because supervisors aren't necessarily required to avoid giving all their employees high (or low) ratings. On the other hand, if you must rank employees, you are forced to distinguish between high and low performers. Thus, harshness/leniency is not a problem with the ranking or forced-choice distribution approaches.

Central tendency. A bias that characterizes the responses to many types of questionnaires is central tendency, which is the tendency to select ratings in the middle of the scale. People seem more comfortable on middle ground than taking a strong stand at either extreme. This bias causes a manager to miss important opportunities to praise or correct employees. Ranking employees instead of using a GRS can avoid the central tendency problem because all employees must be ranked and thus can't all be rated average.

Proximity means nearness. The proximity bias refers to the tendency to assign similar scores to items that are near each other on a questionnaire. If a manager assigns a score of 8 to one appraisal item, this bias might encourage the manager to score the next item as 6 or 7, even though a score of 3 is more accurate. Obviously, this can result in misleading appraisals.

When using a type of appraisal that requires answers to specific questions, a manager might succumb to making random choices. A rating supervisor might do this when uncertain how to answer or when the overall scoring on the test looks undesirable. For example, if a manager thinks an appraisal is scoring an employee too low, he or she might give favorable ratings in some areas where the supervisor has no strong feelings. Managers who catch themselves making random choices should slow down and try to apply objective criteria.

Similarity bias. The similarity bias refers to the tendency to judge others more positively when they are like ourselves. Thus, we tend to look more favorably on people who share our interests, tastes, background, or other characteristics. For example, in appraising performance a manager risks viewing a person's performance in a favorable light because the employee shares her or his interest in sports. Or a rating supervisor might interpret negatively the performance of an employee who is much shyer than the supervisor.

Recency syndrome. The recency syndrome refers to the human tendency to place the most weight on events that have occurred most recently. In a performance appraisal a manager might give particular weight to a problem the employee caused last week or an award the employee just won, whereas he or she should be careful to consider events and behaviors that occurred throughout the entire period covered by the review. The most accurate way to do this is to keep records throughout the year, as described earlier with conducting a critical incident appraisal.

Halo effect. The halo effect refers to the tendency to generalize one positive or negative aspect of a person to the person's entire performance. Thus, if a manager thinks that a pleasant telephone manner is what makes a good customer service representative, he or she is apt to give high marks to a representative with a pleasant voice, no matter what the employee actually says to the customers or how reliable the performance.

Prejudice. Finally, the manager's prejudices about various types of people can unfairly influence a performance appraisal. A manager needs to remember that each employee is an individual, not merely a representative of a group. A manager who believes that African Americans generally have poor skills in using Standard English needs to recognize that this is a prejudice about a group, not a fact to apply to actual employees. Thus, before recommending that a black salesperson needs to improve his or her speaking skills, a supervisor must consider whether the salesperson really needs improvement in that area or whether the supervisor's prejudices are interfering with an accurate assessment. Managers should try to block out the influence of factors such as previous performance, age, or race.

HOW TO AVOID APPRAISAL PROBLEMS

There are at least four ways to minimize the impact of appraisal problems such as bias and central tendency. First, be sure to understand the problems just discussed and the suggestions (like clarifying standards) given for each of them. Understanding the problem can help you avoid it.

Second, choose the right appraisal tool. Each tool, such as the GRS or critical incident method, has its own advantages and disadvantages as noted earlier. Third, train supervisors to eliminate rating errors such as halo, central tendency, and leniency. In a typical training program, raters are shown a videotape of jobs being performed and are asked to rate the worker. Ratings made by each participant are then placed on a flip chart, and the various errors (such as leniency and halo) are explained. Typically, the trainer gives the correct rating and then illustrates the rating errors the participants made (Hedge and Cavanaugh, 1988).

Rater training is no panacea for reducing errors or for improving appraisal accuracy. In practice, several factors, including the extent to which pay is tied to performance ratings, union pressure, employee turnover, time constraints, and the need to justify ratings, may be more important than training. This means that improving appraisal accuracy calls not just for training but also for reducing outside factors such as union pressure and time constraints (Athey and McIntyre, 1987).

A fourth solution—diary keeping—has been proposed and is worth the effort. A recent study illustrates this (DeNisi and Peters, 1996). The conclusion of this and other studies is that you can reduce the adverse effects of appraisal problems by having raters carefully write down positive and negative critical incidents as they occur during the period to be appraised. Maintaining such behavioral records instead of relying on long-term memories is definitely the preferred approach (Sanchez and DeLaTorre, 1996, p. 7). Diary keeping isn't fool proof as some research has shown that in one study while raters were required to keep a diary, contrary to predictions the diary keeping actually undermined the performance appraisal's objectives (Varna, DeNisi, and Peters, 1997).

Most of the appraisal problems we have discussed reflect the fact that performance appraisal is essentially a cognitive, decision-making process. Being familiar with the potential problems, choosing the right appraisal tool, training supervisors, and keeping a diary can help diminish some of the errors that might therefore crop up.

LEGAL AND EFFECTIVE PERFORMANCE APPRAISALS

Performance appraisal plays a central role in equal employment compliance. Since the passage of Title VII, a growing number of courts have addressed issues (including promotion, layoff, and compensation decisions) in which performance appraisals play a significant role (Axline, 1994, p. 62). The EEOC and other federal enforcement agencies make it clear that performance appraisal must be job related and nondiscriminatory.

The elements of a performance appraisal system that can survive court tests can be determined from existing case law. Various cases have provided guidance. The elements of a legally defensible performance appraisal are as follows:

- Performance appraisal criteria based on job analysis
- Absence of disparate impact and evidence of validity
- Formal evaluation criteria that limit managerial validity
- Formal rating instrument
- Personal knowledge of and contact with appraised individual
- Training of supervisors in conducting appraisals
- Review process that prevents one manager acting alone from controlling an employee's career
- Counseling to help poor performers improve

Clearly, the courts are interested in fair and nondiscriminatory performance appraisals. Employers must decide how to design their appraisal systems to satisfy courts, enforcement agencies, and their employees ("Minimize Peformance Appraisal Legal Risks," 1998, p. 10).

In discrimination suits, plaintiffs often allege that the performance appraisal system unjustly discriminated against them because of race or gender. Many performance appraisal measures are subjective, and we have seen that individual biases can affect them, especially when those doing the measuring harbor racial or gender stereotypes.

It is important that organizations develop a system for archiving performance appraisal results. An organization must be able to demonstrate, beyond reasonable doubt, that a given individual employee was sanctioned, rewarded, punished, terminated, or remanded for training on a basis of performance-related reasons rather than nonperformance-related factors such as sex or race.

HOW TO CONDUCT A FORMAL PERFORMANCE APPRAISAL

Conducting a performance appraisal is one of the manager's most important and difficult functions. The first thing a manager can do to conduct an effective formal performance appraisal is to make sure that there are no surprises in store for employees. This means that managers should communicate with their employees on a regular basis about how they are doing with their particular assignments and how well they are collaborating with others.

The formal appraisal session, therefore, should be primarily a way to summarize and continue the informal interaction that has previously taken place between the manager and the employee. It should also be a time to look at how the manager and the employee can continue to work well together in the future. The manager's job in this session is not to tell the employee all the things he or she thinks the employee did wrong over the past year. One reason employees dread these sessions is that managers feel they have to find something to criticize as well as to praise. The manager might then mention a negative comment the employee made or similar trivial points. This hypercritical approach will merely increase the employee's resentment and defensiveness and will make employees feel as though they are powerless to improve.

To make sure the session goes as well as possible and to avoid making it uncomfortable for both the manager and the employee, five general steps should be followed:

1. Refer to past feedback and documented observations of performance.
2. Describe the current performance.
3. Describe the desired performance.
4. Get a commitment to any needed change.
5. Follow up.

Specific guidelines for conducting performance appraisals are described below.

Preparing for the Appraisal Interview Session

Today's manager must recognize that failure to plan for the performance appraisal is planning to fail. Being prepared is key to making sure the discussion with each employee goes smoothly. Before the meeting, the manager needs to do some documentation and planning:

- Create and maintain logs (or documentation) on each employee that include observations of the outcomes of the employee's actions on the job and particular behaviors. Update these logs regularly. Focus on what employees are doing well, and try to understand problems from the systems perspective.

- If a rule infraction has occurred, describe in writing and have the employee sign the written record at the time of the infraction. Keep a record of all discussions that deal with problems that are directly attributable to the employee's performance.

- Review the documentation before the formal appraisal session and highlight important points.

- List the points you want to make, focusing on both strengths and areas for improvement. Be prepared to discuss problems in a manner that focuses on the behaviors that caused the problem and on solutions, not on the person. Be sure to distinguish between problems that are related to the system (e.g., too many assignments) and those that are attributable to the individual.

- Consider the follow-up actions you think might be appropriate to help the employee improve, but be prepared to take the employee's feelings into consideration.

- Think about how you have interacted with the employee and how these interactions might have affected his or her performance. Be prepared to discuss how you and the employee might improve your interactions.

- Set up an appointment with the employee about a week before the performance appraisal session.

- If the employee needs to fill out a self-assessment form, give it to him or her at the time you set up the appointment to meet.

During the Appraisal Interview Session

Here are some ways managers can make the actual session go smoothly:

- Put the employees at ease at the start of the session. Acknowledge that these sessions can be a little nerve wracking, but that their purpose is to help everyone in the team or work group improve and to gather information on how to help these improvement efforts.

- Ask employees what they think of their total performance—not just their strong or weak areas.

- Question employees about what they think are their personal strengths. This gives employees a chance to describe what they do best, which helps them feel positive about the appraisal.

- Tell employees what you believe are their strengths. This demonstrates that you are paying attention to their performance and appreciating their good qualities.

- Describe those areas where you think employees might improve and use documentation to demonstrate why you are making these observations. Then ask employees what they think of your assessment and listen silently to what they have to say. Consider their reasons for poor performance (e.g., lack of equipment, lack of training) in determining appropriate actions to take.

- Assuming that you identify the cause of poor performance, ask employees what you can do together to take care of it.

- Regardless of whether or not an employee receives an average or a good rating, explain why she or he did not get a higher rating. The employee should understand what needs to be done during the next performance period to get a higher rating.

- Set new goals for performance for the next appraisal period.

- Keep a record of the meeting, including a timetable for performance improvement and what each of you will do to work toward your goals.

- Be open and honest, yet considerate of the employee's feelings. The goal is to facilitate improvement, not to make the employee feel bad.

- Be sure to give positive reinforcement to the employee during the discussion, preferably near the end. Being positive helps to motivate the employee to make any necessary change.

After the Appraisal Interview Session

It is vital to follow up on any agreements made during the appraisal sessions. Follow-up indicates that the manager and the organization are serious about improvement. The manager should:

- make appointments to meet with employees individually to review progress;
- set up development opportunities as needed to address skill deficiencies;
- arrange for the employee to get counseling, when available, if a personal problem is involved;
- provide feedback when you see improvements in performance; and
- make him or her aware of the consequences, such as demotion or dismissal, if the employee continues to perform poorly.

Follow-up means more than just working with employees. Managers also have to follow up on themselves. An effective appraisal process requires an ongoing and candid self-assessment by the manager of his or her performance and its effect on employees. Managers can use the following questions to evaluate their own performance and its effect on their employees:

- Do your employees know specifically what you expect?
- Do your employees have written goals and results?
- Have you tracked your employees' performance to see if the trend is up, down, or about the same?
- Have you updated your employees recently about what you are working on and how it affects them?

- Are you maintaining performance documentation?
- Have you scheduled interim reviews with all of your employees?
- Do you frequently—even daily—discuss employee performance?
- Do you frequently "catch" your employees doing something right—and tell them about it?

EFFECTIVE PERFORMANCE MANAGEMENT

An effective performance appraisal system has a strategic importance to the organization. Clearly, the organization must monitor the extent to which it is conducting its performance appraisals effectively, adequately, and appropriately. As with selection, performance appraisal must be free from bias and discrimination.

Also, regardless of which performance appraisal approach is used, an understanding of what performance management is supposed to do is critical. When performance appraisal is used to develop employees as resources, it usually works. When management uses performance appraisal as a punishment or when raters fail to understand its limitations, it fails. The key is not which form or which method is used but whether managers and employees understand its purposes. In its simplest form, a performance appraisal is a manager's observation: "Here are your strengths and weaknesses, and here is a way to shore up the weak areas." It can lead to higher employee motivation and satisfaction if done right.

But in an era of continuous improvement, an ineffective performance management system can he a huge liability (Longnecker and Fink, 1997, p. 28). An effective performance management system will be:

- Consistent with strategic mission of the organization
- Beneficial as a development tool
- Useful as an administrative tool
- Legal and job-related
- Viewed as generally fair by employees
- Useful in documenting employee performance

Most systems can be improved by training supervisors because conducting performance appraisals is a big part of a performance management system. Training should focus on minimizing errors and providing a frame of reference on how raters observe and recall information.

Organizationally, there is a tendency to distill performance into a single number that can be used to support pay raises. Systems based on this concept reduce the complexity of each person's contribution in order to satisfy compensation system requirements (Manzoni and Barsoux, 1998). Such systems are too simplistic to give employees useful feedback or help managers pinpoint training and development needs. In fact, use of a single numerical rating often is a barrier to performance discussions because what is emphasized is attaching a label to a person's performance and defending or attacking that label. Effective performance management systems evolve from the recognition that human behaviors and capabilities collapsed into a single score have a limited use in shaping the necessary range of performance.

EVALUATING THE PERFORMANCE APPRAISAL AND MANAGEMENT PROCESSES

Like recruitment and selection, performance appraisal must be free from bias and discrimination. This means that the organization must monitor the extent to which it is conducting its performance appraisals effectively, adequately, and appropriately.

The performance appraisal system must be doing an effective job of helping the organization identify its low performers so that their deficiencies can be remedied through training or other measures. Even more important, though, the organization must identify its strongest performers so that they can be appropriately rewarded and efforts can be made to retain their employment within the organization. Periodic audits of the performance appraisal system by trained professionals can be an effective method for assessing their effectiveness and the appropriateness of the organization's performance appraisal process.

If the process is working, managers should be able to see real improvements in organizational performance, since performance appraisal feeds into the performance management process. This improvement may take the form of lower levels of absenteeism or turnover, fewer errors in production, fewer returns in sales, and higher appraisals. In the long run, however, these outcomes are not critical to the organization unless they translate into some improvement in the organization's performance. That is, if performance appraisal and the broader performance management, systems are doing what they were designed to do, the organization as a whole should perform better.

SUMMARY

Performance appraisals are important because they help ensure that the recruiting and selection processes are adequate, they play an important role in training, they can help effectively link performance with rewards, they demonstrate that important employment-related decisions have been based on performance, and they can promote employee motivation and development. Performance appraisals also provide valuable and useful information to the organization's HRM planning process. The ultimate goal for any organization using performance appraisals is to be able to improve performance on the job.

Performance appraisals should be done by those familiar with the performance of individual employees. Possibilities include the immediate supervisors, peers, direct reports, customers, and individuals themselves. Multisource, or 360-degree, feedback is increasingly used by organizations to evaluate their employees' performance.

Several methods can be used to assess performance, including written essays, critical incidents, graphic rating scales, behavioral anchored and observation scales, and multiperson comparisons such as paired-comparison and forced-choice approaches. All performance measurement techniques are subject to one or more weaknesses or deficiencies that are often referred to as biases. The most common are harshness bias, leniency bias, similarity bias, proximity bias, central tendency, recency syndrome, and the halo effect. Organizations should undertake efforts to reduce rating error.

Successful performance appraisals are more likely when raters plan and prepare appropriately before the actual appraisal. Additionally, raters should follow specific steps during the appraisal process and include a follow-up phase to ensure that the expected performance improvements are actually coming to fruition.

Today's organizations must monitor the extent to which they are conducting performance appraisals effectively, adequately, and appropriately. As with selection, performance appraisal must be free from bias and discrimination.

REFERENCES

Athey, T., and McIntyre, R. 1987. Effect of rater training on rater accuracy: Levels of processing theory and social facilitation theory perspectives. *Journal of Applied Psychology* 72: 567–572.

Axline, L. 1994. Ethical considerations of performance appraisals. *Management Review* 83: 62.

Cardy, R.L., and Dobbins, G.H. 1997. Performance management. In L.H. Peters, C.R. Greer, and S.A. Youngblood (eds.), *The Blackwell encyclopedia: Dictionary of human resource management*. Malden, MA: Blackwell Publishers.

DeNisi, A., and Peters, L. 1996. Organization of information in memory and the performance appraisal process: Evidence from the field. *Journal of Applied Psychology* 81: 717–737.

Gephart, M. 1995. The road to high performance. *Training and Development* (June): 30–38.

Ghorparde, J., and Chen, M.M. 1995. Creating quality-driven performance appraisal systems. *Academy of Management Executive* 9: 32–39.

Hedge, J., and Cavanaugh, M. 1988. Improving the accuracy of performance evaluations: Comparison of three methods of performance appraiser training. *Journal of Applied Psychology* 73: 68–73.

Jackson, J.H., and Greller, M.M. 1998. Decision elements for using 360-degree feedback. *Human Resource Planning* 20: 18–28.

LaMountain, D.M. 1997. Assessing the value of multisource feedback. *Employment Relations Today* (Autumn): 75–90.

Longnecker, C.O., and Fink, L.S. 1997. Keys to designing and running an effective performance appraisal system. *Journal of Compensation and Benefits* (November–December): 28.

Manzoni, J., and Barsoux, J. 1998. The set-up-to-fail syndrome. *Harvard Business Review* (March–April): 101–114.

Minimize performance evaluation legal risks. 1998. *Journal of Accountancy* (February): 10.

Sanchez, J., and DeLaTorre, P. 1996. A second look at the relationships between rating and behavioral accuracy in performance appraisal. *Journal of Applied Psychology* 81: 7.

Varna, A., DeNisi, A.S., and Peters, L.H. 1996. Interpersonal affect and performance appraisal: A field study. *Personnel Psychology* 49: 341–360.

Chapter 9

Career Development

INTRODUCTION

Traditionally, organizations have engaged in human resources management planning (HRMP) and development. As we noted in Chapter 2, this activity involves managing the organization's employees through various positions and identifying future staffing and development needs. Career development programs, with their great emphasis on the individual, highlight the personal aspect of this process.

Effective career development is integrated with the existing HRM functions and structures in the organization. Integrating career development with other HRM programs creates synergies in which all aspects of HRM reinforce one another. For example, in planning careers, employees need organizational information on strategic planning, HRM planning. Skills inventories can provide this information. Similarly, as they obtain information about themselves and use it in career planning, employees need to know the career paths within the organization and how management views their performance.

The psychological contract between employers and workers has changed. Yesterday, employees "exchanged loyalty for job security." Today, employees instead exchange performance for the sort of training and learning and development that will allow them to remain marketable. This in turn means that the somewhat unidirectional nature of HRM activities such as selection and training is starting to change; in addition to serving the organization's needs, these activities must now be designed so that the employees' long-run interests are served and so that, in particular, the employee is encouraged to grow and realize her or his potential. Exhibit

Exhibit 9.1
HRM Traditional versus Career Development Focus

Activity	Traditional Focus	Career Development Focus
Human resources management planning	(1) Analyzes jobs, skills, and tasks—present and future. (2) Projects needs. (3) Uses statistical data.	Adds information about individual interests, preferences, and the like to data.
Training and development	Provides opportunities for learning skills, information, and attitudes related to the job.	(1) Provides career path information. (2) Adds individual growth orientation.
Performance appraisal	Rating and/or rewards.	Adds development plans and individual goal setting.
Recruitment and placement	Matching the organization's needs with qualified individuals.	Matches individuals and jobs based on a number of variables, including employees' career interests.
Compensation and benefits	Rewards for time, productivity, talent, and so on.	Adds non-job-related activities to be rewarded, such as United Way leadership positions.

9.1 summarizes how activities such as training and performance appraisal can be used to provide more of such a career planning and development focus (Otte and Hutcheson, 1992, p. 10).

Like performance appraisal, training and development, an equally important element of the enhancement of motivation and performance, is the set of activities and processes that constitute career development and planning. This chapter examines career development and its role in developing human potential. We first discuss roles in career development. The discussion then turns to implementing career development. After examining career development issues and challenges for today's diverse workforce, we conclude by discussing how organizations can evaluate career management activities.

MATCHING ORGANIZATIONAL AND INDIVIDUAL NEEDS: THE GOAL OF CAREER DEVELOPMENT

Career development is an ongoing, formalized effort by an organization that focuses on developing and enriching the organization's human resources in light of both the employees' and the organization's needs. Career planning is the process by which an individual formulates career goals and develops a plan for reaching those goals. Thus, career development and career planning should reinforce each other. Career development looks at individual careers from the viewpoint of the organization, whereas career planning looks at careers through the eyes of individual employees. In the end, a career development program should be viewed as a dynamic process that matches the needs of the organization with the needs of employees.

The Organization's Role

The organization has primary responsibility for instigating and ensuring that career development takes place. Specifically, the organization's responsibilities are to develop and communicate career options within the organization to the employee. The organization must carefully advise an employee concerning possible career paths to achieve that employee's career goals.

The organization must supply information about its mission, policies, and plans and provide support for employee self-assessment, training, and development. Significant career growth can occur when individual initiative combines with organizational opportunity. Career development programs benefit managers by giving them increased skill in managing their own careers, greater retention of valued employees, increased understanding of the organization, and enhanced reputations as people-developers. As with other HRM programs, the inauguration of a career development program should be based on the organization's needs as well.

Assessment of needs should take a variety of approaches (surveys, informal group discussions, interviews, etc.) and should involve personnel from different groups, such as new employees, managers, plateaued employees, minority employees, and technical and professional employees. Identifying the needs and problems of these groups provides the starting point for the organization's career development efforts. Organizational needs should be linked with individual career needs in a way that joins personal effectiveness and satisfaction of employees with the achievement of the organization's strategic objectives.

HRM's Role

HRM personnel are generally responsible for ensuring that this information is kept current as new jobs are created and old ones are phased out. Working closely with both employees and their managers, HRM specialists should see that accurate information is conveyed and that interrelationships among different career paths are understood. Thus, rather than bearing the primary responsibility for preparing individual careers plans, the organization should promote the conditions and create the environment that will facilitate the development of individual career plans by the employees.

Like any other HRM activity, if career development is to succeed, it must receive the complete support of top management. Ideally, senior line managers and HRM managers will work together to design and implement a career development system. The system should reflect the goals and culture of the organization, and the HRM philosophy should be woven throughout. An HRM philosophy can provide employees with a clear set of expectations and directions for their own career development. For a program to be effective, managerial personnel at all levels must be trained in the fundamentals of job design, performance appraisal, career planning, and counseling More will be said about management's role in career development shortly.

The Employee's Role

In today's dynamic work environment, individuals are increasingly responsible for initiating and managing their own career planning. Career planning is not something one individual can do for another; it has to come from the individual. Only the individual knows what she or he really wants out of a career, and certainly these desires vary appreciably from person to person.

Career planning requires a conscious effort on the part of the employee; it is hard work, and it does not happen automatically. Each employee must identify his or her own knowledge, skills, abilities, interests, and values and seek out information about career options in order to set goals and develop career plans.

Before employees can engage in meaningful career planning, they must not only have an awareness of the organization's philosophy but they must also have a good understanding of the organization's more immediate goals. Otherwise, they may plan for personal change and growth without knowing if or how their own goals match those of the organization. For example, if the technology of a business is changing and new skills are needed, will the organization retrain to meet this need or hire new talent? Is there growth, stability, or decline in the number of employees needed? How will turnover affect the need? Clearly, an organizational plan that answers these kinds of questions is essential to support individual career planning.

Although an individual may be convinced that developing a sound career plan would be in his or her best interest, finding the time to develop such a plan is often another matter. The organization can help by providing trained specialists to encourage and guide the employee. This can best be accomplished by allotting a few hours of company time each quarter to this type of planning. Individuals and organizations must constantly recognize that individuals, like their organizations, change over time, and their needs and interests change as well. Thus, it would be unrealistic to expect individuals to establish their career goals with perfect understanding of where they are going or, for that matter, where the organization is going. So while goal setting is critical, building in some flexibility is a good idea.

The Manager's Role

It has been said that "the critical battleground in career development is inside the mind of the persons charged with supervisory responsibility" (Randolph, 1981). Although not expected to be a professional counselor, the manager can and should play a role in facilitating the development of a direct report's career. First, and foremost, the manager should serve as a catalyst and sounding board.

Managers should encourage employees to take responsibility for their own careers, offering continuing assistance in the form of feedback on individual performance and making information available about the organization, about the job, and about career opportunities that might be of interest. The manager should show an employee how to go about the process and then help the employee evaluate the conclusions.

Unfortunately, many managers do not perceive career counseling as part of their managerial duties. They are not opposed to this role; rather, they have never considered it as part of their job. To help overcome this and related problems, many organizations have designed training programs to help their managers develop the necessary skills in this area.

Successful career development results from a joint effort by the organization, HRM, the individual, and the immediate manager. The organization provides the resources and structure, the individual does the planning, and the immediate manager provides guidance and encouragement.

IMPLEMENTING CAREER DEVELOPMENT

As suggested in our discussion of HRM planning in Chapter 2, successful organizations must keep a steady watch on their human resources needs and requirements. This ongoing analysis involves an analysis of the competencies or KSAs required for jobs, the progression among related jobs, and the supply of ready (and potential) talent available to fill those jobs.

It is important for an organization to constantly study its jobs carefully in order to identify and assign weights or prioritizations to the KSAs that each one requires. This can be achieved with job analysis and evaluation systems such as those used in compensation programs.

Once the skill demands of the jobs are identified and weighted according to their importance, it is then possible to plan job progressions. A new employee with no experience is typically assigned to a "starting job." After a period of time in that job, the employee can be promoted to one that requires more KSAs. While most organizations concentrate on developing job progressions for managerial, professional, and technical jobs, progressions can be developed for all categories of jobs. These job progressions can then serve as a basis for developing career paths—the lines of advancement within an organization—for individuals. Career pathing will be discussed in more detail later in this chapter.

Although these analyses can be quite helpful to employees—and are perhaps essential for organizations—a word of caution is appropriate here for readers. Many successful careers are not this methodical, nor do they proceed in a lockstep manner. In today's working world, career progressions often occur as much through creating and capitalizing on arising opportunities as they do through rational planning.

It used to be that career development systems were primarily focused on promotions and hierarchical advancement. However, in today's flatter organizations and more dynamic work environment, an individual's career advancement can occur along several different paths: transfers, demotions— even terminations—as well as promotions. HRM policies have to be flexible enough to adapt as well as helpful enough to support the career change.

A promotion is a change of assignment to a job at a higher level in the organization. The new job normally provides an increase in pay and status and demands more KSAs or carries more responsibility. Promotions enable an organization to utilize the KSAs of its personnel more effectively, and the opportunity to gain a promotion serves as an incentive for good performance.

In flatter organizations, there are fewer promotional opportunities and many individuals have found career advancement through lateral moves. A transfer is the placement of an employee in another job for which the duties, responsibilities, status, and renumeration are approximately equal to those of the previous job (although as an incentive, organizations may offer a salary adjustment). Individuals who look forward to change or want a change to learn more may seek out transfers. In addition, transfers frequently provide a broader foundation for individuals to prepare them for an eventual promotion. A transfer may require the employee to change work group, workplace, work shift, or organizational unit; it may even necessitate moving to another geographic area. Transfers make it possible for an organization to place its employees in jobs where there is a greater need for their services and where they can acquire new KSAs.

A downward transfer, or demotion, moves an individual into a lower-level job that can provide developmental opportunities. Although such a move is ordinarily considered unfavorable, some individuals actually may request it in order to return to their "technical roots." It is not uncommon, for example, for organizations to appoint temporary leaders (especially in team environments) with the proviso that they will eventually step down from this position to resume their former position.

Self-Assessment

Many individuals never take the time to analyze their KSAs, interests, and career goals. It isn't that these individuals don't want to analyze these factors; rather, they simply never take the time. While this is not something an organization can do for the individual, the organization can provide the impetus and structure. A variety of self-assessment materials are available commercially; and some organizations have developed tailor-made forms and training programs for the use of their employees. Another option is the use of psychological testing.

An individual's self-assessment should not necessarily be limited by current resources and abilities; career plans today increasingly require that the individual acquire additional training and KSAs. However, this assessment should be based on reality. For the individual, this involves identifying personal strengths—not only the individual's developed abilities but also the financial resources available. More will be said about the organization's role in helping employees identify their potential and the strength of their interests.

Assessing Employee Potential

In conjunction with identifying the career opportunities and requirements for the organization, managers and HRM personnel must also establish a clear understanding of the talent base they have at their disposal. Organizations have several potential sources of information that can be used for assessing employee potential. This typically begins with the use of performance appraisal and moves into other potentially sophisticated methods (i.e., inventorying management talent and using assessment centers).

Identifying and developing talent in individuals is a role that all managers should take seriously. As they conduct formal appraisals, they should be concerned with their direct reports' potential for managerial or advanced technical jobs and encourage their growth in that direction. In addition to immediate managers, there should be others in the organization who have the power to evaluate, nominate, and sponsor employees with promise.

As discussed in Chapter 2, skill inventories are an important tool for succession planning. These inventories provide an indication of the skills employees have as well as their interests and experiences. In this way, they help managers pay better attention to the developmental needs of employees, both in their present jobs and in managerial jobs to which they may be promoted. Organizations often turn to employee personnel records, which reflect information such as education and previous work experience.

An equally important part of this process is identifying high-potential employees who may be groomed as replacements for managers who are reassigned, retire, or otherwise vacate a position.

The assessment center, discussed in Chapter 7, can also be an excellent source of information. The assessment center allows the organization to evaluate individuals as they participate in a series of situations that resemble what they might be called upon to handle on the job. It is usually a good idea for an organization not to depend on any one source of information but to use as many as are readily available. Such an approach provides a natural system of checks and balances.

As noted earlier, the organization's assessment of an individual employee should normally be conducted by HRM personnel and the individual's immediate manager, who serves as a mentor. More about mentoring will be discussed later.

Communicating Career Options

In order to set realistic career goals, employees must know the options and opportunities that are available within the organization. The organization can do several things to facilitate such awareness. Posting and advertising job vacancies as discussed in Chapter 4 is one activity that helps employees get a feel for their career options. Clearly identifying possible paths of advancement within the organization is also helpful. This can be done as part of the performance appraisal process. Another good idea is to share HRM planning forecasts with employees.

Although career management involves a good deal of analysis and planning, the reality is that it needs to provide a set of tools and techniques that help employees gauge their potential for success in the organization. Informal counseling by HRM personnel and supervisors is widely used. Many organizations give their employees information on educational assistance, EEO/AA programs and policies, salary administration, and job requirements. Career pathing and career planning workbooks and workshops are also popular means of helping employees identify their potential and the strength of their interests.

Career Pathing

Career pathing is a technique that addresses the specifics of progressing from one job to another in the organization. It can be defined as a sequence of developmental activities involving informal and formal education, training, and job experiences that help make an individual capable of holding more advanced jobs. Career paths exist on an informal basis in almost all organizations. However, career paths are much more useful when formally defined and documented. Such formalization results in specific descriptions of sequential work experiences as well as how the different sequences relate to one another. This information can be generated by computer.

Traditional career paths have emphasized upward mobility in a single occupation. An alternative to traditional career pathing is to base career paths on real-world experiences and individualized preferences. Paths of this kind would have several characteristics:

1. They would include lateral and downward possibilities, as well as upward possibilities, and they would not be tied to "normal" rates of progress.
2. They would be tentative and responsive to changes in organizational needs.
3. They would be flexible enough to take into account the qualities of individuals.
4. Each job along the paths would be specified in terms of acquirable skills, knowledge, and other specific attributes, not merely in terms of educational credentials, age, or work experience (Jackson, 1999, p. 2).

Realistic career paths, rather than traditional ones, are necessary for effective employee counseling. In the absence of such information, the employee can only guess at what is available.

Career Planning Workbooks and Workshops

Several organizations have prepared workbooks to guide their employees individually through systematic self-assessment of values, interests, abilities, goals, and personal development plans. General Electric has developed an extensive set of manuals for its career development program, including two workbooks to help employees explore life issues that affect career decisions. Other companies prefer to use workbooks written for the general public; for example, Richard N. Bolles's *What Color is Your Parachute 1999: A Practical Manual for Job-Hunters & Career-Changers* (1999) and Julie Griffin Levitt's *Your Career—How to Make It Happen* (1995).

Workshops offer experiences similar to those provided by workbooks. However, they have the advantage of providing a chance to compare and discuss attitudes, concerns, and plans with others in similar situations. Some workshops focus on current job performance and development plans. Others deal with broader life and career plans and values.

A career workshop can help employees assume responsibilities for their careers. It can also help them learn how to make career decisions, set career goals, create career options, seek career planning information, and at the same time build confidence and self-esteem.

Career Counseling

Career counseling is the activity that integrates the different steps in the career-planning process. Career counseling may be performed by an employee's immediate manager, a HRM specialist (or a combination of the two), or outside consultants. In most cases, it is preferable to have the counseling conducted by the immediate manager with appropriate input from HRM personnel. The immediate manager generally has the advantage of practical experience, knows the company, and is in a position to make a realistic appraisal of organizational opportunities.

Some managers are reluctant to attempt counseling because they haven't been trained in the area. However, it is not necessary to be a trained psychologist to be a successful counselor. Generally, managers who are skilled in basic human relations are successful as career counselors. Developing a caring attitude toward employees and their careers is of prime importance. Being receptive to employee concerns and problems is another requirement.

One interesting development in recent years has been the establishment of the Workforce Investment Act of 1998. With the signing of this act, Congress established a new law that consolidates a wide variety of federally sponsored career development and job training programs. Under the new arrangement, one-stop service centers will be set up in cooperation with businesses and local governments to provide jobseekers with a variety of services, including career counseling, skill assessments, training, job search assistance, and referrals to related programs and services (Pantazis, 1999).

Career Self-Management and Training

Career self-management is closely related to the concept of career pathing. Career self-management is the ability to keep pace with the speed at which change occurs within the organization and the industry and to prepare for the future (Meister, 1998). A relatively new concept, career self-management emphasizes the need of individual employees to keep learning because jobs that are held today may evolve into something different tomorrow, or may simply disappear entirely. (The changing nature of jobs is highlighted in Chapter 14.) Career self-management also involves identifying and obtaining new KSAs and competencies that allow the employee to move to a new position. The payoff of career self-management is more highly skilled and flexible employees and the retention of these employees. Career self-management requires commitment to the idea of employee self-development on the part of the organization and the provision of self-development programs and experiences for employees.

In response to the growing view that employees should assume greater responsibility for their own career management many organizations are establishing training programs for employees to teach them how to engage in career self-management. The training focuses on two major objectives: (1) helping employees learn to continuously gather feedback and information about their careers and (2) encouraging them to prepare for mobility.

The training is not geared to KSAs and behaviors associated with a specific job but rather toward their long-term personal effectiveness. Employees often undertake self-assessments to increase awareness of their own career attitudes and values along with a wider viewpoint beyond the next company promotion to broader opportunities in the workplace.

Mentoring

The success of many individuals in their careers can often be tied back to others who influenced them. These individuals frequently mention immediate managers who were especially helpful as career developers. Many of these individuals also mention others at higher levels in the organization who provided guidance and support to them in the development of their careers. These executives and managers who coach, advise, and encourage employees of lesser rank are called mentors.

Generally, the mentor initiates the relationship, but sometimes an employee will approach a potential mentor for advice. Most mentoring relationships develop over time on an informal basis. However, in proactive organizations there is an emphasis on formal mentoring plans that call for the assignment of a mentor to those employees considered for upward movement in the organization. Under a good mentor, learning focuses on goals, opportunities, expectations, standards, and assistance in fulfilling one's potential (Starcevich and Friend, 1999).

Mentoring functions can be divided into two broad categories: career functions and psychosocial functions:

- *Career functions.* Career functions are those aspects of the relationship that enhance career advancement. They include sponsorship, exposure and visibility, coaching, protection, and challenging assignments.
- *Psychosocial functions.* Psychosocial functions are those aspects that enhance the protégé's sense of competence, identity, and effectiveness in a professional role. They include role modeling, acceptance and confirmation, counseling, and friendship.

Both functions are viewed as critical to management development.

Many organizations have developed formal mentoring programs. Alternatively, given the importance of the issue, a number of mentoring organizations have begun to spring up. Often the main purpose of these organizations is to help create and monitor mentoring partnerships so that the right people are matched with one another. When done well, the mentoring process is beneficial for both the pupil and the mentor.

Not surprisingly, mentoring is also being done over the Internet. Known as *e-mentoring*, the process is mediated via Web sites that bring experienced business professionals together with individuals needing counseling. Even though participants in e-mentoring typically never meet in person, many form long-lasting e-mail connections that tend to be very beneficial. Still, most participants see these connections as supplements to—rather than substitutes for—in-company mentors.

Career Plateaus

A career plateau is defined as "the point in a career where the likelihood of additional hierarchical promotion is very low" (Ferrence, Stoner, and Warren, 1977, p. 602). Career plateauing takes place when an employee reaches a position from which he or she is not likely to be promoted further. Virtually all people reach a plateau in their careers; however, some individuals reach their promotional ceiling long before they retire.

Organizations can help employees cope with plateaus by providing opportunities for lateral growth when opportunities for advancement do not exist. Other actions that can aid in managing the plateau process involve: (1) preventing plateauees from becoming ineffective (preventing a problem from occurring); (2) integrating relevant career-related information systems (improving monitoring so that emerging problems can be detected and treated early); and (3) managing ineffective plateauees and frustrated employees more effectively (curing the problem once it has arisen). The first action basically involves helping plateauees adjust to the solid-citizen category and realize they have not necessarily failed. Available avenues for personal development and growth should be pointed out. The second suggestion can largely be implemented through a thorough performance appraisal system. Such a system should encourage open communication between the managers and the person being appraised.

Because plateaued employees often include a significant number of employees who are worth rehabilitating it would pay for most organizations to address this issue seriously. At least five possibilities exist:

- Provide alternative means of recognition. Some possibilities include assigning the employee to a task force or giving other special assignments, participation in brainstorming sessions, representation of the organization to others, and training of new employees.
- Develop new ways to make their current jobs more satisfying. Some possibilities here include relating employees' performance to total organizational goals and creating competition in the job.
- Effect revitalization through reassignment. The idea here is to implement systematic job switching to positions at the same level that require many similar, though not exactly the same, skills and experiences as the present job.
- Utilize reality-based self-development programs. Instead of assigning plateauees to developmental programs designed to help them move into future jobs (which

a majority of development programs do), assign them to development programs that can help them perform better in their present jobs.

- Change managerial attitudes toward plateaued employees. It is not unusual for managers (and supervisors) to give up on and neglect plateaued employees. Such actions are quickly picked up by the affected employees and only compound the problem. (Payne, 1984, p. 42).

Dual-Career Couples

Economic necessity and social forces have encouraged the trend of the employment of both members of a couple. In these dual-career partnerships both members follow their own careers and actively support each other's career development.

As with most lifestyles, the dual-career arrangement has its positive and negative sides. A significant number of organizations are concerned with the problems facing dual-career couples and offer assistance to them. Flexible working schedules are the most frequent organizational accommodation to these couples. Other arrangements include leave policies where either parent may stay home with a newborn, policies that allow work to be performed at home, day care on organization premises, and job sharing.

The difficulties that dual-career couples face include the need for quality child care, the time demands, and the emotional stress. However, the main problem these couples face is the threat of relocation. Many large organizations now offer one kind of job-finding assistance for spouses of employees who are relocated, including payment of fees charged by employment agencies, job counseling firms, and executive search firms. Organizations are also developing networking relationships with other employers to find jobs for the spouses of their relocating employees. These networks can provide a way to "share the wealth and talent" in a community while simultaneously assisting in the recruitment efforts of the participating organizations (Fraze, 1999).

Personal Career Development

As noted at several points throughout this chapter, regardless of whether or not an employer routinely offers development programs, it is essential that employees take responsibility for working out their own development plan. Today, managers and employees who neglect to do this risk stagnation and obsolescence. Even if their KSAs are not outdated, a downsizing or merger may put employees at risk of being terminated. It has happened to many employees already, and there is every indication that this trend will continue in the years to come. Planning for one's career should include an ongoing assessment and consideration of how an individual can demonstrate that he or she makes a difference to the organization. The following suggestions can help individuals make this case if they find that their jobs and careers are vulnerable to the fallout from business decisions such as mergers and downsizings (Kennedy, 1999):

1. Assess yourself—How are your job skills? How do your skills compare with your peers in your organization and in other organizations? How important is your role? Would profits or customer satisfaction be negatively affected if your job or department were eliminated? What do you contribute? Have you become quicker or more productive? Can you show an increase in customer satisfaction associated with your efforts? If you're in a management position, do employees like you and tend to stick with you?

2. Cultivate a positive relationship with your boss and your boss's boss—Can your boss count on you? Is your boss aware of your contributions?

3. Get plugged into the networks—What kind of reputation do you have with others, both inside and outside of the organization? Are others in the organization aware of your skills and contributions? Do you get calls from headhunters suggesting other employment opportunities?

Clearly, in planning a career one should attend to more than simply acquiring specific job knowledge and skills. Job know-how is clearly essential, but as the list above highlights, there are other skills one must develop to be successful as an employee. To succeed as a manager, one must achieve a still higher level of proficiency in such major areas as communications, time management, self-motivation, interpersonal relationships, and the broad area of leadership.

Below is a list of a set of suggestions to help employees enhance their own development and increase their opportunities for advancement. The *development suggestions* focus on personal growth and direction, while the *advancement suggestions* focus on the steps employees can take to improve their promotability in the organization.

Development

1. Create your own personal mission statement that indicates the business you would like to be in and the role you would like to play.

2. Take responsibility for your own direction and growth and avoid placing all of your hopes in an organization-provided development program.

3. Make enhancement, rather than advancement, your priority by constantly searching for opportunities to broaden your skills in the short run.

4. Talk to people in positions to which you aspire and get suggestions on how to proceed to make it to that level.

5. Set reasonable career goals by breaking them into smaller, more manageable goals along the way to your ultimate goal.

6. Make investment in yourself a priority by not neglecting self-development activities.

Advancement

1. Remember that performance in your function is important but interpersonal performance is critical.
2. Set the right values and priorities by aligning your behavior with the organization's values.
3. Provide solutions, not problems, by taking the time to think issues through and to offer potential solutions.
4. Be a team player by working to shine the spotlight on the group's efforts.
5. Be customer-oriented by always keeping in mind that anyone with whom you have an exchange is your "customer."
6. Act as if what you're doing makes a difference by approaching each activity with a positive attitude.

It is important for organizations to understand that a systematic program of career development is a valuable tool in attracting, retaining, and motivating employees. The benefits of such a program are many:

1. Developing an employee's capabilities is consistent with a HRM policy of promotion from within. As noted in Chapter 7, training is important in a career development system.
2. Training enables an employee to acquire the KSAs needed for promotion to higher-level positions. It eases the transition from an employee's present job to one involving greater responsibilities.
3. Training assists in retention. Those organizations that fail to provide training often lose their most promising employees. Frustrated by the lack of opportunity, achievement-oriented employees often seek employment with other organizations that provide training for career advancement.
4. Training can increase an employee's level of commitment to the organization and improve perceptions that the organization is a good place to work. By developing and promoting trained employees, organizations create a competent, motivated, and satisfied workforce.

In general, most organizations have implemented the use of individual development plans (IDPs) for all categories of employees. Special interest programs related to upward mobility for minorities, women, and handicapped workers have also become quite prevalent in these organizations and result from changes in workforce demographics. As suggested throughout this chapter a number of career development tools, techniques, and programs have evolved, including training workshops, individual counseling, career information centers, career ladders, assessment and testing centers, skills inventories, job rotation, and mentoring.

Today's successful organizations should ensure that they have a viable career development system in place that addresses the demands of a changing workforce. It can be an investment with very high returns.

CAREER DEVELOPMENT FOR TODAY'S DIVERSE WORKFORCE

To meet the career development needs of today's diverse workforce, organizations need to break down the barriers some employees face in achieving advancement. The first major study of the glass ceiling in 1991 revealed that women and minorities are held back not only from top executive positions but also from lower-level management positions and directorships. The Department of Labor defines the glass ceiling as "Those artificial barriers based on attitudinal or organizational bias that prevent qualified individuals from advancing upward in their organizations into management level positions" (U.S. Department of Labor, 2001). The study reveals that women and minorities are frequently excluded from informal career development activities such as networking, mentoring, and participation in policymaking committees. In addition to outright discrimination, some of the practices that contribute to their exclusion are informal word-of-mouth recruitment, companies' failure to sensitize and instruct managers about EEO requirements, lack of mentoring, and the too-swift identification of high-potential employees (Kalish, 1992, p. 64).

Barriers to the advancement of women and minorities continue to exist 10 years after the initial government study of the glass ceiling. The Office of Federal Contract Compliance Programs (OFCCP) enforces antidiscrimination laws covering federal contractors. The OFCCP began monitoring the pay and promotion practices of companies doing business with the government in 1991. It has found problems in about half of the companies it has audited. However, some of these difficulties have to do with gender- or race-based pay differences rather than with mobility and promotion opportunities (Swoboda, 1998).

The imbalance in the proportion of women in top management positions and minorities in middle- and top-management positions indicates the ongoing need for special career development programs for both these groups. Systematic on-the-job approaches such as coaching, job rotations and transfers, underway assignments, and mentoring can be particularly helpful. Challenging, successfully completed projects such as troubleshooting, start-ups, and international assignments are especially important to the career progression of executives, and yet women and minorities are less likely to be assigned to those projects. Therefore, careful attention must be paid to

HRM planning and decisions about assignments to ensure that women and minorities have equal opportunities.

Many employers now offer special training to women and minorities who are on a management career path. They may use their own staff or outside firms to conduct the training. Opportunities are also available for women and minorities to participate in seminars and workshops that provide instruction and experiences in a wide variety of management topics. Often these training programs stress the special problems faced by women and minorities in managerial positions. These problems include potential lack of acceptance by their white male counterparts and by direct reports and lack of support from family for women with career aspirations.

Amendments to the Age Discrimination in Employment Act removing ceilings on retirement make it even more important that organizations pay attention to the long-term career development of all employees, including older workers. There are at least four myths about older workers that tend to make them vulnerable to discrimination in training and advancement opportunities.

One myth is that older workers are less motivated, less efficient, and less productive than younger workers. A second myth is that older workers are resistant to change and less flexible than younger workers. A third myth is that older workers tend to have poor attendance records. A fourth myth is that older workers have more accidents. Despite the fact that research has dispelled all of these myths (Mitchell, 1988), subtle discrimination stemming from such myths can, of course, affect the self-confidence and risk taking of older workers and might discourage them from pursuing training opportunities. With people living longer and thus staying in the workforce longer, organizations must recognize the importance of ensuring that their career management systems address the challenges presented by older workers.

Regardless of whether an organization is confronted with a more diverse workforce that is dominated by more women, minorities, older workers or the disabled, it would do well to follow the Glass Ceiling Commission's suggestions for toppling job-advancement barriers if it wishes to remain successful:

- Demonstrate commitment. Top management should communicate its dedication to diversity and enact policies that promote it.
- Hold line managers accountable for progress by including diversity in all strategic business plans. Performance appraisals, compensation incentives, and other evaluation measures should reflect this priority.
- Use affirmative action as a tool to ensure that all qualified individuals compete based on ability and merit.
- Expand your pool of candidates. Look for prospects from noncustomary sources who may have nontraditional backgrounds and experiences.

- Educate all employees about the strengths and challenges of gender, racial, ethnic, and cultural differences.
- Initiate family-friendly programs that help women and men balance their work and family responsibilities (Glass Ceiling, 1991).

If followed, the suggestions from the Glass Ceiling Commission should go a long way toward creating a culture that evaluates, hires, and promotes on the basis of merit.

CAREER DEVELOPMENT ONLINE

Many of today's organizations are developing comprehensive, online career development centers. These online career development centers provide access to a wide variety of services to help employees manage their careers and, in some instances, even find jobs outside their present organization. Online capabilities can provide many types of career-related information on demand. For example, employees can look up the competencies and KSAs required for jobs to which they aspire. Some of the online career planning resources being offered include:

- Information about employment trends and job opportunities.
- Self-assessment tools, such as personality tests and interest indicators, that employees can use to determine which types of jobs they might best pursue.
- Links to online employment resources such as job listings and career development information.
- Individual online job counseling, including advice on preparing for interviews ("Dismantling the Glass Ceiling," 1996).

As noted earlier, in addition to company-sponsored online services, many resources are available on the Internet to help individuals with career development. These resources include job search guides, resume preparation aids, job listings, career-related articles, and other similar services. There is little doubt that career development resources online will continue to expand in the future.

NEW ORGANIZATIONAL STRUCTURES AND CHANGING CAREER PATTERNS

A changing economic environment, increased global competition, and the glut of middle-aged baby boom workers have sparked a further set of changes in organizational structures and employee career paths. Rectructuring, downsizing, or rightsizing have been the norm for many organizations for the past decade and a half. In an effort to reduce labor costs organizations have reduced the size of their permanent full-time staff. These cuts have affected middle managers as well as lower-level employees. Entire levels of management have been abolished to become "flatter," quicker to respond, and closer to the customer. To meet varying labor needs, the new rightsized organizations hire temporary workers or outsource work to smaller organizations and consultants. There also has been a substantial rise in part-time employment, both because part-timers are less expensive and receive fewer fringe benefits and because they provide greater flexibility in scheduling employees for peak demand periods. In general, it is safe to say that for many employees, the "psychological contract" they have with their employer has changed from one of "If you do your job well, we'll employ you until you retire" to "We'll employ you as long as we need your contribution to help us succeed in business."

Consequently, career patterns for individual employees are changing. Research suggests that the traditional linear career path in which one enters an organization near the bottom, works in the same organization for many years, and gradually and predictably moves up, retiring from a fairly high-level position in the same organization may become the exception rather than the rule over the next few decades. The bulge of baby boomers has made climbing the hierarchy much more competitive, the flattening of organizational structures has reduced the number of management positions just as the number of candidates has increased, and massive layoffs have destroyed faith in the employer as a long-term source of security. These changes have caused a great deal of frustration as middle-aged employees fail to advance as they had expected.

In efforts to maintain the motivation and creativity of career-plateaued employees organizations are developing alternatives to the traditional linear career success model. To some extent, the meaning of career success is changing. Some feel that career success now has more to do with self-actualization, skill growth, and self-satisfaction than climbing a fixed ladder of jobs. Balancing family and life commitments with work also seems to be taking on more importance for many employees. Four possible career paths that an employee can follow are: expert, spiral, transitory, and linear (Brousseau, Driver, Eneroth, and Larson, 1996).

An expert, or professional, career ladder rewards growing expertise in a single technical specialty without the need to move into management. Professional ladders allow for career advancement within a single employer, even a "flat" one. For example, scientists and engineers can follow such ladders of increasing technical competence and status (junior engineer, engineer, senior engineer, etc.) without managerial responsibilities.

Another possibility is the spiral career path, which involves a number of lateral moves between functional areas within the same organization. This combines broadening experience and the continuous challenge of new tasks with slower hierarchical progress. For example, one might begin a career in sales, move to operations after several years, move to a different operations job, and then move into the finance area by midcareer. To make these complex spiral career paths work, organizations need to design sophisticated career planning and career information systems to generate and disseminate information about lateral career opportunities throughout the organization (Vaughn and Wilson, 1994).

The transitory career path is another common path. In this approach, the career occurs virtually independent of any single organization. The individual may move into and out of organizations and even occupations on a regular basis, either in search of better jobs and more satisfying challenges or because there is little choice when secure permanent jobs are rare. Some or even most of a transitory career may be spent as a consultant or independent contractor, short-term contract employee, part-timer, or entrepreneur. Individuals on this career path think of themselves as possessing and maintaining a portfolio of competencies that give them security and employability rather than assuming that security and employment are provided by a single organization. Career and development planning is critical for individuals on a transitory career path, but they are more likely to become their own career strategists than rely on input from formal employer-provided career planning systems (Brousseau et al., 1997).

Spiral or transitory career paths may offer another attraction to today's employees; the possibility of staying in one location much longer. With the increasing number of dual-career couples, individuals may prefer to remain in the same community for a longer period, moving between different types of jobs within the same establishment or moving within the same specialty across local employers.

HRM professionals will continue to need to find ways to wrestle with the prevailing "up-or-out" culture of most organizations, which defines lack of upward progress as failure. Traditional linear career planning is less feasible than before, and employer-initiated creative career planning is even more important to effectively utilize talent and provide satisfying careers for today's employees. It has been suggested that the most successful organizations of the future will provide all four types of career paths (linear, expert, spiral, and transitory) in varying proportions to meet the needs of their workforce and to provide the combination of stable and flexible staffing necessary to carry out their business plans (Brousseau et al., 1996).

EVALUATING CAREER MANAGEMENT ACTIVITIES

Career development programs are much more difficult to evaluate than other HRM programs. One of the primary difficulties involves establishing specific objectives. General objectives, such as creating better employees, provide little guidance for evaluation purposes. Even when good objectives are established, it is difficult to design a career development program that can fulfill all of them. Career development tends to be an ongoing process, which compounds the difficulties of evaluation.

One systematic approach to evaluating programs consists of five steps:

1. Determine the history and rationale of the program.
2. Determine the degree to which the program places primary emphasis on its most important goals.
3. Analyze change occurring in employees and the organization; that is, program effectiveness—comparing the outcomes of the program with its stated objectives.
4. Examine the general adaptability of the program.
5. Introduce modifications as required.

Feedback from employees and their managers about the usefulness of specific elements of a career development program is one of the most critical elements of the evaluation process.

While the systematic evaluation process presented above is a start, it is important to understand that the ultimate goal of career management is to have employees who have reached their full potential at work, enjoy productive and satisfying work careers, and then successfully move into retirement. As such, full appreciation of career management activities may not come until after retirement. But as employees are increasingly unlikely to spend their entire careers in a single organization, success in retirement is much more likely to be a function of the individual's own career management efforts as well as the good fortune to remain healthy through retirement years. Furthermore, for many employees (especially those in higher status jobs or those for whom work is an important part of self-image) leaving one's career does not mean the end of work. For these employees managing the transition to what have been called "bridge" jobs (and eventually on to full retirement) is most important for their continued satisfaction (Doeringer, 1990).

Therefore, the success of career management activities can be judged only at one point in time. If an employee is satisfied with her or his career at this point, then career management must be judged successful up to that point. While there is a lot that organizations can do to manage this process, clearly, a great deal depends on the individual's efforts at career management. Employees who go into careers for which they are not well suited (either in terms of abilities or temperament) will obviously be more likely to suffer dissatisfaction with their careers than will those who have made more appropriate career choices. Therefore, although organizational career management efforts are important, the successful management of one's career in today's dynamic world of work depends heavily on each individual's efforts to accurately assess his or her own KSAs and interests and to formulate a plan for what a successful career should look like.

SUMMARY

Today, organizations and individuals need to take a more active, systematic approach to career development. A career development program is a dynamic process that should integrate individual employee needs with those of the organization. The individual employee, the manager, and the employer (especially HRM personnel) all have roles in the individual's career development.

It is the responsibility of the employee to identify her or his own KSAs as well as interests and values and to seek out information about career options. The organization should provide information about its mission, policies, and plans and what it will provide in the way of training and development for the employee.

Organizations must keep a steady watch on their human resources needs and requirements. This ongoing process involves an analysis of the competencies, or KSAs, required for jobs, the progression among related jobs, and the supply of ready (and potential) talent available to fill those jobs. Employees must take responsibility for analyzing their KSAs, interests, and career goals. Organizations must also identify the career opportunities and requirements for the organization and establish a clear understanding of the talent base they have at their disposal. Organizations often rely on various mechanisms to communicate career options, to including posting and advertising job vacancies and sharing HRM planning forecasts with employees.

Career counseling programs are very important to an organization interested in career development for its employees. Such programs usually address a wide variety of career-related issues and are readily accessible to people in the organization. Helping dual-career couples and meeting the challenges for today's workforce require that organizations work to break down the barriers employees face in achieving advancement.

An environment of increasing competition, continuous change, increased globalization, and new organizational structures has resulted in changes in career patterns for individual employees. Organizations have recognized that the traditional career paths are no longer feasible and are increasingly relying on creative career planning to meet the demands of the new world of work.

Unlike other HRM activities, career development and planning are much harder to evaluate. Thus, career management activities can be judged only by individuals at that point in their lives where they feel they have or have not realized their potential.

REFERENCES

Bolles, R. 1999. *What color is your parachute 1999: A practical manual for job-hunters and career-changers.* Berkeley, CA: Ten Speed Press.

Brousseau, K.R., Driver, M.J., Eneroth, K., and Larson, R. 1996. Career pandemonium: Realigning organizations and individuals. *Academy of Management Executive* (November): 52–66.

Dismantling the glass ceiling. 1996. *HRFocus* (May): 12.

Doeringer, P.B. 1990. Economic security, labor market flexibility, and bridges to retirement. In P.B. Doeringer (ed.), *Bridges to retirement*. Ithaca, NY: ILR Press, Cornell University, pp. 3–22.

Ferrence, T.P., Stoner, J.A.E., and Warren, E.K. 1977. Managing the career plateau. *Academy of Management Review* (October): 602–623.

Fraze, V. 1999. Expert help for dual-career spouses. *Workforce* (March): 18–20.

The glass ceiling. 1991. *HRMagazine* (October): 91–92.

Jackson, C. 1999. Career path. *Hospital & Health Networks* (August): 20.

Kalish, B.B. 1992. Dismantling the glass ceiling. *Management Review* (March): 64.

Kennedy, M.M. 1999. How do you prove you make a difference? *Across the Board* 36: 44–48.

Levitt, J.G. 1995. *Your career—how to make it happen*, 3rd ed. Cincinnati, OH: South-Western.

Meister, J.C. 1998. The quest for lifetime employability. *Journal of Business Strategy* (May–June): 25–28.

Mitchell, O.S. 1988. The relation of age to workplace injuries. *Monthly Labor Review* (July): 8–13.

Otte, F.L., and Hutcheson, P.G. 1992. *Helping employees manage careers*. Englewood Cliffs, NJ: Prentice-Hall, p. 10.

Pantazis, C. 1999. The new workforce investment act. *Training and Development* (August): 48–50.

Payne, R.C. 1984. Mid-career block. *Personnel Journal* (April): 42.

Peiperl, M., and Baruch, Y. 1997. The post-corporate career. *Organizational Dynamics* (Spring): 7–22.

Randolph, A.B. 1981. Managerial career counseling. *Training and Development Journal* (July): 54–55.

Starcevich, M., and Friend, F. 1999. Effective mentoring relationships from the mentee's perspective. *Workforce*, supplement (July): 2–3.

Swoboda, F. 1998. US Airways settles "glass ceiling" case. *Washington Post* (December 3), p. E2.

U.S. Department of Labor. 2001. *Glass ceiling report*. www.dol.gov.

Vaughn, R.H., and Wilson, M.C. 1994. Career management using job trees: Charting a path through the changing organization. *Human Resource Planning* 17(4): 43–55.

Chapter 10

Compensation

INTRODUCTION

Organizations exist to accomplish specific goals and objectives. One of the reasons employees go to work in organizations is to get money, which enables them to buy a wide variety of services and goods. It is doubtful, however, whether many employees would continue working were it not for the money they earn. Employees expect organizations to have compensation systems that they perceive as being fair and commensurate with their skills and expectations (LeBlanc and Hulvey, 1998). Pay, therefore, is a major consideration in HRM because it provides employees with tangible reward for their services as well as a source of recognition and livelihood. Compensation is the HRM function that deals with every type of reward individuals receive in exchange for performing organizational tasks. Direct compensation consists of the pay and rewards received by employees in the form of wages and salaries, incentives, bonuses, and commissions. Indirect compensation comprises the many benefits supplied by employers, and nonfinancial compensation includes employee recognition programs, rewarding jobs, and flexible work hours to accommodate personal needs. Typical benefits include vacation, various kinds of insurance, services like child care or elder care, and so forth.

As the business environment becomes increasingly complex and global, the challenge to create and maintain effective compensation programs, given constraints, also requires greater professional expertise, organizational understanding, creativity, and vision than ever before. The system that an organization uses to reward employees can play an important role in the organization's efforts to gain a competitive advantage and to achieve its major objectives. Additionally, both managers and scholars agree that the way compensation is allocated among employees sends a message about what management believes is important and the types of activities it encourages. Furthermore, it is the major cost of doing business for many organizations at the beginning of the twenty-first century (Hackett and McDermott, 1999). In labor-intensive organizations, labor costs typically constitute the single largest proportion of the organization's operating budget. In some organizations, employee remuneration costs may be 70 to 80 percent of operating budget. A strategic compensation program, therefore, is essential so that pay can serve to motivate employee production sufficiently to keep labor costs at an acceptable level. As we will see, compensation includes various elements such as base salary, incentives, bonuses, benefits, and other rewards. In this chapter we cover basic compensation. We start by examining the strategic importance of compensation and the objectives of compensation. Next, we look at factors that must be considered in determining the wage mix for employees. Job evaluation methods and wage and salary surveys used to establish internal and external equity are then introduced and discussed. Legal constraints on compensation and current issues in managing compensation are then highlighted. Before concluding the chapter with a look at HRM's role in compensation, we focus on assessing the effectiveness of compensation.

COMPENSATION PLANNING: THE STRATEGIC IMPORTANCE

Like many other aspects of an organization's approach to managing human resources, compensation can facilitate (or interfere with) achieving many strategic objectives. Today's organizations must increasingly take a strategic approach to planning their compensation efforts. This means that they must compensate employees in ways that enhance motivation, growth, and productivity while, at the same time, they align their efforts with the objectives, philosophies, and culture of the organization. A strategic approach to compensation planning goes beyond determining what market rates to pay employees—although market rates are one element of compensation planning—to purposefully linking compensation to the organization's mission and general business objectives (Tyler, 1998).

A strategic approach to compensation planning also serves to mesh the monetary payments made to employees with specific functions of the HRM program. For example, in the recruitment of new employees, the rate of pay for jobs can increase or limit the supply of applicants. One compensation specialist notes, "The linkage of pay levels to labor markets is a strategic policy issue because it affects the caliber of the workforce and the organization's relative payroll costs" (Risher, 1993, p. 47). In recent years, traditionally low-wage employers like many fast food restaurants have needed to raise their starting wages to attract a sufficient number of job applicants to meet staffing requirements. If rates of pay are high, creating a large applicant pool, then organizations may choose to raise their selection standards and hire better qualified employees. This in turn can reduce employer training costs. When employees perform at exceptional levels, their performance appraisals may justify an increased pay rate. For these reasons and others, an organization should develop a formal HRM program to manage employee compensation.

We will discuss three important aspects of a strategic approach to compensation planning: compensation and organizational objectives, compensation's motivational value, and pay-for-performance standard.

COMPENSATION AND ORGANIZATIONAL OBJECTIVES

Ideally, a compensation or reward system should align individual objectives with important strategic goals of the organization. But for most organizations, the reality falls far short of this idea. The design and implementation of a compensation system constitutes one of the most complex activities for which HRM specialists are responsible. Despite this complexity, today's organizations must manage compensation programs in ways that motivate employees to make meaningful contributions and assume ownership of their jobs.

Because so many organizational funds are spent on compensation-related activities, it is critical for top management and HRM personnel to view the "strategic" fit of compensation with the strategies and objectives of the organization. Increasingly, organizations are recognizing that compensation philosophies must change along with changes in the global marketplace for products and services. For example, in today's business environment many organizations have needed to change their pay philosophy from paying for a specific position or job title to rewarding employees on the basis of their contributions to organizational success. A compensation program, therefore, must be tailored to the needs of the organization and its employees.

Compensation specialists are increasingly speaking of value-added compensation as the most appropriate way for organizations to view compensation (Risher, 1997, p. 16). Also called value-chain compensation, a value-added compensation program is one in which the components of the compensation package (benefits, base pay, incentives, etc.), both separately and in combination, create value for the organization and its employees (Newman and Krzystofiak, 1998). Using a value-added viewpoint, managers will ask questions such as "How does this compensation package benefit the organization?" "Does the benefit offset the administrative cost?" Payments that fail to advance either the employee or the organization are removed from the compensation program.

It is not uncommon for organizations to establish specific goals for joining their organizational objectives to their compensation program. Formalized compensation goals serve as guidelines for managers to ensure that wage and benefit policies achieve their intended purpose ("Stay for Pay," 1998, p. 5). The more common goals of a strategic compensation policy include the following:

- Signaling to employees (and others) the major objectives of the organization—such things as quality, customer focus, and other goals—by emphasizing these through compensation
- Complying with government regulations
- Attracting and retaining the talent the organization needs
- Remaining competitive in the labor market
- Rewarding employees' past performance
- Encouraging employees to develop the KSAs they need
- Controlling the compensation budget
- Reducing unnecessary turnover
- Maintaining salary equity among employees
- Supporting the type of culture (e.g., entrepreneurial) the organization seeks to engender

To achieve these goals, policies must be established to guide management in making decisions. Formal statements of compensation policies typically include the following:

- The rate of pay within the organization and whether it is to be above, below, or at the prevailing community rate.
- The ability of the pay program to gain employee acceptance while motivating employees to perform to the best of their abilities.
- The pay level at which employees may be recruited and the pay differential between new and more senior employees.
- The intervals at which pay raises are to be granted and the extent to which merit and/or seniority will influence the raises.
- The pay levels needed to facilitate the achievement of a sound financial position in relation to the products or services offered.

COMPENSATION'S MOTIVATIONAL VALUE

As noted thus far, compensation has a number of fundamental purposes and objectives. Compensation also has a motivating value. Organizations need to provide appropriate and equitable rewards to employees. Employees want to feel valued and want to be rewarded at a level that is commensurate with their KSAs and other contributions to the organization. In this regard, it is essential, according to the equity theory, that the pay be equitable in terms of those contributions. It is essential also that an employee's pay be equitable in terms of what other employees are receiving for their contributions.

Internal equity. Internal equity in compensation refers to comparisons employees make to other employees within the same organization. In making these comparisons employees question whether they are being equitably paid for their contributions to the organization relative to the way other employees in the organization are paid. Employees expect the president of a company to earn more than the executive vice president, who in turn earns more than the plant manager, and so on. Among other things, compensation is presumed to be correlated with the level of KSAs and experience required to do the job successfully. Thus no one is surprised that people high in the organizational structure earn more than lower-level employees do. Internal equity exists when the pay differentials between different jobs within the organization are perceived as fair—neither too large nor too small. Problems with internal equity can result in conflict among employees, feelings of mistrust, low morale, anger, and perhaps even legal actions if the basis for inequity is perceived to result from illegal discrimination.

External equity. External equity in compensation refers to comparisons employees make with similar employees performing similar jobs at other organizations. For example, when the secretary working for an electrical manufacturer's plant manager worries about external equity, the comparison is likely to be with secretaries at the automobile plant across town rather than with electrical companies nationwide. Problems with external equity may result in high turnover as employees leave for better opportunities elsewhere, generally dissatisfied and unhappy workers, and difficulties in attracting new employees.

Both types of equity are clearly important, but there is one further consideration concerning internal equity. The Equal Pay Act of 1963 stipulates that men and women who perform essentially the same job must be paid the same. Generally speaking, internal equity problems occur when employees in one job believe that they are being undercompensated relative to employees in some other job or jobs within the organization. However, it is illegal to pay a woman less than a man (or vice versa) for performing the same job when there is no objective basis for such a differential. If the organization can prove that such differences are based on differences in performance and/or seniority, the organization will probably avoid litigation, but even then the perception by a woman that she is being paid less than a man doing the same job is likely to lead to problems. Also, if some jobs in the organization are performed mostly by men and others mostly by women, differences in pay between the two jobs (real or perceived) must be attributable to differences in job demands or, again, the organization might face legal problems.

Organizations must understand that how employees view compensation can be an important factor in determining the motivational value of compensation. Furthermore, the effective communication of pay information together with an organizational environment that elicits employee trust in management can contribute to employees' having more accurate perceptions of their pay. The perceptions employees develop concerning their pay are influenced by the accuracy of their knowledge and understanding of the compensation program's strategic objectives.

Pay secrecy. Perceived inequities sometimes occur because employees have inaccurate and/or incomplete information. Misperceptions by employees concerning the equity of their pay and its relationship to performance can be created by secrecy about the pay others receive. There is reason to believe that secrecy can generate distrust in the compensation system, reduce employee motivation, and inhibit organizational effectiveness. Although it's illegal for employers to forbid employee discussions of pay, pay secrecy seems to be an accepted practice in many organizations in both the private and the public sector in the United States.

Managers may justify secrecy on the grounds that most employees prefer to have their own pay kept secret. Probably one of the reasons for pay secrecy that managers may be unwilling to admit is that it gives them greater freedom in compensation management, since pay decisions are not disclosed and there is no need to justify or defend them. Employees who are not supposed to know what others are being paid have no objective base for pursuing complaints about their own pay. Secrecy also serves to cover up inequities existing within the internal pay structure. Further, secrecy surrounding compensation decisions may lead employees to believe that there is no direct relationship between pay and performance.

PAY-FOR-PERFORMANCE STANDARD

A final important aspect of a strategic approach to compensation planning is the pay-for-performance standard. To raise productivity and lower labor costs in today's competitive global economic environment, organizations are increasingly setting compensation objectives based on a pay-for-performance standard. It is agreed that organizations must tie at least some reward to employee effort and performance. Without this standard, motivation to perform with greater effort will be low, resulting in higher wage costs to the organization.

The term "pay-for-performance" refers to a wide range of compensation options including merit-based pay, bonuses, salary commissions, job and pay banding, team/group incentives, and various gainsharing programs. (Gainsharing plans are discussed in Chapter 11.) Each of these compensation systems seeks to differentiate between the pay of average performers and outstanding performers. Some productivity studies show that employees will increase their output by 15 to 35 percent when an organization installs a pay-for-performance program.

Unfortunately, designing a sound pay-for-performance system is not easy. Considerations must be given to how employees' performance will be measured, the monies to be allocated for compensation increases, which employees to cover, the payout method, and the periods when payments will be made (Guinn and Corona, 1991, p. 72). A critical issue concerns the size of the monetary increase and its perceived value to employees. While differences exist as to how large a wage or salary increase must be before it is perceived as meaningful, a pay-for-performance program will lack its full potential when pay increases only approximate rises in the cost of living.

THE BASES FOR COMPENSATION

Organizations have traditionally compensated employees for their work on an hourly basis. This is referred to as hourly work, in contrast to piecework, in which employees are paid according to the number of units they produce. Hourly work, however, is far more prevalent than piecework as a basis for compensating employees.

Employees compensated on an hourly basis are classified as hourly employees, or wage earners. Those whose compensation is computed on the basis of weekly, biweekly, or monthly pay periods are classified as salaried employees. Hourly employees are normally paid only for the time they work. Salaried employees, by contrast, are generally paid the same for each period, even though they occasionally may work more or fewer hours than the regular number of hours in a period. They also usually receive certain benefits not provided to hourly employees.

Another basis for compensation centers on whether employees are classified as nonexempt or exempt under the Fair Labor Standards Act (FLSA). Nonexempt employees are covered by the act and must be paid at a rate of one and one-half times their regular pay for time worked in excess of 40 hours in their workweek. Most hourly workers employed in interstate commerce are considered nonexempt workers under the FLSA. Employees not covered by the overtime provision of the FLSA are classified as exempt employees. Managers and supervisors as well as a large number of white-collar employees are in the exempt category. The U.S. Department of Labor (DOL) imposes a narrow definition of exempt status, and employers wishing to classify employees as exempt must convince the DOL that the job is exempt on the basis of the use of independent judgment by the jobholder and other criteria. Therefore employers should check the exact terms and conditions of exemption before classifying employees as either exempt or nonexempt.

IMPORTANT CONSIDERATIONS FOR WAGE MIX

A combination of internal and external factors can influence, directly or indirectly, the rates at which employees are paid. Each employer has the difficult task of weighting these factors and making numerous decisions that ultimately determine how much a specific employee will be paid. The influence of government legislation on determining the wage mix will be discussed later in this chapter.

External Factors

The major external factors that influence wage rates include labor market conditions, area wage rates, cost of living, collective bargaining if the employer is unionized, and legal requirements.

Labor market conditions. Labor market conditions affect the design of compensation in that they drive decisions about the overall level of pay offered and the mix of pay offered. The labor market reflects forces of supply and demand for qualified labor within an area. These forces help to influence the wage rates required to recruit or retain competent employees. It must be recognized, however, that counterforces can reduce the full impact of supply and demand on the labor market. The economic power of unions, for example, may prevent employers from lowering wage rates even when unemployment is high among union members. Government regulations also may prevent an employer from paying at a market rate less than an established minimum.

Area wage rates. A formal wage structure should provide rates that are in line with those being paid by other employers for comparable jobs within the area. Data pertaining to area wage rates may be obtained from local wage surveys. Wage surveys serve the important function of providing external wage equity between the surveying organization and other organizations competing for labor in the surrounding labor market. Importantly, data from area wage surveys can be used to prevent the rates for jobs from drifting too far above or below those of other employers in the region. When rates rise above existing area levels, an employer's labor costs may become excessive. Conversely, if they drop too far below area levels, it may be difficult to recruit and retain competent personnel. Wage-survey data must also take into account indirect wages paid in the form of benefits.

Cost of living adjustments (COLAs). Because of inflation, compensation rates have to be adjusted upward periodically to help employees maintain their purchasing power. Employers make these changes with the help of the consumer price index (CPI). The CPI is a measure of the average change in prices over time in a fixed "market basket" of goods and services (Bureau of Labor Statistics, 1996). Employers in a number of communities monitor changes in the CPI as a basis for compensation decisions.

Changes in the CPI can have important effects on pay rates. Granting wage increases solely on the basis of the CPI helps to compress pay rates within a pay structure, thereby creating inequities among those who receive the wage increase. Inequities also result from the fact that adjustments are made on a cent-per-hour rather than a percentage basis. For example, a cost-of-living adjustment of 50 cents represents a 7.1 percent increase for an employee earning $7 per hour, but only a 4.2 percent increase for one earning $12 per hour. Unless adjustments are made periodically in employee base rates, the desired differential between higher- and lower-paying jobs will gradually be reduced.

Besides pushing for COLAs unions have also pushed for wage escalation clauses, which increase wages automatically during the life of a contract. These clauses provide for quarterly COLAs in wages based on changes in the CPI. The most common adjustments are 1 cent per hour for each 0.3- or 0.4-point change in the CPI. COLAs are favored by unions during particularly high periods of inflation.

Collective bargaining. Collective bargaining has a major impact on the pay system within given organizations and industries. In a unionized organization, collective bargaining determines the wages for jobs covered by the contract, rules of wage administration for these jobs, and methods for determining the relative worth of jobs. The union's goal in each new collective bargaining agreement is to achieve increases in real wages—wage increases larger than the increase in the CPI—thereby improving the purchasing power and standard of living of its members. This goal includes gaining wage settlements that equal if not exceed the pattern established by other unions within the area.

The agreements negotiated by unions tend to establish rate patterns within the labor market. As a result, wages are generally higher in areas where organized labor is strong. To recruit and retain competent personnel and avoid unionization, nonunion employers must either meet or exceed these rates. The "union scale" also becomes the prevailing rate that all employers must pay for work performed under government contract. The impact of collective bargaining (see Chapter 13 for a more detailed discussion of collective bargaining) therefore extends beyond that segment of the labor force that is unionized.

Internal Factors

The internal factors that influence wage rates are the employer's compensation policy, the worth of a job, an employee's relative worth in meeting job requirements, and an employer's ability to pay.

Organization's compensation policy. Compensation policies and objectives differ widely across large and small organizations as well as across employers in the private and public sectors. For example, an organization's pay objective may be to be an industry pay leader or seek to be wage-competitive. Many organizations will establish numerous compensation objectives that affect the pay employees receive. As a minimum, both large and small employers should set pay policies reflecting: (1) the internal wage relationship among jobs and skill levels, (2) the external competition or an employer's pay position relative to what competitors are paying, (3) a policy of rewarding employee performance, and (4) administrative decisions concerning elements of the pay system such as overtime premiums, payment records, and short-term or long-term incentives.

Worth of a job. Most people would probably agree that some jobs are worth more to an employer than others. For example, negotiating multimillion-dollar contracts with the government is considered to be worth more than emptying wastepaper baskets. Organizations without a formal compensation program generally base worth of jobs on the subjective opinions of people familiar with the jobs. In such instances, pay rates may be influenced heavily by the labor market or, in the case of unionized employees, by collective bargaining. Organizations with formal compensation programs, however, are more likely to rely on a system of job evaluation to aid in rate determination. Even when rates are subject to collective bargaining, job evaluation can assist the organization in maintaining some degree of control over its wage structure.

Employee's relative worth. One employee may be worth more than another in the same job. Sales Manager A consistently sells twice as much as Sales Manager B and is considered of more worth than B to the organization. An organization must take into consideration differences in employee performance. If such things as merit raises are to have their intended value, they must be determined by an effective performance appraisal system that differentiates between those employees who deserve the raises and those who do not. This system, moreover, must provide a visible and credible relationship between performance and any raises received. Unfortunately, too many so-called merit systems provide for raises to be granted automatically. As a result, employees tend to be rewarded more for merely being present than for being productive.

Organization's ability to pay. Unlike their private sector counterparts, for organizations in the public sector, the amount of pay and benefits employees can receive is limited by the funds budgeted for this purpose and by the willingness of taxpayers to provide them. In the private sector pay levels are limited by profits and other financial resources available to employers. Thus an organization's ability to pay is determined in part by the productivity of its employees. This productivity is a result not only of their performance but also of the amount of capital the organization has invested in labor-saving equipment. Generally, increases in capital investment reduce the number of employees required to perform the work and increase an employer's ability to provide higher pay for those it employs.

If an organization has been highly profitable for several years in a row, it is much more likely to pay significantly above-average wages and to grant liberal pay increases than if it is losing money. If an organization is losing money, there is a strong possibility that a reduction in wages and salaries will be one of the options examined.

Economic conditions and competition faced by employers can also significantly affect the rates organizations are able to pay. Competition and recessions can force prices down and reduce the income from which compensation payments are derived. In such situations, employers have little choice but to reduce wages and/or lay off employees or, even worse, to go out of business.

ESTABLISHING INTERNAL EQUITY: JOB EVALUATION SYSTEMS

As discussed previously, an important component of the compensation decision or planning is the worth of jobs. Organizations formally determine the value of jobs through the process of job evaluation. A systematic comparison can define an internal job hierarchy that ranks jobs in terms of their contribution to the organizational objectives. The relative worth of a job may be determined by comparing it with others within the organization or by comparing it with a scale that has been constructed for this purpose. Each method of comparison, furthermore, may be made on the basis of the jobs as a whole or on the basis of the parts that constitute the jobs. In short, this procedure is used to answer such questions as the following: Will technicians be paid more than researchers? If so, how much more? Will word processors be paid more than secretaries, or should both groups receive the same pay? On what basis can these decisions be justified? Most conventional job evaluation plans are variations or combinations of four basic methods: job ranking, job classification, point, and factor comparison.

Job Ranking Method

Job ranking, the simplest and oldest way to evaluate jobs, is used primarily in small organizations. In this method the raters simply rank the various jobs examined. No attempt is made to determine the critical factors in each job. Instead, an overall judgment is made of the relative worth of each job, and the job is ranked accordingly. Job ranking can be done by a single individual knowledgeable about all jobs or by a committee composed of management and employee representatives. The ranking method is simple, inexpensive, fast, and easy to understand. However, it is nonquantitative and rather subjective, for although jobs are compared with each other, there is no explicit set of compensable factors used in this comparison. Additionally, simple ranking gives no information about the distances between jobs, making it difficult to assign salary levels.

Because of the difficulties in ranking a large number of jobs at one time, the paired comparison technique of ranking is sometimes used. With this technique, decisions are made about the relative worth of only two jobs at a time. Since each job is compared with every other job, however, the number of comparisons to be made increases rapidly with the addition of each job to the list. Although this technique is somewhat more systematic than simple ranking, the number of comparisons increases quite rapidly as the number of jobs increases.

Job Classification Method

A second type of job evaluation plan is the job classification method, or job grading. The job classification method is a nonquantitative job evaluation technique that compares the whole job with a predetermined standard. In this approach, jobs are assigned to predefined grades or classes; for example, Grade I, Grade II, Grade III, and so on. These descriptions of each grade feature gradations of job responsibility, skill and education required, and the like. Job descriptions for other jobs in the organization are then examined, and those jobs are classified into grades or levels that seem most appropriate. This method requires a decision at the outset on the number of pay grades to be included in the wage and salary plan. Actual amounts to be assigned to pay grades, of course, may be made after the job evaluation is completed. While this system has the advantage of simplicity, it is less precise than the point and factor comparison methods (discussed in the next sections) because the job is evaluated as a whole. Job grading is common in the public sector. The federal civil service job classification system is probably the best-known system of this type. The job classification method is also widely used by municipal and state governments.

Point Method

The point-factor method breaks the job into components and evaluates each of these job elements against specially constructed scales. A quantitative approach, the point method is rather complex to design but relatively simple to understand and administer once it is in place. It is the most widely used method of job evaluation; well over half the organizations that use job evaluation use the point method. The principal advantage of the point method is that it provides a more refined basis for making judgments than either the ranking or classification methods and thereby can produce results that are more valid and less easy to manipulate.

Using job descriptions as a starting point, managers assign points to various compensable factors that are required to perform that job. Compensable factors are those job dimensions or job requirements that will be the basis for paying employees. For instance, managers might assign points based on the amount of skill that is required to perform a particular job, the amount of physical effort that is needed, the nature of the working conditions involved, and/or the responsibility and authority that are involved in the performance of the job. Job evaluation simply represents the sum of the points that are allocated to each compensable factor for each job.

Organizations select three to 25 compensable factors with the typical point method using about 10 factors. The factors chosen should not overlap with one another, but should be able to immediately distinguish between substantive characteristics of the jobs, be objective and verifiable in nature, and be well understood and accepted by both managers and employees. Given that not all aspects of a particular job may be of equal importance, managers can allocate different weights to reflect the relative importance of these aspects to a job. The weights are usually determined by summing the judgments of a variety of independent but informed evaluators. Thus an administrative job within an organization might result in weightings of required education, 40 percent; required experience, 30 percent; predictability and complexity of the job, 15 percent; responsibility and authority for making decisions, 10 percent; and working conditions and physical requirements for the job, 5 percent.

As the point method is used to evaluate jobs, most organizations also develop a point manual. The point manual is, in effect, a handbook that contains a description of the compensable factors and the degrees to which these factors may exist within the jobs. A manual also will indicate—usually by means of a table—the number of points allocated to each factor and to each of the degrees into which these factors are divided. The point value assigned to a job represents the sum of the numerical degree of values of each compensable factor that the job possesses.

The Factor Comparison Method

The factor comparison method, like the point method, permits the job evaluation process to be accompanied on a factor-by-factor basis. It differs from the point method, however, in that the compensable factors of the jobs to be evaluated are compared against the compensable factors of key jobs within the organization that serve as the job evaluation scale. Key jobs can be defined as those jobs that are important for wage-setting purposes and are widely known in the labor market. Key jobs have the following characteristics:

1. They are important to employees and the organization.
2. They vary in terms of job requirements.
3. They have relatively stable job content.
4. They are used in salary surveys for wage determination.

Key jobs are evaluated against five compensable factors—skill, mental effort, physical effort, responsibility, and working conditions—resulting in a ranking of the different factors for each key job. Normally a committee is selected to rank the criteria across key jobs. Committee members must also assign monetary rates of pay to each compensable factor for each key job. When this task is completed, a factor comparison scale is developed for use in evaluating all other jobs.

COMPENSATION: ESTABLISHING EXTERNAL EQUITY

Job evaluation methods provide for internal equity and serve as the basis for wage rate determination. They do not in themselves determine the wage rate. The evaluated worth of each job in terms of its rank, class, points, or monetary worth must be converted into an hourly, daily, weekly, or monthly rate. Organizations use wage and salary surveys to help set pay or wage rates. In setting wage rates organizations seek to integrate the external information (e.g., labor market conditions, prevailing wage rates, and living costs) with what they have learned through the internal evaluation of jobs. This process is called "pricing the wage structure."

Wage and Salary Surveys

To establish a competitively priced wage structure, organizations typically rely on wage and salary survey data collected from the organization's relevant labor market—local, regional, or national, depending on the job. The labor market is frequently defined as that area from which employers obtain certain types of workers. The labor market for engineers, for example would be national, whereas the labor market for office personnel would be local. It is the wage and salary survey that permits an organization to maintain external equity; that is, to pay its employees wages equivalent to the wages similar employees earn in other establishments.

When job evaluation and wage-survey data are used jointly, they serve to increase the likelihood of both internal and external equity. Although surveys are primarily conducted to gather competitive wage data, they can also collect information on employee benefits or organizational pay practices (e.g., overtime rates or shift differentials).

To design a wage survey, the jobs and area to be studied must be determined, as must the method for gathering data. If the wage survey is done in conjunction with either the point or factor method of job evaluation, the key jobs selected are normally the ones that are surveyed. A good rule of thumb is that a minimum of 30 percent of the jobs in an organization should be surveyed to make a fair evaluation of the organization's pay system. When using the classification or ranking method, the organization should apply the same guidelines followed for selecting jobs with the point and factor comparison methods in choosing the jobs to be surveyed.

A geographic area, an industry type, or a combination of the two may be surveyed. The size of the geographic area, the cost-of-living index for the area, and similar factors must be considered when defining the scope of the survey. The organizations to be surveyed are normally competitors that employ similar types of employees. When they are willing to cooperate, it is often desirable to survey the most important and most respected organizations in the area.

While many organizations conduct their own wage and salary surveys, a variety of "preconducted" pay surveys are available to satisfy the requirements of most public and not-for-profit or private employers. Many trade groups, such as the Dallas Personnel Association, the American Chemical Society, the Administrative Society, and government agencies like the Bureau of Labor Statistics (BLS) publish wage and salary data. Many states conduct surveys on either a municipal or county basis and make them available to employers. While all of these third-party surveys provide certain benefits to their users, they also have various limitations. Two problems with all published surveys are that

1. They are not always compatible with the user's jobs.
2. The user cannot specify what specific data to collect.

To overcome these problems, organizations may collect their own compensation data.

Self-surveys. For an organization that wants to collect and analyze its own data, it is important to obtain information on the characteristics of the responding organizations as well as on both direct and indirect compensation. Organizations wishing to conduct their own wage and salary survey must first select the jobs to be used in the surveys and identify the organizations with whom they actually compete for employees. Since it is not feasible to survey all the jobs in an organization, normally only key jobs, also called benchmark jobs, are used. The survey of key jobs will usually be sent to 10 or 15 organizations that represent a valid sample of other employers likely to compete for the employees of the surveying organization. A diversity of organizations should be selected—small and large, public and private, new and established, and union and nonunion—since each classification of employer is likely to pay different wage rates for surveyed jobs.

After the key jobs and the employers to be surveyed have been identified, the survey organization must decide what information to gather on wages, benefit types, and pay policies. For example, when requesting pay data, it is important to specify whether hourly, daily, or weekly pay figures are needed. In addition, those conducting surveys must state if the wage data are needed for new hires or for senior employees. Precisely defining the compensation data needed will greatly increase the accuracy of the information received and the number of purposes for which it can be used. Once the survey data are tabulated, the compensation structure can be completed.

Wage Surveys, Virtual Jobs, and Wage Curves

As jobs constantly change to match the dynamic needs of the organization and its customers, compensation specialists are asking questions such as, "How do you conduct salary surveys when there are no stable jobs?" "How do you match jobs when there are no jobs to match?" or with the growth of virtual jobs, "How should internal and external pay equity be addressed?" The answers to these concerns lie in developing creative pay surveys to match the organization's compensation strategy. For example, where organizations pay employees on the basis of their competencies and skills, then pay surveys will need to address the compensation of core competencies that span all work and all jobs. The use of maturity-curve surveys is another method to compensate ever-changing job content. Traditionally used to compensate scientific and technical personnel, maturity-curve surveys can also be used to compensate employees on the basis of a relationship between market value and experience.

Wage curves graphically show the relationship between the relative worth of jobs and their wage or salary rates. In addition, these curves can be used to indicate pay classes and ranges for the jobs. Regardless of the job evaluation method used, a wage curve plots the jobs in ascending order of difficulty along the abscissa (x axis) and the wage rate along the ordinate (y axis). If the point method is used for evaluation, the point totals are plotted against their corresponding wage rates to produce a general trend.

To ensure that the final wage structure is consistent with both the job evaluations and the wage survey data, it is sometimes desirable to construct one wage curve based on present wages and one based on the survey data and compare the two. Any discrepancies can be quickly detected and corrected. Points of the graph that do not follow the general trend indicate that the wage rate for that job is too low or too high or that the job has been inaccurately evaluated. Underpaid jobs are sometimes called *green-circle* jobs; when wages are overly high, the positions are known as *red-circle* jobs. These discrepancies can be remedied by granting above- or below-average pay increases for the jobs in question.

Pay Grades and Ranges

From an administrative standpoint, it is generally preferable to group jobs into pay grades and to pay all jobs within a particular grade the same rate or rate range. When the classification system of job evaluation is used, jobs are grouped into grades as part of the evaluation process. When the point and factor comparison method are used, however, pay grades must be established at selected intervals that represent either the point or the evaluated monetary value of these jobs.

The grades within a wage structure may vary in number. The number is determined by such factors as the slope of the wage curve, the number and distribution of the jobs within the structure, and the organization's wage administration and promotion policies. The number utilized should be sufficient to permit difficulty levels to be distinguished but not so great as to make the distinction between two adjoining grades insignificant.

Usually, at the same time pay grades are established, pay ranges are determined for each grade. When this is done, each pay grade is assigned a range of permissible pay, with a minimum and a maximum. The maximum of a pay grade's range places a ceiling on the rate that can be paid to any employee whose job is classified in that grade. Similarly, the minimum of the pay grade's range places a floor on the rate that can be paid. Two general approaches for establishing pay grades and ranges are to have a relatively large number of grades with identical rates of pay for all jobs within each grade and to have a small number of grades with a relatively wide dollar range for each grade. Most pay structures fall somewhere between these extremes.

Ranges within grades are set up so that distinction can be made among employees within grades. Ideally, the placement of employees within pay grades should be based on performance or merit. In practice, however, the distinction is often based on seniority.

On reaching the top of the range for a given grade, an employee can increase her or his pay only by moving to a higher grade. It is not unusual for the ranges of adjacent pay grades to overlap. Under such circumstances, it is possible for an outstanding performer in a lower grade to earn a higher salary than a below-average performer in a higher wage grade.

NEW APPROACHES TO JOB-BASED PAY

Several new perspectives and approaches to determining base pay have evolved over the last several years. This section describes two of the most popular of these approaches: skill-based pay and broadbanding.

Skill-Based Pay

Skill-based pay (also referred to as knowledge-based pay, pay-for-knowledge, or multiskilled base pay) compensates employees for the different skills or increased knowledge they possess rather than for the job they hold in a designated job category. These pay plans encourage employees to earn higher base wages by learning and performing a wider variety of skills (or jobs) or displaying an array of competencies (e.g., a trait or a characteristic that's required by a jobholder to perform that job well) that can be applied to a variety of organizational requirements. As employees learn additional skills, and as the learning is verified through demonstration or tests, they qualify for increments in pay. Skill-based pay is especially compatible with broadbanding because employees can be rewarded for gaining additional skills within a broader array of job activities. Skill-based pay also encourages employees to acquire training when new or updated skills are needed by an organization.

Unfortunately, skill-based pay plans may bring some long-term difficulties. Some plans limit the amount of compensation employees can earn, regardless of the new skills or competencies they acquire. Thus, after achieving the top wage, employees may be reluctant to continue their educational training. Furthermore, employees can become discouraged when they acquire new abilities but find there are no higher-rated jobs to which they can transfer. Unless all employees have the opportunity to increase their pay through the attainment of new skills, employees who are not given this opportunity may feel disgruntled.

Broadbanding

The concept of broadbanding was developed in an effort to make job evaluation more compatible with the downsizing and delayering that characterize many restructured organizations. Organizations that adopt a skill-based or competency-based pay system frequently use broadbanding to structure their compensation payments to employees. Broadbanding simply collapses many traditional salary grades into a few wide salary bands.

An advantage of broadbanding is in the flexibility it provides and the signals it sends to employees. For example, an employee might be interested in a job but be reluctant to explore moving into it if it is not at a higher grade. With broadbanding, the position may be in the same band, so the employee can focus on the content of the job, its challenges, and its developmental opportunities rather than on its grade level. In this way, the employee can learn new skills and better contribute to the team without the possible stigma of a demotion or reduction in pay. Paying employees through broadbands enables organizations to consider job responsibilities, individual skills and competencies, and career mobility patterns in assigning employees to bands.

Broadbanding is not right for all organizations. Managers must be trained to deal with banding's broader salary ranges and fewer control points. Workers may resist the absence of frequent, if small, symbols of their increased value through movement to higher grades.

LEGAL CONSTRAINTS ON COMPENSATION SYSTEMS

Compensation systems, like other areas of HRM, must comply with myriad state and federal regulations. Minimum wage standards and hours of work are two important areas addressed by these laws.

Fair Labor Standards Act (FLSA)

The FLSA of 1938, briefly mentioned earlier in this chapter, is the major law affecting compensation. The FLSA, commonly referred to as the Wage and Hour Act, has been amended several times to raise minimum wage rates and expand employers covered. The FLSA covers those employees who are engaged in the production of goods for interstate and foreign commerce, including those whose work is closely related or essential to such production. The act also covers agricultural workers and employees of certain retail and service establishments whose sales volume exceeds a prescribed amount. Very small, family-owned-and-operated entities and family farms generally are excluded from coverage. Most federal, state, and local government employers are also subject to the provisions of the act, except for military personnel, volunteer workers, and a few other limited groups.

Compliance with FLSA provisions is enforced by the Wage and Hour Division of the U.S. Department of Labor. To meet FLSA requirements employers must keep accurate time records and maintain these records for three years. Inspectors from the Wage and Hour Division investigate complaints filed by individuals who believe they have not received the overtime payments due them. Also, certain industries that historically have had a large number of wage and hour violations can be targeted, and organizations in those industries can be investigated. Penalties for wage and hour violations often include awards of back pay for affected current and former employees for up to two years.

The act has three major objectives:

- Establish a minimum wage floor.
- Discourage oppressive use of child labor.
- Encourage limits on the number of weekly hours employees work through overtime provisions (exempt and nonexempt status).

Minimum wage/wage and hour provisions. The FLSA sets a minimum wage to be paid to the broad spectrum of covered employees. The minimum wage was first set at 25 cents in 1938 to prevent the exploitation of workers and establish a "level playing field" for all employers. The actual minimum wage can be changed only by congressional action. A lower minimum wage level is set for "tipped" employees who work in such organizations as restaurants, but their payment must at least equal the minimum wage when average tips are included.

The minimum wage is one of the most controversial provisions. Basic disagreement about its effects centers on the view of classical economists, who contend that any rise in the minimum wage will soon be offset by an immediate rise in the level of unemployment. Other economists hold that the minimum wage does not raise the level of unemployment in the long run. Rather, it harmlessly raises the wages of the lowest-paid workers. The level at which the minimum wage should be set will obviously continue to lead to significant political discussions and legislative maneuvering. For unskilled workers, the FLSA permits employers to pay a "training wage" of $4.25 per hour for employees younger than 20 years of age during their first 90 days of employment.

As noted earlier in this chapter the overtime provisions of the FLSA require payment of one and one-half the regular hourly rate for work over 40 hours per week. Union contracts may specify greater amounts (e.g., twice the regular hourly rate) or lower thresholds (e.g., overtime after 35 hours per week) that supersede the FLSA provisions.

Employers may pay overtime to exempt employees (e.g., executives and professionals) but are not obligated to do so. Salaried nonexempt employees are covered; to calculate appropriate overtime pay, their salary is converted into an hourly rate. Employers of nonexempt employees are required to keep thorough records of the hours worked to be sure that employees receive overtime payment when it is due.

Child labor provisions. The FLSA forbids the employment of minors between 16 and 18 years of age in hazardous occupations such as mining, logging, woodworking, meatpacking, and certain types of manufacturing. Minors under 16 cannot be employed in any work destined for interstate commerce except that which is performed in a nonhazardous occupation for a parent or guardian or for an employer under a temporary work permit issued by the Department of Labor.

Many employers require age certificates for employees because the FLSA places the responsibility to determine an individual's age on the employer. The certificates may be issued by a representative of a state labor department, a state education department, or a local school district.

Exemptions under the act. The terms exempt and nonexempt are crucial for understanding and complying with the FLSA. Exempt employees include executive, administrative, and professional employees, who are exempt from the minimum wage, work hours, and overtime provisions of the FLSA. Nonexempt employees are subject to the provisions of the FLSA.

The exemption of groups of employees from coverage by the act or from coverage by certain of its provisions creates the most confusion under the FLSA. To be exempt as an executive, an employee must supervise two or more employees, have the authority to hire and fire, and otherwise exercise independent judgment. Administrators need not supervise other employees but do need to exercise independent judgment in carrying out top management policies. Professionals are exempt under the definition of the FLSA if they perform unstandardized artistic or intellectual work of a varied nature that requires independent judgment.

Correctly determining the exempt or nonexempt status of a job is important, although not always easy. For instance, we tend to think of accountants and engineers as professionals, but in some cases they are not professionals under the FLSA guidelines. A lower-level accountant who applies accounting principles with little independent judgment or a newly hired engineer who does setup work for other engineers would not be exempt. Under the law, their employer is liable for overtime pay for these individuals.

A final class of individuals who are exempt from the FLSA includes outside salespeople. An outside salesperson must spend 80 percent or more of the work week away from the employer's place of business, making visits to customers. Outside salespeople need not be paid overtime, and they are often paid only by commission.

Equal Pay Act (EPA)

As mentioned in our discussion of internal equity earlier in the chapter the EPA was passed as an amendment to the FLSA. The EPA requires an organization to offer equal pay for equal work, regardless of the sex of the employee. Thus men and women performing the same job in the same location for the same employer must be offered the same pay, all other things being equal. The use of two job titles for what is essentially the same job as a pretext for paying one group less than the other is not permitted (e.g., calling men "office managers" and women "senior secretaries" when their duties are identical).

The EPA would seem to be a natural basis for pursuing the issue of comparable worth, discussed in more detail later in this chapter. In fact, the rather strict requirements of identical skill, effort, responsibility, and working conditions have made it difficult to use this legislation as the basis for insisting on equal pay for work of comparable worth.

Other Laws Affecting Compensation

Other federal regulations that affect compensation systems have to do with discrimination, wages paid by contractors who work for the U.S. government, and wage garnishment. In addition, some states have their own wage and hour laws.

Title VII of the Civil Rights Act prohibits discrimination on the basis of race, color, sex, national origin, and religion in all aspects of employment, including compensation. Thus it would be illegal to pay minority employees less than similarly qualified nonminority employees for doing the same job in the same location.

The Davis-Bacon Act of 1931, also referred to as the Prevailing Wage Law, requires that the minimum wage rates paid to persons employed on federal public works projects worth more than $2,000 be at least equal to the prevailing rates and that overtime be paid at one and one-half times this rate. The intent of these laws is to prevent the government from buying "Sweatshop" goods and thus indirectly exploiting workers. Some argue that this causes wages to be artificially raised and costs the government more than it would have to pay without this law (Gainer, 1995; Wallace and Fay, 1988). The act is also criticized because the prevailing rates are often the union rates for jobs in the area and are often higher than the average (nonunion) rates (Thieblot, 1996).

The Walsh-Healy Public Contracts Act of 1936 covers workers employed on government contract work for supplies, equipment, and materials worth in excess of $10,000. The act requires contractors to pay employees at least the prevailing wage rates established for the area by the secretary of labor and overtime of one and one-half times the regular rate for all work performed in excess of eight hours in one day or 40 hours in one week, depending on which basis provides the larger premium.

A final law, the Consumer Credit Protection Act of 1968, covers wage garnishment, the procedure by which a creditor can get a court order compelling the employer to pay over a portion of an indebted employee's earnings. The act limits the amount that can be ordered withheld from each paycheck and prohibits an employer from firing an employee for the first incident of garnishment.

CURRENT ISSUES IN MANAGING THE COMPENSATION SYSTEM

Even the best-designed compensation system will be ineffective if it does not gain employee acceptance, and this acceptance is often determined by the way the reward system is administered. This section discusses several major issues associated with the current management of compensation systems. Chief among them is the issue of comparable worth.

Comparable Worth

Equal pay should not be confused with comparable worth, a much more stringent form of legislation enacted in some countries and used in a few public jurisdictions in the United States. In essence, comparable worth is the concept that women should be paid in the same rate range as men for work of comparable worth as well as for equal work. More specifically, comparable worth calls for comparable pay for jobs that require comparable skills, effort, and responsibility and have comparable working conditions, even if the job content is different. For instance, if an organization using the point factor job evaluation method we described earlier finds that the administrative assistant position (held mostly by women) receives the same number of points as the shift supervisor position (held mostly by men), comparable worth legislation would require paying employees in these jobs equally, even though they might be exercising very different skills and responsibilities.

The considerable controversy surrounding comparable worth legislation centers mainly on how it should be implemented rather than on its main goal of pay equity between the sexes. Supporters of comparable worth legislation favor using job evaluation tools to advance pay equity, pointing out that many private organizations already use this method to set wages. Opponents argue that job evaluations are inherently arbitrary and that they do not take sufficient account of a job's market value. For example, comparable worth proponents have often said that markets treat nurses unfairly because society links the profession to women's unpaid nurturing role in the family.

The argument over comparable worth is likely to remain an HRM issue for many years to come. Unanswered questions such as the following will serve to keep the issue alive:

1. If comparable worth is adopted, who will determine the worth of jobs, and by what means?
2. How much would comparable worth cost employers?
3. Would comparable worth reduce the wage gap between men and women caused by labor market supply-and-demand forces?
4. Would comparable worth reduce the number of employment opportunities for women?

Despite all the problems with implementation, comparable worth is already being used in many countries, including Britain, Canada, and Australia.

The compensation gap between women and men will not disappear overnight, but the persistence of comparable worth advocates will help shrink it.

Employee Participation

People tend to be more committed to programs they had a hand in developing. When employees help create compensation plans, there is generally less resistance, and the plan is much more likely to be a successful motivator than a plan imposed by management would be.

It is appropriate to involve employees in many phases of a reward system. For example, a wide variety of employees should serve on job evaluation committees. If a point plan is adopted, it is reasonable to involve employees in identifying the compensable factors to be used and the weight to be assigned to each factor. Employees are also likely to have good insight into which competitor organizations should be included in a wage survey.

There are several mechanisms for employee involvement. At the broadest level, employees can be surveyed to learn their preferences. Employee task forces can help integrate these preferences into a system. Such groups are usually an excellent way to involve employees in the decisions associated with a reward system.

Wage Compression

Wage compression results when wages for new hires are increasing faster than the wages of people already on the payroll. Wage compression is largely an internal pay-equity concern. The problem occurs when employees perceive that there is too narrow a difference between their compensation and that of colleagues in lower-rated jobs.

HRM professionals acknowledge that wage rate compression is a widespread organizational problem affecting diverse occupational groups: white-collar and blue-collar workers, technical and professional employees, and managerial personnel (Schellhardt, 1998). It can cause low employee morale, leading to issues of reduced employee performance, higher absenteeism and turnover, and even delinquent behavior such as employee theft.

Identifying wage compression and its causes is far simpler than implementing organizational policies to alleviate its effect. Organizations wishing to minimize the problem may incorporate the following ideas into their pay policies:

- Give larger compensation increases to more senior employees.
- Emphasize pay-for-performance and reward merit-worthy employees.
- Limit the hiring of new applicants seeking exorbitant salaries.

- Design the pay structure to allow a wide spread between hourly and supervisory jobs or between new hires and senior employees.
- Provide equity adjustments for selected employees hardest hit by pay compression.

Other options include permitting more flexibility in employees' work schedules, including four-day work weeks and work at home.

All-Salaried Workforce

As part of the move to increase employee participation at all organizational levels, many organizations have moved to an all-salaried workforce. All employees, even the blue-collar workers, receive the agreed salary each pay period, and the size of their checks does not depend primarily on the number of hours worked. That is, employees are not docked for lateness or other absences. This policy is meant to eliminate the feeling of hourly employees that they are second-class citizens.

The employer remains responsible for enforcing the FLSA, however, and from this perspective, nonexempt salaried employees are still paid by the hour. Employers must keep a record of hours worked (presumably by less obtrusive means than a time clock) and pay overtime to all nonexempt employees who work more than 40 hours in any one week, whether or not they are otherwise treated as salaried employees by the employer.

ASSESSING COMPENSATION EFFECTIVENESS

Given the enormous cost to an organization of its compensation efforts, it is very important that the organization carefully assess the benefit that accrues to the organization because of those compensation efforts. On the other hand, the organization must provide reasonable compensation and appropriate benefits to its employees. It is important to periodically assess the extent to which compensation costs are in line.

One way of evaluating compensation policies is through the use of wage surveys, as noted earlier in this chapter. Similar comparisons can also be made for wage structures, benefit packages, and so forth. Organizations can most effectively assess their total compensation system by comparing pay levels with those pay levels of other organizations, by analyzing the validity of the organization's job evaluation method, by measuring employee perceptions of pay equity and performance-pay linkages, and by determining individual pay levels within jobs and across jobs.

An organization can also assess the effectiveness of its compensation system and policies by considering how well they help attain strategic business objectives. For example, an organization can have its compensation system tied to its profits. An organization can also audit its overall compensation program to determine whether or not the program is competitive. As part of the recruiting process, it is necessary, of course, for the organization to be seen as an attractive employer in order to hire high-quality human resources. Of course, the attractiveness of an organization as an employer is a function, in part, of the total compensation package, which includes employee benefits, a topic we discuss in Chapter 11.

HRM'S ROLE IN COMPENSATION

In most organizations, the HRM function plays a major role in wage and salary administration. The HRM function is likely to develop the job evaluation system, perhaps with the help of an outside consultant, and will coordinate and manage the system. This includes one or more representatives on a job evaluation committee.

As a rule, HRM personnel conduct surveys of wages and salaries or participate in surveys the department uses in revising the pay structure. Once top management has approved modification of the overall pay structure, the HRM personnel typically monitor compliance with that structure and with the rules that have been established. Generally, individual managers make decisions about the pay of subordinates within the framework of wage and salary plans, and the HRM function ensures that the limits are not exceeded and that the spirit and intent of the plans are adhered to.

SUMMARY

There are a number of purposes and objectives for compensation in today's organizations. The basic purpose is to provide an adequate and appropriate reward system for employees so that they feel valued and worthwhile as organizational members and representatives. Various factors contribute to the compensation strategy an organization develops. Wage or pay surveys are a critical source of information that many organizations use to develop compensation strategies.

There are a variety of well-known methods or techniques for determining the relative value or worth of a job to the organization. Once the job evaluation has been completed, HRM personnel, along with other managers, develop job classes. The wage and salary structure must be administered on an ongoing basis once a wage structure has been developed. Another important aspect of wage and salary administration is pay secrecy. Pay compression is one problem that some organizations occasionally have to confront during wage and salary administration.

Given the enormous costs to an organization of its compensation packages, organizations should conduct regular evaluations of their compensation policies. Paying employees too little or too much can have serious consequences for a business. Therefore, it is important for organizations to have a clear strategy of where they want compensation to be relative to the market and to take regular steps to ensure that they are, in fact, maintaining that desired position. Wage surveys are one way of evaluating compensation policies. Comparisons can also be made for wage structures, benefit packages, and so forth.

REFERENCES

Bureau of Labor Statistics. 1996. *CPI detailed report*. Washington, DC: U.S. Department of Labor, p. 94.

Gainer, D.J. 1995. The Davis-Bacon Act comes under attack by an old alliance. *Wall Street Journal* (May 3), pp. A1, A5.

Guinn, K.A., and Corona, R.J. 1991. Putting a price on performance. *Personnel Journal* (May): 72–78.

Hackett, T.J., and McDermott, D.G. 1999. Integrating compensation strategies that work from the boardroom to the shop floor. *Compensation and Benefits Review* (September–October): 36–43.

LeBlanc, P.V., and Hurley, P.W. 1998. How American workers see the rewards of work. *Compensation and Benefits Review* (January–February): 24–28.

LeBlanc, P.V., and McInerney, M. 1994. Need a change? Jump on the banding wagon. *Personnel Journal* (January): 72–78.

Newman, J.M., and Krzystofiak, F.J. 1998. Value-chain compensation. *Compensation and Benefits Review* (May–June): 60–66.

Risher, H. 1993. Strategic salary planning. *Compensation and Benefits Review* (January–February): 46–50.

Risher, H. 1997. Planning and managing in the new work paradigm. *Compensation and Benefits Review* (January–February): 13–17.

Schellhardt, T.D. 1998. Rookie gains in pay wars rile veterans. *Wall Street Journal* (June 4), p. B-1.

Stay for pay: A retention solution. 1998. *HRFocus* (September): 57.

Thieblot, A.J. 1996. A new evaluation of impacts of prevailing wage law repeal. *Journal of Labor Research* (Spring): 297–322.

Tyler, K. 1998. Compensation strategies can foster lateral moves and growing in place. *HRMagazine* (April): 64–71.

Wallace, M.J., Jr., and Fay, C.H. 1988. *Compensation theory and practice*. Boston: PWS-Kent, pp. 136–138.

Chapter 11

Incentive Compensation and Benefits

INTRODUCTION

Today's organizations are confronted with increased global competition, which poses a difficult challenge for them in general, and for HRM specialists in particular (Brockbank, 1997). The HRM staff must try to develop HRM programs that improve organizational productivity and enhance its effectiveness. Attaining these goals will help ensure that U.S. businesses will be competitive in national and world arenas.

In the previous chapter we emphasized pay based on the worth of a job as a significant factor in determining the pay or wage rate for that job. However, such a narrow focus may fail to motivate employees to perform to their full capacity. Organizations are increasingly trying to get more motivational mileage out of employee compensation by tying it more clearly to organizational objectives and employee performance. In their efforts to raise productivity, organizations are focusing on the many variables that help to determine the effectiveness of pay as a motivator. An organization's reward system includes more than just direct compensation, and direct compensation may include more than just base pay (salary or wage).

This chapter covers some of the additional components that, taken together, make up an organization's reward system. The first part of this chapter discusses the elements of direct compensation that go beyond fixed salary and wages—specifically, various types of individual and group incentive systems. The second part of the chapter focuses on indirect compensation, particularly government-mandated benefits (like Social Security and workers' compensation) and other optional benefits (such as insurance, pensions, vacations, and sick leave). Challenges associated with the implementation and administration of both incentives and benefits are also examined.

THE PURPOSE AND REQUIREMENTS FOR INCENTIVE PLANS

Having determined their goals, objectives, and values, how do organizations signal these elements to their employees? Assuming that an organization has selected the right individuals, has trained these individuals, and has established appropriate work systems, it is still a challenge to have these employees understand what needs to be done. A major mechanism for indicating the organizational goals and objectives is the compensation system. This can best be understood from examples of misalignment:

- What is being signaled to co-workers when well-intentioned but ineffective employees are given above-average merit increases?
- What is being signaled to employees when executives are given large bonuses after the organization has had a below-average year, and only small increases are given to other workers?
- What is being signaled if high commissions and other incentives are paid to field sales representatives, but there is no monitoring of sales practices?
- What is being signaled if an organization has an established bonus system, does not attain the profits necessary to trigger the bonuses in a given year, but decides to pay them anyway "because it was a tough year"?

Basic to the effective functioning of any organization is the way it uses its system of total compensation to communicate to employees both what needs to be done and their role in accomplishing these objectives. The preceding examples of misalignment frequently are well-intentioned actions on the part of organizations but obviously are not consistent with the desired alignment between rewards and organizational objectives. Any system of compensation is highly visible and becomes central to the very fabric of an organization.

An important recent trend in strategic compensation management is the growth of incentive plans, also called variable pay programs, for employees throughout the organization. Variable pay programs establish a performance "threshold" (a baseline performance level) an employee or group of employees must reach in order to qualify for variable payments. One compensation specialist has recently noted that "The performance threshold is the minimum level an employee must reach in order to qualify for variable pay" (Johnson, 1998).

Incentive plans emphasize a shared focus on organizational objectives by broadening the opportunities for incentives to employees throughout the organization. Incentive plans create an operating environment that champions a philosophy of shared commitment through the belief that every individual contributes to organizational performance and success.

INCENTIVE PLANS AND ORGANIZATIONAL OBJECTIVES

Organizations have implemented incentive plans for a variety of reasons: high labor costs, competitive product markets, slow technological advances, and high potential for production bottlenecks. While these reasons are still offered, contemporary arguments for incentive plans focus on pay-for-performance and link compensation rewards to organizational goals. An organization's efforts to mesh compensation and organizational objectives is driven by the hope that employees will assume "ownership" of their jobs, thereby improving their effort and overall job performance. Incentives are designed to encourage employees to put out more effort to complete their job tasks—effort they might not be motivated to expend under hourly and/or seniority-based compensation systems. Financial incentives are therefore offered to improve the market for U.S. goods and services in a global economy. Researchers and HRM professionals have identified the following major advantages of incentive pay programs:

- Incentives focus employee efforts on specific performance targets. They provide real motivation that produces important employee and organizational goals.
- Incentive compensation is directly related to operating performance. If performance objectives (quantity and/or quality) are met, incentives are paid. If objectives are not achieved, incentives are withheld.
- Incentive payouts are variable costs linked to the achievement of results. Base salaries are fixed costs largely unrelated to output.
- Incentives are a way to distribute success among those responsible for producing that success.
- Incentives foster teamwork and unit cohesiveness when payments to individuals are based on team results.

TOWARD SUCCESSFUL INCENTIVE PLANS

As noted previously, today's compensation systems must be strategic in nature, and pay in particular must go beyond individual or group incentive pay and seek to provide a mechanism for an organization to use all elements of compensation, direct (cash compensation) and indirect (benefits), to forge a partnership between the organization and its employees. For an incentive plan to succeed, employees must have some desire for the plan (Bento and White, 1998). This desire can be influenced in part by how successful management is in introducing the plan and convincing employees of its benefits (McKenzie and Shilling, 1998). Encouraging employees to participate in developing and administering the plan is likely to increase their willingness to accept it.

Employees must be able to see a clear connection between the incentive payments they receive and their job performance. This connection is more visible if there are objective quality or quantity standards by which they can judge their performance. Commitment by employees to meet these standards is also essential for incentive plans to succeed. This requires mutual trust and understanding between employees and their supervisors, which can only be achieved through open, two-way channels of communication. Management should never allow incentive payments to be seen as an entitlement. Instead, these payments should be viewed as a reward that must be earned through effort. This perception can be strengthened if the incentive money is distributed to employees in a separate check. Compensation specialists also note the following as characteristics of a successful incentive plan:

- Financial incentives are linked to valued behavior.
- The incentive program seems fair to employees.
- Productivity/quality standards are challenging but achievable.
- Payout formulas are simple and understandable.

Specifying Performance Measures

A valid and transparent measurement system is key to the success of incentive plans because it communicates the importance of established goals. What gets measured and rewarded gets attention. If the performance measurement system focuses on one component of performance and incentives are given for a different component, employees will be confused and managers will wonder why the incentives do not work. For example, if the organization desires to be a leader in quality, then performance indexes may focus on customer satisfaction, timeliness, or being error-free. If being a low-priced producer is the goal, then emphasis should be on cost reduction or increased productivity with lower acceptable levels of quality. While a variety of performance options are available, most focus on quality, cost control, or productivity.

Organizations must do everything possible to avoid relying too heavily on financial performance measures while ignoring other performance indicators that reflect the perspectives of employees, customers, and other strategic partners. Failure to take into consideration other perspectives when it comes to pay for performance can result in a mismatch between the incentive system and the organization's full understanding of what it takes to be effective in the long run.

As more and more organizations consider paying for knowledge or skill acquisition, they come face-to-face with the question of how much value they should place on performance in the current job versus behaviors that prepare employees for future jobs. Finding the right balance between rewarding for current performance versus rewarding for long-term performance is a difficult balancing act. Many critics of performance-based incentive plans point to this as a common problem. Executive incentives that focus attention on short-term movements in the organization's stock price, for example, may lead managers to make decisions that protect the stock price in the short-term but with negative long-term consequences. In sales jobs, balancing short-term and long-term performance objectives also poses a challenge. Traditional commissions focus the attention of a sales staff on the short-term objective of selling goods and services and do nothing to ensure that the customer is satisfied with the purchase. Yet building customer loyalty and repeat business are important strategic objectives for most organizations. Thus, incentives for sales organizations increasingly include measures of customer satisfaction.

An authority on incentive plans notes that the failure of most incentive plans can be traced to the choice of performance measures (Beck, 1992, p. 23). Therefore measures that are quantitative, simple, and structured to show a clear relationship to improved performance are best. Overly quantitative, complex measures are to be avoided. Also, when selecting a performance measure, it is necessary to evaluate the extent to which the employees involved can actually influence the measurement. Finally, employers must guard against "ratcheting up" performance goals by continually trying to exceed previous results. This eventually leads to employee frustration and employee perception that the standards are unattainable. The result will be a mistrust of management and a backlash against the entire incentive program. In the end, organizations should recognize the importance of employees' acceptance of measures of performance, while understanding that objective measures of performance (productivity and cost savings) tend to have greater employee acceptance and credibility.

Managing Incentive Plans

To achieve the full benefit of incentive plans based on productivity, these plans must be carefully thought out, implemented, and maintained. A cardinal rule is that thorough planning must be combined with a "proceed with caution" approach. Compensation specialists stress a number of points related to the effective management of incentive plans. Three of the more important points are, by consensus:

1. Incentive systems are effective only when managers are willing to grant incentives based on differences in individual, team, or organizational performance. Allowing incentive payments to become pay guarantees the defeat of the moti-

vational intent of the incentive. The primary purpose of an incentive compensation plan is not to pay off under almost all circumstances, but rather to motivate performance. Thus, if the plan is to succeed, poor performance must go unrewarded.

2. Annual salary budgets must be large enough to reward and reinforce exceptional performance. When compensation budgets are set to ensure that pay increases do not exceed certain limits (often established as a percentage of payroll or sales), these constraints may prohibit rewarding outstanding individual or group performance.

3. The overhead costs associated with plan implementation and administration must be determined. These may include the cost of establishing performance standards and the added cost of record keeping. The time consumed in communicating the plan to employees, answering questions, and resolving any complaints about it must be included in these costs. (Abosch, 1998)

INCENTIVE COMPENSATION PLANS

Organizations that are sincerely committed to developing a compensation system that is designed around performance will want to consider the use of incentive pay. Typically given in addition to—rather than in place of—the basic wage, incentive plans should be viewed as an additional dimension of the wage or pay structure. Incentives (often referred to as variable pay) can be based on individual, team or group, or organization-wide performance—a pay-for-performance concept. An important feature of these variable pay plans is that incentives increase the cooperation in teams, whereas individual incentives do not.

When individual productivity is measurable, individual incentives are most successful in boosting performance through a fairly direct link between performance and rewards. Individual incentives are given to reward the effort and performance of individuals. Like skill-based pay, discussed in the previous chapter, piece-rate (or piecework) incentives, commissions, and bonuses are popular incentive plans. Each of these will be discussed along with merit pay later in this chapter.

The adoption of individual incentives has accelerated in recent years. Two widely used individual incentives focus on employee safety and attendance. One of the difficulties with individual incentives is that an employee may focus on what is best individually and may block or inhibit performance of other individuals with whom the employee is competing. That competition particularly occurs if only the top performer or winner receives incentives. This is one reason why team or group incentives have been developed.

When an entire group or team is rewarded for its performance, more cooperation among the members is required and usually forthcoming. The most common types of team or group incentives are gainsharing plans where employee teams that meet certain goals share in the gains measured against performance targets. Often, gainsharing programs focus on quality improvement, labor-cost reduction, and other measurable results.

Organization incentives reward people for the performance of the entire organization. This approach reduces individual and team competition and assumes that all employees working together can generate better organizational results that lead to better financial performance. These programs share some of the financial gains to the organization through payments to employees. The payments often are paid as an additional percentage of employees' base pay. Also, organizational incentives may be given as a lump-sum amount to all employees, or different amounts may be given to different levels of employees throughout the organization. The most prevalent forms of organization-wide incentives are profit-sharing plans and employee stock plans. For senior managers and executives, variable pay plans often are established to provide stock options and other forms of deferred compensation that minimize the tax liabilities of the recipients.

Individual Incentives

One of the oldest and most common forms of individual enticement is based on piecework or piece-rate, whether of the straight or differential type. Under a piece-rate incentive plan, the organization pays an employee a certain amount of money for every unit he or she produces. Under the straight piece-rate system, wages are determined by multiplying the number of units produced (such as customers contacted or modules completed) by the piece rate for one unit. The rate per piece does not change regardless of the number of pieces produced. Because the cost is the same for each unit, the wage for each employee is easy to figure, and labor costs can be accurately predicted.

Under a differential piece rate, employees whose production exceeds the standard output receive a higher rate for all of their work than the rate paid to those who do not exceed the standard. Developed by Frederick W. Taylor in the late 1800s, this system is designed to stimulate employees to achieve or exceed established standards of production.

As alluded to earlier, the major shortcoming of the typical piece-rate incentive is that instead of suggesting a partnership between the goals of the individual and those of the organization, it implies that the organization actually distrusts the individual. As a result, a piece-rate system is likely to encourage behaviors opposite to those sought. Workers may restrict output because of the possible adverse consequences associated with high productivity. Piece-rate systems are difficult to use because standards for many types of jobs are difficult and costly to determine. In some instances, the cost of determining and maintaining the standards may be greater than the benefits derived. Jobs in which individuals have limited control over output or in which high standards of quality are necessary also may be unsuited to piecework.

Standard Hour Plan

The standard hour plan is similar to the straight piecework plan except that the standard is set in time units. If employees finish the work in less than the expected time, their pay is still based on the standard time for the job multiplied by their hourly rate. Automobile repair shops often use such systems. If the customer wants to know the cost of replacing an engine component, he or she will be given an estimate based on the mechanic's hourly rate multiplied by the average time needed to replace the component on cars of that type. If the charge is $40 per hour and the replacement of the component requires four hours on average, the expected labor would be $160. This is the labor cost quoted to the customer before work begins. An experienced mechanic may complete the job in three hours. The customer is still charged $160, and the mechanic is paid for four hours' work (the standard time allotted for the job). If the job takes longer than estimated, charges to the customer and payment to the mechanic are still based on four hours' work. Standard hour plans generally are used with longer-cycle operations that are nonrepetitive.

While standard hour plans can motivate employees to produce more, employers must ensure that equipment maintenance and product quality do not suffer as employees strive to do their work faster to earn additional income.

Commissions

Commission reward systems, which are usually found in sales jobs, allow the salesperson to receive a percentage of her or his gross receipts (e.g., 6 percent of all sales). About two-thirds of all salespeople are paid on a commission basis—either straight commission or a base salary plus commission. Notice that these plans put a considerable amount of the salesperson's earnings "at risk." That is, although organizations often have drawing accounts to allow the salesperson to live during lean periods (the person then "owes" this money to the organization), sales representatives who do not perform well will not be paid much. The portion of salary based on commission is not guaranteed and is paid only if sales reach some target level. The unpredictableness in the amount of take-home pay from week to week is a major disadvantage of commission-based compensation.

Bonuses

One of the most popular trends in compensation is the use of bonuses: one-time lump-sum payments given for meeting a performance goal. Bonuses can be based on objective goal attainment or a subjective rating. Generally, bonuses are less costly to the employer than other pay increases because they do not become part of employees' base wages, upon which future percentage increases are figured. A major advantage of a bonus plan is that it is based partly on organizational performance; in a bad year, when corporate performance is down and resources are strained, bonuses will be much smaller or even nonexistent. Individual compensation in the form of bonuses is often used at the executive levels of an organization, but its usage is also spreading to lower-level jobs.

Bonuses can also be used to reward employees for contributing new ideas, developing skills, or obtaining professional certifications. When the skills or certification requirements are acquired by an employee, a pay increase or a one-time bonus may follow. For example, a financial services firm might provide the equivalent of two weeks' pay to employees who master job-relevant computer skills.

When some special employee contribution is to be rewarded, a spot bonus is used. A spot bonus, as the name implies, is given "on the spot," normally for some employee effort not directly tied to an established performance standard. For example, a customer service representative might receive a spot bonus for working long hours to fill a new customer's large order.

Merit Pay

One popular and almost universally used incentive system is merit pay. Merit pay is a major motivational device for employees at all levels—managerial, professional, and hourly. Under a merit plan, employees who receive merit increases have a sum of money added to their base salary. Somewhat likened to a cost-of-living raise, merit pay differs in that the percentage of increase to the base wage rate is attributable solely to performance. Those who perform better generally receive more merit pay. For example, during periods of low inflation and competitive pressures on organizations' costs, a top performer may receive a 5 percent increase, whereas an average performer receives 3 percent and a below-average performer receives no increase.

Merit raises may not always achieve their intended purpose. Unlike a bonus, a merit raise may be perpetuated year after year even when performance declines. When this happens, employees come to expect the increase and see it as being unrelated to their performance. Furthermore, employees in some organizations are opposed to merit raises because, among other reasons, they do not really trust management. What are referred to as merit raises often turn out to be increases based on seniority or favoritism, or raises to accommodate increases in cost of living or in area wage rates.

While there are problems with merit pay, it is likely to remain a staple of compensation systems. At the same time, it is likely that in the future merit programs will be supplemented with other types of individual or group incentives. Organizations will rely on merit pay for the broad range of adjustments but will reward top performers with individual bonuses or all employees with a group incentive based on company performance.

Executive Compensation

A major function of incentive plans for executives is to motivate them to develop and use their abilities and contribute their energies to the fullest possible extent. Incentive plans should also facilitate the recruitment and retention of competent executive employees. This can be accomplished with plans that will enable them to accumulate a financial estate and to shelter a portion of their compensation from current income taxes.

Organizations commonly have more than one compensation strategy for executives in order to meet various organizational goals and executive needs. For example, chief executive officers (CEOs) may have their compensation packages heavily weighted toward long-term incentives because CEOs should be more concerned about the long-term impact of their decisions than the short-term implications. Group vice presidents, on the other hand, may receive more short-term incentives, since their decisions affect operations on a six- to 12-month basis. Regardless of the mix, executive compensation plans consist of four basic components: (1) base salary, (2) short-term incentives or bonuses, (3) long-term incentives or stock plans, and (4) perquisites. Another important element in compensation strategy is the compensation mix to be paid to managers and executives accepting overseas assignments.

Bases for executive salaries. The levels of competitive salaries in the job market exert perhaps the greatest influence on executive base salaries. An organization's compensation committee—normally members of the board of directors—will order a salary survey to find out what executives earn in comparable enterprises. Comparisons may be based on organization size, sales volume, or industry grouping. By analyzing the data from published studies, along with self-generated salary surveys, the compensation committee can determine the equity of the compensation package outside the organization.

Bases for short-term incentives or bonuses. Bonuses play an important role in today's competitive executive payment programs. This type of incentive is usually a short-term one (annual) and is based on performance. Consequently, the definition of performance is especially critical.

There are almost as many bonus systems as there are companies using this form of executive compensation. In some systems, the annual bonus is tied by formulas to objective measures such as gross or net profits, earnings, share price, or return on investment. Other executive bonus plans are based on the subjective judgment of the board of directors and CEO. More complex systems establish certain targets—for example, a 10 percent increase in corporate earnings from the previous year—and generally set aside a bonus pool for when the target is attained. The bonus is then distributed, either in accordance with a preset formula or on the basis of subjective judgments.

Bases for executive long-term incentives. Publicly held organizations in the United States have been criticized for their focus on the short-term (i.e., quarterly profit) goals to the detriment of long-term survival and growth objectives. Therefore, organizations have adopted compensation strategies that tie executive pay to long-term performance measures.

The most popular approach is to give stock or stock options to executives. The options are valuable as long as the price of the stock keeps increasing. However, the stock purchased (or the right to buy stock) can decrease in value and even become worthless if the company goes bankrupt. Executives of many large companies have suffered this fate in recent years.

Stock options are also attractive to shareholders. First, an option is not a bonus. Executives must use their own resources to exercise their right to purchase stock. Second, the executives are assuming the same risk as all other shareholders—namely, that the price could move in either direction. Options are a form of profit sharing that links the executive's financial success to that of the shareholders. Finally, stock options are one of the few ways to offer large rewards to executives without the embarrassment of "millions of dollars of obvious money changing hands" (Quinn, 1986). Nevertheless, the risk factor in this type of incentive may be too great for it to be attractive to executives.

Executive perquisites. In addition to incentive programs, executive employees are often given special benefits and perquisites. Perquisites, better known as "perks," are the extras that frequently go with executive status. Perks range from such amenities as special parking and plush offices to pay for vacation travel, automobile expenses, and company-paid memberships in clubs. More personal perks, such as low-cost loans and personal use of company facilities (e.g., airplanes) have been slowly disappearing over the last decade as various tax regulatory agencies have ruled that their value must be included in the executive's taxable income. However, the list of perks is long and will remain an expected feature of the upper levels of the executive ladder.

Clearly, executives in the United States earn substantial compensation. Although there may be complete justification for any given executive compensation package—even one that looks enormous—organizations should also appreciate the concern and sensitivity that others have about these compensation packages and ensure that to the extent possible everyone is being rewarded appropriately for her or his level of performance.

TEAM AND GROUP INCENTIVE PLANS

The emphasis on total quality management and cost reduction has led many organizations to implement a variety of group incentive plans. These plans are designed to accomplish the same objectives as individual incentives—that is, to link rewards to performance. Group plans enable employees to share in the benefits of improved efficiency realized by major organizational units or various individual teams. These plans encourage cooperative, rather than individualistic, spirit among all employees and reward them for their total contribution to the organization. Such features are particularly desirable when working conditions make individual performance difficult, if not impossible, to measure.

Team compensation. The growing use of work teams in organizations has implications for compensation of the teams and their members. Interestingly, while the use of teams has increased significantly in the past few years, the question of how to equitably compensate the individuals who compose the team remains one of the biggest challenges. Team incentive plans reward team members with an incentive bonus when agreed-upon performance standards are met or exceeded. Furthermore, the incentive will seek to establish a psychological climate that fosters team cooperation.

Gainsharing. Gainsharing is used in many organizations. Gainsharing programs are designed to share with employees the cost savings from productivity improvements. The underlying assumption of gainsharing is that employees and the employer have the same goals and thus should appropriately share in incremental economic gains.

In general, organizations that use gainsharing start by measuring team- or group-level productivity. This measure must be valid, reliable, and truly reflective of current levels of performance. The team or work group itself is then given the charge of attempting to lower costs and otherwise improve productivity through any measures that its members develop and its manager approves. Any cost savings or productivity gains that result are quantified and translated into dollar values, and a predetermined formula is used to allocate these dollar savings between the employer and the employees. A typical formula for distributing gainsharing savings is to provide 25 percent to the employees and 75 percent to the company.

Although gainsharing is a popular reward system for employees, experience with these techniques has pointed up a number of factors that contribute either to their success or to their failure. For example, the success or failure of incentive programs begins with the culture of the organization. Putting a gainsharing program in autocratically or in desperation to save a badly managed firm virtually guarantees failure. Inadequate systems, severe external competitive conditions, and government constraints also inhibit the success of gainsharing programs. Simply offering gainsharing payouts may not be enough to generate much participation in the plan.

Negative attitudes toward the gainsharing plan and management can lead to nonparticipation by the employees. However, gainsharing certainly can work to improve performance.

One specific type of gainsharing plan is called the Scanlon Plan. The Scanlon Plan has the same basic strategy as gainsharing plans in that teams or groups of employees are encouraged to suggest strategies for reducing cost. However, the distribution of these gains is usually tilted much more heavily toward employees, with employees usually receiving between two-thirds and three-fourths of the total cost savings that the plan achieves. Furthermore, the distribution of cost savings resulting from the plan are not given just to the team or group that suggested and developed the ideas but are instead distributed across the entire organization.

Improshare. A number of gainsharing-type plans have been devised. One is Improshare, which stands for Improved Productivity through Sharing. Improshare was created by Mitchell Fein, an industrial engineer. It is similar to a piece-rate plan except that it rewards all workers in the organization. Input is measured in hours and output in physical units. A standard is calculated and weekly bonuses are paid based on the extent to which the standard is exceeded. Generally, Improshare programs have resulted in productivity gains.

The Rucker Plan. The share-of-production plan (SOP), or Rucker Plan, normally covers just production workers but may be expanded to cover all employees. As with the Scanlon Plan, committees are formed to elicit and evaluate employee suggestions. The Rucker Plan, however, uses a far less elaborate participatory structure. As one authority noted, "It commonly represents a type of program that is used as an alternative to the Scanlon Plan in firms attempting to move from a traditional style of management toward a higher level of employee involvement" (Ost, 1989, p. 94).

The financial incentive of the Rucker Plan is based on the historic relationship between the total earnings of hourly employees and the production value that employees create. The bonus is based on an improvement in this relationship that employees are able to realize. Thus, for every 1 percent increase in production value that is achieved, workers receive a bonus of 1 percent of their total payroll costs.

Earnings-at-risk programs. These plans place a portion of an employee's base pay at risk. The philosophy behind these programs is that employees should not expect substantial rewards without assuming some risk for their performance. These plans, however, allow employees to recapture lower wages, or reap additional income above full base pay when quality, service, or productivity goals are met or exceeded. An employee's base pay might be set at 90 percent (i.e., 10 percent below market value—the risk part), the loss to be regained through performance. For example, total employee compensation might be made up of base pay, risk pay, and reward pay. The risk/reward incentive would encourage team members to continuously improve job performance. The risk portion of pay might require that 10 percent of base pay be withheld until specific organizational performance goals are met. When these goals are achieved, the money withheld would be paid back in, say, a quarterly lump sum. The reward portion of compensation is paid only if the risk goals are met. The maximum achievable reward could then be something like $10,500. Production rewards could be paid quarterly and profitability rewards paid annually.

ORGANIZATION-WIDE INCENTIVE PLANS

An organization-wide incentive system compensates all employees in the organization based on how well the organization as a whole performs over an extended period of time—normally one year, but the period can be longer. Organization incentive plans seek to create a "culture of ownership" by fostering a philosophy of cooperation and teamwork among all organizational members. Thus, the purpose of these plans is to produce teamwork. For example, conflict between production and marketing can be overcome if management uses an incentive system that emphasizes organizational profit and productivity. Common organizational incentive systems include profit sharing, stock options, and employee stock ownership plans (ESOPs).

Profit Sharing

Probably no incentive plan has been the subject of more widespread interest, attention, and misunderstanding than profit sharing. As the name implies, profit sharing distributes a portion of organizational profits to employees. Profit sharing plans differ from gainsharing in two respects:

1. They are often implemented corporation-wide, whereas gainsharing is often at the unit level.
2. They use a formula based on profit rather than on productivity improvement.

The usual profit sharing program establishes a base-level profit target. After this target is achieved, a percentage of additional profits is set aside in a bonus pool to be distributed to participants. Sometimes the bonus pool is distributed in equal dollar shares to all employees. At other times the distribution is made according to organizational level salary/wages.

Profit sharing plans differ in the proportion of profits shared with employees and in the distribution and form of payment. The amount shared with employees may range from 5 to 50 percent of the net profit. In some profit sharing plans, employees receive portions of the profits at the end of the year; in others, the profits are deferred, placed in a fund, and made available to employees on retirement or on their leaving the organization.

In spite of their potential advantages, profit sharing plans are also prone to certain weaknesses. For example, when companies have had a bad year, even good employees may go unrewarded. Low profits may be due to factors beyond the employees' control, such as economic conditions. Another drawback is that deferred payout plans may have less incentive value because of the long time lapse between the good performance and the eventual payment. If a plan fails to pay off for several years in a row, this can have an adverse effect on productivity and employee morale.

Stock Options

In addition to offering stock options to executives, stock option programs are sometimes implemented as part of an employee benefit plan or as part of a corporate culture linking employee effort to stock performance. However, organizations that offer stock option programs to employees do so with the belief that there is some incentive value to the systems. By allowing employees to purchase stock, the organization hopes they will increase their productivity, assume a partnership role in the organization, and thus cause the stock price to rise. Furthermore, stock option programs have become a popular way to boost morale of disenfranchised employees caught in mergers, acquisitions, and downsizing.

Stock option plans grant to employees the right to purchase a specific number of shares of the company's stock at a guaranteed price (the option price) during a designated time period. Although there are many types of options, most options are granted at the stock's fair market value. Not uncommon are plans for purchasing stock through payroll deductions. For example, full-time employees can receive options to purchase a set amount of company stock at a fixed price. When the company's stock price reaches a certain level, employees can exercise a portion of the option and collect the cash.

Employee Stock Ownership Plans

Like profit sharing, employee stock ownership plans (ESOPs) are based on the entire organization's performance—in this case as measured by the organization's stock price. Employee stock ownership plans reward employees with company stock, either as an outright grant or at a favorable price that may be below market value.

Under an ESOP employees are gradually given a major stake in ownership of the organization. The typical form of this plan involves the company taking out a loan that it uses to buy a portion of its own stock in the open market. Once the loan repayment begins through the use of company profits, a certain amount of stock is released and allocated to an employee stock ownership trust (ESOT). Employees are assigned shares of company stock kept in the trust, based on length of service and pay level. On retirement, death, or separation from the organization, employees or their beneficiaries can sell the stock back to the trust or on the open market, if the stock is publicly traded.

Employee stock ownership plans are subject to certain tax laws. Generally, the employers who treat all employees alike are most advantaged. Those that provide different levels of benefits for different groups of employees are penalized in the tax laws. As was seen with profit sharing, especially deferred profits, the link between employee effort and company results is frequently weak. With ESOPs, this relationship is further diminished because success is not only a function of profits but also of the whims of Wall Street with respect to the valuation the financial markets put on companies—a factor employees find difficult to control. Another potential problem with ESOPs is that as more retirement income comes from these plans, the more dependent a pensioner becomes on the price of company stock. Future retirees are vulnerable to stock market fluctuations as well as to management mistakes. Also, unlike traditional pension plans, ESOP contributions are not guaranteed by the federally established Pension Benefit Guaranty Corporation, a major drawback to employees should their employer face serious financial setbacks or closure.

NEW APPROACHES TO PERFORMANCE-BASED REWARDS

Some organizations have started to recognize that they can leverage the value of the incentives they offer to their employees and to groups in their organizations by allowing those individuals and groups to have a say in how rewards are distributed. For example, an organization could grant salary-increase budgets to work groups and then allow the members of those groups to determine how to allocate the rewards. This strategy would appear to hold considerable promise if everyone understands the performance arrangements that exist in the work group and everyone is committed to being fair and equitable. Unfortunately, it can also create problems if people in a group feel that rewards are not being distributed fairly.

Organizations are also getting increasingly innovative in their incentive programs. For example, some now offer stock options to all their employees rather than just to top executives. Regardless of the method used, however, it is also important that organizations effectively communicate what rewards are being distributed and the basis for that distribution. That is, if incentives are being distributed on the basis of perceived individual contributions to the organization, then members of the organization should be informed of that fact. This information will presumably help them to understand the basis on which pay increases and other incentives and performance-based rewards have been distributed.

THE ROLE OF EMPLOYEE BENEFITS IN COMPENSATION SYSTEMS

Our discussion has thus far been restricted to the issue of pay. However, in today's marketplace organizations must do more than offer a "fair day's pay" to compete for quality employees. Employees also want a good benefits package. In reality, employees have grown accustomed to generous benefits programs and have come to expect them. We now discuss the various benefit options that may be offered by employers.

Once a largely neglected issue, the topic of benefits has become front-page news during the last decade. Child care, health care costs and coverage, flexible benefits, and changes in pension benefits are among the most dynamic compensation topics today. Whereas the issue of executive compensation has receded some from the front page over time, issues related to benefits continue as news of the day.

A major reason for the increased attention to benefits is costs. Fifty years ago, indirect compensation cost less than 5 percent of the direct compensation offered to most employees. More recently, benefits equal 44 percent of the cost of direct compensation for companies with 500 or more employees (Bureau of Labor Statistics, 1998). Most of the increase does not reflect new benefits but rather the higher costs of legally required payments (e.g., the employer's share of Social Security) and of optional benefits (especially health insurance). The costs for both doubled over a 20-year period.

Because benefits are contingent on membership in the organization, they help an organization attract and retain employees. Benefit programs do not directly motivate increased employee performance, for the link between performance level and benefit level is virtually zero. All employees receive similar benefit coverage, regardless of their performance levels.

Employees gain several advantages by receiving part of their compensation in this indirect form. For example, even though employees may contribute to or even pay the entire cost of benefits such as insurance, the cost associated with the group coverage of all employees is likely to be considerably lower than equivalent insurance purchased individually. In addition, some benefits are given favorable tax treatment; the employee need not pay tax on the value of health insurance, for example. The following section reviews many of the common benefit plans currently in use and discusses related issues such as cost containment and legal considerations.

TYPES OF BENEFITS

The major categories of benefits include mandatory protection programs, pay for time not worked, private retirement plans, and a wide variety of other services.

Mandated Protection Plans

Protection plans are benefits designed to protect employees when their income is threatened or reduced by illness, disability, unemployment, or retirement. Several of these benefits are provided to employees because either the federal or the state government legislatively mandates them. The Federal Insurance Contribution Act (FICA) of 1935, better known as the Social Security Act is the most notable required protection program.

Social Security. The Social Security Act provides an insurance plan designed to protect covered individuals against loss of earnings resulting from various causes. These causes may include retirement, unemployment, disability, or in the case of dependents, the death of the worker supporting them. Thus, as with any type of casualty insurance, Social Security does not pay off except in the case where a loss of income is actually incurred through loss of employment.

The Social Security program is supported by means of a tax levied against employees' earnings that must be matched by the employer in each pay period (Coy, 1998). The tax revenues are used to pay three major types of benefits: (1) old-age insurance benefits, (2) disability benefits, and (3) survivors' insurance benefits. Because of the continual changes that result from legislation and administrative rulings, as well as the complexities of making determinations of an individual's rights under Social Security, we will describe these benefits only in general terms.

To qualify for old-age insurance benefits, a person must have reached retirement age and be fully insured. A fully insured person has earned forty credits—a maximum of four credits a year for ten years, based on annual earnings of $2,360 (a figure adjusted annually) or more. Having enough credits to be fully insured makes one eligible for retirement benefits, but it does not determine the amount. The amount of monthly Social Security retirement benefits is based on earnings, adjusted for inflation, over the years an individual is covered by Social Security.

To receive old-age insurance benefits, covered individuals must also meet the retirement earnings test. Persons under 70 years of age cannot be earning more than the established annual exempt amount through gainful employment without a reduction in benefits. This limitation on earnings does not include income from sources other than gainful employment, such as investments or pensions.

The Social Security program provides disability benefits to workers too severely disabled to engage in "substantial gainful work." To be eligible for such benefits, however, an individual's disability must have existed for at least six months and must be expected to continue for at least 12 months or be expected to result in death. After receiving disability payments for 24 months, a disabled person receives Medicare protection. Those eligible for disability benefits, furthermore, must have worked under Social Security long enough and recently enough before becoming disabled. Disability benefits, which include auxiliary benefits for dependents, are computed on the same basis as retirement benefits and are converted to retirement benefits when the individual reaches the age of 65.

Survivors' insurance benefits represent a form of life insurance paid to members of a deceased person's family who meet the eligibility requirements. As with life insurance, the benefits that the survivors of a covered individual receive may greatly exceed their cost to this individual. Survivors' benefits can be paid only if the deceased worker had credit for a certain amount of time spent in work covered by Social Security. The exact amount of work credit needed depends on the worker's age at death. Generally, older workers need more years of Social Security work credit than younger workers, but never more than forty credits. As with other benefits discussed earlier, the amount of benefit survivors receive is based on the worker's lifetime earnings in work covered by Social Security.

Unemployment compensation. Another benefit required by law is unemployment compensation, established as part of the Social Security Act of 1935. Unlike Social Security, which is managed by the federal government, unemployment compensation is handled by the states in accordance with federal guidelines. Each state operates its own compensation system, and provisions differ significantly from state to state. In most states, employers finance this benefit by paying a small tax on the first $7,000 of an employee's wages. The size of the employer's contribution varies on the basis of past claims against that employer, thus providing an incentive to employers to avoid frequent layoffs. The experience-based tax rate also provides an inducement for employers to keep careful records of the reasons that employees leave and to document all discharges due to misconduct.

The amount of compensation that workers are eligible to receive is determined by their previous wage rate and previous period of employment. Unemployment compensation laws in most states disqualify workers from receiving benefits under the following conditions: (1) quitting one's job without good cause, (2) being discharged for misconduct connected with work, or (3) refusing suitable work while unemployed.

Workers' compensation. Workers' compensation provides benefits to persons injured on the job. State laws require most employers to provide workers' compensation coverage by purchasing insurance from a private carrier or state insurance fund or by providing self-insurance. Employers that self-insure are required to post a bond or deposit securities with the state industrial commission. State laws usually require that employers have a minimum number of employees before they are permitted to self-insure. Group self-insurance is permitted in some states and is useful for groups of small businesses. U.S. government employees are covered under the Federal Employees' Liabilities Act, administered by the Department of Labor.

The workers' compensation system requires employers to give cash benefits, medical care, and rehabilitation services to employees for injuries or illnesses occurring within the scope of their employment. Employees are entitled to quick and certain payment from the workers' compensation system without proving that the employer is at fault. In exchange, employees give up the right of legal actions and awards; so employers enjoy limited liability for occupational illnesses and injury.

A major concern to employers nationwide is the high cost of workers' compensation claims. The direct cost of claims to U.S. businesses has been around $70 billion annually. Swelling medical costs and benefits paid to workers are the major factors. In addition, there are more disorders today that are harder to assess objectively, such as back pain. Then too, claims are sometimes made for ailments that may have little to do with the workplace, such as hearing loss, stress, and cancer (Lattanzio, 1997). Steps that organizations and survivors can take to control workers' compensation costs are:

- Perform an audit to assess high-risk areas within a workplace.
- Prevent injuries by proper ergonomic design of the job and effective assessment of job candidates.
- Provide quality medical care to injured employees by physicians with experience and preferably with training in occupational health.
- Reduce litigation by effective communication between the employer and the injured worker.
- Manage the care of an injured worker from the injury until return to work. Keep a partially recovered employee at the work site.
- Provide extensive worker training in all related health and safety areas.

Efforts to reduce workplace injuries and illnesses can reduce workers' compensation premiums and claims costs. Many of the safety and health management suggestions discussed in Chapter 12 can be used to reduce workers' compensation costs.

Private Plans

In addition to the pension benefits that are guaranteed under the Social Security Act, many companies elect to establish private pension plans for their employees. These prearranged plans, administered by the organization, provide income to the employee upon her or his retirement. Contributions to the retirement plan may come from either the employer or the employee but in most cases are actually supported by contributions from both parties. A variety of retirement plans are available, including individual retirement accounts, or IRAs, and employee pension IRAs. In addition, a 401(k) plan allows employees to save money on a tax-deferred basis by entering into salary deferral agreements with their employer.

Legal constraints on pension plans. Companies establish pension plans voluntarily, but once established, the Employment Retirement Income Security Act (ERISA) requires that employers follow certain rules. The act ensures that employees will receive the pension benefits due them even if the company goes bankrupt or merges with another organization. Employers must pay annual insurance premiums to a government agency in order to provide funds from which guaranteed pensions can be paid. Additionally, ERISA requires that employers inform workers about what their pension-related benefits include.

There are two basic types of pension plans: defined benefit plans and defined contribution plans. Under defined benefit plans the size of the benefits is precisely known and is usually based on a simple formula using such input as years of service. This type of plan is often favored by unions and is closely monitored under ERISA. Although the employee may contribute to these plans, the amount of the contribution has no bearing on the benefits. Under defined contribution plans the size of the benefit depends on how much money is contributed to the plan. This money can be contributed either by the employer alone (noncontributory plans) or by the employer and the employee (contributory plans).

The use of traditional defined-benefit plans, with their fixed payouts, is in decline. Defined-benefit plans are less popular with employers because they cost more and because they require compliance with complicated government rules. Most new pension plans are contributory, defined contribution plans. However, some experts believe that employers may want to consider returning to defined-benefit plans, which allow for flexibility in plan design such as opening paths for the advancement of younger employees while enabling older workers to retire.

Along with 401(k) saving plans, the largest development in pension planning has been cash-balance saving plans. Pension experts predict that in less than 10 years most larger corporations will convert their traditional pension plan to a cash-balance program. Cash-balance plans offer large monetary savings to employers while providing financial security to employees (Schultz, 1998).

Cash-balance plans work by having the employer make a yearly contribution into an employee's retirement savings account. Contributions are based on a percentage of the employee's pay—typically 4 percent. Additionally, the employee's account earns annual interest, often tied to the 30-year Treasury rate. For example, an employee earning $35,000 a year would receive a yearly contribution of $1,400 to his or her account. After a year, the account would receive an interest credit, typically 5 percent. Employees can normally roll the balance of their account into an IRA should they change jobs.

Whether an individual employee benefits from a cash-balance retirement plan depends on the employee's age and years of service with the company. Employees in their twenties and thirties with low years of service can build substantial retirement savings starting at an early age. However, employees in their forties, fifties, or sixties, with lengthy years of service, can lose from 20 to 50 percent of their pension by switching from a traditional pension plan to a cash-balance program (Schultz, 1998). Why? With a traditional pension plan, employee benefits rise sharply during later years of employment. Remember, typical pension formulas multiply years of service by the highest final years of pay. With a cash-balance plan, all employees receive the same steady annual credit; thus older employees lose those last big years of accruals. Companies reap financial savings because pension contributions for older employees are significantly reduced.

To lessen the financial impact on older employees, some companies may increase the annual pay credit for older employees as compared with younger workers. Others have allowed older employees to remain in the traditional pension plan until retirement, or they grant older employees a "boost" in their opening cash-balance account.

Health Benefits

The benefits that receive the most attention from employers today because of high costs and employee concern are health care benefits (e.g., medical or health insurance). The goal of health insurance is to provide partial or complete coverage of medical expenses incurred by the employee and the employee's family. In practice, this means either paying directly or reimbursing the employee for hospital charges, surgery, and other personal or family medical expenses. In the past, health insurance plans covered only medical, surgical, and hospital expenses. Today many employers include prescription drugs as well as dental, optical, and mental health care benefits in the package they offer their workers.

The Consolidated Omnibus Budget Reconciliation Act of 1984 (COBRA) provides for a continuation of health insurance coverage for a period of up to three years for employees who leave a company through no fault of their own. Such employees are required to pay the premiums themselves, but at the company's group rate.

Cost containment. With the significant rise in health care costs, it is understandable that employers seek relief from these expenses. The approaches used to contain the costs of health care benefits include reductions in coverage, increased deductibles or copayments, and increased coordination of benefits to make sure the same expense is not paid by more than one insurance reimbursement. Other cost-containment efforts involve alternatives to traditional medical care: the use of health maintenance organizations and preferred providers, incentives for outpatient surgery and testing, and mandatory second opinions for surgical procedures. Employee assistance programs and wellness programs may also allow an organization to cut the costs of its health care benefits.

A health maintenance organization (HMO) provides complete medical care for employees and their families at a fixed annual fee. Supplemental policies typically cover hospitalization for those HMOs not associated with hospitals. Since doctor visits are not charged on a per visit basis, individuals are more likely to seek preventive care, thus reducing the incidence and costs of more serious illness.

Although HMOs have clearly lowered health costs, there is growing concern that quality care is being sacrificed in the name of cost savings. Increasing health care competition, price battles, high usage rates, and in some cases medical apathy are all cited causes of lower-quality HMO health care. Fortunately, employers can monitor the quality of care provided by the HMO by conducting a process evaluation of the providers' effectiveness.

A preferred provider organization (PPO) is a limited group of physicians and hospitals that agrees to provide services in accordance with competitive fee schedules negotiated in advance. The physicians and hospitals benefit from knowing that they have a guaranteed customer base. Employees are free to use any physicians or hospital that is part of the PPO or another provider if they are willing to pay any difference. Many employers have organized PPOs in communities located near their facilities. Since employees and the federal government will continue to push for improved health care, employers will find it necessary to have an active managed care program for their employees, emphasizing both quality service and cost containment.

Another important medical cost-containment program is the medical savings account (MSA). Employer-offered MSA plans provide employees with comprehensive medical insurance carrying high deductibles. Employers establish a fund from which to pay employee medical costs "before" the deductible is satisfied. The benefits of an MSA include: (a) the employer pays lower medical care premiums; (b) employees retain discretion over medical spending; and (c) employees can "shop" for the best cost/quality medical care available commensurate with their individual needs.

Employees of small businesses find MSAs particularly beneficial to their health care needs. Under the Health Insurance Portability Act of 1996, employees of small employers may establish a tax-free, interest-bearing MSA. Under the MSA, individuals enrolled in a high-deductible plan may make tax-free contributions to an account created primarily for the purpose of paying for qualified medical expenses.

Other Health Benefits

Dental plans are designed to help pay for dental costs and to encourage employees to receive regular dental attention. Like medical plans, dental care plans may be operated by insurance companies, dental service corporations, those administering Blue Cross/Blue Shield plans, HMOs, and groups of dental care providers. Typically, the insurance pays a portion of the charges, and the subscriber pays the remainder.

Optical care insurance is another, relatively new benefit that many employers are offering. Coverage can include visual examinations and a percentage of the costs of lenses and frames.

COMPENSATION FOR TIME NOT WORKED

Almost all employers provide full-time employees with some payments for time not worked. The "payment for time not worked" category of benefits (e.g., supplemental pay benefits) includes paid vacations, bonuses given in lieu of paid vacations, payments for holidays not worked, paid sick leave, military and jury duty, and payments for absence due to a death in the family or other personal reasons. Supplemental pay benefits are typically one of an employer's most expensive benefits because of the large amount of time off that many employees receive.

Vacation. It is generally agreed that vacations are essential to the well-being of an employee. Eligibility for vacations varies by industry, locale, and organization size. To qualify for longer vacations of three, four, or five weeks, one may expect to work for seven, 15, and 20 years, respectively. A majority of employers stagger vacation schedules to remain well staffed throughout the year, whereas some schedule a plant shutdown and have all employees take vacation at that time.

Paid holidays. Both hourly and salaried workers can usually expect to be paid for 10 holidays a year. The type of business tends to influence both the number and observance of holidays. Virtually all employers pay employees for major national holidays. Some employers have additional holidays, such as President' Day (February), Columbus Day (October), or Veterans' Day (November), whereas others observe religious holidays such as Good Friday and Rosh Hashanah. Many employers give workers an additional two or three personal days off to use at their discretion.

Sick leave. There are several ways in which employees may be compensated during periods when they are unable to work because of illness or injury. Many employers accrue sick leave in proportion to days worked. For instance, one-half day of paid sick leave may be given for each 15 days worked. Some organizations allow unused sick leave to accumulate over the years, to be used in case of extended illness. Another popular alternative is to pay employees for unused sick leave as an incentive to come to work regularly and to use sick leave only when it is really needed.

Severance pay. A one-time payment is sometimes given to employees who are being terminated. Known as severance pay, it may cover only a few days' wages or wages for several months. The pay received is usually dependent on the employee's years of service. However, severance pay can also be based on the reason for termination, the salary or grade level of the employee, the title or level in the organization, or a combination of factors. Employers that are downsizing often use severance pay as a means of lessening the negative effects of unexpected termination of employees. Other triggers for severance pay include job elimination, voluntary separation programs, or refusal of reassignment or relocation.

Other Leaves

In 1993, the Family and Medical Leave Act (FMLA) became law. This act mandates unpaid leave of up to 12 weeks, with benefits and reinstatement rights, in the event of the birth or adoption of a child or serious illness in the immediate family, including parents. Health benefits must be maintained for employees on this type of leave. Leave is available to employees who have worked at least 1,250 hours in the previous 12 months of employment with the same employer.

Additional leave benefits can include medical, civic, and bereavement leave. Medical leave allows employees extended time off for major medical reasons. Frequently, such leave is unpaid and takes effect when all sick leave days have been exhausted. Leave for civic obligations includes time off for jury duty, part (or all) of the day off to vote in national elections, and leave for military duty, such as National Guard or reserve military service. Bereavement leave allows the employee time off for a death in the immediate family.

Supplemental Unemployment Benefits

While not required by law, in some industries unemployment compensation is augmented by supplemental unemployment benefits (SUBs). In some industries (such as automaking), shutdowns to reduce inventories or to change machinery are common, and in the past employees were laid off or furloughed and had to depend on unemployment insurance. Supplemental unemployment benefits are paid by the company and supplement unemployment benefits, thus enabling the workers to better maintain their standards of living. Supplemental benefits are becoming more prevalent in collective bargaining agreements. They provide benefits over and above state employment compensation for three categories: layoffs, reduced workweeks, and relocations. Such benefits are most popular in heavy manufacturing operations such as in the auto and steel industries. Here, weekly or monthly plant shutdowns are normal, and some plan for guaranteeing minimum annual income is more appropriate.

Life Insurance

One of the oldest and most popular employee benefits is group term life insurance, which provides death benefits to beneficiaries and may also provide accidental death and dismemberment benefits. The premium costs are normally paid by the employer, with the face value of the life insurance equal to two times the employee's yearly wages. These programs frequently allow employees to purchase additional amounts of insurance for nominal charges. Where employers operate a cafeteria-style benefits program, selection of extra insurance may be one of the choices offered employees.

OTHER BENEFITS

In addition to protection plans and paid time off, many organizations also offer a growing array of other kinds of benefit programs, some of which provide innovative opportunities for employees. This section discusses some of the other important benefits.

Employee assistance programs (EAPs). Many organizations have established EAPs to help employees cope with a variety of problems that interfere with the way they perform their jobs. An EAP typically provides diagnosis, counseling, and referral for advice or treatment when necessary for problems related to alcohol or drug abuse, emotional difficulties, and financial or family difficulties. (EAPS will be discussed in detail in Chapter 12.) The main intent is to help employees solve their personal problems or at least to prevent problems from turning into crises that affect their ability to work productively. To handle crises, many EAPs offer 24-hour hot lines.

Wellness programs. As noted earlier, many organizations have been struggling with ways to reduce health care costs. In addition to the attempt described earlier, these efforts have resulted in a new type of benefit known as wellness programs. These programs concentrate on keeping employees from becoming sick rather than simply paying expenses when they become sick. In some organizations these programs may be simple and involve little more than organized jogging or walking during lunch breaks. More elaborate programs might include smoking cessation programs, high blood pressure and cholesterol screening, and stress management programs. Some organizations actually have full-fledged health clubs on site and provide counseling and programs for fitness and weight loss. Although these programs typically take place after work hours (or before), the companies often provide the services either for free or at cost.

Adoption benefits. Many employers have had maternity and paternity benefits for employees who give birth to children. In the interest of fairness, a growing number of organizations provide benefits for employees who adopt children. In comparison to those giving birth, a relatively small number of employees adopt children, but there is a fairness issue that employers have addressed by providing adoption benefits. For example, some organizations give a cash benefit and a certain number of weeks paid leave to employees who adopt children.

An additional group of benefits is often referred to collectively as life cycle benefits. The most common of these are child care and elder care benefits. Thus they are targeted at different stages in an employee's life.

Child care. Balancing work and family responsibilities is a major challenge for many workers. It is likely that every major company will soon consider offering child care assistance as an employee benefit. Such assistance can take the form of on-site child care, financial assistance, or information and referral. Relatively few on-site facilities have been established, primarily because of costs and concerns about liability and attracting sufficient employee use. However, for a number of firms, providing on-site child care has had a positive impact on employees who use the service (Armour, 1998). Having on-site child care also has been an advantage in recruiting workers in tight labor markets.

Other options for child care assistance include:

- Providing referral services to aid parents in locating child care providers
- Establishing discounts at day care centers, which may be subsidized by the employer
- Arranging with hospitals to offer sick-child programs partially paid for by the employer
- Developing after-school programs for older school-age children, often in conjunction with local public and private school systems

Elder care. An important family-related issue of growing importance is caring for elderly relatives. Various organizations have surveyed their employees and found that as many as 30 percent of them have had to miss work to care for an aging relative. The responsibilities associated with caring for elderly family members have resulted in reduced work performance, increased absenteeism, and more personal stress for the affected employees.

Interest in and demand for elder care programs will increase dramatically as baby boomers move into their fifties and find themselves managing organizations and experiencing elder care problems with their own parents.

Educational assistance. Another important benefit is educational assistance. Typically, employees are reimbursed for tuition and possibly for books or other associated costs. In general, educational assistance is limited to courses or degree programs that are job related.

Benefits for spousal equivalents. An increasing number of organizations extend "spousal" benefits to same-sex partners and to unmarried opposite-sex partners. Usually, to be eligible, unmarried partners of the same sex must live together and share financial obligations. If they break up, the employee must wait one year before registering a new partner. In addition to health, some plans include life insurance, relocation expenses, bereavement leave, and a death benefit. Such benefits are optional for most employers, but they are required for some.

Relocation and housing. As housing costs continue to sour more employers are considering housing assistance as an employee benefit. Relocation assistance traditionally has consisted of financial help for travel expenses and the cost of moving possessions. If needed, the company might also pay for furniture storage for a limited time as well as for temporary housing. A growing number of firms also offer a variety of allowances and services for transferred employees and high-demand new hires. These benefits include cost allowances for selling a house, expenses for finding a new residence, assistance in finding employment for a spouse, and temporary living expenses.

Flexible Benefit Options

One way to increase employee satisfaction with benefits and overall job satisfaction without increasing the cost of the compensation package is by offering a flexible benefit package, also termed a cafeteria-style benefit plan. Under this plan, employees are automatically given a core plan with minimum coverage in medical insurance and retirement benefits. In addition, they receive benefit credits each year, which they can "spend" on additional benefits of their choice (e.g., more vacation time, more life insurance, more dental insurance, and so on).

Flexible benefit plans are very effective and popular because they recognize that employees of different ages and life situations have differing personal needs. Flexible benefits allow individual employees to choose the benefits they want. Most companies provide a request form annually, allowing employees to modify their package.

A flexible benefit program involves several additional costs. First, communication of benefit options is more difficult. As many organizations can attest, it is extremely difficult to get the word out on a single benefit package. When there are multiple packages, as with flexible benefits, the communication problem is far more difficult. Administrative costs also increase with the number of options.

For companies willing to invest extra effort to ensure that flexible benefit programs will work, the advantages outweigh the disadvantages. Flexible benefit programs enhance an organization's reputation for progressive treatment of its employees.

ADMINISTERING AN EFFECTIVE BENEFITS PROGRAM

When organizations make decisions about benefits and services, they must consider the following facts (Grossman, 2000):

- Mandated programs must be funded.
- There is little evidence that benefits and services really motivate performance. Nor do they necessarily increase satisfaction.
- Most employees view benefits and services as entitlements.
- Unions, competitors, and industry trends continue to pressure organizations to provide or increase voluntary benefits.
- Costs of benefits and services continue to escalate dramatically.

To administer a benefits program effectively, certain steps are necessary. Four of these are discussed next.

Step 1: Set objectives and strategy for benefits. There are three strategies for benefits:

1. Pacesetter strategy. Be first with the newest benefits employees desire.
2. Comparable benefits strategy. Match the benefits programs similar organizations offer.
3. Minimum benefits strategy. Offer the mandatory benefits and those that are most desired and least costly.

The decision about which strategy to use is made on the basis of management goals. The third strategy may be chosen because of inability to pay more benefits or because management believes the employees want more pay and fewer benefits. Before costly benefits and services are offered, management must set objectives that fit its benefits strategy.

Step 2: Involve employees and unions. Whatever strategy may be chosen, it makes sense for organizations to find out what those involved desire in benefits and services. Yet, in most organizations, top managers alone judge which benefits the employees prefer. Without getting some input on employees' preferences, it is impossible to make these decisions intelligently. This is similar to a marketing manager trying to decide on consumers' preferences with no market research.

Therefore, it is wise to permit (and encourage) employee participation in decision making about benefits and services. When employees share in these decisions, they show more interest in them. One way to let employees participate in the decisions is to poll them with attitude surveys. Another is to set up employee benefits advisory committees.

When the organization is unionized, it is vital that the union leadership be involved. Many times, the leadership knows what employees want in benefits. Sometimes, however, the leadership tries to maximize benefits without having determined what employees want. It is useful to involve the union leadership in preference studies so that all parties are seeking benefits desired by the employees.

Step 3: Communicate benefits. The main goal of both direct and indirect compensation should be to achieve company goals by providing rewards that are valued by employees. Communication is critical for the successful administration of benefits. Organizations that do not invest effort in communicating a specific benefit might be better off not offering the benefit in the first place.

Communicating about benefits is not an easy task. Plans and options can be quite complex, and employees tend to have little interest in benefits until they need to use them. In an effort to improve communication about benefits, many employers have instituted special benefits communication systems to inform employees about the value of the benefits they provide. There are several specific ways organizations can improve communications about benefits. First, written communication should be in plain language, not insurance jargon. Second, communication should be frequent and timed to occur when employees are likely to listen. Describing benefits when employees first begin work is unlikely to be effective because new employees have many more pressing issues to attend to in the first few weeks on the job. Finally, communication should be directed not just to the employee but also to other consumers of the benefit—most commonly, the spouse.

Step 4: Monitor costs closely. In addition to considering costs involved in the choice of benefits, it is vital that managers make sure the programs are administered correctly. Review of insurance claims is especially important. More efficient administration procedures using computerized methods also can lead to greater savings and more satisfied employees.

Together, these four steps will make any benefits program more effective.

EVALUATING INDIRECT COMPENSATION AND BENEFIT PLANS

Given the enormous cost to the organization of benefit packages, organizations must carefully assess the benefit that accrues to the organization from those packages. On the one hand, the organization must provide appropriate benefits to its employees. At the same time, the best interest of stockholders and other constituents of the organization require the company to manage its resources wisely. Thus it is important to periodically assess the extent to which costs are in line. One way of doing so is through the use of the wage surveys mentioned in Chapter 10. Although these surveys typically ask about wages for specific jobs, questions about benefits can be included as well. Any organization, for example, can learn the average insurance premium costs that other organizations are paying, and even if it cannot match these premiums, the company can nevertheless get a better feel for how close its costs are to those of other organizations.

Likewise, some organizations might audit their benefit programs to determine whether or not they are providing a competitive package. As a part of the recruiting process, of course, the organization wants to be seen as an attractive employer so that it can hire quality human resources. Thus if other organizations in the labor market are providing special benefits that the organization is not providing, it might have to reconsider this policy. On the other hand, the organization may be providing more benefits than its competitors are providing and might be able to scale back in some areas as a way of controlling costs.

There is one final issue to consider relative to evaluating benefit programs. In many cases these programs are not effectively communicated to employees. It is not unusual for some employees to know less than they should about their benefits. Organizations must take every opportunity to increase their employees' understanding of their benefits and the cost to the organization. An organization can never expect to gain the full advantage of its benefit program when employees don't completely understand their benefits or underestimate the cost of their benefits.

Given the cost and significance of benefits, organizations must do a thorough job of evaluating the effectiveness and costs of the benefits they are providing to their employees. As a center of expertise, the HRM function should take the lead role in evaluating the effectiveness of the organization's benefit program as well as in communicating the significance of those benefits to all employees in the organization.

In the end, organizations should consider conducting a cost-benefit analysis of benefits. The cost of benefits can be calculated fairly easily:

1. Total cost of benefits annually for all employees.
2. Cost per employee per year—basis 1 divided by number of employee hours worked.
3. Percentage of payroll—basis 1 divided by annual payroll.
4. Cost per employee per hour—basis 2 divided by employee hours worked.

The benefits side of the equation is another issue, however. There continues to be little significant empirical research on the effects of benefits on productivity.

SUMMARY

Pay can be linked to performance at the individual, group, or organizational levels. Individual plans can be used only where individual performance is measurable. Individual plans include piecework, commissions, individual bonuses, and merit pay increases. In addition, an increasing number of organizations are basing pay on the number of different skills or jobs mastered as a way of motivating continued employee learning and productivity.

Group systems are important where employee cooperation and coordination are necessary. Group incentives may be piece rates based on group output, gainsharing, or profit sharing plans. Profit sharing is an incentive system in which designated employees share the business profits. Gainsharing plans include the Scanlon Plan, Improshare, and the Rucker Plan, all of which seek employee suggestions to cut costs and then share the savings with the employees.

Executives are especially important to organizations and thus usually operate with a somewhat different system of compensation and incentives. Frequently, executive reward packages include bonus plans based on organizational performance and long-term incentives in the form of stock options.

Employee benefits include mandatory protection programs, compensation for time not worked, optional protection programs, and private retirement (pension) plans. In the last 25 years, there have been a variety of federal laws and regulations regarding benefits. For example, COBRA requires the extension of group medical benefits to terminated employees, at the employees' expense.

Several important issues related to benefits include cost containment, flexible benefit options, and work-family issues. As benefit costs have increased more rapidly than inflation, employers have had to resort to innovative ways of containing costs. Flexible benefits provide an important means of tailoring benefits to employee needs. Finally, as with other HRM activities, organizations must continually look for ways to assess their compensation programs and overall program administration.

REFERENCES

Abosch, K.S. 1998. Variable pay: Do we have the basics in place? *Compensation and Benefits Review* (July–August): 12–22.

Armour, S. 1998. School bells at the work site. *USA Today* (August 26), pp. 1B–2B.

Beck, D. 1992. Implementing a gainsharing plan: What companies need to know. *Compensation and Benefits Review* (January–February): 21–33.

Bento, R.F., and White, L.F. 1998. Participants' values and incentive plans. *Human Resource Management* (Spring): 47–59.

Brockbank, W. 1997. HR's future on the way to a presence. *Human Resource Management* 36(1): 65–69.

Bureau of Labor Statistics. 1998. *Employer costs for employee compensation* (March 1997). Available at: http://stats.bls.gov/ecthome.htm, p. 13 (April 3, 1998).

Coy, P. 1998. Social security: Let it be. *Business Week* (November 30): 34–35.

Grossman, R.J. 2000. Measuring up. *HRMagazine* (January): 28–35.

Johnson, S.T. 1998. Plan your organization's reward strategy through pay-for-performance dynamics. *Compensation and Benefits Review* (May–June): 67–72.

Lattanzio, S. 1997. What can an employer do to influence the cost of its workers' compensation program? *Compensation and Benefits Review* (May–June): 20–28.

McKenzie, F.C., and Shilling, M.D. 1998. Ensuring effective incentive design and implementation. *Compensation and Benefits Review* (July–August): 57–65.

Ost, E. 1989. Gain sharing's potential. *Personnel Administrator* (July): 92–96.

Quinn, J.B. 1986. Slow profits, slow pay. *Newsweek* (December 22): 52.

Schultz, E.E. 1998. Ins and outs of cash-balance plans. *Wall Street Journal* (December 4), p. C-1.

Chapter 12

Employee Safety and Health

INTRODUCTION

Today most organizations are concerned about providing a safe and healthy workplace for their employees. But meeting that general goal is not easy; nor can all situations affecting employee health and safety always be anticipated. Nevertheless, organizational managers and HRM personnel have responsibilities for the health and safety issues of their organization. Part of this concern is simple humanitarianism. Few organizations would knowingly send unprotected employees into a dangerous situation. Aside from altruism, there are two other reasons for organizational concern about the work environment. First, there are bottom-line performance consequences of mental and physical health. Second, state and federal laws require that reasonable levels of safety be maintained in the work environment.

In today's successful organizations, safety and health management concerns go beyond the physical condition of the workplace to a regard for employees' mental and emotional well-being and a commitment to protecting the surrounding community from pollution and exposure to toxic substances. As a consequence of the importance of safety and health, employees at all levels of the company are now involved.

This chapter is about safety and health in the workplace. The chapter emphasizes the fact that an unsafe work environment will have a negative effect on the employee's ability and motivation to be productive. This chapter will cover the current issues related to employee safety and health and discuss some of the steps organizations are taking to improve their employee safety and health performance records. The chapter describes occupational and safety and health legislation like the Occupational Safety and Health Act. We then emphasize the responsibilities and right of employers and employees under the Occupational Safety and Health Act. Following a discussion of the changing nature of the Occupational Safety and Health Administration (OSHA), we focus on the causes of occupational accidents and on ways to minimize occupational health risks. Next we highlight other safety and health concerns, including AIDS in the workplace, smoking at work, substance abuse, stress, and violence in the workplace. Before concluding with a discussion on evaluating safety and health programs, we cover organizational programs to promote safety and health.

COSTS OF WORK-RELATED ACCIDENTS AND ILLNESSES

The costs of work-related accidents and occupational diseases to American industry are known to be in the billions of dollars annually and are increasing in certain areas. These costs are both tangible and intangible.

The tangible costs are measurable financial expenses. One major category of these costs is directly related to lost production. This category includes costs incurred as a result of work slowdown, damaged or idle equipment, damaged or ruined products, excessive waste, and any profit forgone due to lost sales. A closely related cost is the cost incurred for training new or temporary replacements.

Another category covers insurance and medical costs. These costs are increasing due to large claims and other expenses incurred as a result of work-related accidents. This category includes the costs of workers' compensation insurance, accident insurance, and disability insurance.

The intangible costs of work-related accidents and illnesses include lowered employee morale, less favorable public relations, and a weakened ability to recruit and retain employees. It is only natural that employee morale will suffer in an unsafe environment. If a member of a maintenance team is injured, the harmony of the team may be impaired by the absence of the injured employee. A bad safety record may also be a major reason for poor employee relations with management. If employees perceive that their managers are unconcerned about their physical welfare, employee–manager relations can deteriorate. In fact, safety is often a primary reason for unionizing. A poor safety record is also harmful to an organization's public relations. It may deter customers from purchasing a business's products or services. Frequently organizations ignore or are not aware of these and other "hidden" costs of occupational illness or injury. In general, the more serious the accident, the greater the costs.

SAFETY AND HEALTH: LEGAL REQUIREMENTS

Complying with a variety of federal and state laws is fundamental for organizations developing a safe and healthy workforce and working environment. Some major legal areas are discussed below.

Workers' Compensation

At this time, all states have workers' compensation laws in some form. Under these laws, employers contribute to an insurance fund to compensate employees for injuries received while on the job. Premiums paid reflect the accident rates at each employer. Also, these laws usually provide payments for lost wages, for medical bills, and for retraining if the employee cannot go back to the old job.

Before the passage of workers' compensation laws, an employee might not recover damages for an injury, even if it was caused by hazards of the job or through the negligence of a fellow worker. Employees who died or became disabled as a result of occupational injury or disease received no financial guarantees for their families. Employers (and society) assumed that safety was the employee's responsibility. Employers once viewed accidents and occupational diseases as unavoidable by-products of work. This idea was replaced with the concept of using prevention and control to minimize or eliminate safety and health risks in the workplace.

Workers' compensation coverage has been expanded in many states to include emotional impairment that may have resulted from physical injury, as well as job-related strain, stress, anxiety, and pressure. Some cases of suicide also have been ruled to be job-related, with payments due under workers' compensation. However, the most common injuries are back problems, broken bones, cuts, and carpal tunnel syndrome. The most common illnesses are stress and allergies. These are examples of injuries and illnesses typically covered by workers' compensation.

A new focus of workers' compensation coverage is the increase in telecommuting by employees. It is not widely known that in most situations while working at home for an employer, individuals are covered under workers' compensation laws. Therefore, if an employee is injured while doing employer-related work at home, the employer is liable for the injury. Some employers inspect home offices and give telecommuters training courses.

Workers' compensation costs have increased dramatically in the past and have become a major issue in many states. Employers must continually monitor their workers' compensation expenditures. To reduce accidents and workers' compensation costs, an employer should have a well-managed safety and health program. These programs typically result in a reduction of insurance premiums, savings on litigation costs, less money paid to injured workers for lost work time, lowered expenses for training new workers, decreased overtime, and increased productivity.

Efforts to reduce workplace injuries and illnesses can reduce workers' compensation premiums and claims costs. Many of the safety and health management suggestions discussed in this chapter can be part of an effort to reduce workers' compensation costs.

Child Labor Laws

Another area of safety concern is reflected in restrictions affecting younger workers, especially those under the age of 18. Child labor laws, found in Section XII of the Fair Labor Standards Act (FLSA), set the minimum age for most employment at 16 years. For "hazardous" occupations, 18 years is the minimum. Some of the occupations that the federal government considers hazardous for children who work while attending school are:

- Manufacturing or storing explosives
- Driving a motor vehicle and being an outside helper
- Coal mining
- Logging and sawmilling
- Operating power-driven hoisting apparatus
- Mining, other than coal mining
- Using power-driven bakery machines
- Manufacturing brick, tile, and related products
- Wrecking, demolition, and shipbreaking operations

Americans with Disabilities Act (ADA) and Safety

The ADA is an entirely new form of regulation for safety and health. The ADA has created some problems for employers. For example, employers sometimes try to return injured workers to "light-duty" work in order to reduce workers' compensation costs. However, under the ADA, in making accommodations for injured employees through light-duty work, employers may be undercutting what really are *essential job functions*. Making such accommodations for injured employees for extended periods of time may require an employer to make accommodations for job applicants with disabilities.

Safety and health record-keeping practices have been affected by the following provision in the ADA:

> Information from all medical examinations and inquiries must be kept apart from general personnel files as a separate confidential medical record available only under limited conditions specified in the ADA.

As interpreted by attorneys and HRM practitioners, this provision requires that all medical-related information be maintained separately from all other confidential files. Also, specific access restrictions and security procedures must be adopted for medical records of all types, including employee medical benefit claims and treatment records.

In addition to complying with workers' compensation, ADA, and child labor laws, most employers must comply with the Occupational Health and Safety Act of 1970. This act has had a tremendous impact on the workplace. Therefore, any person interested in HRM must develop knowledge of the provisions and implications of the act, which is administered by OSHA.

THE OCCUPATIONAL SAFETY AND HEALTH ACT

In 1969, in the aftermath of a tragic explosion that claimed the lives of 78 coal miners and amid reports of a high incidence of black-lung disease among miners, Congress passed the Coal Mine Health and Safety Act. The following year, continuing public and governmental concern about safety and health in the workplace was reflected in passage of the Occupational Safety and Health Act. Its stated purpose is "to assure so far as possible every working man and woman in the nation safe and healthful working conditions and to preserve our human resources." Thus the Occupational Safety and Health Act was designed to enforce safety and health standards to reduce the incidence of occupational injury, illness, and death.

Agencies Created by the Occupational Safety and Health Act

The Occupational Safety and Health Act created three autonomous but related agencies to ensure occupational safety and health. These three agencies are the Occupational Safety and Health Review Commission (OSHRC), the National Institute for Occupational Safety and Health (NIOSH), and as already noted, the Occupational Safety and Health Administration (OSHA).

OSHRC is based in the Department of Labor. This commission plays a judicial role in administering workplace safety and health. Organizations can appeal a safety or health citation by requesting a review by OSHRC. If dissatisfied with an OSHRC ruling, an employer may appeal through the federal court system.

NIOSH has primary responsibility for conducting and coordinating research on workplace safety and health. This research could involve determining safe levels of particular chemicals in the atmosphere or what decibel level of machine noise requires hearing protection to prevent injury. NIOSH's research provides the basis for making recommendations to OSHA concerning possible regulations. The NIOSH homepage is available at http://www.cdc.gov/niosh.

OSHA, an agency of the U.S. Department of Labor (DOL), enforces the Occupational Safety and Health Act, which covers nearly all businesses with one or more employees. OSHA was created to:

- Encourage employers and employees to reduce workplace hazards and to implement new safety and health programs or improve existing programs.
- Provide for research to develop innovative ways of dealing with occupational safety and health problems.
- Establish "separate but dependent responsibilities and rights" for employers and employees to achieve better safety and health conditions.
- Maintain a reporting and record-keeping system to monitor job-related injuries and illnesses.
- Establish training programs to increase the number and competence of occupational safety and health personnel.
- Develop mandatory job safety and health standards and enforce them effectively.
- Provide for the development, analysis, evaluation, and approval of state occupational safety and health programs. (U.S. Department of Labor, 1995, p. 2).

Accident prevention is a major goal of safety and health management. OSHA requires employers to keep a log of on-the-job accidents, and accident investigation and measurement can supply useful data for developing effective safety programs and improving working conditions. These data can be useful to company safety specialists as well as to worker–management safety committees.

State occupational safety and health programs are found in those states that have assumed responsibility for administration of the Occupational Safety and Health Act. Under special plans negotiated with the DOL, states agree to establish programs of inspection, citation, and training that meet or exceed the minimum standards enforced on the federal level.

Inspections

OSHA standards are enforced through inspections and (if necessary) citations. OSHA may not conduct warrantless inspections without an employer's consent. It may, however, inspect after acquiring a judicially authorized search warrant or its equivalent.

OSHA inspections are conducted by compliance officers. These inspectors are men and women from the safety and health field who have attended at least four weeks of specialized training at OSHA's Training Institute at Des Plaines, Illinois, or at one of 11 other training centers. They also take additional training courses once each year in specialized areas such as industrial hygiene, construction, or maritime safety and health.

OSHA has a list of inspection priorities. Imminent danger situations get top priority. These are conditions in which it is likely that a danger exists that can immediately cause death or serious physical harm. Second priority is given to catastrophes, fatalities, and accidents that have already occurred. (Such situations must be reported to OSHA within 48 hours.) Third priority is given to valid employee complaints of alleged violation of standards.

Next in priority are periodic special-emphasis inspections aimed at high-hazard industries, occupations, or substances. Finally, random inspections and reinspections generally have last priority. Most inspections result from employee complaints.

OSHA no longer follows up every employee complaint with an inspection. The focus now is on high-priority problems. Under its priority system, OSHA conducts an inspection within 24 hours when a complaint indicates an immediate danger, and within three working days when a serious hazard exists. For a "nonserious" complaint filed in writing by a worker or a union, OSHA will respond within 20 working days. Other nonserious complaints are handled by writing to the employer and requesting corrective action.

The inspection process starts with the presentation of the compliance officer's credentials and a meeting with the appropriate employer representative. If the inspection has resulted from an employee complaint the compliance officer should give the employer a copy of the complaint, with the complainant's name withheld, as well as copies of any applicable laws and safety and health standards.

Before an inspection tour, the compliance officer will also want to meet with a representative of the employees if the company is unionized. If it is not, an employee representative will be selected by the members of the plant safety committee or by the employees as a whole. Both the employee and employer representatives typically accompany the compliance officer during the inspection. In addition to a plant inspection, the compliance officer is permitted to interview various employees at his or her discretion about safety and health conditions. OSHA gives the compliance officer the right to take photographs, make instrument readings, and examine safety and health records. Compliance officers must keep any trade secrets they observe confidential, however, or face a $1,000 fine and/or one year in jail.

After the inspection, the officer should discuss any observations with the employer and review possible OSHA violations. The employer should estimate the time needed to correct any hazardous conditions noted by the officer. Citations and penalties are not issued at this time, nor can the officer order that any part of the business be closed down immediately. If an imminent danger exists, the compliance officer will ask the employer to abate the hazard and remove endangered employees. If the employer does not comply, OSHA administrators can go to the appropriate federal district court for an injunction prohibiting further work as long as unsafe conditions exist.

Violations and Citations

If after the inspection tour an OSHA standard is found to have been violated, the OSHA area director determines what citations and penalties, if any, will be issued as well as a proposed time period for abatement. An employer who believes the citation is unreasonable or the abatement period is insufficient may contest it. The act provides an appeal procedure and a review agency, OSHRC, which operates independently from OSHA.

OSHA may impose civil penalties up to $7,000 for each violation. Criminal penalties are levied in the most serious cases. For example, a willful violation that results in the death of an employee can bring a court-imposed fine of up to $250,000 (or $500,000 if the employer is a corporation) or imprisonment for up to six months, or both. A second conviction can double these penalties. Falsifying records can result in a fine of up to $10,000 and six months in jail. Multiple violations or failure to correct prior violations can add up to enormous fines.

In general, OSHA calculates penalties based on the gravity of a particular violation and usually takes into consideration such factors as the size of the business, the organization's compliance history, and the employer's good faith. In practice, OSHA must have a final order from the independent OSHRC to enforce a penalty. While that appeals process has been speeded up of late, an employer who files a notice of contest can still drag out an appeal for years.

Not all OSHA inspections are performed by OSHA. OSHA allows a state to take over responsibility for inspections and enforcement of workplace safety if its laws are at least as stringent as the federal standards. Twenty-five states currently run their own safety programs in partnership with OSHA.

Record-keeping Requirements

The Occupational Safety and Health Administration recently revised the rule on record-keeping to improve the system employers use to track and record workplace injuries and illnesses. OSHA's record-keeping requirements, in place since 1971, were designed to help employers recognize workplace hazards and correct hazardous conditions by keeping track of work-related injuries and illnesses and their causes. The revised rule that became effective on January 1, 2002, affected approximately 1.3 million establishments. The rule is expected to produce better information about occupational injuries and illnesses while simplifying the overall record-keeping system for employers. The rule is also intended to better protect employees' privacy.

Like the former rule, employers with 10 or fewer employees are exempt from most requirements of the new rule, as are a number of industries classified as low-hazard-retail, service, finance, insurance, and real estate sectors. The new rule updated the list of exempted industries to reflect recent industry data. (All employers covered by the Occupational Safety and Health Act must continue to report any workplace incident resulting in a fatality or the hospitalization of three or more employees.)

The revised rule includes a provision for recording needlestick and sharp injuries that is consistent with recently passed legislation requiring OSHA to revise its bloodborne pathogens standard to address such injuries. This provision is expected to result in a significant increase in recordable cases annually.

The new record-keeping rule also conforms with OSHA's ergonomics standard published in November 2000. It simplifies the manner in which employers record musculoskeletal disorders (MSDs), replacing a cumbersome system in which MSDs were recorded using criteria different from those for other injuries or illnesses. The revised forms have a separate column for recording MSDs, which will improve the compilation of national data on these disorders.

One of the least understood concepts of record-keeping has been restricted work; the new rule clarifies the definition of restricted work or light duty and makes it easier to record those cases. Work-related injuries are also better defined to ensure the recording only of appropriate cases while excluding cases clearly unrelated to work.

The revised rule also promotes improved employee awareness and involvement in the record-keeping process, providing workers and their representatives access to the information on record-keeping forms and increasing awareness of potential hazards in the workplace. Privacy concerns of employees have also been addressed; the former rule had no privacy protections covering the log used to record work-related injuries and illnesses.

Written in plain language using a question and answer format, the regulation for the first time uses checklists and flowcharts to provide easier interpretations of record-keeping requirements. Finally, employers are given more flexibility in using computers and telecommunications technology to meet their record-keeping requirements. OSHA's record-keeping requirements provide the source data for the Bureau of Labor Statistics (BLS) Occupational Injury and Illness Survey, the primary source of statistical information concerning workplace injuries and illnesses. The Bureau of Labor Statistics collects the data and publishes the statistics, while OSHA interprets and enforces the regulation.

The new record-keeping rule updates three record-keeping forms:

- OSHA Form 300 (Log of Work-Related Injuries and Illnesses); simplified and printed on smaller, legal-sized paper.
- OSHA Form 301 (Injury and Illness Incident Report); includes more data about how the injury or illness occurred.
- OSHA Form 300A (Summary of Work-Related Injuries and Illnesses); a separate form updated to make it easier to calculate incidence rates.

No one knows how many industrial accidents go unreported. It may be many more than anyone suspects, despite the fact that OSHA has increased its surveillance of accident-reporting records. OSHA guidelines state that facilities whose accident record is below the national average rarely need inspecting.

Accident frequency rate. Accident frequency and severity rates must be calculated. Regulations from OSHA require organizations to calculate injury frequency rates per 100 full-time employees on an annual basis. Employers compute accident severity rates by figuring the number of lost-time cases, the number of lost workdays, and the number of deaths. These figures are then related to total work hours per 100 full-time employees and compared with industry-wide rates and other employers' rates.

Reporting injuries and illnesses. Four types of injuries or illnesses have been defined by the Occupational Safety and Health Act of 1970:

- Injury- or illness-related deaths.
- Lost-time or disability injuries: These include job-related injuries or disabling occurrences that cause an employee to miss his or her regularly scheduled work on the day following the accident.
- Medical care injuries: These injuries require treatment by a physician but do not cause an employee to miss a regularly scheduled work turn.
- Minor injuries: These injuries require first-aid treatment and do not cause an employee to miss the next regularly scheduled work turn.

OSHA's Hazard Communication Standard

Because of the threats posed by chemicals, OSHA has established a Hazard Communication Standard (HCS). This standard is also known as the "right to know" rule. The basic purpose of the rule is to ensure that employers and employees know what chemical hazards exist in the workplace and how to protect themselves against those hazards. The goal of the rule is to reduce the incidence of illness and injuries caused by chemicals. The HCS establishes uniform requirements to ensure that the hazards of all chemicals imported into, produced by, or used in the workplace are evaluated and that the results of these evaluations are transmitted to affected managers and exposed employees.

The HCS specifically requires that employers maintain complete and updated material safety data sheets (MSDSs), for each hazardous material. MSDSs provide information on the nature of the hazards involved and include appropriate handling procedures and remedies for unexpected exposure. Employers, manufacturers, or importers involved with the hazardous material may prepare MSDSs.

RESPONSIBILITIES AND RIGHTS OF EMPLOYERS AND EMPLOYEES UNDER THE OCCUPATIONAL SAFETY AND HEALTH ACT

Both employers and employees have responsibilities and rights under the Occupational Safety and Health Act. Employers, for example, are responsible for meeting their duty to provide "a workplace free from recognized hazards" and for being familiar with mandatory OSHA standards. Employers have the right to seek advice and off-site consultation from OSHA, to request and to receive proper identification of the OSHA compliance officer before inspection, and to be advised by the compliance officer of the reason for an inspection.

The Occupational Safety and Health Act has an impact on the entire organization. In addition to employer responsibilities, it also places certain responsibilities on supervisors and front-line managers. Although supervisors cannot be familiar with all of the thousands of pages of OSHA regulation interpretations, they do need to understand what kinds of practices are required to preserve health and safety in their departments. In addition, OSHA regulations impose some specific responsibilities on supervisors and managers.

First, OSHA requires that supervisors keep specific records. Second, managers are often asked to accompany OSHA officials while they inspect the organization's facilities. Third, managers should be familiar with the OSHA regulations affecting their departments and ensure that the employees follow all safety rules.

Employees also have rights and responsibilities but cannot be cited for violations of their responsibilities. They are responsible, for example, for complying with all applicable OSHA standards, for following all employer safety and health rules and regulations, and for reporting hazardous conditions to the supervisor.

It appears that the Occupational Safety and Health Act will continue to be important in regulating health and safety in the workplace. As its provisions become more generally known, more employees are likely to exercise their rights concerning business hazards under the act. These include the:

- Right to request an OSHA inspection.
- Right to be present during the inspection.
- Right to protection from reprisal for reporting the company to OSHA.
- Right to access to the individual's personal medical records held by the company.
- Right to refuse to work if there is a real danger of death or serious injury or illness from job hazards.

In short, employees have a right to demand safety and health on the job without fear of punishment. Employers are forbidden to punish or discriminate against workers who complain to OSHA about job safety and health hazards.

CHANGING NATURE OF OSHA

OSHA has become one of the most controversial federal agencies with which HRM personnel must deal. Few laws have evoked as much negative reaction as the Occupational Safety and Health Act. While most people would support its intent, many have criticized the manner in which it has been implemented. The sheer volume of regulations has been staggering, and many of them are vaguely worded. For example, OSHA developed the following 39-word single-sentence definition of the word *exit* (*Code of Federal Regulations*, 1988, p. 126):

That portion of a means of egress which is separated from all other spaces of the building or structure by construction or equipment as required in this subject to provide a protected way of travel to the exit discharge.

In addition, many OSHA standards have been criticized as unacceptable, arbitrary, trivial, unattainable, excessively detailed, costly, or petty. Additionally, other critics have argued that OSHA has had an overly adverse effect on small businesses.

As a result of these criticisms, OSHA has made several changes in its policies and procedures. Small businesses with 10 or fewer employees no longer have to file accident reports or undergo routine inspections, and the accident report itself has been simplified and condensed. As mentioned, OSHA inspectors must also now obtain warrants before entering an employer's premises (Hammer, 1985).

Similarly, on July 16, 1998, former president Clinton signed two OSHA reform bills. The overall aim is to help OSHA focus on achieving its aims through cooperation rather than through confrontation. One bill requires OSHA to focus on criteria such as reduced injuries and illnesses as indicators of OSHA compliance, rather than on such measures as numbers of inspections or citations and fines. The other bill authorizes OSHA to fund state-administered programs to help employers identify and correct violations (Bureau of National Affairs, 1998, p. 236).

On the whole, OSHA in fact seems to be moving toward achieving its aim through cooperation. One example is its Cooperative Compliance Program (Bureau of National Affairs, 1997b), implemented in 1998 and aimed at getting employers to voluntarily provide safe workplaces (Bureau of National Affairs, 1997c, p. 416).

To the chagrin of some employers, OSHA is also becoming more technologically advanced in reporting its inspection results. For example, you can find on OSHA's Web site (www.osha.gov) easy access to your company's (or your competitor's) OSHA enforcement history. All the details are there, including the results of inspections conducted at small and large organizations.

THE CAUSES OF OCCUPATIONAL ACCIDENTS

There are three causes of workplace accidents: unsafe employee acts, unsafe work conditions, and chance occurrences. Chance occurrences (such as walking past a door just as someone opens it) contribute to accidents but are more or less beyond management's control. We will therefore focus on unsafe employee acts and unsafe conditions.

Unsafe Employee Acts

Some experts point to the employee as the pivotal cause of accidents. People cause accidents, and no one has found a surefire way to eliminate unsafe employee acts such as:

- Distracting, teasing, abusing, startling, quarreling, and horseplay
- Lifting improperly
- Throwing materials
- Using unsafe procedures in loading, placing, mixing, or combining
- Operating or working at unsafe speeds—either too fast or too slow
- Making safety devices inoperative by removing, adjusting, or disconnecting them
- Taking unnecessary chances

Unsafe employee acts such as these can undermine even the best attempts on your part to minimize unsafe conditions. It is difficult to determine why employees behave unsafely. There probably is no single reason. Some employees may be suffering from fatigue, boredom, stress, poor eyesight. Others may be daydreaming, be in a rush, or have physical limitations. However, these reasons do not explain why some employees intentionally neglect to wear prescribed safety equipment or to follow safety procedures. These employees may wish to impress others or project a certain image. They may think that accidents always happen to someone else. That attitude can easily lead employees to be careless or show off.

Employees with low morale also tend to have more accidents than employees with high morale; low morale is likely to be related to employee carelessness. A company's poor safety record can adversely affect morale.

Finally, a reason often given for accidents is that certain people are accident-prone. It seems to be true that due to their physical and mental makeup, some employees are more susceptible to accidents than are others. Accident-proneness may result from inborn traits, but it often develops as a result of the individual's environment. Given the right set of circumstances, anyone can be accident-prone. For example, a "normal" employee who was up all night with a sick child might very well be accident-prone the next day. A tendency to be accident-prone should not be used to justify an accident, however. Employees who appear to be accident-prone, even temporarily, should be identified and receive special attention.

Unsafe Work Conditions

Accidents can and do happen in all types of environments: in offices, retail stores, factories, and lumberyards. Accidents are more likely to occur in certain locations than others, however. Listed in order of decreasing accident frequency, these locations are:

1. Wherever heavy, awkward material is handled using hand trucks, forklifts, cranes, and hoists.
2. Improper handling and material lifting (about one-third of workplace accidents).
3. Around any type of machinery that is used to produce something else. Among the most hazardous are metalworking and woodworking machines, power saws, and machines with exposed gears, belts, chains, and the like. Even a paper cutter or an electric pencil sharpener has a high accident potential.
4. Wherever people walk or climb, including ladders, scaffolds, and narrow walkways. Falls are a major source of accidents.
5. Wherever people use hand tools, including chisels, screwdrivers, pliers, hammers, and axes.
6. Wherever electricity is used other than for the usual lighting purposes. Among the places where electrical accidents occur are near extension cords, loose wiring, and portable hand tools.
7. Near outdoor power lines.

Just as there are certain locations in which accidents occur more frequently, certain conditions of the work environment also seem to result in more accidents. Some of these unsafe conditions are:

- Serious understaffing in which there are not enough people to do the job safely
- Unguarded or improperly guarded machines
- Defective equipment and tools
- Hazardous procedures in, on, or around machines or equipment
- Improper illumination—glare, insufficient light
- Poor or improper ventilation

- Improper dress, such as clothing with loose and floppy sleeves worn when working on a lathe or any machine with moving parts
- Loose tile, linoleum, or carpeting
- Sharp burrs or edges on materials
- Reading while walking
- Poor housekeeping, such as cluttered aisles and stairs, dirty or wet floors that are slippery or have small, loose objects lying on them, and improperly stacked materials

The basic remedy here is to eliminate or minimize the unsafe conditions. OSHA standards address the mechanical and physical conditions that cause accidents. Furthermore, a checklist of unsafe conditions can be useful for spotting problems.

While accidents can happen anywhere, there are some high-danger zones. About one-third of industrial accidents occur around forklift trucks, wheelbarrows, and areas where handling and lifting activities occur. The most serious accidents usually occur near metal and woodworking machines and saws, or around transmission machinery like gears, pulleys, and flywheels (Bureau of National Affairs, 1997c, p. 416). Falls on stairs, ladders, walkways, and scaffolds are the third most common cause of industrial accidents. Hand tools (like chisels and screwdrivers) and electrical equipment (extension cords, electric droplights, and so on) are other big causes of accidents.

OCCUPATIONAL DISEASE

Potential sources of work-related diseases are as distressingly varied as the symptoms of those diseases. Occupational disease can be defined as a job-related disturbance of the normal functioning of the body or of a person's mental and emotional capacities. Examples of common occupational diseases are silicosis from breathing silica dust, rashes from handling insecticides, impaired hearing from exposure to noisy machines, and lead poisoning from exposure to lead in paint. Excessive and prolonged job stress, which is beginning to be recognized as a serious problem in many contemporary organizations and is discussed separately in the next section, can also be considered an occupational disease.

Potential lawsuits and criminal charges are reason enough to interest organizations in the prevention of occupational disease. The costs of occupational diseases are also of major concern. It has been estimated that American businesses pay half of the nation's health care bills, and any reasonable preventive measures they can take would seem to make economic sense.

Causes of Occupational Disease

Some of the common causes of occupational illness are exposure to toxic substances, dangerous chemicals, radiation, cigarette smoke, excessive noise, inadequate lighting, and harmful fumes and vapors aggravated by poor ventilation. The rapidly growing use of visual display terminals (VDTs) is associated with such ailments as eyestrain, neck pain, and disorders of the hand and wrist nerves, including carpal tunnel syndrome, a painful wrist disorder caused by repeated hand or wrist motions.

Indoor Air Quality (IAQ)

Over the last 10 years, more and more employees have expressed concerns over the quality of the indoor office environment. Two important terms in this context are *indoor air quality* (IAQ) and *sick-building syndrome*. Indoor air quality refers to the quality of the air in a business environment. Sick-building syndrome refers to illnesses with a wide range of symptoms that are believed to be caused by the building itself. The reason that employees blame poor IAQ for their symptoms is that those symptoms are often alleviated by leaving the building. For example, one office building near Washington, D.C., had to be evacuated several times because of a noxious odor that was making employees violently ill.

Sick-building syndrome has been linked to several factors. These include inadequate ventilation and chemical contaminants from indoor sources like adhesives, carpeting, upholstery, copy machines, pesticides, and cleaning agents. One employee recently developed a recurrence of asthma due to a solvent used to remove old carpet and the glue used to lay the new carpet. Other factors are chemical contaminants from outdoor sources (motor vehicle exhaust fumes, etc.); biological contaminants (bacteria, molds, pollen, and viruses); uncomfortable temperatures; and high levels of humidity. Pollutants that are most frequently in the news include secondhand smoke, asbestos, and radon. Poor building environment can also be caused by discomfort, noise, poor lighting, ergonomic stresses such as poorly designed equipment, and job-related psychological stresses.

Workers' compensation claims based on IAQ have become increasingly frequent. Typically, a wide spectrum of symptoms are reported: headaches, unusual fatigue, itching or burning eyes or skin, nasal congestion, dry throat, and nausea.

NIOSH evaluates potential health hazards in the workplace through its Health Hazard Evaluation (HHE) Program. Any employer, employee, employee representative, state or local government agency, or federal agency can ask NIOSH investigators to conduct an evaluation. Solutions to problems with IAQ and sick-building syndrome usually include combinations of the following: removal of the pollutant, modification of ventilation through increasing rates and locations of air distribution, cleaning the air, installing particle control devices, and banning smoking. Education and communication are also important elements of both remedial and preventive IAQ control.

Minimizing Occupational Health Risks

The major problem with reducing the occurrence of occupational diseases is the difficulty of detecting them and then pinpointing their cause. Thus, in some way avoiding occupational disease is more difficult for organizations than avoiding accidents. In the first place, occupational diseases are frequently diagnosed only in their advanced stages. Workers may not notice the small, incremental changes in their physical condition that may occur from week to week or even year to year. There is often no way to identify with certainty the precise moment the disease began or what were the precise circumstances at that time. It may be unclear whether an occupational disease is attributable to repeated exposure and progressive debilitation over time or whether one exposure produced the disease. Thus, the organization's strategy for minimizing health risks may need to be very complex and expensive, and may not be recognized as necessary until some damage has already been done.

Typically, the disease is linked to the workplace through statistics. Researchers compare the percentage of employees who have the disease with the percentage of people in the general population who have the disease. If the percentage is significantly greater for the employees than for the general population, researchers suggest that something at the workplace may have caused the disease.

Even if an organization is able to determine that its employees are suffering from an illness related to their occupation, the difficulties are not over. Next, the company must determine exactly what aspect of the work environment and/or the job caused the illness. Statistics and medical research help in this process, but the detective work may have to be done up to 40 years after the exposure.

Of course, the detection of occupational diseases is not always difficult. Medical science aids the process through studies of the impact of various environmental factors on health, and sometimes the cause is apparent, as in the case of hearing loss from sustained exposure to loud noises. When an illness is determined to be caused by something in the work environment, the organization is just as responsible in cases where the cause is not readily apparent as it is in more obvious cases.

As more is learned about the connections between industrial environments and medical consequences, employers will undoubtedly be required to shoulder more of the responsibility for both initial and cumulative exposure prevention as well as for compensation of victims. It is also likely that health and safety departments will need to devote more time and expense to maintaining records of employees' exposure to hazardous materials, monitoring cumulative exposure effects on a routine basis, and checking the degree to which safety measures are routinely applied.

OTHER SAFETY AND HEALTH CONCERNS

Besides accidents, several common concerns about safety and health in the workplace are especially significant because they are widely occurring, or at least widely discussed. These include AIDS in the workplace, substance abuse, smoking in the workplace, stress, and violence.

Alcohol and drug abuse, prolonged job stress, and emotional illness are among the enormously costly problems that need to be addressed through programs within organizations as well as through broader community programs. The costs of these other safety and health concerns are of various kinds, and they include losses stemming from absenteeism, lowered productivity, and treatment expenses. What cost figures do not show, of course, is the mental and emotional anguish these problems cause fellow workers, friends, family members, and others. Obviously, drug, alcohol, and emotional problems off the job carry over into the job setting and vice versa.

AIDS in the Workplace

Individuals infected with HIV-AIDS are protected under the Americans with Disabilities Act discussed in Chapter 3 and earlier in this chapter. But the disease is quite different from most other disabilities. Because of the complex nature of the infection and the multiplicity of AIDS-related illnesses, greater understanding is required of the general medical symptoms of AIDS, and it may be difficult for supervisors and other managers to determine just how to comply with the law. It must be noted, however, that few jobs exist where having HIV-AIDS prohibits an employee from performing essential job functions. Should such a situation arise, the employer is expected to provide reasonable accommodations, which might include changes in equipment or work assignments.

In general, organizations can follow three approaches in trying to deal with AIDS from a management perspective. One strategy is to include AIDS under a comprehensive life-threatening illness policy. For example, one organization identifies all resources available through the company's HRM department for any employees facing a life-threatening illness and has adopted 10 guidelines for supervisors of stricken employees.

Another strategy is to form an AIDS-specific policy, which includes guidelines created especially to deal with AIDS-afflicted employees. Contemplating this type of policy is a completely legal action, as long as neither the intent nor the implementation of the policy results in discrimination against people on the basis of AIDS. In general, most organizations that form an AIDS-specific policy do so in an affirmative way. That is, the essence of the policy is to affirm the organization's stance that employees with AIDS are still entitled to work, receive benefits, and be treated comparably to all other employees.

Finally, the third approach that some companies take is to have no policy at all. If the no-policy approach is chosen, the workforce must be kept informed about AIDS and told that people with AIDS are entitled to remain employed. Unfortunately, far too many companies take this approach. The problem here is that the organization doesn't want to confront the necessity for having an AIDS policy, is afraid to confront the need for such a policy, or doesn't know how to approach such a policy. In any of these events, managerial ignorance can potentially result in serious problems for both the employer and the employees of an organization.

Hot lines, job flexibility, part-time work, flexible hours, and working at home are other approaches adopted by employers to keep the employee with AIDS gainfully employed. In addition, the federal government suggests that employers establish guidelines on accidents involving the handling of blood or other body fluids to control the spread of the infection.

Smoking at Work

Arguments and rebuttals characterize the smoking-at-work controversy, and statistics are rampant. A multitude of state and local laws have been passed that deal with smoking in the workplace and public places. Passage of these laws has been viewed by many employers positively, because they relieve employers of the responsibility for making decisions on smoking issues. But many courts, unlike state legislatures, have been hesitant to address the smoking-at-work issue. They clearly prefer to let employers and employees resolve their differences rather than prohibiting or supporting the right to smoke.

As a result of health studies, complaints by nonsmokers, and state laws, many employers have established no-smoking policies throughout their workplaces. Although employees who smoke tend to complain initially when a smoking ban is instituted, they seem to have little difficulty adjusting within a few weeks, and many quit smoking or reduce the number of cigarettes they use each workday. Employers have also offered smoking cessation workshops and even cash incentives to employees who quit smoking, and these measures do seem to reduce smoking by employees.

Substance Abuse

There are millions of substance abusers in the workplace, and in the United States alone, substance abusers cost employers about $30 billion annually in lost production and account for 40 percent of all industrial fatalities. Increasingly, alcohol abuse is seen as a disease. In cases where alcohol abuse is suspected, many organizations refer the employees for counseling prior to subjecting them to disciplinary action. In discharge cases involving alcoholism, arbitrators tend to disapprove of the imposition of severe penalties unless counseling and treatment have been tried first. On the other hand, arbitrators tend to support discipline in cases involving drugs.

Denial is a typical response of the alcoholic or addicted person. But the problem must be confronted before treatment can be effective.

More and more employers are concerned about drugs in the workplace and the potential for serious accidents caused by drug-impaired employees. Recognizing the huge direct and indirect costs of substance abuse to the American society, in 1988 Congress passed a law that is having far-reaching implications for organizations with federal contracts and their supervisors. The Drug-Free Workplace Act of 1988 (a subsection of the Anti-Drug Abuse Act) requires federal contractors to establish anti-drug policies and procedures and to make a "good-faith" effort to sustain a drug-free working environment. Employees are required to notify the employer within five days after any substance abuse conviction, and the employer is required to notify the appropriate federal government agency within 10 days after receiving notice from the employee of any such conviction.

Many employers are testing applicants or current employees for drug abuse. It is important that organizations have appropriate policies for testing either applicants or current employees. Such policies need to involve (1) informed consent, (2) scheduling, (3) assurance of test validity, and (4) confidentiality. Such screening is likely to increase as drug use continues to be a problem for the larger society and the liability associated with having an employee under the influence of drugs is a cost companies are expected to bear.

The legal issues surrounding drug testing are complex and still evolving. In the public sector, some of these issues center on constitutional rights pertaining to search and seizure, privacy, and due process. In the private sector, legal issues center on equal employment opportunity laws, disability discrimination laws, and liability for defamation and wrongful discharge. The courts clearly tend to approve drug testing when there is a "reasonable individualized suspicion" that an employee's performance is being affected by drugs.

Stress

Concerns about stress and how to manage it have become major safety and health issues. Stress runs rampant at most workplaces. The problem is not stress itself but prolonged and unchecked stress. When the body remains in an excited state after a crisis has passed, harmful effects begin to set in. Studies indicate that prolonged stress is linked to subsequent physical injury, debilitation, and disease, including heart disease. Cardiovascular diseases are responsible for more than half of all deaths in the United States, and heart attacks are the leading cause of death among males over the age of 35. Further, there are links between stress and gastrointestinal diseases, arthritis, and rheumatism, which are major sources of employee disability.

Excessive stress tends to occur in jobs in which there are heavy psychological demands but the employee has little control over how to get the job done. These include jobs in which employees have little control over how to relate to the client, such as telephone operators, nurse's aides, and cashiers. Postal work also appears to be a high-stress job. Stress appears to be a factor in—and certainly a result of—homicides that have occurred at post offices.

The courts have established four categories of on-the-job stress for which individuals may be allowed to file for workers' compensation ("The Cost of Safety," 1980). The first category involves medical stimuli from the job that result in a physical illness—for example, when consistent stress causes a heart attack. The second category consists of physical stimuli on the job that result in a psychological illness—for example, a work injury that causes anxiety so severe that the employee cannot go back to work. The third category covers situations in which a mental stimulus on the job causes a psychological illness. One example would be a person who suffers from depression and loss of self-esteem because of on-the-job stress and consequently is unable to perform his or her job.

The final category relates to a slightly different pattern of circumstances. The courts have maintained that individuals may obtain damage awards when they experience distress due to intentional or reckless acts of the employer that degrade or humiliate the employee. This principle may cover a wide range of possible actions, including sexual harassment. Employers should be aware of their potential liabilities for stress-related illnesses, as well as the loss in employee productivity that can occur when workers are overstressed for a long period. Conscientious employers can help to prevent stress from turning into a serious health problem.

Unfortunately, organizations cannot always eliminate all sources of job stress; some stress may be inherent in the job. For instance, some jobs are dangerous (e.g., logging, police work, firefighting), and some place the worker in demanding interpersonal situations (e.g., customer relations specialists). When job stresses cannot be relieved, the employee must learn to cope with them. An organization can help by offering employees stress counseling or by providing them the opportunity to "work off" their stress through physical exercise. Some of the organizational interventions described later, such as the use of employee assistance programs (EAPs) and wellness programs, can be helpful in this regard.

Violence in the Workplace

Historically, safety programs have focused on the prevention of accidents in the workplace. Recently, however, violence in the workplace has become an increasing safety and health concern. Violence is the second most common cause of death among employees and the most common for female employees. Workplace homicides may be committed by fellow workers, former employees, clients, robbers, or sometimes an employee's dissatisfied partner. Violence short of murder may include harassment, threats, intimidation, hostage taking, and physical injury. OSHA has adopted standards for preventing violence against health care and social service workers, who are at the greatest risk. They also have recommended voluntary guidelines for night retail establishments, where employees are at great risk of crime.

Employers can reduce the risk of violence by outsiders with improved security and access controls, better visibility of work locations, surveillance cameras, and physical barriers such as bulletproof glass enclosures. Violence by employees against other employees can be reduced by preemployment screening, by supervisor vigilance, and by a policy of zero tolerance to any workplace harassment or violence.

While there is no way to guarantee that an organization will be free from violence, a violence prevention program can greatly increase that probability. Violence prevention programs are described in the next section.

PROGRAMS TO PROMOTE SAFETY AND HEALTH

Many organizations have instituted formal programs to promote the safety and health of employees. This section will discuss safety programs, violence prevention programs, EAPs, and wellness programs.

Safety Programs

Management's first duty should be to formulate a safety policy and then implement and sustain this policy through a safety or loss control program. The heart of any safety program is accident prevention. It is obviously much better to prevent accidents than to react to them. A major objective of any safety program is to get the employees to "think safety"—to keep safety and accident prevention on their minds. These programs may include training, safety meetings, the posting of safety statistics, awards for safe performance, contests, and safety and health committees. Although these programs may be time-consuming, supervisors will ultimately benefit if their employees use good safety practices. Not only will there be budgetary and morale advantages but increased safety will decrease the time a supervisor spends filling out accident reports, attending meetings to investigate injuries, and making recommendations.

Many approaches are used to make employees more safety conscious. However, the following elements are present in most successful safety programs.

• All employees are trained in safety procedures and understand relevant company rules.
• Management is willing to spend money and budget for safety.
• Safety programs have the support of top and middle management.
• Managers and supervisors follow safety rules and conform to regulations.
• Responsibility for safety is an integral part of managers' jobs.
• Positive attitude toward safety is maintained throughout the organization.
• Safety efforts are monitored and evaluated regularly.

More will be said about evaluation of safety efforts later.

In short, organizations show their concern for loss control by establishing a clear safety policy and by assuming the responsibility for its implementation. Organizations that fail to implement safety policies or fail to report job-related illnesses and injuries face fines from OSHA for unsafe practices as well as potential lawsuits or workers' compensation claims by employees.

STRATEGIES FOR PROMOTING SAFETY

Organizations have tried a variety of strategies directed at reducing or eliminating unsafe behaviors at work. Some specific suggestions for promoting safety within organizations are provided below.

One way to encourage employee safety is to involve employees at various times in safety training sessions and committee meetings and to have these meetings frequently. In addition to safety training, continuous communication to develop safety consciousness is necessary. Merely sending safety memos is not enough. Posting safety policies and rules is part of this effort. Contests, incentives, and posters are all ways to heighten safety awareness. Changing safety posters, continually updating bulletin boards, and posting safety information in visible areas are also recommended. Safety films and videotapes are additional ways to communicate safety ideas.

Uninteresting work often leads to boredom, fatigue, and stress, all of which can cause accidents. In many instances, job enrichment can be used to make the work more interesting and results in fewer accidents. Job enrichment attempts to increase both the number of tasks a worker does and the control the worker has over the job. Simple changes can often make work more meaningful to the employee. Job enrichment attempts are usually successful if they add responsibility, challenge, and similar qualities that contribute to the employee's positive inner feelings about the job.

Employees frequently are involved in safety planning through safety committees, often composed of workers from a variety of levels and departments. The safety committee is a way to get employees directly involved in the operation of the safety program. A rotating membership of five to 12 members is usually desirable, including both management and operating employees. Usually, at least one member of the committee is from the HRM unit. The normal duties of a safety committee include inspecting the work site, observing work practices, investigating accidents, and making recommendations. The safety committee may also sponsor accident prevention contests, help prepare safety rules, promote safety awareness, review safety suggestions from employees, and supervise the preparation and distribution of safety materials.

Reinforcing behaviors that reduce the likelihood of accidents can be highly successful. Reinforcers include non-monetary reinforcers such as feedback, activity reinforcers such as time off, material reinforcers such as company-purchased doughnuts during the coffee break, and financial rewards for attaining desired levels of safety.

The behavioral approach relies on specifying and communicating the desired performance to employees, measuring that performance before and after interventions, monitoring performance at unannounced intervals several times a week, and reinforcing desired behavior several times a week with performance feedback.

Management by objectives (MBO) can also be used in the safety area. MBO is a process in which managers and employees identify common goals, specify ways employees will contribute to the accomplishment of those goals, and agree to use the measured results to evaluate employees' performance. Behavior modification programs are often linked successfully to MBO programs that deal with occupational health. There are seven basic steps in these programs:

1. Identify hazards and obtain information about the frequency of accidents.
2. Based on this information, evaluate the severity and risk of the hazards.
3. Formulate and implement programs to control, prevent, or reduce the possibility of accidents.
4. Set specific goals that are challenging, but attainable regarding the reduction of accidents or safety problems.
5. Consistently monitor results of the program.
6. Provide positive feedback to promote correct safety procedures.
7. Monitor and evaluate the program against the goals.

Violence Prevention Programs

As noted earlier, violence against employees has become an enormous problem at work. Employers should eliminate such violence on humanitarian grounds, but there are legal reasons for doing so as well. For example, an employer may be sued by the victim of a violent employee on the theory that the employer negligently hired or retained someone who the employer should reasonably have known could act violently. And even if the employee was not negligently hired or retained, employers may still in general be liable for employees' violent acts when the employees' actions were performed within the scope of employment.

A set of OSHA guidelines released in 1995, "Guidelines for Preventing Workplace Violence for Health Care and Social Service Workers," can serve as a guide for organizations to develop a written workplace violence prevention program as part of an overall safety and health program. Some of the guidelines' main recommendations include the following:

- Establish a policy of zero tolerance for workplace violence.
- Encourage employees to report incidents of workplace violence.
- Develop a plan for workplace security.
- Appoint a person with program responsibility and provide adequate resources to run the program.
- Ensure management commitment to employee safety.
- Hold employee meetings on safety issues.

Managers play an important role in the success of violence prevention programs. Managers need to take responsibility for reducing or eliminating violence in the workplace. To this end, they must be sensitive to the causes of workplace violence. Many people feel pressured in their jobs and fear layoffs. When other stresses are added to these, such as negative performance appraisals, personality conflicts with co-workers or managers, or personal problems such as divorce, a potentially dangerous person may emerge.

Screening out potentially explosive employees and applicants is an important line of defense for employers. At a minimum this means instituting a sound preemployment investigation. Obtain a detailed employment application and solicit an applicant's employment history, educational background, and references. A personal interview, personnel testing, and a review and verification of all information provided should also be included. Sample interview questions to ask might include, for instance, "What frustrates you?" and "Who was your worst supervisor and why?" Interviewers might also ask job candidates to describe how they reacted to a past management decision with which they disagreed, and why. The responses to these questions and follow-up questions could be quite revealing.

Finally, managers should learn the proper organizational procedures for reporting and dealing with different types of potentially violent situations. Comprehensive violence prevention programs can be beneficial.

Employee Assistance Programs (EAPs)

Many organizations offer employee assistance programs (EAPs) in an attempt to improve performance and retention by helping employees solve personal problems. EAPs address a variety of employee problems ranging from drug abuse to marital problems to bereavement. Direct assistance or help through referrals for these employees is essential for humane reasons and for reasons of organizational effectiveness.

Many organizations create EAPs because they recognize their ethical and legal obligations to protect not only their workers' physical health but their mental health as well. Ethical obligations stem from the fact that the work climate, job change, work rules, work pace, management style, work group characteristics, and so forth, are frequently the causes of behavioral, psychological, and physiological problems for employees. Ethical obligations become legal obligations when employees sue the company or file workers' compensation claims for work-related illness.

The success of EAPs depends on how well they are planned and implemented. There is also some evidence that EAPs are more successful with some types of problems than with others. For instance, EAPs appear to be more effective at dealing with alcoholism than with drug addiction.

It is especially important that EAPs be available when dealing with a potentially violent employee, one involved with substance abuse, or one with a life-threatening illness or suffering from extreme stress. All these employees can be referred to EAPs.

Wellness Programs

As health care costs have skyrocketed over the last two decades, organizations have become more interested in preventive programs focused on maintaining worker health. Employers' desires to improve productivity, decrease absenteeism, and control health care costs have come together in the "wellness" movement. Companies are encouraging employees to lead healthier lives, and are attempting to reduce health care costs through formal employee wellness programs. While EAPs focus on treating troubled employees, wellness programs focus on preventing health problems in the first place.

Wellness programs may be as simple and inexpensive as providing information about stop-smoking clinics and weight-loss programs or as comprehensive and expensive as providing professional health screening and multimillion-dollar fitness facilities.

A number of organizations have developed fitness programs to involve employees in some form of controlled exercise or recreational activities. Fitness programs range from subsidized membership at a local health club to company softball teams to very sophisticated company-owned facilities.

STEP-COUNTER PEDOMETER

Remove battery spacer before use
to operate the pedometer.

This pedometer is useful to those who
frequently walk and would like a way of
measuring the number of steps taken in their
workout period.

Features:
1. Step Counter(0-99,999 steps)
2. Foldout, large-digit display that is easily
   viewed without removing it from your body.
3. Long-life Lithium Cell battery change
   easily with a removable battery cover.
4. Counter reset with the touch of a button.

Changing the Battery:
To change the battery, simply remove the
cover off the pedometer near the RESET
button. Insert new battery and replace cover.

NOTE: Magnetic or Mechanical Pedometers
measure levels of physical activity, and they
are not highly accurate. There is a +/- 10%
deviation in accuracy on instruments of this
type.
Measurements will be influenced by the
sensitivity settings, placement on the body
and overall stride of the wearer, pedometer
must be placed on the waistband, not the
pocket to work properly.

EVALUATION OF SAFETY AND HEALTH PROGRAMS

Safety and health programs have begun to receive more attention in recent years. The consequences of inadequate programs are measurable: increases in workers' compensation payments, more lawsuits, greater insurance costs, fines from OSHA, and pressures from unions. Evaluation of a safety management program requires indicator systems such as accident statistics, effective reporting systems, clear safety rules and procedures, and management of the safety effort.

A safety and health program can be evaluated fairly directly in a cost-benefit sense. The most cost-effective safety programs need not be the most expensive. Programs that combine a number of approaches—identifying safety criteria such as improvements in job performance and decreases in sick leave, safety training, safety meetings, providing medical facilities, and strong participation by top management—work when the emphasis is on the engineering aspects of safety.

Conducting a cost-benefit analysis can be helpful in improving programs. An organization can calculate the costs of safety specialists, new safety devices, and other safety measures. Savings due to reductions in accidents, lowered insurance costs, and lowered fines can be weighed against these costs. Programs can be judged by other measurable criteria as well, such as improvements in job performance, decreases in sick leave, and reductions in disciplinary actions and grievances. At the same time, supervisors must realize that cause-and-effect relationships may be complex and difficult to measure accurately. In addition, not all benefits of a health and safety program are measurable; many benefits are intangible.

SUMMARY

Management's primary responsibility toward safety is to establish an environment where safety is emphasized. Organizations have a legal responsibility to ensure that the workplace is free from recognized hazards and that working conditions are not harmful to employees' physical or mental health. Managers also have responsibilities to listen to employee complaints and suggestions, work closely with the safety committee (if there is one), and provide safety instruction.

The basic purpose of any safety program is to prevent accidents. Since getting employees to "think safety" is one of the more effective ways to prevent accidents, this is a major objective of most programs. Many strategies are available for promoting safety within an organization. These include making the work interesting, establishing a safety committee, periodically holding safety training, and rewarding employee participation.

Indoor environmental quality, HIV-AIDS, substance abuse, stress and occupational diseases are common concerns about safety and health. Occupational disease is a particularly difficult problem for many reasons in today's organizations, including the fact that the onset of some disease is gradual and hard to detect. It is likely that organizations will be required to shoulder more responsibility for prevention in the future. Prolonged stress is associated with enough health and accident problems for stress to be an important area of concern for organizations, which need to help employees manage or reduce stress. Employee assistance programs (EAPs) provide avenues for supervisors and organizations to offer help to employees with problems in their personal and work lives. Wellness programs provide opportunities for employers to reduce health care costs.

REFERENCES

Bureau of National Affairs. 1997a. Workplace fatalities. *BNA Bulletin to Management* (August 28): 276–277.

Bureau of National Affairs. 1997b. OSHA seeks cooperative compliance. *BNA Bulletin to Management* (September 4): 288.

Bureau of National Affairs. 1997c. OSHA's cooperative program shoves off. *BNA Bulletin to Management* (December 25): 416.

Bureau of National Affairs. 1998. Initial OSHA reform bills become law. *BNA Bulletin to Management* (July 30): 236.

Code of federal regulations. 1988. Washington, DC: U.S. Government Printing Office, p. 126.

The cost of safety. 1980. *Wall Street Journal* (July 10), p. 18.

Hammer, W. 1985. *Occupational safety management and engineering*, 3rd ed. Upper Saddle River, NJ: Prentice Hall, pp. 62–63.

Selye, H. 1974. *Stress without distress.* New York: The New American Library, p. 151.

U.S. Department of Labor. 1995. *All about OSHA*, rev. ed. Washington, DC: U.S. Department of Labor, p. 2.

Yarborough, M.H. 1994. Securing the American workplace. *HRFocus* (September): 1, 4–5.

Chapter 13

Managing Labor Relations and Collective Bargaining

INTRODUCTION

The beginning of the twenty-first century presents the labor unions of the United States with a different environment. The new century presents a highly competitive global economy featuring free trade. The result is a global search for efficient, low-cost labor, larger mergers, deregulation, and privatization.

In the United States, the economy is rapidly moving from a manufacturing to a service orientation. Despite this transition many organizations still have to contend with one of the most significant challenges facing them today—dealing with organized labor in ways that optimize the needs and priorities of both the organization and its employees. The reality is that when this is done effectively and constructively, both sides benefit. But when relationships between an organization and its unions turn sour, both sides can suffer great costs. While some organizations have enjoyed relatively positive relationships with their unions in recent years, others have not fared well. And the costs have been enormous.

Although union membership has decreased substantially during the past decade and a half, unions are still an important influence upon organizations. Whether or not managers approve of labor organizations, they will not become unimportant in the United States. Even if they did, labor organizations are still very important in many nations around the world in which U.S. organizations do business. Today's organizations and managers, whether in a unionized or nonunionized environment, will always need to consider good employer–employee relations as a top priority if they want to be successful.

This chapter begins with an overview of the labor relations context in the United States. This includes some history of unionization and a discussion of the legal context of union activities. We then focus on the structure of unions in the United States and the process of unionizing, including why and how employees unionize. The collective bargaining process is then discussed, including issues involved in negotiating and administering labor agreements. Finally, the chapter discusses the importance of assessing the entire collective bargaining process and the union–management relationship.

Labor Unions' Role in Organizations

Labor relations is the process of dealing with employees who are represented by a union. A labor union can be defined as an organization of employees that uses collective action to advance its members' interests in regard to shared job-related goals, including items such as higher pay, shorter working hours, enhanced benefits, and/or better working conditions. Collective bargaining, a specific aspect of labor relations discussed more fully later in this chapter, is the process by which unions seek to manage their working environment. More specifically, collective bargaining is the process by which managers and union leaders negotiate acceptable terms and conditions of employment for workers represented by unions.

When unions are not present, employers usually set employment terms and conditions unilaterally (i.e., without consulting employees), within the constraints imposed by market conditions and the Fair Labor Standards Act. Although collective bargaining is a term that technically and properly is applied only in settings where employees are unionized, similar processes, of course, often exist in nonunionized settings as well. In these cases, however, they are likely to be labeled employee relations.

Because unions want to participate in setting important employment conditions and to affect government policy through political channels, they are the source of ongoing controversy and opposition. The history of their development in the United States has had many ups and downs. Today, unions as a whole face some serious challenges. Among organizations in the private sector, union membership is declining, and employers are more aggressively resisting the unionization of their employees and demanding concessions from unions at the bargaining table. On the other hand, increased unionization among government employees has offset some of the decline in the private sector since the mid-1960s. More will be said about this later in this chapter.

A BRIEF HISTORY OF THE DEVELOPMENT OF UNIONS IN THE UNITED STATES

To understand what unions are and what they want, it is useful to understand "where they've been" in the United States. Unions have a long history that closely parallels the history of the country itself. For example, the earliest unions in the United States emerged during the Revolutionary War. As early as 1790, skilled craftsmen (shoemakers, tailors, printers, and so on) organized themselves into trade unions. They posted their "minimum wage" demands and had "tramping committees" go from shop to shop to ensure that no member accepted a lesser wage. The Journeyman Cordwainers Society of Philadelphia was one of the first unions formed by shoemakers. The union's goal was to enhance the pay and working conditions of all shoemakers.

Many of the earliest unions were local and often confined their activities to a single setting. But in 1834 the first national unions in the United States began to emerge. Throughout the remainder of the nineteenth century, one major union after another began to appear. Among the most significant were the National Typographical Union in 1852, the United Cigarmakers in 1856, and the National Iron Molders in 1859. As the nineteenth century ended, there were 30 national unions with a combined membership of around 300,000 individuals.

The first union to achieve significant size and influence was the Knights of Labor, formed around 1869. This group attracted employees and local unions from all crafts and occupational areas. The Knights had two objectives: (1) to establish one large union for all employees regardless of trade, and (2) to replace the American political and economic system of capitalism with socialism. The strength of the Knights of Labor was diluted because it failed to integrate the industrial and craft needs and interests of skilled and unskilled members. By 1885 it had 100,000 members, which (as a result of winning a major strike against a railroad) exploded to 700,000 members the following year. Partly because of their focus on social reform, and partly due to a series of unsuccessful strikes, the Knights' membership dwindled rapidly thereafter. By 1893 when the Knights were dissolved, there were virtually no members.

In 1886 Samuel Gompers formed the American Federation of Labor (AFL). It consisted mostly of skilled workers and, unlike the Knights, eschewed social reform for practical bread-and-butter gains for its members. Also unlike the Knights of Labor, the AFL served as an umbrella organization, with members joining individual unions that were affiliated with the AFL, as opposed to directly joining the AFL itself.

Growth in the union movement was slow from 1886 to 1935. In 1935, the Congress of Industrial Organizations (CIO) was formed by John L. Lewis, president of the United Mine Workers, in cooperation with a number of union presidents expelled from the AFL. The CIO grew quickly, using the industrial union structure to organize employees in mass production jobs. Craft, semiskilled, the unskilled employees within an industry, such as assembly-line workers, machinists, and assemblers, could be members of the same CIO-affiliated union. Soon, the AFL began to offer membership to unskilled workers as well. Competition for new members led to bitter conflicts between the AFL and CIO until they merged in 1955, forming the AFL-CIO (http://www.aflcio.org/) with a total membership of around 15 million employees. Union membership since that time, however, has been quite erratic.

THE "NEW FACE" OF LABOR

As alluded to earlier, the last decade or so has seen a dramatic decrease in the number of union workers in the United States. Many union members are still traditional blue-collar workers, but unions increasingly appeal to white-collar workers, too. For instance, federal, state, and local governments have seen a substantial increase in the number of their employees becoming union members. Additionally, while union membership in other countries is declining, it is still very high. In an effort to respond to the changes in union membership the AFL-CIO entered the twenty-first century prepared to be a more sophisticated, relevant, and open organization with a vision of what the workplace of America should become. They believe workplaces should be for the good of workers, consumers, owners, and managers.

This vision will be accomplished through "workplace democracy." The AFL-CIO sees this as a process by which workers help to influence worker educational and training programs, employment needs, how work is organized, technology in the workplace, definition of quality, and investments needed to remain productive. They believed these worker-influenced decisions will result in basic business strategy required for organizations to remain successful.

Although their vision represents a challenge of thinking for the business community, it also presents a challenge to the HRM personnel. Human resource management's challenge is that the AFL-CIO will be taking a more active role in HRM functions as they attempt to implement their vision in smoothing relations between employers and unions.

As Nancy Milk, director of the AFL-CIO's Center for Workplace Democracy at the union's headquarters building, points out, HRM is part of the real strategic business planning process and that it is also their interest. Director Milk believes HRM's input for planning strategies for recruitment, education, and training is critical for job creation. These issues are the interest and focus of organized labor in the twenty-first century. She believes organized labor will now be working with HRM professionals to achieve these mutual goals (Leonard, 1999).

Whether this union's "new face" will be effective remains to be seen. However, the Bureau of Labor Statistics reported in the first month of the twenty-first century that U.S. labor unions gained more members in 1999 than they had in any year for the past 20 years.

Although some states, such as New Jersey, lost union members, California led the nation gaining 132,000, with 74,000 of the total being home care workers. The highest rate of union membership is in the government, with 37 percent, compared to the private-sector rate of 9.4 percent. This results in the overall national unionization rate of 13.9 percent (Cleeland, 2000).

THE LEGAL CONTEXT OF UNIONS IN THE UNITED STATES

Owing in part to the tumultuous history of union–management relations in the United States, a variety of laws and other regulations have been passed, some of which are intended to promote unionization and union activities, whereas others are intended to limit or curtail them. As early as 1806 the local courts in Philadelphia declared the cordwainers union to be, by its very existence, in restraint of trade and illegal. The *Cordwainer Doctrine*, as it became known, dominated the law's view of unions until 1843 when the Massachusetts Supreme Court, in *Commonwealth v. Hunt*, ruled that unions were not by their very nature in restraint of trade but that this charge had to be proven in each individual case. This decision led to increased union activity, but organizations responded by simply firing union organizers. Further, after the Sherman Antitrust Act was passed in 1890, business once again sought (successfully) court injunctions against unions for restraint of trade. By the 1920s organizations also sought to identify union leaders as communists in order to reduce public sympathy and give the government an excuse to move on the unions.

By the end of the 1920s, the country was in the grips of the Great Depression, and the government soon intervened in an attempt to end work stoppages and start the economy on the road to recovery. Three major pieces of labor legislation enacted during the 1920s and 1930s have withstood constitutional challenge: the Railway Labor Act of 1926, the Norris-LaGuardia Act of 1932, and the National Labor Relations Act of 1935. The Railway Labor Act, as amended, gave railroad (and later, airline) employees the right to form unions, bargain collectively, and strike. The Norris-LaGuardia Act established severe limitations on the judicial issuance of injunctions to halt labor activity and also outlawed the "yellow dog" contract (an effort to forbid employees from joining unions or even speaking to union organizers).

The next significant piece of legislation was the National Labor Relation Act (NLRA) passed in 1935. The NLRA, known as the Wagner Act, placed the protective power of the federal government firmly behind employee efforts to organize and bargain collectively through representatives of their choice (Kaufman and Lewin, 1998). The basic purpose of the Wagner Act was to grant power to labor unions and to put unions on a more equal footing with management in terms of the rights of employees. Among its most important provisions are the legal right of employees to form unions, the legal right to bargain collectively with management, and the legal right to engage in group activities such as strikes to accomplish their goals.

The Wagner Act also created the National Labor Relations Board (NLRB) to administer its provisions. The NLRB serves the public interest by reducing interruptions in production or service caused by labor–management strife. Today the NLRB still administers most labor law in the United States.

The most important piece of legislation in the years following World War II was the Labor Management Relations Act, also known as the Taft-Hartley Act, passed in 1947. The Taft-Hartley Act was designed to better the balance of power between unions and management. Many politicians, employers, and even some union leaders felt that the Wagner Act went too far in regulating and limiting management, while leaving union actions unconstrained. In response, Taft-Hartley specified several unfair labor practices of unions, created the Federal Mediation and Conciliation Service to aid in the resolution of disputes, and provided a mechanism for handling strikes that create a national emergency (Taylor and Whitney, 1987). Unfair labor practices of unions according to the Taft-Hartley Act include: (1) restraint or coercion of employees in the exercise of their rights, (2) restraint or coercion of employees in the selection of the parties to bargain on their behalf, (3) persuasion of employers to discriminate against any of their employees, (4) refusal to bargain collectively with an employer, (5) participation in secondary boycotts and jurisdictional disputes, (6) attempt to force recognition from an employer when another union is already the certified representative, (7) charge of excessive initiation fees and dues, and (8) "featherbedding" practices that require payment of wages for services not performed. In short, the passage of the Taft-Hartley Act meant that the law could no longer be criticized as favoring unions.

A final significant piece of legislation affecting labor relations is the Landrum-Griffin Act passed in 1959. Officially called the Labor Management Reporting and Disclosure Act, this law focused on eliminating various unethical, illegal, and undemocratic union practices. For instance, the Landrum-Griffin Act requires national labor unions to elect new leaders at least once every five years and states that convicted felons cannot hold national union office (which is why Jimmy Hoffa was removed as the president of the teamsters). It also requires unions to file annual financial statements with the Department of Labor. And finally, the Landrum-Griffin Act stipulates that unions provide certain information regarding their internal management and finances to all members.

THE STRUCTURE OF UNIONS IN THE UNITED STATES

Large labor unions, like all organizations, have unique structures. But most unions have some basic structural characteristics in common. The cornerstone of most labor unions, regardless of their size, is local unions, more frequently referred to as "locals." Locals are unions that are organized at the level of a single company, plant, or small geographic region. Each of these 70,000 or so local unions, varying in size up to 40,000 members, elects a president, a secretary-treasurer, and perhaps one or two other officers from the membership. In the larger locals, a business representative is hired as a full-time employee to handle grievances and contract negotiation. Locals also elect their own shop steward. The shop steward is a regular employee who functions as a liaison between union members and supervisors. The steward protects the rights of the worker, by filing grievances when the employer has acted improperly.

Local unions are usually clustered by geographic region and coordinated by a regional officer. These regional officers, in turn, report to and are a part of a national governing board of the labor union.

The major umbrella organization for labor unions in the United States is the national (or international) union, a body that organizes, charters, and controls member locals. Each national union is represented in proportion to its membership. The national affairs of a large union are generally governed by an executive board and a president, who are usually elected by the union members. This election takes place at an annual national convention that all union members are invited to and are encouraged to attend.

The president is almost always a full-time union employee and may earn as much money as a senior manager of a business. The executive board functions much more like a board of directors and is generally composed of individuals who serve on the board in addition to their normal functions as employees of an organization. And just as a large business has various auxiliary departments such as public relations and a legal department, large national unions have auxiliary departments as well. These auxiliary departments may handle such things as legal affairs of the union, oversee collective bargaining issues, and provide a variety of assistance and services to the local unions as requested and needed.

The national union collects dues and has its own boards, specialized publications, and separate constitutions and bylaws. National unions determine broad union policy and offer services to local union units. They also help maintain financial records and provide a base from which additional organizing drives may take place.

THE PROCESS OF UNIONIZING

Individually, employees may be able to exercise relatively little power in their relations with employers. The treatment and benefits they receive depend in large part on how their employers view their worth to the organization. Of course, if they believe they are not being treated fairly, they have the option of quitting. However, another way to correct the situation is to organize and bargain with the employer collectively. The laws discussed earlier, as well as various regulations, prescribe a very specific set of steps that employees must follow if they want to establish a union. These laws and regulations also dictate what management can and cannot do during an effort by employees to organize and form a union.

Why Employees Unionize

Since the middle of the nineteenth century, a substantial amount of research and theory has been devoted to discovering why employees join, form, and support unions. There have been sociological, political, economic, psychological, and even sociobiological theories advanced as to why unions develop. A detailed understanding of these perspectives is beyond the scope of this book. However, the simplest answer is very straightforward: employees believe that they are somehow better off as a result of joining a union than they would be by not joining a union (Fullagar, Clark, Gallagher, and Gordon, 1994).

But the real reason is much more complex. In the early days of labor unions, people chose to join them because working conditions were in many cases so unpleasant. In the eighteenth and nineteenth centuries, for example, in their quest to earn ever-greater profits, some business owners treated their workers with no respect. For instance, they often forced their employees to work long hours, there were no minimum wage laws or other controls, and there were no safety standards. As a result, many employees worked 12, 15, or 18 hours a day and sometimes were forced to work seven days a week. The pay was sometimes just pennies a day, and they received no vacation time or other benefits. Moreover, they worked totally at the whim of their employer, and if they complained about working conditions, they were dismissed. Thus people initially chose to join labor unions because of the strength that lay in the numbers associated with the large-scale labor unions.

In many parts of the United States, and in many industries, these early pressures for unionization became an ingrained part of life. Union values and union membership expectations were passed from generation to generation. This trend typified many industrialized northern cities such as Pittsburgh, Cleveland, and Detroit. In general, parents' attitudes toward unions are still an important determinant of whether an employee will elect to join a union (Barling, Kelloway, and Bremermann, 1991). And as noted earlier, strong unionization pressures still exist in some industries, such as the automobile industry, the steel industry, and other economic sectors that rely on heavy manufacturing.

Contemporary views of why employees join unions note that employees are more likely to unionize when they are dissatisfied with some aspect of their job, believe that a union could help make this aspect of the job better, and are not philosophically opposed to unions or to collective action

(Youngblood, DeNisi, Molleston, and Mobley, 1984). Thus, employees generally join unions to satisfy needs that are important to them. Although needs and their importance differ among individuals, some of the more prevalent needs include the following: job security, socialization and group membership, safe and healthy working conditions, communication link to management, and fair compensation. Consistent with these needs, the conditions in the workplace that are most likely to trigger union organizing are lack of job security, low wages, the use of subcontracting, hostile supervisory practices, and inadequate health care or other benefits.

HOW WORKERS BECOME UNIONIZED

The amended National Labor Relations Act (NLRA) establishes procedures by which employees may form and join a union. Employees must first have some interest in joining a union. In some cases this interest may arise because current employees are dissatisfied or unhappy with some aspect of the employment relationship. In other instances existing labor unions may send professional union organizers to nonunionized plants or work facilities to create interest in unionization.

Petition Phase

During the petition phase, employees express initial interest in union representation by signing authorization cards that empower a union to represent them in collective bargaining. The wording on these cards must state that the signer is authorizing bargaining rights to the union and not simply expressing an interest in holding a certification election. These cards serve as evidence of the desire of employees to form a union. Under NLRA rules, at least 30 percent of the employees in a proposed bargaining unit must sign the cards for the NLRB to consider a petition for an election. In practical terms, though, a union has little chance of winning an election if less than 50 percent of the workers sign the authorization cards. This is why most union organizers do not petition for an election unless they have managed to obtain signatures from more than 50 percent of employees during the authorization card campaign. The union's rationale is that during the election campaign, it is likely to face employer opposition that could convince some workers not to support the union. Thus, if the union receives less than 50 percent of employee support, it may drop the organizing effort or start a new authorization campaign later.

The petition phase culminates when the union asks the employer for recognition as the bargaining representative of the workers. Such a request is often accompanied by some form of evidence (usually the signed authorization cards) that a majority of the employees want collective bargaining. If management grants such recognition, it will be legally required to bargain in good faith over the terms and conditions of employment. However, most employers deny such requests, forcing the union to petition the NLRB to hold a certification election.

Election Phase

The election phase consists of three steps. First, the NLRB conducts representation hearings to determine the appropriate bargaining unit. The bargaining unit refers to the specifically defined group of employees who will be eligible for representation by the union. More specifically, the bargaining unit consists of those jobs or positions in which two or more employees share common employment interests and working conditions (e.g., similar duties, hours of work, compensation, production methods, and overall supervision). When a common set of interests exists, those workers may be reasonably grouped together to bargain collectively.

The second step of the election phase involves campaigning by both the union and the employer. Unions are at a disadvantage here because they have less access to workers in the bargaining unit than employers do. Therefore, employers must provide the union the names, addresses, and telephone numbers of their employees within seven days after the parties consent to an election. Most union organizing activity within organizations takes place on the employees' own time and in nonwork areas. Union organizers make home visits to employees and distribute literature (handbills) at plant gates.

NLRB rules closely regulate employer conduct during anti-union campaigns. Employers may not give employees false or misleading information about the union. While employers may certainly communicate their views about unionization (i.e., express clear preferences for staying nonunion), they may not threaten or punish employees for pro-union activities. Nor may employers promise benefits to employees if they reject the union. Further, employers are forbidden to interrogate employees about their union sentiments.

The third step is the election itself, which is typically held on-site at the company. The NLRB requests the union and the employer to supply election observers to ensure that voters are members of the sanctioned bargaining unit. No one may be present in the polling area during the election except NLRB representatives and designated observers.

Certification Phase

The NLRB certifies the results of the election. As long as the NLRB does not find misconduct, a simple majority by either party is required to win the election. If a simple majority of those voting approve union certification, then the union becomes the official bargaining agent of eligible employees. The organizers also elect officers, establish a meeting site, and begin to recruit membership from the labor force in the bargaining unit. But if a majority fails to approve certification, the process ends. In this instance organizers cannot attempt to have another election for at least one year.

Either the employer or the union may file objections to the election within five days. These objections may be related to conduct by either party that affects the outcome of elections.

After its deliberations, the NLRB may dismiss the charges and certify the election results, or it may order a rerun election. If the NLRB holds a rerun election, it may require the guilty party to publicly acknowledge misconduct during the initial campaign. If the NLRB finds evidence of gross misconduct on the part of the employer during the campaign, it may issue a bargaining order. A bargaining order directs an employer to accept collective bargaining with the union even if the employer won the election. The NLRB reasons that when an employer is guilty of outrageous and pervasive unfair labor practices, it not only undermines the union's authorization card majority but also intimidates workers to the point that a fair return election is not possible. The Supreme Court upheld the right of the NLRB to issue bargaining orders in a 1969 decision (*NLRB v. Gisel Packing Company*).

Decertification of Union

Just because a union becomes certified, however, does not necessarily mean that it will exist in perpetuity. Indeed, under certain conditions an existing labor union may be decertified. A company's workers for example, might become disillusioned with the union and may even come to feel that they are being hurt by the presence of the union in their organization. For example, they may believe that management of the organization is trying to be cooperative and to bargain in good faith but that the union itself is refusing to cooperate.

For decertification to occur, two conditions must be met. First, a labor contract cannot be in force (that is, the previous agreement must have expired and a new one not yet approved). And second, the union must have served as the official bargaining agent for the employees for at least one year. If both of these conditions are met, employees or their representatives can again solicit signatures on decertification cards. As with the certification process, if 30 percent of the eligible employees in the bargaining unit sign, then the NLRB conducts a decertification election. And again, a majority decision determines the outcome. Thus, if a majority of those voting favor decertification, the union is removed as the official bargaining agent for the unit. Once a union has been decertified, a new election cannot be requested for certification for at least one year.

THE COLLECTIVE BARGAINING PROCESS

Once a union has been legally certified, it becomes the official bargaining agent for employees that it represents. At this point, the union has the right to approach management for the purpose of negotiating a contract for members of the bargaining unit with respect to "rates of pay, wages, hours of employment, or other conditions." Collective bargaining is generally an ongoing process that includes both the drafting and the administration of a labor agreement.

Collective bargaining is a system for governing relations between representatives of employers and employees through bilateral negotiations to reach mutual agreement about employment terms. This mutual agreement, called a collective bargaining agreement, covers all members of the bargaining unit, regardless of whether they are members of the union.

Those unfamiliar with contract negotiations often view the process as an emotional conflict between labor and management, complete with marathon sessions, fist pounding, and smoke-filled rooms. In reality, negotiating a labor agreement entails long hours of extensive preparation combined with diplomatic maneuvering and the development of bargaining strategies (Baker, 1996). Furthermore, negotiation is only part of the collective bargaining process. Collective bargaining may include the use of economic pressures in the form of strikes and boycotts by a union. Lockouts, plant closures, and the replacement of strikers are similar pressures used by an employer. In addition, either or both parties may seek support from the general public or from the courts as a means of pressuring the opposing side.

Negotiating a Collective Bargaining Agreement

Collective bargaining can take many forms. No one form is more effective; each was developed to deal with the particular characteristics of given industries and their unions. For instance, in some industries, such as coal mining, a single union negotiates a master contract with representatives of the various employers. In the automotive industry, "pattern bargaining" takes place: The agreement negotiated with one company is used as a prototype for other bargaining agreements. For example, the United Auto Workers (UAW) selects one of the Big Three automakers as a target for negotiations. The agreement worked out in those negotiations is expected to be ratified by the other companies, perhaps with a few minor changes. Yet another form of bargaining takes place at major metropolitan newspapers, which traditionally bargain with as many as a dozen different unions, such as Photoengravers, Pressmen, and American Newspaper Guild.

Preparing for Collective Bargaining

By definition, collective bargaining involves two sides: management representing the employing organization and the labor union representing its employees. The collective bargaining process is aimed at agreement on a binding labor contract that will define various dimensions of the employment relationship for a specified period of time. Thus, both management and union leaders must be adequately prepared for a bargaining and negotiation period, since the outcome of a labor negotiation will have long-term effects on both parties.

Both management and unions do a lot of preliminary work before actual negotiations ever start. Management can prepare for collective bargaining in a number of ways. For example, the organization can look closely at its own financial health to provide a realistic picture of what it can and cannot do in terms of wages and salaries for its employees. Management can also do comparative analysis to see what kinds of labor contracts and agreements exist in similar companies and research what this particular labor union has been requesting—and settling for—in the past.

The union can and should also undertake a number of actions to prepare for collective bargaining. It should examine the financial health of the company through public financial records and other such sources. And like management, labor can also carefully determine what kinds of labor agreements have been reached in other parts of the country and what kinds of contracts other divisions of the company or other businesses owned by the same corporation may have negotiated in recent times.

Establishing Strategies

Both parties establish a bargaining agenda by identifying issues about which they want to bargain. NLRB rulings and various labor laws have defined three categories of bargaining items:

1. Illegal bargaining items are matters about which bargaining is not permitted by law. For example, union security arrangements (e.g., closed and open shops) cannot be negotiated in right-to-work states.
2. Mandatory bargaining items are issues that must be negotiated if either party brings these matters to the table. Refusal to bargain about a mandatory item is considered an unfair labor practice. The NLRB has declared approximately 70 items to be mandatory—for example, wages, hours of work, plant rules, work and production standards, pension and employee benefit plans, grievance procedures, etc.
3. Voluntary or permissive bargaining items (e.g., pensions and other benefits for persons previously retired, union participation in the establishment of company

product prices, industry promotion plans, interest arbitration clause, etc.) become part of the negotiations only if both parties agree to discuss them. Neither party can be compelled against its wishes to negotiate permissive items, and refusal to discuss these matters is not considered an unfair labor practice. Should the parties decide to negotiate a permissive item, failure to reach an accord on the matter cannot delay concluding a contract.

Choosing a Bargaining Strategy

Before actual negotiations take place, each party must decide on its priorities among bargaining items. Obviously, each party must attempt to conceal its priorities, although as the bargaining proceeds, the relative importance of each item will become apparent to experienced negotiators for the other side.

Priorities play a major role in determining bargaining strategy. For example, two items about which an employer may wish to bargain could be health benefits and staffing rules that mandate work crew size. If the employer gives health benefits a greater priority than staffing, it may drop its demands for changes in staffing levels if the union agrees to make concessions on the health benefit issue.

Each party must also establish a range of bargaining objectives when preparing for negotiations. Using all of the information at its disposal about factors that influence settlement levels, each party estimates the following three bargaining objectives for each item to be negotiated:

1. The realistic bargaining objective is the expected value of the final settlement on a particular bargaining issue. Based on assessment of the climate for the negotiations (e.g., the degree of conflict apparent between the parties prior to the start of bargaining) and patterns or trends in other contracts in related companies, the realistic objective represents the settlement level perceived to be most likely for a particular bargaining item.

2. The optimistic bargaining objective indicates the most favorable settlement level perceived as possible by each party. Though not as likely to be achieved as the realistic objective, the optimistic objective is within the realm of possibility if negotiations unfold favorably.

3. The pessimistic bargaining objective represents the least favorable settlement that a party is willing to accept on a given negotiated issue. If the bargaining goes poorly for one of the parties, it will reluctantly settle at this pessimistic objective.

Engaging in Good Faith Bargaining

Once bargaining begins, an employer is obligated to negotiate in good faith with the union's representative over conditions of employment. Good faith requires the employer's negotiators to meet with their union counterparts at a reasonable time and place to discuss these conditions. It requires also that the proposals submitted by each party be realistic. In discussing the other party's proposals, each side must offer reasonable counterproposals for those it is unwilling to accept.

The Taft-Hartley Act and its interpretation by the NLRB over the years has provided a number of guidelines for interpreting the meaning of the term good faith. For example, the act does not specifically compel either party to agree to a proposal or grant concessions in order to bargain in good faith. Further, the NLRB typically evaluates the totality of conduct by a party during the negotiations before determining whether it is bargaining in good or bad faith.

One type of bad faith bargaining is "surface bargaining"—presenting obviously unacceptable proposals or offering no alternative counterproposals. Bad faith bargaining may also include such tactics as complicating the scheduling of bargaining sessions or refusing to provide pertinent information. Finally, if the employer bypasses the official union bargaining representative and attempts to negotiate directly with its members, it would also be guilty of bargaining in bad faith.

Resolving Impasses

If labor and management have reached an impasse, either or both sides can do a number of things in an attempt to break the impasse. The basic objective of most of these tactics is to force the other side to alter or redefine its bargaining zone so that an accord can be reached. The bargaining zone of an organization includes the employer's (or union's) maximum limit, the employer's expectations, and the employer's desired result on items being negotiated. For example, the organization might have as a desired result a zero increase in wages and benefits (also known as management's "target point"). But the organization also recognizes that this outcome is very unlikely and actually expects to provide a modest increase in wages and benefits totaling perhaps 4 to 5 percent. But if preparations are done thoroughly, managers also know the maximum amount they are willing to pay, which might be as high as 7 or 8 percent (management's "resistance point"). Note that in this example management would rather suffer through a strike than agree to more than an 8 percent pay increase.

The most potent weapon that the union holds is the potential for a strike. A strike occurs when employees walk off their jobs and refuse to work. In the United States most strikes are called economic strikes because they are triggered by impasses over mandatory bargaining items such as salaries and wages. During a strike, workers representing the union frequently march at the entrance to the employer's facility with signs explaining their reasons for striking. This action is called picketing and is undertaken to elicit sympathy for the union and to intimidate management.

Two less extreme tactics that unions sometimes use are boycotts and slowdowns. A boycott occurs when union members agree not to buy the products of a targeted employer. A slowdown occurs when instead of striking, workers perform their jobs at a much slower pace than normal. A variation on the slowdown occurs when union members agree, sometimes informally, to call in sick in large numbers on certain days. For example, pilots at American Airlines engaged in a massive "sick out" in early 1999, causing the airline to cancel thousands of flights before a judge ordered the pilots back to work.

Some kinds of strikes and labor actions are illegal. Foremost among these is the so-called wildcat strike. A wildcat strike occurs during the course of a labor contract and is usually undertaken in response to a perceived injustice on the part of management. Because strikes are not legal during the course of a binding labor agreement, a wildcat strike is also, at least theoretically, unauthorized by the strikers' union.

Management also has certain tactics that it may employ in its efforts to break an impasse. One possibility is called a lockout. A lockout occurs when the employer denies access to the workplace. Managers must be careful when they use lockouts, however, because the government closely regulates this practice. An organization cannot lock out its employees simply to deprive them of wages in an effort to gain power during the labor negotiation. But suppose, however, the employer has a legitimate business need for locking out its employees. If this business need can be carefully documented, then a lockout might be legal. For example, almost half of the 1998–1999 National Basketball Association season was lost when team owners locked out their players over contract issues. Management also occasionally uses temporary workers or replacements for strikers. These individuals are called strikebreakers. Conflict sometimes erupts between strikebreakers attempting to enter an employer's workplace and picketers representing the interest of the union at the employer's gates.

Sometimes the various tactics described above are successful in resolving the impasse. For instance, after workers have gone out on strike, the organization may change its position and indeed modify its bargaining zone to accommodate potentially larger increases in pay. After experiencing a strike, the organization may realize that the costs of failing to settle are greater than it believed and so is willing to give more to avoid a longer strike (in other words, the company's resistance point has shifted). But in many situations other alternatives to resolve an impasse, such as the use of mediation and arbitration, are also available.

In mediation a neutral third party, called the mediator, listens to and reviews the information presented by both sides. Having no power to impose a solution, the mediator attempts to facilitate the negotiations between union and management. The mediator may make suggestions and informed recommendations and perhaps adds objectivity to the often emotional negotiations. To have any success at all, the mediator must have the trust and respect of both parties and have sufficient expertise and neutrality to convince the union and employer that she or he will be fair and equitable.

The U.S. government operates the Federal Mediation and Conciliation Service (FMCS) to make experienced mediators available to unions and companies. A program called Relationships by Objectives is offered by the FMCS to eliminate the causes of recurrent impasses and to increase the likelihood of a cooperative relationship between union and management.

Yet another alternative for resolving impasses is arbitration. Arbitration is a procedure in which a neutral third party studies the bargaining situation, listens to both parties and gathers information, and then makes a determination that is binding on the parties. The arbitrator, in effect, determines the conditions of the agreement.

In final-offer arbitration, the arbitrator can choose between the final offer of the union and the final offer of the employer. The arbitrator can't alter these offers but must select one as it stands. Since the arbitrator chooses the offer that appears most fair, and since losing the arbitration decision means settling for the other's offer, each side is pressured to make as good an offer as possible. By contrast, in conventional arbitration, the arbitrator is free to fashion any award deemed appropriate. Professional baseball uses final-offer arbitration to resolve contract disputes between individual players and owners.

The arbitration process that deals with the contract terms and conditions is called interest arbitration. This type of arbitration is relatively infrequent in the private sector. It is more common in the public sector, where it becomes a necessary quid pro quo for foregoing the strike option. Only about 20 states have compulsory interest arbitration procedures.

Once the contract impasse is removed, union and management have an agreement. Abiding by it is the essence of contract administration; however, at times, arbitration will again be necessary, namely, when a grievance is filed. This type of arbitration is referred to as rights arbitration or grievance arbitration.

ADMINISTERING A COLLECTIVE BARGAINING AGREEMENT

Once a collective bargaining agreement is in place, it is a legally binding contract. Because the parties are likely to interpret contract provisions differently, disputes often arise. These are referred to as rights disputes (as distinct from interest disputes) because they involve legally enforceable rights under the contract. Therefore, both sides need some mechanism for fairly interpreting the language of the agreement in specific situations.

Grievance Procedures

Contract disputes are resolved through a grievance system. Grievance systems are contractual provisions included in almost all collective bargaining agreements that provide due process for claims of contract violations. A grievance, which can be filed by either employees or employers, is an allegation that contract rights have been violated. Consider the following example:

Suppose that a contract contains a provision that states that an employee will only be discharged for "just cause." A union member by the name of Sarah Washington insults her immediate supervisor in front of a number of other workers and managers. The company may believe that it has just cause for firing Sarah, while Sarah may believe that such an extreme disciplinary action is unjust. This incident is likely to result in the union filing a grievance on Sarah's behalf.

The grievance procedure is considered by some authorities to be the heart of the bargaining agreement, or the safety valve that gives flexibility to the whole system of collective bargaining (Elkouri and Elkouri, 1985).

When negotiating a grievance procedure, one important concern for both sides is how effectively the system will serve the needs of labor and management. A well-written grievance procedure will allow grievances to be processed expeditiously and with as little red tape as possible. Furthermore, it should serve to foster cooperation, not conflict, between the employer and the union.

Union grievance procedures differ from organization to organization. Some contain simple two-step procedures. Here the grievant, union representative, and company representative first meet to discuss the grievance. If a satisfactory solution is not found, the grievance is brought before an independent third-party arbitrator, who hears the case, writes it up, and makes a decision. Arbitration is the final step in virtually all grievance procedures. Support for the concept of grievance arbitration may be found in the Taft-Hartley Act:

Fair adjustment by a method agreed upon by the parties is hereby declared to be the desirable method for settlement of grievance disputes arising out of the application or interpretation of an existing collective-bargaining agreement. (Taft-Hartley/Labor Management Relations Act, Section 203(d), 1947)

At the other extreme, the grievance procedure may contain six or more steps. The first step might be for the grievant and shop steward to meet informally with the grievant's supervisor to try to find a solution. If one is not found, a formal grievance is filed and a meeting scheduled among the employee, shop steward, and the supervisor's boss. The next steps involve the grievant and union representatives meeting with higher and higher level managers. Finally, if top management and the union can't reach agreement, the grievance may go to arbitration.

What if grieving employees believe that they have not been properly represented by the union? May they appeal an arbitrator's decision to the courts? The courts will generally refuse to hear such cases, unless employees can prove the union was grossly negligent in handling the grievance. Unions typically win such complaints.

In a unionized setting, an important determinant of the outcome of any grievance is the climate of labor relations. Grievances are more likely to be settled favorably when the climate is positive. When the climate is cooperative and harmonious, the chance that grievances will be granted at lower levels in the process is increased tremendously. However, when the relationship is distant or hostile, more grievances are denied or withdrawn. More will be said about this in the final section of this chapter.

ASSESSMENT OF COLLECTIVE BARGAINING

The effectiveness of the entire collective bargaining process and the union–management relationship can be measured by the extent to which each party attains its goals. But this approach has its difficulties. Because goals are incompatible in many cases and can therefore lead to conflicting estimates of effectiveness, a more useful measure may be the quality of the system used to resolve conflict. Conflict is more apparent in the collective bargaining process, where failure to resolve the issues typically leads to strikes. Another measure of effectiveness is the success of the grievance process, or the ability to resolve issues developing from the bargaining agreement.

Effectiveness of Negotiation

Because the purpose of negotiations is to achieve an agreement, the agreement itself becomes an overall measure of bargaining effectiveness. A healthy and effective bargaining process encourages the discussion of issues and problems and their subsequent resolution at the bargaining table. In addition, the effort required to reach agreement is a measure of how well the process is working. Some indications of this effort are the duration of negotiations, the outcome of member ratification votes, the frequency and duration of strikes, the use of mediation and arbitration, the need for government intervention, and the quality of union–management relations (whether conflict or cooperation exists). Joint programs for productivity and quality-of-work-life improvements could be regarded as successes resulting from effective union–management relations.

Effectiveness of Grievance Procedures

The success of a grievance procedure may be assessed from different perspectives. Management may view the number of grievances filed and the number settled in its favor as measures of effectiveness, with a small number filed or a large number settled in its favor indicating success. Unions may also consider these numbers, but from their point of view, a large number filed and a large number settled in their favor may indicate success.

An overall set of measures to gauge grievance procedure effectiveness may be related to the disagreements between managers and employees. Measures that might be included are frequency of grievances; the level in the grievance procedure at which grievances are usually settled; the frequency of strikes or slowdowns during the term of the labor agreements; the rates of absenteeism, turnover, and sabotage; and the necessity for government intervention.

The success of arbitration is often judged by the acceptability of the decisions, the satisfaction of the parties, the degree of innovation, and the absence of bias in either direction. The effectiveness of any third-party intervention rests in part on how successfully strikes are avoided because the motivation for such intervention is precisely to avert this extreme form of conflict resolution. As noted in the final section, HRM plays an important role in developing a positive labor–management climate.

HRM's ROLE IN LABOR RELATIONS

Obviously, there is a great deal for HRM professionals to know about labor law and labor relations. NLRB and court decisions interpreting relevant acts frequently fine-tune the requirements on management. Unionized organizations need someone with expertise in this area to guide their practices. In most organizations, the HRM function provides labor relations expertise. Larger establishments will have industrial or labor relations (LR) specialists within the HRM department, whereas in smaller organizations the HRM generalist may do most of the work.

When a union is present, HRM and labor relations experts are responsible for educating management and supervisors on the details of the contract and how to comply with it. They also liaise with the union if changes in work procedures are envisioned, such as implementing joint employee–management committees or reengineering. Prior to contract negotiations, HRM/LR experts will have a large role in helping to develop the bargaining position of the organization. This may involve holding meetings with supervisors to discover problems of working under the present contract and suggestions for modifying work rules. It also will include research and meetings with top management to develop a position on pay and other expensive benefits. HRM/LR experts are also often involved in face-to-face negotiations and in advising management on proposed settlements.

In organizations without unions, the HRM function of dealing with the day-to-day management and maintenance of hourly workers is often called employee relations. Organizations in which only some of the hourly employees are unionized may have both employee relations and labor relations functions for dealing with the two types of employees.

When operating without a union, HRM experts and all other managers need to be aware of the law so that they do not accidentally commit an unfair labor practice such as threatening or firing an employee who starts to discuss the possibility of unionizing. HRM experts also need to ensure that wages are fairly administered and competitive with other employers. In all areas, employer practices should be scrupulously fair and consistent and in line with written policies. Employees should have a "voice mechanism" to bring their complaints forward. A nonunion grievance procedure can fill this role, as can an open-door policy by all management, and perhaps an HRM ombudsman to respond to employee concerns.

It has been said that organizations "get the union they deserve." This means that good, fair, conscientious HRM can either prevent employees from feeling the need for a union to protect them or result in smooth and cooperative relations with an existing union because there are few issues on which employees feel mistreated. Employment practices seen as arbitrary, unfair, or exploitative are likely to lead to the formation of a more militant union.

While unions are taking a smaller role in many organizations, every HRM member needs to be conversant with labor law and highly attuned to preventing employee discontent that could grow into active conflict with a union.

SUMMARY

Labor relations is the process by which organizations deal with employees who are represented by a union. A labor union is a legally constituted group of individuals working together to achieve shared job-related goals. Collective bargaining is the process by which managers and union leaders negotiate acceptable terms and conditions of employment for those workers represented by the unions.

Unions have a long and uneven history in the United States. A variety of laws and other regulations have been passed, some of which are intended to promote unionization and union activities, whereas others are intended to limit or curtail union activities. And like any large organization, labor unions also have structures that facilitate their work.

Since the mid-1950s, labor unions in the United States have experienced increasing difficulties in attracting new members. Increasingly, unions recognize that they don't have as much power as they once held and that it is in their own best interests, as well as in the best interests of the workers they represent, to work with, not against, management. Bargaining perspectives have also altered in recent years. The direction unions will take is not clear. Employees continue to express dissatisfaction about their jobs and job security. Certainly, unions will continue to represent workers' economic concerns; however, the future impact of unions is uncertain.

There are specific steps employees must follow if they want to establish a union. If all the steps are successfully followed and enough eligible workers in the bargaining unit sign authorization cards, then the NLRB conducts an election, which may or may not result in the union becoming certified. Under certain conditions an existing labor union may be decertified.

Collective bargaining involves management representing the employing organization and the labor union representing employees. The collective bargaining process is aimed at agreement on a binding labor contract that will define various dimensions of the employment relationship for a specified period of time. Organizations and unions must work together to address any impasses that might occur during collective bargaining. If an impasse cannot be resolved, third-party involvement may be necessary.

A key clause in the labor contracts that are negotiated between management and labor is precise agreement on how the terms of the contract will be enforced. Although some enforcement issues are relatively straightforward, others may not be. To settle disagreements over contract administration during the life of a contract, the grievance system may be used.

REFERENCES

Baker, J.G. 1996. Negotiating a collective bargaining agreement: Law and strategy—A short course for non-labor lawyers. *Labor Law Journal* (April): 253–267.

Barling, J., Kelloway, E.K., and Bremermann, E.H. 1991. The role of family socialization and work beliefs. *Journal of Applied Psychology* 75: 725–731.

Bureau of National Affairs. 1995. *Grievance guide*, 9th ed. Washington, DC: Bureau of National Affairs.

Cleeland, N. 2000. Union ranks up in '99, led by California. *Los Angeles Times* (January 20), p. A1.

Elkouri, F., and Elkouri, E.A. 1985. *How arbitration works*, 4th ed. Washington, DC: Bureau of National Affairs.

Fullagar, C., Clark, D., Gallagher, D., and Gordon, M.E. 1994. A model of the antecedents of early union commitment: The role of socialization experiences and steward characteristics. *Journal of Organizational Behavior* 15: 517–533.

Kaufman, B.E., and Lewin, D. 1998. Is the NLRA still relevant to today's economy and workforce? *Labor Law Journal* (September): 114–117.

Leonard, B. 1999. The new face of organized labor. *HRMagazine* (July): 55–65.

NLRB v. Gisel Packing Company, 395 U.S. 575, 1969.

Taft-Hartley/Labor-Management Relations Act, Section 203(d), 1947.

Taylor, B.J., and Whitney, F. 1987. *Labor relations law*. Englewood Cliffs, NJ: Prentice-Hall, chap. 2.

Youngblood, S., DeNisi, A., Molleston, J., and Mobley, W. 1984. The impact of worker attachment, instrumentality beliefs, perceived labor union image, and subjective norms on voting intentions and union membership. *Academy of Management Journal* 27: 576–590.

Chapter 14

International Human Resources Management

INTRODUCTION

It is clear that the multinational corporation (MNC) is playing an increasingly major role in the world economy. Such a corporation is usually defined as a company with operations in more than one country (Porter, 1990, p. 18). Multinational corporations can be viewed as having an interlocking network of subsidiaries in several countries, whose executives view the whole world as its theater of operations, and who therefore obtain and allocate financial, material, technical, and managerial resources in a manner conducive to the achievement of total enterprise objectives. Shell, Colgate-Palmolive, Bechtel, and Philips are typical MNCs.

International business is not a new phenomenon. Indeed, its origins can be traced back literally thousands of years as merchants plied their wares along ancient trade routes linking southern Europe, the Middle East, and the Orient. Silks, spices, grains, jade, ivory, and textiles were among the most popular goods forming the basis for early trade. Wars have been fought over issues arising from international commerce, and the British Empire was built around the financial and business interests of the British nobility.

In the 1950s and 1960s, most large MNCs operating in the world were American (Phatak, 1978). These organizations operated in a world economy relatively safe from competition from firms of other nationalities. The world of international business became far more complex and competitive in the 1970s and particularly in the 1980s. Since the 1990s, the nature of international business has truly become global as firms from many countries are competing for their share of an ever-increasing world market of goods and services. International business and global competitiveness have become almost commonplace for most larger organizations today, and more and more medium-size and smaller businesses are engaged in international business as well.

As emphasized at various points throughout this book, one important source of competitive advantage and success for an organization is its human resources. The competitive value of effective HRM in multinational firms is certainly great, if not greater than in purely domestic organizations.

This chapter examines issues involved in managing human resources in MNCs. This process is referred to as international human resources management (IHRM). We begin with a discussion of the differences between HRM in domestic and international environments and then look at HRM planning and approaches to IHRM that MNCs can take and the factors that affect the choice of approach. The remainder of the chapter considers specific HRM functions within an MNC, such as staffing, training and development, performance appraisal, and compensation.

Domestic HRM versus IHRM

The internationalization of U.S. corporations has grown at a faster pace than the internationalization of many organizations' HRM efforts and staff. Broadly defined, IHRM is the process of procuring, allocating, and effectively utilizing human resources in a multinational corporation. HRM managers in MNCs must achieve two somewhat conflicting strategic objectives. First, they must integrate HRM policies and practices across a number of subsidiaries in different countries so that overall corporate objectives can be achieved. At the same time, the approach to HRM must be sufficiently flexible to allow for significant differences in the types of HRM policies and practices that are most effective in different business and cultural settings. This problem of balancing integration (control and coordination from headquarters) and differentiation (flexibility in policies and practices at the local subsidiary level) has long been acknowledged as a common dilemma facing HRM and other functional managers in multinational corporations (Bartlett and Ghoshal, 1989).

Although some argue that IHRM is not unlike HRM in domestic settings, others suggest that IHRM differs from domestic HRM in several ways. In broad terms, IHRM involves the same activities as domestic HRM (e.g., procurement refers to HRM planning and staffing); however, domestic HRM is involved with employees within only one national boundary. For example, IHRM necessarily places a greater emphasis on functions and activities such as relocation, orientation, and translation services to help employees adapt to a new and different environment outside their own country. Most larger corporations have a full-time staff of HRM managers devoted solely to assisting globalization. McDonald's, for example, has a team of HRM directors who travel around the world to help country managers stay updated in international concerns, policies, and programs.

Others suggest that there are more significant differences between IHRM and domestic HRM. Specifically, compared with domestic HRM, IHRM (1) encompasses more functions, (2) has more heterogeneous functions, (3) involves constantly changing perspectives, (4) requires more involvement in employees' personal lives, (5) is influenced by more external sources, and finally, (6) involves a greater level of risk than typical domestic HRM (Schuler, Dowling, and DeCieri, 1991, p. 430).

When compared to domestic HRM, IHRM requires a much broader perspective on even the most common HRM activities. This is particularly so for HRM managers operating from the MNC's headquarters location. The number and variety of IHRM activities are daunting. International HRM staff must deal with issues as varied as international taxation; international relocation and orientation; various other administrative services for expatriates; selecting, training, and appraising local and international employees; and managing host-government relations in a number of countries around the world. Even when dealing with a particular HRM activity like compensation, international HRM personnel are faced with a great variety of national and international pay issues. For example, when dealing with pay issues, the headquarters-based HRM personnel must coordinate pay systems in different countries with different currencies that may change in relative value to one another over time. In the case of fringe benefits provided to host-country employees, some interesting complications might arise. For example, it is common in the United States for companies to provide health insurance benefits to the employee and the employee's family, which usually means spouse and children. In some countries, however, the term "family" may encompass a more extended group of relatives— multiple spouses, aunts, uncles, grandparents, nephews, and nieces. How does the organization's benefit plan deal with these different definitions of family? (Morgan, 1986).

A final aspect of the broader scope of HRM is that headquarters-based managers deal with employee groups that have very different cultural backgrounds. The headquarters manager must coordinate policies and procedures to manage expatriates from the firm's home country (parent country nationals, PCNs), host country nationals (HCNs), as well as third country nationals (TCNs; e.g., a German manager working for an American MNC in the firm's Chilean subsidiary) in subsidiaries around the world. Although such issues are important for the headquarters-based manager, they are also relevant to the HRM personnel located in the subsidiary. The HRM personnel must develop HRM systems that are not only acceptable in the host country but also compatible with the company-wide systems being developed by his or her headquarters-based counterpart. These policies and practices must effectively balance the needs and desires of local employees, PCNs, and TCNs as well.

It is at the subsidiary level that the increased involvement of IHRM in the personal lives of employees becomes particularly apparent. Often subsidiary HRM personnel are involved in arranging housing, health care, transportation, education, and recreational activities for expatriate and local staff. Subsidiary HRM personnel may even find themselves dealing with expatriates who have marital and/or alcohol problems, acting as counselor and legal advisor (Solomon, 1995).

IHRM activities are also influenced by a greater number of external forces than are domestic HRM activities. The headquarters-based HRM personnel may have to set EEO policies that meet the legal requirements of both the home country and a number of host countries. Because of the visibility that MNCs tend to have in foreign countries (especially in developing countries), subsidiary HRM personnel may have to deal with government ministers, other political figures, and a greater variety of social and economic interest groups than would normally be encountered in purely domestic HRM.

Levels of risks and consequences associated with HRM decisions is the final difference between domestic HRM and IHRM. There certainly are major risks associated with HRM in domestic situations. Unfair hiring practices may result in a firm's being charged with violation of EEO laws and subjected to financial penalties. The failure to establish constructive relationships with domestic unions can lead to strikes and other forms of labor actions. However, IHRM personnel face these same risks as well as some additional ones that are unique and more threatening. Depending on the countries where the MNC operates, headquarters and subsidiary HRM personnel may have to worry about the physical safety of employees (i.e., in some countries kidnapping and terrorism are of concern to IHRM personnel).

Frequently, the human and financial consequences of failure in the international arena are more severe than in domestic business. For example, expatriate failure (the premature return of an expatriate from an international assignment) is a potentially high-cost problem for international companies. Direct costs (salary, training costs, and travel and relocation expenses) per failure to the parent firm may be as high as three times the domestic salary plus relocation expenses, depending on currency exchange rates and location of assignments. Indirect costs such as loss of market share and damage to international customer relationships may be considerable. Clearly, if managers do not perform well and must be recalled to the home country, their failure represents a huge financial loss for the firm.

A final risk is that of expropriation or seizure of the MNC's assets in a foreign country. If HRM policies antagonize host country unions or important political groups, the MNC may be asked to leave the country, have its assets seized, or find the local government taking majority control of its operation. Again, this is not the sort of risk that most domestic HRM personnel face.

Increasingly, domestic HRM is taking on some of the flavor of IHRM as it deals more and more with a multicultural workforce, given the changing demographics in the United States. Thus, some of the current focus of domestic HRM on issues of managing workforce diversity may prove to be beneficial to the practice of IHRM. While not necessarily transferable to a multinational context the management of diversity within a single national context at least lays the foundation for appreciating the challenges of being an MNC.

HRM Planning

The importance of HRM planning was highlighted in Chapter 2. HRM planning is particularly important in MNCs with strategic global objectives. Planning for the efficient use of human resources is essential if the MNCs are to meet their goals. However, the implementation of HRM planning procedures may be more difficult in some subsidiaries than in others. In cultures where people are viewed as basically subjugated to nature, there is very little need for HRM planning. The implementation of extensive HRM planning systems in cultures where people are unable to determine what happens would be met with bemusement at best and significant resistance at worst. Likewise, cultures that are oriented toward the present would not view long-term planning as valuable. In cultures oriented toward the past, planning would tend to focus on purely historical data and the use of these data in predicting future HRM needs. Such an approach might be appropriate for organizations that operate in relatively stable environments but would not work well for organizations in highly variable environments where the past has little to do with the future.

With more employees abroad as organizations have gone global, HRM departments have had to tackle new global challenges in their efforts to be successful in their HRM planning. Typical HRM planning challenges center on (1) deployment, (2) knowledge and innovation dissemination, and (3) identification and development of talent on a global basis (Roberts, Kossek, and Ozeki, 1998). Easily getting the right skills to where they are needed in the organization regardless of geographical location is a deployment issue that HRM planning must address. Additionally, spreading state-of-the art knowledge and practices throughout the organization, regardless of where they originate, must be part of a proactive HRM planning process that recognizes the need to disseminate knowledge and innovation to enhance organizational success. Finally, identifying who has the ability to function effectively in a global organization and developing these abilities is an important component of HRM planning. Without a process for identifying and developing talent on a global basis organizations will not be able to develop and sustain a competitive advantage.

Dealing with such challenges means most organizations have had to scramble to develop HRM policies and procedures just for handling international assignments. This process itself can be very complex. For example, consider some of the factors an organization needs to address just in deciding whom to deploy to overseas assignments and how to pay those people. From a practical point of view, the organization would have to address issues such as:

- *Candidate identification, assessment, and selection.* In addition to the required technical and business skills, key traits to consider for global assignments include, for instance: cultural sensitivity, interpersonal skills, and flexibility.
- *Cost projections.* The average cost of sending an employee and family on an overseas assignment is reportedly between three and five times the employee's predeparture salary. As a result, quantifying total cost for a global assignment and deciding whether to use an expatriate or a local employee are essential in the budgeting process.
- *Assignment letters.* The assignee's specific job requirements and associated pay will have to be documented and formally communicated in an assignment letter.
- *Compensation, benefits, and tax programs.* As will be noted later in this chapter there are many ways to compensate employees who are transferred abroad, given the vast differences in living expenses around the world. Some common approaches to international pay include home-based plus a supplement and destination-based-pay.
- *Relocation assistance.* The assignee will probably have to be assisted with such matters as maintenance of the person's home and automobiles, shipment and storage of household goods, and so forth.
- *Family support.* Cultural orientation, language training, education assistance, and emergency provisions are just some of the matters to be addressed here before the family is shipped abroad.

And that's just the tip of the iceberg. Cross-cultural, technical, and language training programs will probably be required. The complex and differentiated tapestry of labor laws and rules from country to country and provisions for reassimilating the expatriate when he or she returns home are some of the other issues the organization has to address in its IHRM planning efforts.

Approaches to IHRM Planning

Any international firm must develop an IHRM strategy. There are a number of strategic approaches available to MNCs in the planning and management of international human resources. We will focus on four of these in this section. In the ethnocentric approach, the MNC simply exports HRM practices and policies used in the home country to subsidiaries in foreign locations. Expatriates from the MNC's home country manage the foreign subsidiaries, and the MNC's headquarters maintains tight control over the subsidiaries' policies.

In the polycentric approach, the subsidiaries are basically independent from headquarters. HRM policies are adapted to meet the circumstances in each foreign location. Local managers in the foreign sites are hired to manage HRM activities.

The regiocentric approach represents a regional grouping of subsidiaries. HRM polices are coordinated within the region to as great an extent as possible. Subsidiaries may be staffed by managers from any of the countries within the region. Coordination and communication within the region are high, but they are quite limited between the region and the MNC's headquarters.

In the geocentric approach, HRM policies are developed to meet the goals of the global network of home country locations and foreign subsidiaries. This may include policies that are applied across all subsidiaries as well as policies adapted to the needs of individual locations—depending on what is best to maximize global results. An attempt is made to identify the HRM practices from both the home and host countries and apply them in an integrative manner where most appropriate around the world. The organization is viewed as a single international business entity rather than a collection of individual home-country and foreign business units. Human resources management and other activities throughout the MNC are managed by individuals who are most appropriate for the job regardless of their nationality (Hennan and Perlmutter, 1979). Thus an organization might find a French manager handling HRM activities in the London office of a Dutch MNC.

COUNTRY CULTURE, ORGANIZATIONAL CHARACTERISTICS, AND HRM PRACTICES

Culture is a society's set of assumptions, values, and rules about social interaction. A country's culture can be defined as the set of values, symbols, beliefs, and languages that guide behavior within that culture. The culture in which one is raised programs the mind to react to the environment in certain ways. In essence, culture provides people with a mental road map and traffic signals (Black, Gergersen, and Mendenhall, 1992). The road map depicts the goals to be reached and the ways to get there; the traffic signals indicate who has the right of way, when to stop, and so on.

In other words, people have within their minds a kind of "cultural software" (Hofstede, 1980). They don't have to wake up in the morning and figure out how to greet people, how to behave in a classroom, how to dress, how to behave when invited to someone's house, or whether to eat with silverware or their hands. All of this is programmed in, and people are free to go about their day pursuing goals within the confines of their culture's boundaries.

A culture does not necessarily coincide precisely with national boundaries, but these two different constructs tend to be relatively similar in terms of geographic area and domain. All employees in an international business need to be aware of cultural nuances, since by definition HRM personnel are concerned with people. Further, they must be especially cognizant of the role and importance of cultural differences and similarities in workers from different cultures.

As suggested thus far, culture is important to IHRM. While this statement may seem obvious, its relevance may be lost in a country like the United States, where many of the best-known theories of management practice are firmly rooted in Western culture. Numerous studies indicate that cultural differences do affect how managers manage and how direct reports react to different management styles (Easterby-Smith, Malina, and Yuan, 1994). Several researchers have spent considerable time identifying the aspects, or dimensions, of culture that vary from one culture to another. In 1961, two researchers suggested that cultures vary from one another in how they view some very basic issues. These dimensions are presented in Exhibit 14.1 (Kluckhohn and Strodtbeck, 1961). In addition, Hofstede's work on four dimensions of culture is important in understanding similarities and differences in culture. These dimensions, along with definitions are presented in Exhibit 14.2 (Hofstede, 1980).

The information in Exhibits 14.1 and 14.2 have enormous implications for MNCs. Differences in culture based on Kluckhohn and Strodtbeck's and Hofstede's dimensions may significantly affect HRM practices. As businesses move out of their home countries and employ people with potentially different orientations or cultural values, it is essential that corporations consider the inevitable clash between their "exported" HRM practices and the national culture.

As a general principle, the more an HRM practice contradicts the prevailing societal norms, the more likely it will fail. For instance, Hofstede describes management by objectives (MBO) as "perhaps the single most popular management technique 'made in the U.S.A.' " (Hofstede, 1980). Because it assumes (1) negotiation between the boss and employee, or a not-too-large power distance; (2) a willingness on the part of both parties to take risks, or weak uncertainty avoidance; and (3) that both supervisors and subordinates see performance and its associated rewards as important. Because all three of these assumptions are prominent features of U.S. culture, MBO "fits" the United States. But in other countries—France, for example—MBO has generally run into problems because of cultural incompatability:

Exhibit 14.1
Kluckhohn and Strodtbeck's Dimensions of Culture

Dimension	Orientation	Definition
Basic nature of human beings	Good	Left to their own devices, people are basically good and will act in a reasonable and responsible manner.
	Evil	People are basically evil and cannot be trusted.
	Mixed	People are a mixture of good and evil.
Relationships among people	Individualistic	The primary responsibility of an individual is to him/herself. Individual characteristics and abilities are of most concern.
	Group	Responsibility to family and group is most important. Ability to fit into the group rather than individual ability is paramount.
	Hierarchical	Basically the same orientation as for group, with the addition that distinct differences in status are expected and respected.
Activity orientation	Being	The point of life is to live and understand. Activity, in and of itself, is not important.
	Doing	The point of life is to do things, be involved in activities, and accomplish objective goals.
Relation to nature	Subjugation	Human activities are determined by nature and the environment.
	Harmony	Humans should live in harmony with their environment.
	Domination	Humans can control their destiny and can exert domination over their environment.
Time orientation	Past	History is important in determining our present actions.
	Present	Our actions should focus on the present, and the current situation should determine what we do.
	Future	Our actions should focus on the future and the attainment of future goals.

Exhibit 14.2
Hofstede's Dimensions of Culture

Dimension	Definition
Power distance	The degree to which power is unequally distributed in a society or organization.
Uncertainty avoidance	The degree to which a society considers itself threatened by uncertain events and ambiguous situations and tends to avoid these types of situations or tries to control them through formal means.
Individualism-collectivism	The extent to which society emphasizes the importance of the individual versus the group.
Masculinity-femininity	The extent to which society values masculine characteristics of aggressiveness, assertiveness, and not caring for others; also, the extent to which male and female roles are clearly defined.

The high power distance to which the French are accustomed from childhood ultimately has thwarted the successful utilization of MBO as a truly participative process. . . . The problem is not necessarily with MBO per se but the French managers . . . who are unaware that they are trying to exert control through the implementation of the objectives of MBO almost by fiat. (Jaeger, 1986)

The following section and subsections on intercountry differences describe the difficulties faced by organizations in the design and implementation of HRM programs in diverse cross-cultural settings. Many of these differences stem from cultural differences. They are discussed along with other problems facing HRM specialists that are not exclusively cultural in nature.

INTERCOUNTRY DIFFERENCES AND HRM

As evidenced by our discussion to this point, organizations operating only within the borders of the United States have the luxury of dealing with a relatively limited set of economic, cultural, and legal variables. Notwithstanding the range from liberal to conservative, for instance, the United States is basically a capitalist, competitive society. And while a multitude of cultural and ethnic backgrounds are represented in the U.S. workforce, various shared values (such as an appreciation of democracy) help to blur the otherwise sharp cultural differences. While the different states and municipalities certainly have their own laws affecting HRM, a basic framework of federal laws, also helps produce a fairly predictable set of legal guidelines regarding matters such as employment discrimination, labor relations, and safety and health.

An organization operating multiple units abroad is generally not blessed with such relative homogeneity. For example, minimum legally mandated holidays may range from five weeks in Luxembourg to none in the United Kingdom. And while there are no formal requirements for employee participation in Italy, employee representatives on boards of directors are required in Denmark for companies with more than 30 employees. The point is that the management of the HRM function in MNCs is complicated enormously by the need to adapt personnel policies and procedures in their IHRM planning to the differences among countries in which each subsidiary is based. The following are some factors in intercountry differences that demand such adaptation (Schuler, Dowling, and DeCieri, 1993).

Cultural Factors

As noted above, wide-ranging cultural differences from country to country require corresponding differences in HRM practices among a company's foreign subsidiaries. For instance, incentive plans in Japan still tend to focus on the work group, while in the West the more usual prescription is still to focus on individual worker incentives. Similarly, in a study about managers from Hong Kong, the People's Republic of China, and the United States, U.S. managers tended to be most concerned with getting the job done, while Chinese managers were most concerned with maintaining a harmonious environment; Hong Kong managers fell between these two extremes (Ralston et al., 1992).

The mix of cultures in the subsidiaries of an MNC and the level of cultural difference among the subsidiaries will restrict the IHRM approach taken by an organization. As the number and level of cultural differences among subsidiaries increase, it becomes much more difficult for HRM staff at the MNC's headquarters to formulate and implement consistent HRM practices worldwide. Thus, even though an MNC might prefer an ethnocentric approach to managing human resources, the policies and practices formulated at headquarters may be totally inappropriate and unacceptable in particular subsidiary locations. A more polycentric or regiocentric approach may be necessary.

In the end, the role of HRM personnel is to develop HRM practices that are (1) acceptable within the local culture and (2) acceptable to management at the MNC's headquarters. The balancing of these two requirements is a difficult task. Whether subsidiary HRM personnel are home-, host-, or third-country nationals, they bring their "own cultural baggage," which may affect their ability to accommodate cultural differences in the host workforce. Employees in a subsidiary may consist of a mixture of home-, host-, and third-country nationals—all with their own distinct cultural backgrounds and preferences. The subsidiary's HRM personnel must help all employees adapt to the HRM practices operating in the subsidiary, even though these practices may be derived from cultures very different from their own.

Political Policies, Legal Regulations, and Industrial Relations Factors

Industrial relations, and specifically the relationship between the worker, the union, and the employer, vary dramatically from country to country. In Germany, for instance, codetermination is the rule. Here, employees have the legal right to a voice in setting company policies. In this and several other countries, workers elect their own representatives to the supervisory board of the employer, and there is also a vice president for labor at the top-management level.

In many other countries the state interferes little in the relations between employers and unions. In the United States, for instance, HRM policies on most matters such as wages and benefits are set not by the state but by the employer, or by the employer in negotiations with its labor unions. In Germany, on the other hand, the various laws on codetermination, including the Works Constitution Act (1972), largely determine the nature of HRM policies in many German firms.

Organizations that take an ethnocentric approach to IHRM and would prefer to use many expatriates to manage and staff their subsidiaries may find themselves restricted by government policies and legal regulations in the host country. Policies limiting expatriates and requiring extensive employment of host-country nationals are put into place to encourage MNCs to hire, train, and develop local employees, particularly managerial and technical staff. This is especially likely in developing countries, where management and technical training within the host country's education system is rudimentary and the local government views the presence of MNCs in the country as a means of developing local expertise.

Economic Factors

Differences in economic systems among countries also translate into intercountry differences in HRM practices. In free enterprise systems, for instance, the need for efficiency tends to favor HRM policies that value productivity, efficient workers, and staff cutting where market forces dictate. Moving along the scale toward more socialist systems, HRM practices tend to shift toward preventing unemployment, even at the expense of sacrificing efficiency.

Managerial, Educational, and Technological Development in the Host Country

An MNC opening subsidiaries in Europe faces a much different IHRM challenge than one opening subsidiaries in a country in western Africa. In Europe, the available workforce is likely to be well educated and have considerable technical and management experience. Therefore, the opportunity to develop polycentric, regiocentric, or geocentric IHRM strategies is available. In west African countries, management and technical education is likely to be limited, and the bulk of the workforce may lack basic skills needed to deal with modern production processes or service activities. A more centralized IHRM strategy is necessary, with careful on-site monitoring by home-country personnel.

Labor Cost Factors

Closely related to the last factor are labor cost factors. Intercountry differences in labor costs are substantial. Hourly compensation costs can range in U.S. dollars for production workers from $1.50 in Mexico to $5.80 in Taiwan, to $13.77 in the United Kingdom, $17.20 in the United States, and $31.88 in Germany, for instance (Bureau of National Affairs, 1997). There are other comparative labor costs to consider. For example, wide gaps exist in hours worked, amounts of severance pay to departing employees, and vacation time for employees.

International Experience of the Organization

Organizations with extensive international experience have had the opportunity to develop more diverse methods of maintaining coordination and control over their foreign operations. Thus they may focus less on centralized control of HRM functions than firms with little international experience. Newcomers to the global marketplace may view the international business environment as more unpredictable, higher in ambiguity and uncertainty, and perhaps more threatening than more experienced global players. Construction of control, that is, a tendency toward centralizing decision-making and coordination functions, is common in ambiguous, uncertain, and threatening situations.

How the Subsidiary Is Established

The method used to establish operations in foreign locations also may affect HRM policies. In the case of foreign operations that are acquired by merger or acquisition, the presence of existing HRM practices in the acquired/merged operations likely will reduce the wholesale exportation of home country HRM systems into the subsidiary. In "Greenfield" sites, it may be more likely that HRM practices and policies from the home country will be implemented.

Technology and the Nature of the Product

This factor interacts with the two factors mentioned earlier. For technologically sophisticated products or services, the need to maintain specific production standards and quality control necessitates a greater degree of centralization of HRM functions at the MNC's headquarters location and the use of home-country managers and technical personnel to monitor these standards. This is the case particularly when the subsidiaries involved are located in host countries with low levels of technological and managerial expertise. On the other hand, some products must be adapted to host-country tastes in order to succeed in the local market. For example, some food items that are highly popular in the United States would be viewed as quite repulsive in other countries. In this case, reliance on local talent to adapt the product to suit the host-country market may require a very different approach to managing the subsidiary's recruiting activities.

INTERNATIONAL STAFFING POLICY

The staffing challenges for international assignments are broader in scope than those for domestic staffing. As noted earlier, MNCs can approach the management of IHRM in a number of ways: ethnocentric, polycentric, regiocentric, and geocentric. These approaches to IHRM are translated from an organization's corporate values. For example, in the ethnocentric corporation, "the prevailing attitude is that home country attitudes, management style, knowledge, evaluation criteria, and managers are superior to anything the host country might have to offer" (Perlmutter, 1989, p. 129). In the polycentric corporation, "there is a conscious belief that only host country managers can ever really understand the culture and behavior of the host country market; therefore, the foreign subsidiary should be managed by local people" (Phatak, 1989). Geocentrism assumes that management candidates must be searched for on a global basis, on the assumption that the best manager (or other employee) for any specific position anywhere on the globe may be found in any of the countries in which the organization operates. For our purposes we will only focus on these three approaches.

These three sets of multinational values translate into three broad international staffing policies or sources for staffing international operations. First, the company can send people from its home country. These employees are often referred to as expatriates, or home-country nationals. Second, it can hire host-country nationals, natives of the host country, to do the managing. Third, it can hire third-country nationals, natives of a country other than the home country or the host country.

Each of these three sources of overseas workers provides certain advantages and certain disadvantages. Some of the more important advantages are as follows: (1) host-country nationals—less cost, preference of host-country governments, intimate knowledge of environment and culture, and language facility; (2) home-country nationals (expatriates)—talent available within company, greater control, company experience, mobility, and experience provided to corporate executives; and (3) third-country nationals—broad experience, international outlook, and multilingualism. Most corporations use all three sources for staffing their multinational operations, although some companies exhibit a distinct bias for one or another of the three sources (Tung, 1998).

At early stages of international expansion organizations often send home-country expatriates to establish activities (particularly in less-developed countries) and to work with local governments. At later stages of internationalization there is typically a steady shift toward the use of host-country nationals. There are three reasons for this trend:

1. Hiring local citizens is less costly because the organization does not have to worry about the costs of home leaves, transportation, and special schooling allowances.
2. Since local governments usually want good jobs for their citizens, foreign employers may be required to hire them.
3. Using local talent avoids the problem of employees having to adjust to the culture.

Subsidiary HRM personnel ought to use a hiring process that fits the local labor market. For example, an MNC may need the services of a local personnel selection agency to identify the sources of skilled employees.

In general, employee recruitment in other countries is subject to more government regulation than it is in the United States. Regulations range from those that cover procedures for recruiting employees to those that govern the employment of foreign labor or require the employment of the physically disabled, war veterans, or disabled persons. Many Central American countries, for example, have stringent regulations about the number of foreigners that can be employed as a percentage of the total workforce.

Multinational corporations tend to use the same kinds of internal and external recruitment sources as are used in their home countries. At the executive level, companies use search firms. At lower levels more informal approaches tend to be useful. While unskilled labor may be readily available in a developing country, recruitment of skilled workers may be more difficult. Many employers have learned that the best way to find workers in these countries is through referrals and radio announcements because many people lack sufficient reading or writing skills.

The laws of many countries require the employment of locals if adequate numbers of skilled people are available. In these cases, recruiting is limited to a restricted population. Specific exceptions are granted (officially or unofficially) for contrary cases, as for Italian, Spanish, Greek, and Turkish workers in Germany and the Benelux (Belgium, the Netherlands, and Luxembourg) countries and for Mexican farmworkers in the United States.

Just as local employment laws must be adhered to, premium salaries may have to be offered to lure highly qualified individuals away from local firms. Additionally, as suggested in point two above, in some countries hiring may require using a government-controlled labor bureau. This may be particularly prevalent in hierarchical cultures with high power distance. In Vietnam, for example, local labor bureaus are heavily involved in the hiring process. Thus, while top managers may have preferences for one source of employees over another, the host country may place pressures on them to restrict their choices. Such pressure takes the form of sophisticated government persuasion through administrative or legislative decrees to employ host-country individuals. In short, important staffing issues may have to be approved by very high government officials.

The development of a selection system may be complicated by the fact that selection tests used in the home country of the MNC may be culturally biased and inappropriate elsewhere. For example, many personality tests were developed using Western samples. The personality profiles provided by such tests, and certainly their normative data, would be meaningless in trying to understand the behavior of Chinese or Malaysian job applicants.

Even if the concepts measured by the tests are applicable, there are difficulties in getting many tests adequately translated into the host-country language. Further, issues of race, age, and sex discrimination can cause considerable difficulties for the subsidiary HRM personnel. For example, in Singapore, a fairly hierarchical and masculine culture, it is acceptable and legal to place job advertisements that specifically state the race, age range, and sex of employees being sought.

The methods of selection commonly used by corporations operating internationally are interviews, assessment centers, and tests. While some companies interview only the candidate, others interview both the candidate and the spouse, lending support to the fact that companies are becoming increasingly aware of the significance of the spouse's adjustment to a foreign environment and the spouse's contribution to managerial performance abroad.

Clearly, selection practices vary around the world. In the United States managers tend to emphasize merit, with the best-qualified person getting the job. In other countries, however, organizations tend to hire on the basis of family ties, social status, language, and common origin. The candidate who satisfies these criteria may get the job even if otherwise unqualified. While much of this is changing as a result of the growing realization among some organizations in other nations that greater attention must be given to hiring those most qualified, there still exist a number of challenges that subsidiary HRM personnel must be cognizant of in their international staffing efforts.

TRAINING AND DEVELOPMENT

While an organization may have been successful in staffing for international work, the employee may then require special training to achieve the desired level of performance. Over time, given the rapidity of change in an international setting, employees may also need to upgrade their skills as they continue on the job. Such training may be provided within the organization or outside it in some type of educational setting.

One of the major problems associated with hiring in less developed countries is that the skill level of individuals may be less than desired. In such circumstances, it is important to invest considerable time and effort in the selection process and to provide increased training to local employees when they arrive on the job (Desatnick and Bennett, 1978). However, much like the problem of transferring headquarters-based selection procedures to subsidiaries, training programs designed in the home country to teach employees the skills needed to perform their jobs may be inappropriate for use in other cultures. Translating training materials may be difficult. In addition, how people learn and the methods of training with which they are comfortable vary across cultures. For example, the Chinese, whose culture is very hierarchical, are taught respect and deference for teachers. As a result, Chinese students see themselves as the "receivers" and the teachers as the "givers" of knowledge (Kirkbride, Tang, and Shae, 1989). Chinese students rarely ask questions or challenge a teacher's statements. To do so would be disrespectful. Consequently, Chinese students take a passive role in learning, and the very active, high-participation methods often used in Western training programs would be inappropriate.

Good training programs help MNCs attract needed employees from the host countries. In less developed countries especially, individuals are quite eager to receive the training they need to improve their work skills. Oftentimes, however, an organization's human capital investment does not pay off. It is very common, for example, for locally owned companies to hire away those workers who have been trained by the foreign-owned organizations.

Apart from developing local resources, most MNCs recognize that to be successful in an international setting, managers and other employees need to receive special training for overseas assignments. One organization specializing in such programs prescribes a four-step approach (Adler, 1994,

p. 30). Level 1 training focuses on the impact of cultural differences and on raising trainees' awareness of such differences and their impact on business outcomes. Level 2 aims at getting participants to understand how attitudes (both negative and positive) are formed and how they influence behavior. (For example, unfavorable stereotypes may subconsciously influence how a new manager responds to and treats her or his new foreign subordinates.) Level 3 training provides factual knowledge about the target country, while Level 4 provides skill building in areas like language and adjustment and adaptation skills.

Successful MNCs recognize that if they are to achieve their strategic objectives their managers need to be educated and trained in global management skills. For example, one organization has identified the following six skill categories for the global manager, or the manager equipped to run an international business (Rothwell, 1993): (1) ability to seize strategic opportunities, (2) ability to manage highly decentralized organizations, (3) awareness of global issues, (4) sensitivity to issues of diversity, (5) competence in interpersonal relations, and (6) skill building community. Organizations that are serious about succeeding in the global business environment are tackling these problems head-on by providing intensive training. Companies like Bechtel, Procter & Gamble, Texas Instruments, and others with large international staffs prepare employees for overseas assignments. The biggest mistake managers can make is to assume that people are the same everywhere. An organization that makes a concerted effort to ensure that its employees understand and respect cultural differences will realize the impact of its effort on its sales, costs, and productivity (Kemper, 1998).

Training and development programs that prepare employees for working internationally typically include: (1) language training, which includes not only learning the language of the host country but also how the people think and act in their relations with others; (2) cross-cultural training, which includes understanding one's own cultural conditioning, understanding cultural differences, and understanding work attitudes and motivations in other cultures; (3) assessing and tracking career development, which includes maximizing the career benefits of foreign assignments and repatriation (i.e., process of employee transition home from an international assignment); and (4) managing personal and family life in the form of culture shock (e.g., perpetual stress experienced by people who settle overseas). In addition to providing training to employees in advance of overseas assignments, successful MNCs also provide more training to employees (and their families) after the overseas assignment has ended. All family members must reacclimate to life in the United States or home country.

PERFORMANCE APPRAISAL

In evaluating employee performance in international environments, cultural difference is an important factor. Culture helps determine what aspects of performance should be appraised and how that appraisal should be conducted. For instance, the cultural differences between the United States and England are not as great as those between the United States and China. Thus, hostility or friendliness of the cultural environment in which one works (or manages) should be considered when appraising employee performance.

There is also the issue of who will be responsible for the evaluations: the host-country management or the parent-country management. In many cases, an individual working internationally has at least two allegiances: one to his or her home country (the office that made the assignment) and the other to the host country in which the employee is currently working. Superiors in each location frequently have different information about the employee's performance and may also have very different expectations about what constitutes good performance. For these reasons, the multirater (360-degree) appraisal discussed in Chapter 8 is gaining favor among MNCs.

Although local management would generally be considered a more accurate gauge, it typically evaluates expatriates from its own cultural perspectives and expectations, which may not reflect those of the parent country. That is, cultures may influence one's perception of how well an individual is performing. For example, in some countries, hierarchical values make it a disgrace to ask employees for ideas. In this and other situations, participative decision making may be viewed either positively or negatively, depending on the culture. Such cultural biases may not have any bearing on an individual's true level of effectiveness. In addition, local management frequently does not have enough perspective on the entire organization to know how well an individual is truly contributing to the organization as a whole. This could vastly alter a supervisor's performance appraisal (Dowling, Schuler, and Welch, 1994).

Domestic managers are frequently unable to understand expatriate experiences, value them, or accurately measure their contribution to the organization. Geographical distances pose severe communication problems for expatriates and home-country managers. Instead of touching base regularly, there is a tendency for both expatriates and domestic managers to work on local issues rather than coordinate across time zones and national borders. Information technology has improved this situation, and it is far easier to communicate globally today than it was just a few years ago (Martinsons, 1997). But even when expatriates contact their home-country offices, it is frequently not to converse with their superiors. More likely they talk with peers and others throughout the organization.

Confusion may arise from the use of home-country evaluation forms if they are misunderstood, either because the form has been improperly translated, not translated at all, or the evaluator is uncertain what a particular question means. The home-office management, on the other hand, is often so remote that it may not be fully informed on what is going on in an overseas office. Because they lack access and because one organization may have numerous foreign operations to evaluate, home-office managements often measure performance by quantitative indices, such as profits, market shares, or gross sales (Oddou and Mendenhall, 1991). However, "simple" numbers are often quite complex in their calculations and data are not always comparable. Further, even when the measurements are comparable the comparison country will have an effect. Additionally, depending on where the supervisor's results are compared, different outcomes may occur. Accordingly, such issues complicate home-country management performance evaluations by numerical criteria, or indices.

Clearly, an individual's success or failure is affected by a host of technical and personal factors. Many of these factors should be considered in developing appropriate criteria. For instance, the goals and responsibilities inherent in the job assignment are among the most important criteria used to evaluate an individual's performance. As suggested above, superiors often resort to using "easy" criteria such as productivity, profits, and market share. These criteria may be valid—but they are still deficient if they do not capture the full range of an expatriate's responsibility.

Many of the performance appraisal methods discussed earlier in this text focus on the assessment of individual performance (e.g., behaviorally anchored rating scales, behavioral observation scales). Most of these procedures were developed in the United States, a very individualistic society. By contrast, in China and Japan group performance is critical, and singling out individuals for praise or criticism is highly threatening. Employees in such collective cultures gain much of their sense of identity from membership in work groups. Individually oriented appraisals serve to separate individuals from those sources of identity.

A culture's standing on individualism–collectivism also determines how "good performance" is defined. In Japan, behaviors directed toward maintaining group harmony and cohesiveness (e.g., helping resolve conflicts among group members) may be valued as much as, if not more than, behaviors focused on more objective performance activities (e.g., producing more widgets). Task performance at the expense of group harmony certainly would be viewed as inappropriate. A similar situation may exist in feminine cultures, in which maintenance of good personal relationships is valued. Managers who maintain good personal networks and develop warm, trusting relationships with their subordinates may be viewed as better managers than those with higher levels of objective task performance. Researchers have found marked differences in the criteria used by Chinese and British organizations. In British organizations, the focus was on bottom-line delivery, evidence of experience in more than one business area, and experience in another country. In Chinese organizations, criteria included loyalty to the Communist Party, good quality of relationships, evidence of being a hard worker, and good "moral" practice (Easterby-Smith, Malina, and Yuan, 1994).

Performance feedback in an international setting is clearly a two-way street. Although the home-country and host-country superiors may tell an expatriate how well he or she is doing, it is also important for expatriates to provide feedback regarding the support they are receiving, the obstacles they face, and the suggestions they have about the assignment. More than in most any other job, expatriates are in the very best position to evaluate their own performance.

Given the pros and cons of home-country and host-country evaluations, most observers agree that performance evaluations should try to balance the two sources of appraisal information (Harvey, 1997). Two other recommendations have been suggested on the subject of international performance appraisal:

- Modify the normal performance criteria of the evaluation sheet for a particular position to fit the overseas position and site characteristics. Expatriates who have been returned from a particular site or the same country can provide useful input into revising performance criteria to reflect the possibilities and constraints of a given location.
- Include a current expatriate's insights as part of the evaluation. This means that nonstandardized criteria, which are difficult to measure, will be included, perhaps on a different basis for each country. This creates some administrative difficulties at headquarters, but in the long run it will be a more equitable system. (Dowling et al., 1991)

Successful MNCs recognize that they cannot simply use standard appraisal criteria overseas and expect valid results. They take the time to construct criteria according to each subsidiary's unique situation, use the appropriate evaluation form, and conduct performance appraisals individually or based upon group performance, depending on the culture of each subsidiary. Successful performance appraisal in international assignments means that the organization uses multiple raters and makes sure that some of those raters have lived and worked in the country in which the expatriate is working.

COMPENSATION

One of the most complex areas of IHRM is compensation. The whole area of international compensation presents some tricky problems. On the one hand, there is a certain logic in maintaining company-wide pay scales and policies so that, for instance, divisional marketing directors throughout the world are all paid within the same narrow range. This reduces the risk of perceived inequities and dramatically simplifies the job of keeping track of disparate country-by-country wage rates.

Adapting pay scales to local markets can present the HRM personnel with more problems than it solves. The fact is that it can be enormously more expensive to live in some countries (like Japan) than others (like Greece). If these cost-of-living differences aren't considered, it may be almost impossible to get managers to take "high-cost" assignments.

However, the answer is usually not just to pay, say, marketing directors more in one country than in another. For one thing, you could thereby elicit resistance when telling a marketing director in Tokyo who's earning $3,000 per week to move to your division in Spain, where his or her pay for the same job will drop by half (cost of living notwithstanding). One way to handle the problem is to pay a similar base salary company-wide and then add on various allowances according to individual market conditions (Mazur, 1995).

Determining equitable wage rates, or for that matter compensation systems, in many countries is no simple matter. There are a variety of factors that affect compensation systems within MNCs. MNC compensation systems are influenced by internal business factors such as varying wage costs, levels of job security, and differing business strategies. Compensation is affected by differences in prosperity and spending power related to the strength of national economies and currencies. Social factors such as the extent to which pay differences are considered acceptable, the appreciation of different forms of pay, and the acceptance of different forms of compensation and appraisal (e.g., stock options, incentive pay based on performance) also affect MNC compensation systems within a particular country. Wage and other legislation, along with the influence of unions, has an impact on compensation systems as well.

It is beyond the scope of this chapter to discuss the myriad of influences on MNC compensation practices around the world. Suffice it to say that subsidiary HRM personnel must know or have access to information about these issues. Regulations concerning pensions, social security, medical insurance, and other benefits are critically important and vary greatly. In some countries, benefits such as housing, transportation, and year-end bonuses are common; in others they are not.

Issues relating to gender-based or racially based wage differentials are of particular concern for subsidiaries of U.S. organizations. Even though such differentials may be acceptable in countries where U.S. MNCs operate, they are certainly not consistent with U.S. HRM policies. U.S. HRM specialists in foreign subsidiaries must make decisions as to whether it is ethical to have discrimination in one part of the MNC but not in another. Union influences may play an important role in determining wage policies in some countries but not in others. For example, Australia has had for some years now a national wage-setting system in which the government and unions negotiate pay rates for workers that apply country-wide. In Hong Kong, by contrast, labor unions are extremely weak, and wage rates are determined by the free market.

Compensating host-country employees is another basic managerial or administrative issue that must be addressed when an organization establishes operations overseas. More specifically, host-country employees are generally paid on the basis of productivity, time spent on the job, or a combination of these factors. In industrialized countries, pay is generally by the hour; in developing countries, by the day. The piece-rate method is quite common. In some countries, including Japan, seniority is an important element in determining employees' pay rates. When organizations commence operations in a foreign country, they usually set their wage rates at or slightly higher than the prevailing wage for local companies. Eventually, though, they are urged to conform to local practices to avoid "upsetting" local compensation practices.

Employee benefits in other countries are frequently higher than those in the United States. In Italy, for example, benefits are about 92 percent of wages and in France 70 percent, compared with 40 percent in the United States. Whereas in the United States most benefits are awarded to employees by employers, in other industrialized countries most of them are legislated or ordered by governments. Some of these plans are changing. Defined contribution plans are on the rise, sex equality is becoming important, and stock ownership is being tried (Sullivan, 1996).

Compensation of expatriate managers is another issue that MNCs must address. Compensation plans for expatriate managers must be competitive, cost-effective, motivating, fair and easy to understand, consistent with international financial management, easy to administer, and simple to communicate. To be effective, an international compensation program must:

- Provide an incentive to leave the United States
- Allow for maintaining an American standard of living
- Facilitate reentry into the United States
- Provide for the education of children
- Allow for maintaining relationships with family, friends, and business associates (Gould, 1999)

The most common approach to formulating expatriate pay is to equalize purchasing power across countries, a technique known as the balance sheet approach (Fraeze, 1998). The basic idea is that each expatriate should enjoy the same standard of living he or she would have had at home. With the balance sheet approach, four main home-country groups of expenses—income taxes, housing, goods and services, and reserve—are the focus of attention. The employer estimates what each of these four expenses is for the expatriate's home country and also what each is expected to be in the expatriate's host country. Any differences—such as additional income taxes or housing expenses—are then paid by the employer.

In practice this usually boils down to building the expatriate's total compensation around five or six separate components. For example, base salary will normally be in the same range as the manager's home-country salary. In addition, however, there might be an overseas or foreign service's premium. This is paid as a percentage of the executive's base salary, in part to compensate the manager for the cultural and physical adjustments he or she will have to make. There may also be several allowances, including a housing allowance and an education allowance for the expatriate's children. Income taxes represent another area of concern. In many cases a U.S. manager posted abroad must pay not just U.S. taxes but also income taxes in the country to which she or he is posted.

As with performance appraisal systems, cultural preferences may influence the type of compensation system that is appropriate. If we relate specific cultural dimensions to pay systems, in high power distance cultures, compensation systems should reflect hierarchical divisions within the organization. Pay should reflect job and status differences, with large differences in the pay levels of the highest- and lowest-level workers. In contrast, compensation systems in low power distance cultures should be more egalitarian, with relatively small differences between the top and bottom earners. In individualistic cultures, compensation systems should reward individual achievement, and in collective cultures, pay should be group based or seniority based (Gomez-Meia and Wellbourne, 1991).

In the end, it is important for MNCs to understand that the "trick in designing compensation systems in international environments is to understand what motivates employees in each culture, and to design the system around those motivations. Money, praise, or external symbols (a corner office, a personal parking space), while attractive to American employees, may not hold the same attraction for members of other cultures. Simply superimposing American compensation and reward systems onto a foreign subsidiary oftentimes will not only fail to work but may actually damage the productivity of the workers in that subsidiary.

INTERNATIONAL LABOR RELATIONS

Multinational corporations opening subsidiaries abroad will find substantial differences in labor relations practices among the world's countries and regions. First, each country has a different history of unionism, and each government has its own view of its role in the labor relations process.

This role is often reflected in the types and nature of the regulations in force. While the U.S. government generally takes a "hands-off" approach toward intervention in labor–management matters, the Australian government, to which the labor movement has very strong ties, is inclined to be more involved. Thus, not only must the MNC industrial relations office be familiar with the separate laws of each country, it also must be familiar with the environment in which those statutes are implemented. Understanding international labor relations is vital to an organization's strategic planning and potential success in the global arena. Unions affect wage levels, which in turn affect competitiveness in both labor and product markets. Unions and labor laws may limit employment-level flexibility through security clauses that tightly control layoffs and terminations (or redundancies). This is especially true in such countries as England, Germany, France, Japan, and Australia where various laws place severe restrictions on employers.

Since labor relations can affect the strategic planning initiatives of MNCs, it is necessary to consider the issue of headquarters' involvement in host-country international union relations. The organization must assess if the labor relations function should be controlled globally from the parent company or if it would be more advantageous for each host country to administer its own operation. There is no simple means of making this assessment. However, MNCs must decide whether or not to keep labor relations centrally located at corporate headquarters or to adapt to host-country standards and have the labor relations function decentralized. Many European countries have opted for decentralization of labor relations, while American organizations are more inclined to centralization of labor relations.

The national attitude toward unions is another divergence among MNCs in labor relations. Generally, Europeans have had greater experience with unions, are accustomed to a larger proportion of the workforce being unionized, and are more accepting of the unionization of their own workers. American MNCs, on the other hand, view unions negatively at home and try to avoid unionization of the workforce (Woodruff, 1997). In Japan, as in other parts of Asia, unions are often closely identified with an organization (Cole and Deskins, 1988).

There are also significant differences in countries outside the United States in the collective bargaining process. The collective bargaining process is typically carried out in companies operating in the United States. When we look at other countries, we find that the whole process can vary widely, especially with regard to the role that government plays. In the United Kingdom and France, for example, government intervenes in all aspects of collective bargaining. Government involvement is only natural where parts of industry are nationalized. Also, in countries where there is heavy nationalization there is more likely to be acceptance of government involvement, even in the nonnationalized companies. In developing countries it is common for the government to have representatives present during bargaining sessions to make sure that unions with relatively uneducated leaders are not disadvantaged in bargaining with skilled management representatives.

Clearly, some important differences exist in the area of labor relations between the United States and other countries. Any company that wants to be successful in the global arena must be aware of what is happening and pending in labor legislation and fully understand and comply with the host country's laws and customs.

SAFETY AND HEALTH

It is important to know the safety and health environments of each country in which an organization operates. Generally, corporations in western Europe, Japan, Canada, and the United States put great emphasis on the health and welfare of their employees. However, most businesses in less developed countries have limited resources and thus cannot establish awareness or protection programs.

Most countries have laws and regulatory agencies that protect workers from hazardous work environments. It is important for American organizations to learn the often complex regulations that exist as well as the cultural expectations of the local labor force. Manufacturing operations, in particular, where there are myriad potentially hazardous situations, must design and establish facilities that meet the expectations of the local employees—not necessarily those of Americans.

Having employees abroad does raise some unique safety and fair treatment issues, however. For example, "kidnapping has become a way of life in some countries south of the U.S. border, and in many places—Brazil, Nigeria, the Philippines, Russia, and New Guinea, to name a few—street crime is epidemic, although tourists and business people are rarely kidnapped or assassinated." As one security executive at an oil company put it, "It's crucial for a company to understand the local environment, local conditions and what threat exists" (Greengard, 1997). Keeping business travelers out of crime's way is a specialty all its own that MNCs have had to address in developing their IHRM policies and practices.

Making provisions to ensure employee safety and health doesn't stop at a country's borders. MNCs must ensure that they are just as safety and health conscious with workers abroad as they are with those at home. There is a strong need for IHRM staff to be vigilant in identifying the unique aspects of HRM programs in an international business environment that may impact the organizations potential success. It is also just as important for IHRM personnel to assess the costs and benefits of IHRM programs. The basic nature of the factors that contribute to the value added are the same as for domestic HRM activities. However, the magnitude of these costs and potential benefits may be considerably different in the international context. In addition, there are some HRM activities that should be assessed for value added that are not typically found in domestic operations. Examples of these include:

- The costs and benefits of repatriation programs.
- The ability of IHRM policies to provide an appropriate mix of PCN, HCN, and TCN managers for optimal organizational efficiency and effectiveness.
- The costs and subsequent benefits of localization programs (reducing expatriate and increasing local employees) in foreign subsidiaries.
- The costs and benefits of customizing HRM activities to suit particular national cultures and legal systems.
- The costs and benefits of HRM programs developed to deal with the special problems of foreign taxation and social security systems. (Florkowski and Schuler, 1994)

This list is not intended to be exhaustive in nature. It does exemplify, however, the need for IHRM personnel to recognize the important role they play in helping their organization succeed in both the domestic and international business environment.

SUMMARY

The topic of international HRM is so important that a whole chapter has been dedicated to its discussion. As with the rest of this book, the goal has been to show some of the best practices for managing an organization's most valuable resource—its people at work. Much of what has been discussed throughout this book can be applied to both domestic and internationally successful organizations that are able to sustain and prolong their success through the way they manage their human resources.

International human resources management is distinct from domestic HRM because of its broader perspective, the greater scope of activities included in IHRM, and the higher level of risk associated with IHRM activities. Multinational corporations may take any one of a number of different approaches to HRM, with the choice depending on political and legal regulations; the managerial, educational, and technology development in the host country; and differences between the home and host cultures.

The headquarters-based managers must coordinate IHRM operations in a variety of countries, each with its own local cultural, legal, and traditional influences. The headquarters policies must be flexible enough to allow for these local variations. However, policies also must be developed to help achieve the overall strategic global objectives of the MNC.

Care must be taken in developing the various HRM activities to ensure that they take into consideration each local country's cultural nuances. Staffing, training and development, performance appraisal, compensation, and the use of expatriates versus locals are of paramount concern to successful IHRM.

Multinational corporations must pay particular attention to assessing the costs and benefits of IHRM programs. The basic nature of the factors that contribute to success are the same as for domestic HRM activities. However, the magnitude of these costs and potential benefits may be considerably different in the international context. In addition, there are some HRM activities that should be assessed for value added that are not typically found in domestic HRM operations.

As with all of the other HRM activities discussed throughout this book, organizations must recognize the important role that effective management of human resources plays in the organization's success in the international arena. Recruiting, selecting, evaluating, training and developing, and compensating employees all play important roles in developing and sustaining competitive advantages for an organization. As noted in the first chapter, today and in the future an organization's ability to attract, develop, and retain a talented workforce will be a critical factor in developing a high-performance, successful organization.

REFERENCES

Adler, N. 1994. Women managers in a global economy. *Training and Development* (April): 30–36.

Bartlett, C.A., and Ghoshal, S. 1989. *Managing across borders: The transnational solution*. London: Century Business.

Black, J.S., Gergersen, H.B., and Mendenhall, M.E. 1992. *Global assignments: Successfully expatriating and repatriating international managers*. San Francisco: Jossey-Bass.

Bureau of National Affairs. 1997. Labor costs in manufacturing by nation. *BNA Bulletin to Management*: 116–117.

Cole, R.E., and Deskins, D.R., Jr. 1988. Racial factors in site location and employment patterns of Japanese auto firms in America. *California Management Review* (February): 9–22.

Desatnick, R.L., and Bennett, M.L. 1978. *Human resource management in the multinational company*. New York: Nichols.

Dowling, P.J., Schuler, R.S., and Welch, D.E. 1994. *International dimensions of human resource management*, 2nd ed. Belmont, CA: Wadsworth, pp. 103–120.

Easterby-Smith, M., Malina, D., and Yuan, L. 1994. How culture-sensitive is HRM? A comparative analysis of practice in Chinese and UK companies. *The International Journal of Human Resource Management* 6(1): 32–59.

Florkowski, G., and Schuler, R.S. 1994. Auditing human resource management in the global environment. *The International Journal of Human Resource Management* 5(4): 827–851.

Fraeze, V. 1998. Is the balance sheet right for your expats? *Global Workforce* (September): 19–26.

Gomez-Mejia, L., and Wellbourne, T. 1991. Compensation strategies in a global context. *Human Resource Planning* 14(1): 29–41.

Gould, C. 1999. Expat pay plans suffer cutbacks. *Workforce* (September): 40–46.

Greengard, S. 1997. Mission possible: Protecting employees abroad. *Workforce* (August): 30–32.

Harvey, M. 1997. Focusing the international performance appraisal process. *Human Resource Development Quarterly* (Spring): 41–62.

Hennan, D., and Perlmutter, H.V. 1979. *Multinational organization development.* Reading, MA: Addison-Wesley.

Hofstede, G. 1980. *Culture's consequences: International differences in work-related values.* Beverly Hills, CA: Sage Publications.

Jaeger, A. 1986. Organization development and national culture: Where's the fit? *Academy of Management Review* 11: 178–190.

Kaeter, M. 1995. International development. *Training* (May): 23–29.

Kemper, C.L. 1998. Global training's critical success factors. *Training and Development* (February): 35–37.

Kirkbride, P.S., Tang, S.F.Y., and Shae, W.C. 1989. The transferability of management training and development: The case of Hong Kong. *Asia Pacific Human Resource Management* 21(1): 7–20.

Kluckhohn, F., and Strodtbeck, F.L. 1961. *Variations in value orientations.* Evanston, IL: Row, Peterson.

Martinsons, M.G. 1997. Human resource management applications of knowledge-based systems. *International Journal of Information Management* (February): 35–53.

Mazur, L. 1995. Entropay. *Across-the-Board* (January): 40–43.

Morgan, P.V. 1986. International HRM: Fact or fiction. *Personnel Administrator* 31(9): 43–47.

Oddou, G., and Mendenhall, M. 1991. Expatriate performance appraisal: Problems and solutions. In M. Mendenhall and G. Oddou (eds.), *Readings and Cases in international human resource management.* Boston: PWS-Kent, pp. 366–374.

Perlmutter, H. 1989. The tortuous evolution of the multinational corporation. *Columbia Journal of World Business* (January–February), pp. 11–14, as discussed in A. Phatak, *International dimension of management.* Boston: PWS-Kent, p. 129.

Phatak, A.V. 1978. *Managing multinational corporations.* New York: Praeger, pp. 21–22.

Phatak, A.V. 1989. *International dimension of management.* Boston: PWS-Kent.

Porter, M.E. 1990. *The competitive advantage of nations.* New York: Free Press, p. 18.

Ralston, D., Elsass, P., Gustafson, D., Cheung, F., and Tepstra, R. 1992. Eastern values: A comparison of managers in the United States, Hong Kong, and the People's Republic of China. *Journal of Applied Psychology* 7(5): 664–671.

Roberts, K., Kossek, E., and Ozeki, C. 1998. Managing the global workforce: Challenges and strategies. *Academy of Management Executive* 12(4): 93–106.

Rothwell, S. 1993. Leadership development and international HRM. *Manager Update 4* (Summer): 20–32.

Schuler, R., Dowling, P., and DeCieri, H. 1991. An integrative framework of strategic international human resource management. *Journal of Management* 19(2): 419–459.

Schuler, R.S., Dowling, P., and DeCieri, H. 1993. An integrative framework of strategic international human resource management. *The International Journal of Human Resource Management* 4(4): 717–764.

Solomon, C.M. 1995. Danger below! Spot failing global assignments. *Personnel Journal* 76(11): 78–85.

Sullivan, M. 1996. European benefit issues: Costs to the multinational employers. *Compensation and Benefits Management* (Spring): 54–60.

Tung, R.L. 1998. American expatriates abroad: From neophytes to cosmopolitans. *Journal of World Business* (Summer): 125–144.

Woodruff, D. 1997. The German worker is making a sacrifice. *Business Week* (July 28): 46–47.

Index

281; commissions, 280; employee stock ownership plans (ESOPs), 287–288; evaluating, 303–304; executive, 282–283; gainsharing, 284–285; individual, 279–280; managing, 278–284; merit pay, 281; organizational objectives, 275; performance-based rewards, 288; profit sharing, 286–287; purpose of, 274–275; standard hour plan, 280; stock options, 287; team and group, 284; toward successful, 275–278
International Harvester, 10
International human resources management (IHRM), 7–8; compensation and, 379–382; country culture and, 365–368; domestic versus, 360–363; HRM planning and, 363–365; intercountry differences and, 368–372; labor relations and, 382–384; MBO and, 366; multinational corporations (MNCs) and, 8, 359–366, 369; performance appraisal and, 377–379; safety and health and, 384–385; staffing policy challenges and, 372–375; training and development and, 375–377
Interviews: job analysis, 85–86; performance appraisal and, 213–216; recruitment and, 133; selection and placement and, 155–157, 171

Job analysis, 79–102; changing nature of jobs and, 99–100; data collection, 81–87; future of, 100–101; HRM planning and, 74, 79; line managers and, 81; major uses of, 77–81; methods, 87–98; nature of, 74; performance appraisal and, 80; recent trends in, 98; recruitment and, 79; selection and, 79, 141; uniform guidelines and, 75–77; work redesign and, 81
Job Analysis Handbook of Business, 84
Job classification, 77–78
Job descriptions, 77
Job design, 78–79, 182

Job enrichment, 182, 329
Job evaluation, 78
Job posting and bidding, 119–120
Job rotation, 182
Job specifications, 77
Johnson, Lyndon, 48
Journal of Applied Psychology, 84

Kirkpatrick, Donald, 194
Knights of Labor, 337

Labor Management Relations Act of 1947, 340. *See also* Taft-Hartley Act
Labor Management Reporting and Disclosure Act. *See* Landrum-Griffin Act of 1959
Labor relations: AFL-CIO, 337–338; employee reasons for unionizing, 342–343; history of, 336–338; HRM's role in, 354–355; IHRM and, 382–384; labor relations and, 336; legal context of, 339; NLRB and, 343–345, 354; process of unionizing, 341–345; structure of, 340–341; unions and, 336–343
Landrum-Griffin Act of 1959, 340. *See also* Labor Management Reporting and Disclosure Act
Learning theory, 177–181

Management by objectives (MBO), 208; IHRM and, 366; safety and, 330
Maslow, Abraham, 11–12
McDonnell-Douglas Corp. v. Green, 61
Mentoring, 231–232
Mercedes Benz, 25
Microsoft, 156
Milk, Nancy, 338

National Cash Register Company, 8
National Institute for Occupational Safety and Health (NIOS), 311; indoor air quality and, 322–323
National Iron Molders, 337
National Labor Relations Act (NLRA) of 1935, 339
National Labor Relations Board

About the Author

RONALD R. SIMS is the Floyd Dewey Gottwald Senior Professor of Business Administration in the Graduate School of Business at the College of William & Mary, Williamsburg, Virginia. He holds a doctorate in organizational behavior and consults widely with organizations in the private, public, and not-for-profit sectors. Dr. Sims is author or coauthor of more than 75 scholarly and professional articles and more than 17 books, 10 published by Quorum. Among his more recent ones are *The Challenge of Front-Line Management* (2000), *Keys to Employee Success in Coming Decades* (1999, with John G. Veres III), and *Reinventing Training and Development* (1998).